DESIGNING EFFECTIVE DIGITAL LEARNING ENVIRONMENTS

Bringing together the research of leading international scholars in the field of digital learning, *Designing Effective Digital Learning Environments* discusses cutting-edge advancements in digital technology and presents an evidence-informed summary of best practices for effective design principles and implementation within educational settings.

Readers will benefit from a synthesis of research evidence from previous meta-analyses on how to design digital environments that support learning, motivation, and collaboration. Divided into eight thematic parts, chapters unpack:

- An introduction to the design of digital learning environments
- Learning with multimedia, with particular emphasis on digital reading comprehension environments and GeoGebra software
- Digital videos for learning, including dynamic visualizations, instructional videos, and eye movement modeling examples
- Simulated realities, including learning with pedagogical agents and immersive virtual reality environments
- Game-based and sensor-based learning in digital environments
- Digital learning in social contexts, including a discussion of CSCL, social media, and audience response systems
- Design of digital classrooms, including flipped classroom approaches and synchronous online learning
- A concluding section discussing the efficacy and design of digital learning environments

This edited volume is an essential read for any scholar, researcher, Ph.D., or Masters student working in the field of digital learning.

Andreas Gegenfurtner is a Professor of Methods in Learning Research at the University of Augsburg. He currently serves as editor of *Frontline Learning Research* and is on the editorial boards of the EARLI journals *Educational Research Review* and *Learning and Instruction*.

Ingo Kollar is a Professor of Psychology with a special emphasis on Educational Psychology at the University of Augsburg. He also serves on the editorial boards of *Instructional Science, International Journal of Computer-Supported Collaborative Learning*, and *Psychology Learning and Teaching*.

New Perspectives on Learning and Instruction

Editor in Chief – Isabel Raemdonck
(Leiden University – The Netherlands)

New Perspectives on Learning and Instruction is published by Routledge in conjunction with EARLI (European Association for Research on Learning and Instruction). This series publishes cutting-edge international research focusing on all aspects of learning and instruction in both traditional and non-traditional educational settings. Titles published within the series take a broad and innovative approach to topical areas of research, are written by leading international researchers and are aimed at a research and post-graduate student audience.

Also available:

Motivation and Emotion in Learning and Teaching across Educational Contexts: Theoretical and Methodological Perspectives and Empirical Insights
Edited by Gerda Hagenauer, Rebecca Lazarides and Hanna Järvenoja

Designing Effective Digital Learning Environments
Edited by Andreas Gegenfurtner and Ingo Kollar

For a full list of titles, please visit: https://www.routledge.com/New-Perspectives-on-Learning-and-Instruction/book-series/EARLI

DESIGNING EFFECTIVE DIGITAL LEARNING ENVIRONMENTS

Edited by Andreas Gegenfurtner and Ingo Kollar

LONDON AND NEW YORK

First published 2025
by Routledge
4 Park Square, Milton Park, Abingdon, Oxon OX14 4RN

and by Routledge
605 Third Avenue, New York, NY 10158

Routledge is an imprint of the Taylor & Francis Group, an informa business

British Library Cataloguing-in-Publication Data
A catalog record for this book is available from the British Library

Library of Congress Cataloging-in-Publication Data
Names: Gegenfurtner, Andreas, editor. | Kollar, Ingo, editor.
Title: Designing effective digital learning environments / Edited by Andreas Gegenfurtner and Ingo Kollar.
Description: Abingdon, Oxon ; New York, NY : Routledge, 2025. | Series: New perspectives on learning and instruction | Includes bibliographical references and index.
Identifiers: LCCN 2024036738 (print) | LCCN 2024036739 (ebook) | ISBN 9781032478197 (hardback) | ISBN 9781032478180 (paperback) | ISBN 9781003386131 (ebook)
Subjects: LCSH: Web-based instruction--Design. | Instructional systems--Design. | Educational innovations.
Classification: LCC LB1044.87 .D479 2025 (print) | LCC LB1044.87 (ebook) | DDC 371.33/44678--dc23/eng/20240813
LC record available at https://lccn.loc.gov/2024036738
LC ebook record available at https://lccn.loc.gov/2024036739

ISBN: 978-1-032-47819-7 (hbk)
ISBN: 978-1-032-47818-0 (pbk)
ISBN: 978-1-003-38613-1 (ebk)

DOI: 10.4324/9781003386131

Typeset in Sabon
by SPi Technologies India Pvt Ltd (Straive)

CONTENTS

FIGURES

TABLES

CONTRIBUTORS

Lidia Altamura is a Ph.D. student of the Reading and Comprehension program at the University of Valencia, Spain. She is part of the interdisciplinary research group dedicated to reading processes ERI Lectura. She has been a visiting researcher at the Hochschule der Medien of Stuttgart, Germany. Her research interests and work are oriented to the study of reading processes, on paper and on screen, and their interaction with reading and multitasking habits.

Svenja Bedenlier is a Professor for education with a focus on digitization in higher and adult education at Friedrich-Alexander-Universität Erlangen-Nürnberg, Germany. Her research revolves around digital learning in the context of open and distance education and the intersection of internationalization and digitization in higher education. She also currently works on research syntheses and their application in education research.

Maik Beege is a tenure-track professor for digital media in education at the University of Education in Freiburg, Germany. His research interests include the influence of social processes on learning. Furthermore, he focuses on the optimization of instructional videos, as well as the promotion of cognitive activation during learning. He is particularly interested in suing complex models to investigate causal influences of multimedia design on processes during learning and consequently, on learning outcomes.

Isaac D. Dunmoye obtained his B.Eng. degree from the University of Ilorin, Nigeria where I graduated with first-class honors. I obtained my master's degree in Electrical Engineering from University of Cape Town, South Africa, and proceeded to University of Georgia, Athens, USA for my Ph.D. program in Engineering Education and Transformative Practices.

Christian Ebner is a research associate at the DIT (Deggendorf Institute of Technology), where he works in the department for digital teaching. His research mainly focuses on digital learning and students' perceptions of innovative teaching methods. He gives training to professors and other teaching staff at the DIT on how to integrate digital teaching methods (e.g., online-tools) into their lectures. Furthermore, he is involved in the conception of new 'innovative classrooms' at the DIT, where lecturers and students can experiment with new forms of teaching.

Selina Emhardt obtained her Ph.D. (2022) at the Faculty of Educational Sciences of the Open University of the Netherlands. Her research focuses on expertise development, example-based learning, and ways to enhance the design of instructional videos using eye-tracking technology. She is currently working at the Amsterdam University of Applied Sciences, The Netherlands, where she advises lecturers on topics related to blended learning.

Taiwo R. Feyijimi, a current master's student in Electrical and Computer Engineering at the University of Georgia, holds an associate degree in Electrical And Electronics Technology, as well as a BS and an education degree in Physics. His passion lies in Automation Engineering and utilizing machine learning/AI to tackle diverse STEM/Engineering problems.

Andreas Gegenfurtner is a Professor of methods in learning research at the University of Augsburg, Germany. His research focuses on digital learning, student heterogeneity, and visual expertise in the professions. He is particularly interested in using mixed-method and multi-method approaches to examine affective, cognitive, and motivational correlates of synchronous digital learning, for example in flipped classrooms and webinars. Andreas serves as editor for the EARLI journal Frontline Learning Research.

Libby Gerard is a Research Professor at the University of California, Berkeley School of Education. Her research examines how learning technologies can capture student ideas and help teachers use those ideas to make decisions about classroom instruction. Libby's recent projects explore the use of machine learning to provide personalized guidance for student science explanations and to support teachers' customization of instruction. Libby designs and leads professional development by using student data and the knowledge integration framework to inform instructional customization and resource allocation. Libby's research is published in leading peer-reviewed journals including Science and the Review of Educational Research.

Laura Gil is an Associate Professor of the Department of Developmental and Educational Psychology at the University of Valencia, Spain. She is a member of the ERI Lectura, a research unit focused on the study of reading. She did her Ph.D. in educational Psychology with international mention. In addition, she was a postdoctoral student Juan de la Cierva with the Research Group "Thought, understanding and working memory" at National Distance Education University, Spain. Her research career has focused on the analysis, evaluation, and intervention of reading comprehension processes of single and multiple texts.

Martin Greisel is a psychologist working as an Assistant Professor in educational psychology at the University of Augsburg, Germany. His research is centered around regulation behavior in the contexts of self-regulated learning, collaborative learning, peer feedback, and evidence-informed reasoning of pre-service teachers.

Raija Hämäläinen works in the field of technology-enhanced learning at the Center for Research for Learning and Teaching at the University of Jyväskylä, Finland. Hämäläinen's research interests include collaboration and creativity in technology-enhanced learning settings, workplace learning, and teacher–student interaction. She is a well-recognized keynote speaker on novel methods (e.g. EARLI 2021), an associate editor of Educational Research Review, and WP leader in Center of Excellence (InterLearn). Hämäläinen has wide international networks (member of the Earli EC, community committee of CSCL, Earli Sig 14 coordinator).

Marion Händel is a Professor of media psychology with a focus on media education and research on media use at Ansbach University of Applied Sciences, Germany. Her research focuses on digital learning, for example, via videoconferencing, as well as self-regulated learning. Marion is interested in learning in school and higher education, especially on metacognitive, motivational, and cognitive processes. She is a scientific board member of the international journal Metacognition and Learning.

Byron Havard is a Professor in the Department of Instructional Design and Technology at the University of West Florida. His research interests include online collaboration and communication media, instructional strategies for emerging technologies, and social and cultural dimensions in instructional technology.

Emely Hoch works as a postdoctoral researcher in the Multiple Representations Lab at the Leibniz-Institut für Wissensmedien (Tübingen, Germany). Her research focuses on technology-enhanced learning and teaching. In particular, she is interested in metacognitive processes and the underlying mechanisms of self-regulated learning, as well as how to support learners' self-regulation in the context of multimedia learning and technology-enhanced learning.

Markus Hohenwarter is a full Professor of mathematics education at the Johannes Kepler University Linz, Austria. His research focuses on the use of technologies for learning and teaching mathematics.

Vincent Hoogerheide is an Assistant Professor at the Department of Education at Utrecht University, the Netherlands. His research has three main foci. The first research line investigates the conditions under which studying instructional videos enhances learning and motivation. The second research line focuses on the question of whether and why making an instructional video for someone else is an effective learning activity. The third main research line deals with the important issue of (supporting) self-regulated learning. Vincent is a coordinator of the EARLI special interest group 7 (technology-enhanced learning and instruction) and serves as associate editor at Applied Cognitive Psychology.

Markus Huff is a full Professor of psychology holding a joint position as head of both the Applied Cognitive Psychology research group at Eberhard Karls Universität Tübingen and the Perception and Action Lab at Leibniz-Institut für Wissensmedien (IWM). The primary focus of his research is processes of human perception and action in digital environments. Markus studied psychology, mathematics, and computer science, receiving his doctorate at IWM and Uni Tübingen. After a postdoctoral fellowship at IWM, Uni Tübingen, and Washington University in St. Louis, he became a junior professor at Tübingen before heading the research infrastructures department at the DIE in Bonn.

Nathaniel J. Hunsu is an Assistant Professor of Engineering Education at the University of Georgia. He has a Ph.D. in Educational Psychology from Washington State University. His research interests are in learning and cognition, students' engagement in their learning contexts, and the assessment of learning and engagement in engineering classrooms.

Halszka Jarodzka is Professor of Instructional Design for Online Learning at the Faculty of Educational Sciences of the Open University of the Netherlands. She studied Psychology and obtained her Ph.D. in Psychology (2011) at the University of Tübingen, Germany. Her research focuses on how eye tracking can help to understand and improve visual expertise development in professionals (e.g., teachers and physicians) as well as the design of multimedia materials for instruction, learning, and testing in online environments. She co-founded and co-coordinated EARLI SIG 27 'Online measures of learning processes'.

Özün Keskin is a Ph.D. student at the University of Augsburg, Germany. Her research focuses on teacher professional vision, eye tracking in the context of teacher professionalism, and professionalism in managing heterogeneity in classrooms. She is interested in using mixed-method approaches to examine affective and cognitive processes in the school context.

Ellen Kok is an Assistant Professor at the Department of Education at Utrecht University, The Netherlands. She holds a Ph.D. from Maastricht University (2016). Her research focuses on the use of eye tracking in educational research, specifically to enhance learning. She investigates how gaze visualizations can be used as feedback to learners, as input for teachers to tailor their instructions to learners' needs, and to enrich instructional videos (i.e., eye movement modeling examples).

Ingo Kollar is a Professor of psychology with a special emphasis on educational psychology at the University of Augsburg, Germany. His research focuses on technology-enhanced learning, collaborative learning, and evidence-informed reasoning of pre-and in-service teachers. He is a scientific board member of Instructional Science, the International Journal of Computer-Supported Collaborative Learning, and Psychology Learning and Teaching.

Edith Lindenbauer is a college Professor at the University College of Education Upper Austria. Currently, her research focuses on the integration of digital materials in mathematics education at the secondary level from various perspectives.

Marcia C. Linn is the Evelyn Lois Corey Professor of Instructional Science at the Berkeley School of Education, specializing in science and technology. She is a member of the National Academy of Education and a Fellow of the American Association for the Advancement of Science (AAAS), the American Psychological Association, the Association for Psychological Science, the American Educational Research Association, and the International Society of the Learning Sciences (ISLS). She has served as President of ISLS, Chair of the AAAS Education Section, and on the boards of AAAS, Educational Testing Service, and the National Science Foundation Education Human Resources Directorate.

Guido Makransky is a Professor of Educational Psychology and the founder of the Virtual Learning Lab at the Department of Psychology, University of Copenhagen. His current research focuses on understanding the mechanisms of learning and behavior change in immersive learning environments.

Amelia Mañá is an Associate Professor of the Department of Developmental and Educational Psychology at the University of Valencia, Spain. She is a part of the ERI Lectura, a research structure focused on the interdisciplinary study of reading. She did her Ph.D. in Educational Psychology. She has been a visiting researcher at University of Memphis, USA, and the University of Poitiers, France. Her research focuses on the analysis and evaluation of metacognitive and motivational processes involved in reading comprehension.

Richard E. Mayer is a Distinguished Professor of Psychological and Brain Sciences at the University of California, Santa Barbara (USA). His research interests are in applying the science of learning to education, with a focus on how to help people learn in ways so they can transfer what they have learned to new situations. His research is at the intersection of cognition, instruction, and technology, with current projects on multimedia learning, computer-supported learning, computer games for learning, learning in immersive virtual reality, learning with animated pedagogical agents, and instructional video.

Martin Merkt is head of the junior research group Audiovisual Instruction and Information at the German Institute for Adult Education in Bonn. His main research interest lies in the optimization of dynamic audiovisual learning materials from a cognitive psychological perspective. After receiving his diploma in psychology at the University of Tübingen, Martin finished his Ph.D. at the Leibniz-Institut für Wissensmedien in Tübingen, where he also worked as a postdoc until 2017.

Steve Nebel is a Professor of Media Education at the University of Potsdam, Germany. He investigates various ways of teaching with different multimedia materials and regarding the use of media. He puts special emphasis on innovative technological approaches, such as educational video games.

Manuel Ninaus is a tenure-track Professor of digital technologies and psychology at the University of Graz, Austria. His general research interests include educational technologies and multimodal learning analytics. He is particularly interested in the cognitive, emotional, and neurofunctional foundations of game-based learning. Therefore, in his research, he combines behavioral and cognitive measures, such as user log data, performance, and reaction times, but also state-of-the-art psychophysiological and neuroimaging methods.

Tugce Özbek is a Ph.D. student with a special emphasis on educational psychology at the University of Augsburg, Germany. Her research focuses on technology-enhanced learning.

Gustav Bøg Petersen is a Ph.D. student at the Department of Psychology, University of Copenhagen. His work primarily focuses on using virtual agents and avatars for learning purposes.

Julia Pirklbauer did her Master of Education in mathematics, psychology, and philosophy. She is now working as Website Product Owner at GeoGebra.

Günter Daniel Rey leads the Chair of Psychology of Learning with Digital Media at Chemnitz University of Technology (Germany). He investigates various applications of learning with digital media using a quantitative and experimental approach. His research includes a broad range of topics from the field of multimedia learning and focuses on cognitive, emotional, and social aspects of learning with digital media.

Maximilian Sailer is a Professor of educational sciences at the University of Passau, Germany. His areas of academic interest include technology-enhanced learning (TEL), blended learning, and empirical educational research.

Michael Sailer is a postdoctoral scholar at the Chair of Education and Educational Psychology at LMU Munich, Germany. His research interests are gamified learning, simulation-based learning, as well as the use of AI in education and the digital transformation of K-12 and higher education.

Ladislao Salmerón is Full Professor of Educational Psychology at the University of Valencia, Spain. He conducts his research at the ERI Lectura, a research unit focused on the study of reading in its multiple facets. He did his Ph.D. in cognitive psychology at the University of Granada, Spain. He was a Fulbright scholar at the Institute of Cognitive Science at the University of Colorado Boulder, USA. His research focuses on digital literacies in different populations.

Stefanie Schallert-Vallaster is a postdoctoral researcher at the University College of Virtual Teacher Education in Austria. Her research focuses on technology-enhanced learning.

Katharina Scheiter is Professor for Digital Education at the University of Potsdam, Germany. In her research, she focuses on the design of educational technology, its integration into classrooms as well as the necessary competencies of teachers for teaching with technology. For her use-inspired research, she has received the Erik de Corte Award of EARLI (2009) and the Franz-Emanuel-Weinert Award of the German Psychological Association (2022). She serves on various boards and committees dealing with technology-enhanced learning and teaching and is particularly interested in the transfer of scientific evidence into educational practice.

Ruben Schlag is a research assistant at the Chair of Educational Sciences at the University of Passau, Germany. His research focuses on technology-enhanced learning in higher education. This includes gamified learning and (online) flipped classroom designs.

Sascha Schneider is a Professor of Educational Technology at the University of Zurich, Switzerland. Sascha Schneider's research focuses on cognitive, emotional, motivational, social, and metacognitive processes when learning with digital media such as text- and image-based materials, but also dynamic or interactive media. He also examines retrieval processes that become necessary when working on learning tasks or quizzes.

Anne Schüler is postdoc and deputy head of the Multiple Representations Lab at the Leibniz-Institut für Wissensmedien (Tübingen, Germany). Her research focuses on the cognitive foundations of multimedia learning (e.g., mental text-picture integration; automatic reactivation, and validation processes) and instructional methods to support the processes underlying learning with multimedia (e.g., Eye Movement Modeling Examples). Furthermore, she studies the processing and impact of conflicting information in videos and social media. She is a member of the international editorial advisory board of Learning and Instruction.

Stoo Sepp is a Lecturer in the School of Education at the University of New England, Australia. His research focuses on how instructional media affect learning and cognition, as well as how embodied activities such as hand gestures can support learning in digital environments. Additionally, he explores novel methods of quantifying physical interactions with learning materials, related to work in Multimodal Learning Analytics (MMLA).

Laura Spang is a Ph.D. student with a special emphasis on educational psychology at the University of Augsburg, Germany. Her main research interest lies in co-regulation in collaborative learning.

Daniel Tolks is a Professor of medical and health education at the Medical School Hamburg, Germany. His research interests are gamification and serious games for health, digital learning, and teaching in health care, as well as the use of AI in medical education. He is editor of the Journal for Medical Education and chairs the digitalization committee of the German Society for Medical Education (GMA).

Detlef Urhahne is Professor of psychology with a special emphasis on educational psychology at the University of Passau, Germany. His research focuses on teacher education, motivational psychology, gifted education, science education, and the use of educational technology in the classroom. He is working as an associate editor for Educational Psychology: An International Journal of Experimental Educational Psychology.

Antoine van den Beemt is an Associate Professor in the Eindhoven School of Education at Eindhoven University of Technology, working in the domain of STEM-teacher professional development. His research focuses on innovation in higher education, which he explores in two directions. First, technology-enhanced learning, emphasizing blended learning and the use of learning analytics to improve learning and teaching. Second, challenge-based learning (CBL), with special attention to teacher roles, learner experience, and theorizing CBL. Antoine participates in university-wide programs for educational innovations with ICT, and for the development and implementation of CBL.

Tamara van Gog is Professor of Educational Sciences at the Department of Education at Utrecht University, The Netherlands, and distinguished international professor at the LEAD graduate school and research network of the University of Tübingen, Germany. She studied Educational Psychology at Tilburg University (2001) and holds a Ph.D. from the Open University of The Netherlands (2006). Her research focuses on instructional design to foster example-based learning, self-regulated learning, multimedia learning, and critical thinking. She regularly applies eye tracking in her research as a tool to study and enhance learning processes.

Tim van Marlen obtained his Ph.D. (2019) at the Department of Education at Utrecht University, The Netherlands, where he continued to work as postdoc until 2022. His research focuses on the design of video modeling examples, including eye movement modeling examples.

Freydis Vogel is Professor for digitalization in education at the University of Hamburg, Germany. Her research topics are about digital teaching and learning with a particular focus on collaborative learning processes. She is a scientific board member of Instructional Science and the International Journal of Computer-Supported Collaborative Learning.

Marlene Wagner is a postdoctoral researcher at the University for Continuing Education Krems, Austria. Her research focuses on the effectiveness of digital learning environments, such as flipped classrooms or hybrid virtual classrooms, and on the professional development of teachers in terms of technology integration practices in the classroom.

Robert Weinhandl is a postdoctoral researcher at Johannes Kepler University Linz, Austria. His research focuses on using technologies for learning mathematics at the secondary level and exploring the characteristics of mathematics students.

PREFACE

Over the past decades, the rapid advancement of digital technology has offered new ways to support learning across a broad range of educational settings, from pre-school all the way to adult education. Simultaneously, the investigation of the effects of different kinds of digital technology on learning has become an increasingly important topic of educational and psychological research on learning and instruction, as well as research in different subject-matter didactics. For an individual scholar and practitioner, it is sometimes a challenge to read and keep up with the rapidly growing number of individual study reports. As a remedy, this volume provides an overview of the empirical effects of a wide collection of digital technologies on learning-relevant processes and outcomes, summarized in 19 chapters. Following an introductory piece, the chapters are organized thematically as they relate to (a) learning with multimedia, (b) learning with digital videos, (c) learning from simulated realities, (d) game-based and sensor-based learning in digital environments, (e) digital learning in social contexts, and (f) designing digital classrooms. To arrive at reliable recommendations for educational practice on when and how to use different digital technologies to stimulate learning, the empirical evidence that is reported in the single chapters predominantly originates from meta-analytic syntheses. Ultimately, the chapters and their evidence-based recommendations for designing effective digital learning environments are discussed by two renowned experts in the field to provide directions for further educational research and practice.

ACKNOWLEDGMENTS

The volume editors would like to thank the following scholars (in alphabetic order) for their invaluable support when peer-reviewing the chapter drafts. Their feedback has significantly contributed to strengthen and improve the quality of this volume. Thank you.

Jean-Michel Boucheix
Chris Dede
Yiannis Dimitriadis
Eleonora Faggiano
Paul Ginns
Martin Greisel
Marion Händel
Steffi Heidig
Rene Kizilcec
Marie-Christin Krebs
Pantelis Papadopoulos
Annelies Raes
Martin Rehm
Helge Strømsø
David van Alten

PART I

Introduction

1

DESIGN OF DIGITAL LEARNING ENVIRONMENTS

Evidence from meta-analyses

Andreas Gegenfurtner and Ingo Kollar

Digital technologies have dramatically changed the way we live and work over the past decades (Kasneci et al., 2023; Säljö & Mäkitalo, 2022). It is therefore no surprise that also educators have more and more exploited the vast possibilities that digital technologies offer to support learning and teaching in all stages of education, including preschool settings (McPake et al., 2013), K12 learning (Wagner et al., 2021), higher education (Daumiller et al., 2021), and adult education (Tynjälä et al., 2014). Such efforts are often strongly pragmatically oriented and follow a trial-and-error rather than a more systematic, evidence-based approach (Wekerle & Kollar, 2022). This is unfortunate, given the fact that educational research has accumulated a very rich body of empirical research that can inform practitioners what technologies to use for what educational purposes, how to use them, and how to embed them in their teaching practices.

Yet, it has to be acknowledged that it is, arguably, an unrealistic demand to expect teachers and instructors to gain an overview of the thousands of research studies that focus on digitally supported learning and teaching. For example, as of March 2023, a search for "computer-supported collaborative learning" alone (which is just one – albeit very lively – area of research on digitally supported learning and teaching) in a scientific database such as Web of Science produces more than 6,000 results. For other lines of research, these numbers are even higher (e.g., for multimedia learning: More than 16,000 hits). Even researchers in these areas are typically overwhelmed by the sheer amount of research on different (sub-)topics of technology-enhanced learning.

Against this background, educational science has therefore increasingly produced meta-analyses to arrive at clear statements regarding the effects of

DOI: 10.4324/9781003386131-2

different aspects when designing and implementing digital environments in education. The basic idea of a meta-analytic synthesis is to find all studies on a specific research question (such as: What is the effect of learning with animations compared to learning from textbooks?), document the effects that were found in each of these studies, and aggregate effect sizes across studies (with studies with larger samples receiving a higher weight than studies with smaller samples; Schmidt & Hunter, 2015). The benefits of this approach are clear: First, statements on the effects of certain kinds of digital technologies are based on a much larger sample size than can ever be achieved in one primary study. Second, since related primary studies typically vary with regard to various study features such as target group, learning materials, and test procedures, meta-analytical statements can be regarded as much more robust than statements that can be made on the basis of a single primary study. And third, the variability of primary studies with respect to different study features affords the opportunity to identify so-called "moderator variables" – variables that can explain why some realizations of a given technology have larger (or smaller) effects than others – which is a useful strategy to explore the boundary conditions when designing digital learning environments. Therefore, the value of meta-analytical evidence for the purpose of informing educational practice on what, when, and how technologies to use to support learning and teaching is extraordinarily high.

The present volume therefore attempts to provide an overview over the (predominantly, but not exclusively) meta-analytical evidence on the effects of a wide collection of different kinds of technology on various learning outcomes. It does this in eight parts. After this introductory editorial in the first section of the volume, Part II focuses on learning with multimedia: Anne Schüler, Emely Hoch, and Katharina Scheiter review important principles that contribute to the effectiveness of learning with multimedia (Chapter 2); Ladislao Salmerón, Lidia Altamura, Laura Gil, and Amelia Mañá elaborate on the design of effective digital reading comprehension environments (Chapter 3); and Robert Weinhandl, Edith Lindenbauer, Stefanie Schallert-Vallaster, Julia Pirklbauer, and Markus Hohenwarter present GeoGebra as a comprehensive tool for learning mathematics (Chapter 4).

Part III focuses on learning with digital videos: Martin Merkt and Markus Huff discuss meta-analytic evidence on how to overcome challenges and seize opportunities when learning with dynamic visualizations (Chapter 5); Vincent Hoogerheide and Stoo Sepp then identify six evidence-informed tips on how to optimize learning from instructional videos (Chapter 6); and Tamara van Gog, Ellen Kok, Selina Emhardt, Tim van Marlen, and Halszka Jarodzka discuss research syntheses on learning with eye movement modeling examples, an emerging approach that bridges eye tracking and video examples (Chapter 7).

Part IV highlights learning from simulated realities: Maik Beege, Steve Nebel, Günter Daniel Rey, and Sascha Schneider first reflect on the empirical evidence and theoretical models when learning with pedagogical agents in digital environments (Chapter 8); and Gustav Bøg Petersen and Guido Makransky then present evidence-based recommendations for designing effective immersive virtual reality learning environments (Chapter 9).

Part V centers on game-based and sensor-based learning in digital environments: Ruben Schlag, Michael Sailer, Daniel Tolks, Manuel Ninaus, and Maximilian Sailer discuss theory and evidence on the effectiveness of gamification in education (Chapter 10), followed by Byron Havard, who reflects in his chapter on the use of sensors and wearables as emerging tools used in digital learning environments (Chapter 11).

Part VI focuses on digital learning in social contexts: Ingo Kollar, Martin Greisel, Tugce Özbek, Laura Spang, and Freydis Vogel reflect on meta-analyses of design principles in computer-supported collaborative learning (Chapter 12); Antoine van den Beemt discusses social media in class as a problem or a panacea (Chapter 13); and Nathaniel J. Hunsu, Isaac D. Dunmoye, and Taiwo R. Feyijimi examine the effects of clickers and audience response systems for effective learning and instruction in the classroom (Chapter 14).

Part VII is devoted to designing digital classrooms: Marlene Wagner, Andreas Gegenfurtner, and Detlef Urhahne present meta-analytic evidence of design elements aimed at increasing the effectiveness of flipped classrooms (Chapter 15); Andreas Gegenfurtner, Svenja Bedenlier, Christian Ebner, Özün Keskin, and Marion Händel discuss a number of meta-analyses examining principles for designing effective synchronous online learning (Chapter 16); and Libby Gerard and Marcia C. Linn reflect on the impacts of web-based inquiry learning environments aligned with knowledge integration pedagogy (Chapter 17).

Finally, Part VIII includes two reflective discussions of the chapters in this edited volume: Richard E. Mayer focuses on Parts II, III, and IV and how the presented evidence helps educational practitioners and instructional designers to increase the effectiveness of digital learning (Chapter 18); Raija Hämäläinen then focuses on the chapters in Parts V, VI, and VII and how the summarized evidence-based recommendations help inform the design of digital learning environments, balancing theoretical, methodological, empirical, and technological approaches (Chapter 19).

Overall, we strongly believe that the chapters in this volume provide an extremely valuable resource for practitioners aiming to improve their teaching with the aid of digital technologies. Yet, it is clear that the results of meta-analytical findings cannot take the burden from teachers completely, as deriving concrete actions from highly aggregated effect sizes can at times be far from easy and straightforward (Schildkamp, 2019). Nevertheless, meta-analytical evidence can be a strong foundation for initial decisions on how to use digital technologies in the classroom. To turn these decisions into actions, though, teachers should also be aware of primary studies (including qualitative and mixed-method research), as the descriptions of actual implementations of digitally enhanced learning environments will be more specific, particularly on the social and material affordances of learning environments.

To conclude, we hope that the chapters of this volume can support educational practitioners with general guidance on what, when, and how to use educational technology in their classrooms. Still, though, it is the teachers' task to evaluate these findings, apply them to their current situations, and make informed decisions on whether, how, and when to use them to improve learning and teaching.

References

Daumiller, M., Rinas, R., Hein, J., Janke, S., Dickhäuser, O., & Dresel, M. (2021). Shifting from face-to-face to online teaching during COVID-19: The role of university faculty achievement goals for attitudes towards this sudden change, and their relevance for burnout/engagement and student evaluations of teaching quality. *Computers in Human* Behavior, *118*, 106677. https://doi.org/10.1016/j.chb.2020.106677

Kasneci, E., Seßler, K., Küchemann, S., Bannert, M., Dementieva, D., Fischer, F., et al. (2023). ChatGPT for good? On opportunities and challenges of large language models for education. *Learning and Individual Differences, 103,* 102274. https://doi.org/10.1016/j.lindif.2023.102274

McPake J., Plowman, L., & Stephen, C. (2013). Pre-school children creating and communicating with digital technologies in the home. *British Journal of Educational Technology, 44*(3), 421–431. https://doi.org/10.1111/j.1467-8535.2012.01323.x

Säljö, R., & Mäkitalo, Å. (2022). Learning and development in a designed world. In N. Veraksa & I. Pramling Samuelsson (Eds.), *Piaget and Vygotsky in XXI century*. Springer. https://doi.org/10.1007/978-3-031-05747-2_3

Schildkamp, K. (2019). Data-based decision-making for school improvement: Research insights and gaps, *Educational Research, 61*(3), 257–273. https://doi.org/10.1080/00131881.2019.1625716

Schmidt, F. L., & Hunter, J. E. (2015). *Methods of meta-analysis: Correcting error and bias in research findings* (3rd ed.). Sage.

Tynjälä, P., Häkkinen, P., & Hämäläinen, R. (2014). TEL@work: Toward integration of theory and practice. *British Journal of Educational Technology, 45*(6), 990–1000. https://doi.org/10.1111/bjet.12164

Wagner, M., Gegenfurtner, A., & Urhahne, D. (2021). Effectiveness of the flipped classroom on student achievement in K-12 education: A meta-analysis. *Zeitschrift für Pädagogische Psychologie, 35*(1), 11–31. https://doi.org/10.1024/1010-0652/a000274

Wekerle, C., & Kollar, I. (2022). Using technology to promote student learning? An analysis of pre- and in-service teachers' lesson plans. *Technology, Pedagogy and Education, 31*(5), 597–614. https://doi.org/10.1080/1475939X.2022.2083669

PART II
Learning with Multimedia

2

THE EFFECTIVENESS OF LEARNING WITH MULTIMEDIA

Anne Schüler, Emely Hoch and Katharina Scheiter

Multimedia learning materials, that is, learning materials consisting of text presented together with corresponding pictures (Mayer, 2021), are widely used. Whether in textbooks, informal learning settings such as museums, or digital learning environments (the subject of the present book), we encounter multimedia materials everywhere.

The present chapter first offers an overview of the cognitive foundations for learning with multimedia. We then provide an overview of seven multimedia design principles formulated based on the human cognitive system. For each principle, we explain its underlying assumptions, summarize the empirical evidence (based on existing meta-analyses or reviews when possible), and describe its most important boundary conditions. We conclude with some implications regarding the integration of multimedia into educational settings.

Theoretical Foundations for Learning with Multimedia

The most influential theories regarding learning with multimedia are the cognitive theory of multimedia learning (CTML; e.g., Mayer, 2021) and the integrated model of text and picture comprehension (Schnotz & Bannert, 2003). Both theories make similar assumptions on how the cognitive system works (e.g., that multimedia materials are processed in two channels with limited capacity). In the following, we will describe the assumptions of the CTML in more detail.

Based on Baddeley's (1992) working memory model and Paivio's (1990) dual coding theory, the CTML postulates that humans possess two separate channels for processing information from text and pictures—an auditory–verbal channel and a visual-pictorial channel (in the following we use the

DOI: 10.4324/9781003386131-4

term auditory channel to refer to the auditory part of the auditory–verbal channel, and so on). Both channels are assumed to be limited in their capacity. A prerequisite for successful multimedia learning is that learners actively select relevant information from text and pictures in sensory memory, organize the selected information into mental representations in working memory, and integrate these mental representations with each other and with prior knowledge into a coherent mental model stored in long-term memory.

According to the theory, there exist different processing paths for pictures, spoken text, and written text:

Pictures are processed in the visual-pictorial channel. Learners select information from the picture, which is then represented as an image base (i.e., a mental representation of the selected images) in the visual channel. Then, learners build meaningful connections among the selected images, that is, they organize the images into a coherent pictorial mental model, which is located in the pictorial channel.

Spoken text is processed in the auditory–verbal channel. Learners select information from the spoken text, which is then represented as a word sound base (i.e., a mental representation of the selected sounds) in the auditory channel. Then, learners build meaningful connections among the selected sounds, that is, they organize the sounds into a coherent verbal mental model, which is located in the verbal channel.

According to CTML, the written text takes the most complicated path, as it is assumed to be processed initially in the visual–pictorial channel but is then transferred to the auditory–verbal channel. First, learners select information from the written text, which is then represented as images in the visual channel (but see Rummer et al., 2011 for a critical discussion of this assumption). Second, through the process of mental articulation, it is transferred to the auditory channel, where it is represented as a word sound base. Third, learners organize the sounds into a verbal mental model located in the verbal channel.

After the learners have constructed the verbal and pictorial models, learners integrate them with each other and with relevant prior knowledge reactivated from long-term memory. According to CTML, this integration is crucial for successful learning, as the resulting integrated mental model reflects a deeper understanding necessary, for instance, to reason and solve novel problems.

Based on the assumptions described above, multimedia design principles have been derived, which are assumed to support the selection, organization, and integration of information. They aim at reducing extraneous, that is, unnecessary processing (Fiorella & Mayer, 2022a), managing essential, that is, necessary processing (Mayer & Fiorella, 2022), as well as inducing generative activities relevant to mental model construction (Fiorella & Mayer, 2022b). In a meta-analysis of meta-analyses, Noetel et al. (2022)

reported a medium effect ($g = 0.38$) of these multimedia design principles on learning outcomes.

In the following, we provide an overview of seven multimedia design principles formulated based on the aforementioned assumptions on how the human cognitive system works. If possible, we refer to current meta-analyses or systematic reviews and report the associated effect sizes.

The Animation Principle

According to the animation principle, the use of dynamic representations, which portray change over time directly and explicitly, can have educational benefits (Lowe & Schnotz, 2014). When learning from a (series of) static picture(s), learners need to mentally imagine how an object would change over time, for instance, by changing its appearance or position. Thus, especially for moving objects (e.g., a hopping kangaroo, a pulley system), learners would have to mentally animate the object to build a mental model that adequately reflects their dynamics (Hegarty, 1992). Mental animation, however, is an error-prone and cognitively demanding process. Accordingly, dynamic representations make mental animation unnecessary and are hence assumed to reduce cognitive processing demands. However, at the same time, dynamic representations are transient. Accordingly, learners may fail to attend to relevant information at the right time, especially in the case of multiple things changing simultaneously, and therefore miss the information; moreover, they may experience difficulties in integrating information across time into one coherent mental model (cf. the animation processing model, Lowe & Boucheix, 2008, and the cognitive theory of visual expertise, Gegenfurtner et al., 2022; for more detailed accounts of [visual] processing demands). For these reasons, the actual benefits of learning from animation are often far less than what has been envisioned and depend on certain boundary conditions explained below.

The first meta-analysis published by Höffler and Leutner (2007) found a small effect of learning from animations over learning from static pictures ($d = 0.37$, 76 pairwise comparisons). About 10 years later, Berney and Bétrancourt (2016) replicated this effect in a meta-analysis based on a larger body of evidence (small effect of $g = 0.22$, 140 pairwise comparisons). Ploetzner et al. (2020) extended this database to a total of 194 studies and identified an important moderator based on its reanalysis, namely, the nature of change portrayed in the animation and how it relates to the learning goal. In particular, they found that the use of animation did not affect learning when the displayed changes were irrelevant to learning ($g = 0.004$), whereas the effect sizes increased with the complexity of changes that had to be understood. For simple changes (e.g., changes in position, changes in an object's length), the effect size favoring animation was small to medium ($g = 0.34$), whereas it was large ($g = 0.65$) for complex changes (e.g., changes in velocity, non-linear motion, irregular transformations of objects). Thus, animation supports learning only if the change is relevant to understanding and if this change cannot easily be portrayed in a static picture.

Based on findings suggesting that animations may be challenging to process because of their transience, there have been many attempts to scaffold learners' processing of animations (see Lowe et al., 2022, for an overview). For instance, animations have been enriched with interactive features to allow learners to control the speed of presentation; moreover, their display has been augmented by signaling relevant information or segmenting the animation into manageable and meaningful parts. Finally, learners have been asked to perform additional tasks when learning from animations (e.g., gesturing, drawing). However, while for each of these scaffolding measures, there are studies showing positive effects, their overall effectiveness appears to be limited. Accordingly, animation should be used sparingly and only when required by the learning task.

The Modality Principle

According to the modality principle (Mayer, 2021), text accompanying pictures should be presented in spoken and not in written format. Based on CTML, Mayer (2021) assumes that when pictures are presented together with written text, the visual channel is likely to become overloaded. On the other hand, when pictures are presented together with spoken text, the verbal information is offloaded to the auditory channel, which should result in more cognitive capacity available and better performance. However, this explanation has been questioned in the literature (see for example, Rummer et al., 2011) as it is not fully in line with Baddeley's (1992) conception of working memory, which is one of the foundations of the CTML.

Alternative explanations for the modality principle assume that with written text and pictures, a less contingent presentation is given than with spoken text and pictures (i.e., written text and pictures do not allow for simultaneous perception but require visual research processes instead), and that with written text and pictures, less attention might be dedicated to the picture (cf. Schüler et al., 2011). The latter explanation is supported by a systematic review of eye-tracking research on multimedia learning (Alemdag & Cagiltay, 2018), where the authors concluded that the most prevalent result of seven studies investigating the modality effect via eye tracking was that learners with spoken text spent more time viewing the picture than learners with written text.

Ginns conducted a meta-analysis in 2005 on the modality effect and reported a medium to large effect size of $d = 0.72$ for 39 between-subjects effects. Six years later, Reinwein (2012) conducted a meta-analysis on the modality effect, considering 86 between-subject effects. He reported small to medium effect sizes between $d = 0.38$ and 0.50, depending on the unit of analysis and the type of outcome used in the analysis. When correcting for publication bias, he reported a small, but still positive effect size of $d = 0.20$ in favor of spoken text and pictures. In a recent overview, Mayer and Fiorella (2022) summarize 76 experimental comparisons concerning transfer performance, resulting in a medium median effect size of $d = 0.65$ favoring spoken text and pictures. Obviously, the reported effect sizes differ depending on the empirical studies, the unit of analysis, and the type of outcome considered. This could be an indication that boundary conditions play an important role in the modality principle.

Indeed, several moderators have been identified by the meta-analyses mentioned above. Hence, the modality effect is more likely to occur when the materials are rather high in element interactivity (Ginns, 2005), the presentation is system-paced (Ginns, 2005; Reinwein, 2012), the texts are rather short (Reinwein, 2012), or dynamic rather than static pictures are used (Reinwein, 2012).

The Signaling Principle

According to the signaling (or cueing) principle, learning from text and pictures is more effective when relevant information is highlighted (van Gog, 2022). Signals are means that are aimed to emphasize the importance of information and its structure. For instance, signals can be advanced organizers, headers, or different types of formatting devices (e.g., boldface print) in the printed text, arrows, circles, and moving spotlights in (dynamic) visual displays, or color coding to indicate correspondences of information in the text and the picture. Accordingly, the term signaling is used for a variety of different devices that, while different in their realization properties, have similar functions for learning. In particular, signals help to allocate attention to relevant information at the right time, thereby aiding the selection of information and reducing the need for unnecessary search processes. Moreover, signals aimed at supporting learners in identifying correspondences between information presented in the text and the picture foster text-picture integration (multimedia integration signals, Richter et al., 2018). Signals do not add information to the multimedia message; rather, they support the processing of information already contained therein. Accordingly, once the signals are removed from a multimedia message, it will still be meaningful.

A number of meta-analyses have confirmed the effectiveness of signaling to enhance learning (Alpizar et al., 2020; Richter et al., 2016; Schneider et al., 2018). Alpizar et al. (2020) reported a small effect size ($d = 0.38$) in favor of signaling in multimedia messages based on 44 effect sizes. Studies included text-based and picture-based signaling as well as signaling in both media. Signaling effects varied by realization property, with all variants being effective —with the exception of "focus by effect" signaling, where the relevant information in a picture or animation is highlighted by adjusting the presentation itself (e.g., zooming in, using a spotlight). This corresponds to findings from an earlier meta-analysis by Richter et al. (2016) that focused exclusively on the effects of multimedia integration signals. Based on 45 effect sizes, they found a small effect size of $r = .17$. Finally, Schneider et al. (2018) re-analyzed studies on the signaling effect across various media, including but not limited to multimedia. In their meta-analysis of 145 effect sizes, they obtained a medium to large effect ($g = 0.53$); in addition, they found positive effects on student motivation and their self-reported cognitive load. Moreover, 12 out of 14 studies provided evidence that signaling leads to more intense processing of signaled information. At a descriptive level, effects on learning outcomes varied by realization, with positive effects obtained for text organization signals, color coding in visual displays, and pointing gestures (in descending order). A number of signaling devices made no difference (e.g., referencing the picture in the text, use of labels or spotlights in visual displays), while flashing had even negative effects on learning outcomes. Schneider et al. (2018) reanalyzed many studies investing signaling only in text, which may explain why they found a larger effect size than the two meta-analyses focusing on learning with multimedia. Apparently, text signaling is more effective (as corroborated also by the moderator analysis).

All three meta-analyses also considered prior knowledge as a potential moderating factor—with divergent results, however. While in the two studies focusing exclusively on multimedia learning (Alpizar et al., 2020; Richter et al., 2016), the effects of signaling were evident only for low prior knowledge students, but not for high prior knowledge students, Schneider et al. (2018) observed no moderation. However, in the prior meta-analyses, there were only very few studies containing high-prior knowledge students. Richter et al. (2018) ran a study explicitly designed to test the moderation effect with secondary students learning with different variants of a digital textbook on introductory chemistry. They found a significant signaling effect for students with low prior knowledge, which, however, reversed for students with medium and high levels of prior knowledge. Thus, signaling may even be harmful to the latter students, possibly because it suppresses their active processing of information aimed at identifying text–picture correspondences on their own.

The Contiguity Principle

According to the contiguity principle (Mayer, 2021), text and corresponding pictures should be presented near (i.e., contiguous) in time and space. Based on this recommendation, two contiguity principles have been postulated: First, the temporal contiguity principle, which recommends presenting spoken text and pictures simultaneously (i.e., close in time) and not successively (i.e., separated in time). Based on CTML, the simultaneous presentation of spoken text and corresponding picture supports the integration process as both, the verbal mental representation as well as the pictorial mental representation, are more likely to be simultaneously available in working memory (Mayer, 2021).

Second, the spatial contiguity principle recommends presenting written text and pictures spatially close together and not spatially separated. This should support learning because no resource-demanding search processes are necessary and because the verbal and the pictorial mental representation are more likely simultaneously available in working memory, thereby facilitating integration (Mayer, 2021). This assumption is supported by the review of eye-tracking research in multimedia learning (Alemdag & Cagiltay, 2018), which showed that spatially contingent presentations enhanced the attentional focus as well as increased the number of integrative transitions between the spatially close representations.

Ginns (2006) examined both kinds of contiguity (i.e., spatial and temporal) together in a meta-analysis and found a large positive effect of contiguity in general (overall $d = 0.85$). In a subsequent moderator analysis, he found positive large effects for both spatial ($d = 0.72$) as well as temporal ($d = 0.78$) contiguity. Furthermore, the meta-analysis revealed that the contiguity of multimedia presentation is especially relevant when the learning material is complex (i.e., high in element interactivity). However, what remains unclear from Ginns's meta-analysis is whether complexity affects the spatial and temporal contiguity principle differently, since the two principles were synthesized in the moderator analyses.

Regarding the spatial contiguity principle, a recent meta-analysis by Schroeder and Cenkci (2018) reported a large positive effect of spatially near-text picture presentations, $g = 0.63$. Further, a number of potential moderators were tested. Noteworthy, they could not replicate Ginns' finding (2006) that complexity moderates the contiguity principle for the spatial contiguity principle. A possible explanation could be that element interactivity was coded differently in both studies. Moreover, the spatial contiguity effect appeared with low text-picture overlap, but also when the picture overlapped with the text, but the text was understandable without the picture. It did not, however, appear when the text overlapped with the picture, but the picture was understandable without the text.

Regarding the temporal contiguity principle, no current meta-analysis exists. Mayer (2021) reports a large median effect size of $d = 1.31$ based on a review of eight studies conducted by him and his colleagues. Based on single empirical studies, it seems that the temporal contiguity principle especially applies when longer segments of verbal or pictorial information are presented and the presentation is system-paced (cf. Fiorella & Mayer, 2022a).

The Verbal Redundancy Principle

According to the verbal redundancy principle (Mayer, 2021), pictures should only be presented with spoken text. The presentation of pictures together with highly redundant (i.e., identical) spoken and written text should be avoided.

Based on CTML (Mayer, 2021), the presentation of highly redundant verbal information is harmful to learning for two reasons: First, learners must reconcile what they hear with what they read. This requires mental resources, which are then no longer available for meaningful learning processes. Second, the written text and the picture are both initially processed within the visual channel. Hence, they compete for the limited resources, resulting in reduced learning outcomes (see modality principle).

The empirical evidence for the redundancy effect is mixed. Whereas an (unsystematic) review by Mayer and Fiorella (2014) reports a large median effect size of $d = 0.86$ in favor of non-redundant presentations, a meta-analysis by Adesope and Nesbit (2012) reports an overall small effect size of $g = 0.15$—in favor of redundant presentations! A closer look at both reviews provides at least a partial explanation for these inconsistent findings. Mayer and Fiorella (2014) only considered studies in their review that used identical spoken and written text and that presented redundant texts together with pictures. Adesope and Nesbit (2012), on the other hand, also incorporated studies not using pictures and with different degrees of redundancy (e.g., identical text vs. partial redundant text).

The moderator analyses by Adesope and Nesbit (2012) showed several interesting moderating effects: First, verbal redundancy enhanced learning only when compared to groups using spoken text (small effect: $g = 0.29$). When compared to groups using written text, verbal redundancy did not enhance learning ($g = -0.04$). Please note, however, that in this comparison studies using pictures and studies not using pictures are still compiled. As redundancy had an effect only compared to only-spoken text groups, Adesope and Nesbit (2012) report the further moderator analyses just for these comparisons. It revealed that redundancy was helpful when only text was presented, but not when pictures were presented (which corroborates the verbal redundancy principle); that it was helpful with system-paced presentations, but not with learner-paced presentations; that it was helpful for readers at different reading fluency levels, but especially for second-language (L2) learners; and that it was helpful for learners with low prior knowledge, but not for learners with high prior knowledge. Unfortunately, no moderation analyses are reported for pure multimedia presentations, which would be of particular importance for the present book chapter. However, what is interesting is that the meta-analytic overview shows that redundancy did even not hinder learning when pictures were presented.

The Segmenting Principle

According to the segmenting principle, multimedia learning materials should be presented in manageable, meaningful parts that are presented sequentially under the control of the learner (learner pacing) rather than being presented as a whole, continuous learning unit (Mayer, 2021). The segmenting principle is based on the limited capacity assumption and specifically refers to the situation when the amount of essential cognitive processing necessary to understand the to-be-learned material exceeds the learners' cognitive capacity. This, for instance, is the case with complex multimedia instruction that is presented at a fast pace. Presenting such materials learner-paced and in bite-sized segments helps learners perceive the underlying structure of the content and provides them sufficient time to cognitively process the essential material at the pace they need (Mayer, 2021).

Overall, there is empirical evidence for a positive effect of applying the segmenting principle in multimedia learning. In an (unsystematic) review including 14 experiments a medium median effect size of $d = 0.60$ is reported for performance in transfer tests when multimedia materials were presented in segments over presenting materials continuously (Mayer & Fiorella, 2022). Furthermore, another (unsystematic) review that specifically looked at segmenting in computer-based multimedia instruction even found a medium to large effect size (median effect size $d = 0.77$; Mayer, 2017). However, a meta-analysis that included 56 empirical studies also showed evidence supporting the segmenting effect but could only reveal small to medium effect sizes for learning performance (retention performance: $d = 0.32$, transfer performance $d = 0.36$; Rey et al., 2019).

Based on the reviews, it is assumed that the segmenting principle especially applies to complex learning content (i.e., with high element interactivity) that is fast-paced, as well as when the working memory capacity of learners is low (Mayer, 2021; Mayer & Fiorella, 2022). The meta-analysis found mixed evidence for moderators (Rey et al., 2019): Whereas the segmenting effect was confirmed for system-paced segmenting, learner-paced segmenting only improved performance in transfer tests. Also, prior knowledge was a moderator for retention performance—with larger effects for high prior knowledge learners—but did not moderate the effect for transfer performance. Finally, the reviews as well as the meta-analysis conclude that research is needed to determine what constitutes the optimal size of segments (Mayer, 2021; Mayer & Fiorella, 2022; Rey et al., 2019).

The Coherence Principle

According to the coherence principle, information that is not needed to achieve the instructional objective (i.e., extraneous information) should rather be excluded than included in a multimedia message (Mayer, 2021). In contrast to essential content information, extraneous information refers to additional relevant but nonessential details (e.g., additional interesting facts), or additional interesting but irrelevant details (i.e., seductive details, e.g., non-relevant background stories). The theoretical rationale for the coherence principle is that processing extraneous information comes at the expense of processing essential information and thus impedes learning (Fiorella & Mayer, 2022a; Mayer, 2021). This is in line with the limited capacity assumption of the CTML (Mayer, 2021) as it is assumed that adding extraneous information distracts the learner from the actual to-be-learned content and may lead to an overload of working memory. This rationale is supported by a review of eye-tracking research in multimedia learning, which has shown that seductive details draw learners' attentional focus away from essential content and hinder the integration process (Alemdag & Cagiltay, 2018).

In an overview of his 19 experiments on the coherence principle, Mayer (2021) reported a large effect (median effect size of $d = 0.86$) showing that excluding extraneous information improved learning outcomes. However, most research more specifically focused on the effect of removing seductive details (Rey, 2012; Sundararajan & Adesope, 2020). First, in a meta-analysis based on 39 experimental effects, Rey (2012) found that removing seductive details from multimedia learning material led to positive small to medium effects on retention performance ($d = 0.30$) and transfer performance ($d = 0.48$). In a second, more recent meta-analysis (68 independent effect sizes) these findings of excluding seductive details were confirmed again with a small to medium effect ($g = 0.33$) on learning performance (Sundararajan & Adesope, 2020).

Several boundary conditions were identified by the meta-analyses or discussed in literature reviews: Adding seductive details to multimedia messages seems to be particularly harmful when they impose a high cognitive load (Eitel et al., 2020; Rey, 2012) as well as when learners have low working memory capacity or low ability to control their attention (Fiorella & Mayer, 2022a; Rey, 2012). Furthermore, learning is hampered when seductive details are particularly distracting or interesting (Rey, 2012; Sundararajan & Adesope, 2020), or when instruction was paper-based rather than presented on-screen (Sundararajan & Adesope, 2020).

Integration of the Multimedia Design Principles in Educational Settings

The overview of the multimedia design principles shows that they differ in terms of the size of the effects and the consistency with which similar effect sizes were reported. For example, for the spatial contiguity principle and the temporal contiguity principle the existing meta-analyses (Ginns, 2006;

Schroeder & Cenkci, 2018) and reviews (Mayer, 2021) report consistently large effect sizes. For the animation principle, the reported effect sizes were also consistent across the meta-analyses, with albeit small effects (Berney & Bétrancourt, 2016; Höffler & Leutner, 2007; Ploetzner et al., 2020). Regarding other multimedia design principles, like the modality principle (Ginns, 2006; Mayer & Fiorella, 2022; Reinwein, 2012), the signaling principle (Alpizar et al., 2020; Richter et al., 2016; Schneider et al., 2018), the segmenting principle (Mayer, 2017; Mayer & Fiorella, 2022; Rey et al., 2019), and the coherence principle (Mayer, 2021; Rey, 2012; Sundararajan & Adesope, 2020) the reported effect sizes vary between small, medium, and large effects. A special case occurs for the redundancy principle—here the literature reports both large effects in favor of non-redundant material (Mayer & Fiorella, 2014) as well as small effects in favor of redundant material (Adesope & Nesbit, 2012). The reported inconsistencies are due to the fact that different studies are incorporated in the meta-analyses and reviews—sometimes because more empirical studies were available in the meantime (e.g., Ginns, 2005; Reinwein, 2012), in some cases, however, because the underlying selection criteria were different (e.g., Adesope & Nesbit, 2012). In a nutshell, especially the contiguity principles seem to be rather stable effects with associated large effect sizes. For the integration into educational settings, this means that texts and associated pictures should be presented as spatially and temporally close as possible. For example, if a teacher presents a picture on the smartboard, and wants to explain it to the class, this should be done simultaneously. Further, in textbooks or digital learning environments, written explanations should be integrated into the picture.

The meta-analyses and reviews also show that the effectiveness of multimedia principles often depends on certain boundary conditions. The boundary conditions most often identified were pacing (redundancy principle, modality principle, temporal contiguity principle, segmenting principle), prior knowledge (redundancy principle, signaling principle, segmenting principle), and complexity (modality principle, contiguity principles). Based on the findings it can be recommended (1) to implement the redundancy principle, the modality principle, the temporal contiguity principle, and the segmenting principle rather when system-paced learning environments are used, and (2) to implement the modality principle and contiguity principles when the complexity of the learning materials is high. For prior knowledge, the evidence is less clear: Whereas the redundancy and the signaling principle seem to be especially helpful for low prior knowledge learners, the segmentation principle is especially helpful for high prior knowledge learners, at least when retention was used as the dependent variable. Furthermore, there is empirical evidence from single studies (Kalyuga et al., 1998; Richter et al., 2018) that the positive effects of the multimedia design principles might even reverse for high prior knowledge learners (cf. expertise reversal effect,

Kalyuga et al., 2003). Especially in the latter case, we need to identify the turning point where instructional support should be reduced to enhance learning for high prior knowledge learners (cf. Renkl, 2002, SEASITE principles). Once such turning points have been identified, optimal support of learners might be achieved through adaptive learning environments (Aleven et al., 2017) that can adjust the presentation of material to learner characteristics (such as prior knowledge).

To put the multimedia design principles successfully into practice, it is important that the relevant stakeholders (e.g., teachers, instructional designers, publishers) are aware of the multimedia design principles and their effectiveness as well as the associated boundary conditions. Furthermore, especially teachers are faced with the challenge that (digital) multimedia learning materials should not replace teaching itself. Instead, (digital) multimedia learning materials have to be orchestrated in the context of classroom instruction. This makes it a necessary requirement for teachers to be familiar with the effectiveness and particular boundary conditions of the multimedia design principles.

There are, of course, open questions that future research should address. For example, most of the reported studies used short learning units and conducted the research in the laboratory. Therefore, we know little about the effectiveness of multimedia design principles if they are embedded into more comprehensive curricula. Since, for instance, motivation and self-regulation could play a major role in this context, it is unclear how this influences the effectiveness of multimedia design principles in complex, comprehensive curricula.

To conclude, even though there is some variability in the availability of evidence and some cases even contradictions, by and large the integration of multimedia design principles should be recommended. They support rather than hinder learning and, in many cases, they are not associated with larger production costs, thereby rendering them an efficient means to support student achievement.

Evidence-Based Practice Recommendations

- Learning materials that are designed according to the multimedia design principles can support learning.
- There is considerable variability in the size of the effects associated with the multimedia design principles; contradictory findings are reported for the redundancy principle.
- The multimedia design principles are particularly effective in system-paced learning environments and with high material complexity.
- Learners' prior knowledge moderates the occurrence of many of the multimedia design principles.

References

Adesope, O. O., & Nesbit, J. C. (2012). Verbal redundancy in multimedia learning environments: A meta-analysis. *Journal of Educational Psychology, 104*(1), 250–263. https://doi.org/10.1037/a0026147

Alemdag, E., & Cagiltay, K. (2018). A systematic review of eye tracking research on multimedia learning. *Computers & Education, 125,* 413–428. https://doi.org/10.1016/j.compedu.2018.06.023

Aleven, V., Connolly, H., Popescu, O., Marks, J., Lamnina, M., & Chase, C. (2017). An adaptive coach for invention activities. In E. André, R. Baker, X. Hu, M. Rodrigo, & B. du Boulay (Eds.), *Artificial intelligence in education. AIED 2017. Lecture notes in computer science* (Vol. 10331, pp. 3–14). Springer. https://doi.org/10.1007/978-3-319-61425-0_1

Alpizar, D., Adesope, O. O., & Wong, R. M. (2020). A meta-analysis of signaling principle in multimedia learning environments. *Educational Technology Research and Development, 68*(5), 2095–2119. https://doi.org/10.1007/s11423-020-09748-7

Baddeley, A. (1992). Working memory. *Science, 255*(5044), 556–559. https://doi.org/10.1126/science.1736359

Berney, S., & Bétrancourt, M. (2016). Does animation enhance learning? A meta-analysis. *Computers & Education, 101,* 150–167. https://doi.org/10.1016/j.compedu.2016.06.005

Eitel, A., Endres, T., & Renkl, A. (2020). Self-management as a bridge between cognitive load and self-regulated learning: The illustrative case of seductive details. *Educational Psychology Review, 32*(4), 1073–1087. https://doi.org/10.1007/s10648-020-09559-5

Fiorella, L., & Mayer, R. E. (2022a). Principles for reducing extraneous processing in multimedia learning: Coherence, signaling, redundancy, spatial contiguity, and temporal contiguity principles. In R. E. Mayer & L. Fiorella (Eds.), *The Cambridge handbook of multimedia learning* (3rd ed., pp. 185–198). Cambridge University Press. https://doi.org/10.1017/9781108894333.019

Fiorella, L., & Mayer, R. E. (2022b). The generative activity principle in multimedia learning. In R. E. Mayer & L. Fiorella (Eds.), *The Cambridge handbook of multimedia learning* (3rd ed., pp. 339–350). Cambridge University Press. https://doi.org/10.1017/9781108894333.036

Gegenfurtner, A., Gruber, H., Holzberger, D., Keskin, Ö., Lehtinen, E., Seidel, T., Stürmer, K., & Säljö, R. (2022). Towards a cognitive theory of visual expertise: Methods of inquiry. In C. Damşa, A. Rajala, G. Ritella, & J. Brouwer (Eds.), *Re-theorizing learning and research methods in learning research.* Routledge.

Ginns, P. (2005). Meta-analysis of the modality effect. *Learning and Instruction, 15*(4), 313–331. https://doi.org/10.1016/j.learninstruc.2005.07.001

Ginns, P. (2006). Integrating information: A meta-analysis of the spatial contiguity and temporal contiguity effects. *Learning and Instruction, 16*(6), 511–525. https://doi.org/10.1016/j.learninstruc.2006.10.001

Hegarty, M. (1992). Mental animation: Inferring motion from static displays of mechanical systems. *Journal of Experimental Psychology: Learning, Memory, and Cognition, 18*(5), 1084–1102. https://doi.org/10.1037/0278-7393.18.5.1084

Höffler, T. N., & Leutner, D. (2007). Instructional animation versus static pictures: A meta-analysis. *Learning and Instruction, 17*(6), 722–738. https://doi.org/10.1016/j.learninstruc.2007.09.013

Kalyuga, S., Ayres, P., Chandler, P., & Sweller, J. (2003). The expertise reversal effect. *Educational Psychologist*, 38(1), 23–31. https://doi.org/10.1207/S15326985EP3801_4

Kalyuga, S., Chandler, P., & Sweller, J. (1998). Levels of expertise and instructional design. *Human Factors: The Journal of the Human Factors and Ergonomics Society*, 40(1), 1–17. https://doi.org/10.1518/001872098779480587

Lowe, R. K., & Boucheix, J.-M. (2008). Learning from animated diagrams: How are mental models built? In G. Stapleton, J. Howse, & J. Lee (Eds.), *Diagrammatic representation and inference* (pp. 266–281). Springer.

Lowe, R. K., & Schnotz, W. (2014). Animation principles in multimedia learning. In R. E. Mayer (Ed.), *The Cambridge handbook of multimedia learning* (2nd ed., pp. 513–546). Cambridge University Press. https://doi.org/10.1017/CBO9781139547369.026

Lowe, R. K., Schnotz, W., & Boucheix, J.-M. (2022). The animation composition principle in multimedia learning. In R. E. Mayer & L. Fiorella (Eds.), *The Cambridge handbook of multimedia learning* (3rd ed., pp. 313–323). Cambridge University Press. https://doi.org/10.1017/9781108894333.033

Mayer, R. E. (2017). Using multimedia for e-learning. *Journal of Computer Assisted Learning*, 33(5), 403–423. https://doi.org/10.1111/jcal.12197

Mayer, R. E. (2021). *Multimedia learning* (3rd ed.). Cambridge University Press. https://doi.org/10.1017/9781316941355

Mayer, R. E., & Fiorella, L. (2014). Principles for reducing extraneous processing in multimedia learning: Coherence, signaling, redundancy, spatial contiguity, and temporal contiguity principles. In R. E. Mayer (Ed.), *The Cambridge handbook of multimedia learning* (2nd ed., pp. 279–315). Cambridge University Press. https://doi.org/10.1017/CBO9781139547369.015

Mayer, R. E., & Fiorella, L. (2022). Principles for managing essential processing in multimedia learning: Segmenting, pre-training, and modality principles. In R. E. Mayer & L. Fiorella (Eds.), *The Cambridge handbook of multimedia learning* (3rd ed., pp. 243–260). Cambridge University Press. https://doi.org/10.1017/9781108894333.025

Noetel, M., Griffith, S., Delaney, O., Harris, N. R., Sanders, T., Parker, P., del Pozo Cruz, B., & Lonsdale, C. (2022). Multimedia design for learning: An overview of reviews with meta-meta-analysis. *Review of Educational Research*, 92(3), 413–454. https://doi.org/10.3102/00346543211052329

Paivio, A. (1990). *Mental representations*. Oxford University Press. https://doi.org/10.1093/acprof:oso/9780195066661.001.0001

Ploetzner, R., Berney, S., & Bétrancourt, M. (2020). A review of learning demands in instructional animations: The educational effectiveness of animations unfolds if the features of change need to be learned. *Journal of Computer Assisted Learning*, 36(6), 838–860. https://doi.org/10.1111/jcal.12476

Reinwein, J. (2012). Does the modality effect exist? and if so, which modality effect? *Journal of Psycholinguistic Research*, 41(1), 1–32. https://doi.org/10.1007/s10936-011-9180-4

Renkl, A. (2002). Learning from worked-out examples: Instructional explanations supplement self-explanations. *Learning and Instruction*, 12, 529–556.

Rey, G. D. (2012). A review of research and a meta-analysis of the seductive detail effect. *Educational Research Review*, 7(3), 216–237. https://doi.org/10.1016/j.edurev.2012.05.003

Rey, G. D., Beege, M., Nebel, S., Wirzberger, M., Schmitt, T. H., & Schneider, S. (2019). A meta-analysis of the segmenting effect. *Educational Psychology Review*, *31*(2), 389–419. https://doi.org/10.1007/s10648-018-9456-4

Richter, J., Scheiter, K., & Eitel, A. (2016). Signaling text-picture relations in multimedia learning: A comprehensive meta-analysis. *Educational Research Review*, *17*, 19–36. https://doi.org/10.1016/j.edurev.2015.12.003

Richter, J., Scheiter, K., & Eitel, A. (2018). Signaling text–picture relations in multimedia learning: The influence of prior knowledge. *Journal of Educational Psychology*, *110*(4), 544–560. https://doi.org/10.1037/edu0000220

Rummer, R., Schweppe, J., Fürstenberg, A., Scheiter, K., & Zindler, A. (2011). The perceptual basis of the modality effect in multimedia learning. *Journal of Experimental Psychology: Applied*, *17*(2), 159–173. https://doi.org/10.1037/a0023588

Schneider, S., Beege, M., Nebel, S., & Rey, G. D. (2018). A meta-analysis of how signaling affects learning with media. *Educational Research Review*, *23* (November 2017), 1–24. https://doi.org/10.1016/j.edurev.2017.11.001

Schnotz, W., & Bannert, M. (2003). Construction and interference in learning from multiple representation. *Learning and Instruction*, *13*(2), 141–156. https://doi.org/10.1016/S0959-4752(02)00017-8

Schroeder, N. L., & Cenkci, A. T. (2018). Spatial contiguity and spatial split-attention effects in multimedia learning environments: A meta-analysis. *Educational Psychology Review*, *30*(3), 679–701. https://doi.org/10.1007/s10648-018-9435-9

Schüler, A., Scheiter, K., & Schmidt-Weigand, F. (2011). Boundary conditions and constraints of the modality effect. *Zeitschrift Für Pädagogische Psychologie*, *25*(4), 211–220. https://doi.org/10.1024/1010-0652/a000046

Sundararajan, N., & Adesope, O. (2020). Keep it coherent: A meta-analysis of the seductive details effect. *Educational Psychology Review*, *32*(3), 707–734. https://doi.org/10.1007/s10648-020-09522-4

van Gog, T. (2022). The signaling (or cueing) principle in multimedia learning. In R. E. Mayer & L. Fiorella (Eds.), *The Cambridge handbook of multimedia learning* (3rd ed., pp. 221–230). Cambridge University Press. https://doi.org/10.1017/9781108894333.022

3

DESIGN OF EFFECTIVE DIGITAL READING COMPREHENSION ENVIRONMENTS

Ladislao Salmerón, Lidia Altamura, Laura Gil and Amelia Mañá

Design of effective digital reading comprehension environments

Educational institutions across the world have moved rapidly to integrate digital reading tools in the classroom to support comprehension and learning. As is the case with many educational innovations, that move has been quicker than our understanding of how to best design digital environments to foster reading comprehension. Recent meta-analytical and large-scale data show that the transition from paper to digital reading can bring serious risks to students. Plain digital texts, as compared to printed versions, are comprehended slightly poorly, as documented by meta-analyses that synthesize primary studies focusing on children (Furenes et al., 2021), as well as by those that focus on a wide range of ages (Clinton, 2019; Delgado et al., 2018; Kong et al., 2018). In the same vein, a higher frequency of use of digital reading tools in the classroom negatively correlates with students' comprehension skills, as documented in two large representative samples of 4th and 8th grade US students, even after controlling for the potential confounding effects of a relevant set of students' and teachers' factors (Salmerón et al., 2022). In conclusion, we cannot just assume that the introduction of any digital reading activity in schools will be, at best, neutral for students' reading comprehension. On the contrary, given that digital-based reading is an integral part of the current educational realm, a strong effort should be made to select and design digital environments that may support students' skill development.

In the following, we review current literature on how to design effective digital reading environments to support students' comprehension and learning, and discuss relevant individual factors that must be considered in their design.

DOI: 10.4324/9781003386131-5

Finally, we discuss how students could benefit from hybrid reading environments, which take the best of well-designed printed and digital reading.

Features of digital texts

In trying to identify effective designs for digital reading environments, we should first start by defining what we mean by digital texts. There are at least four major definitions of digital reading that have shaped researchers' efforts to understand how design can support comprehension (Coiro, 2021; Salmerón et al., 2018): 1) screen reading; 2) Internet reading; 3) multimodal text reading; and 4) interactive digital reading. While these conceptions refer to non-exclusive definitions of digital reading (e.g. Internet reading can only take place on a screen), research tended to emphasize specific design aspects particularly relevant to each scenario.[1] In this subsection, we revise the literature concerning the design based on these major definitions and conclude with recommendations to support students' self-regulation during digital reading.

Screen reading

In its simplest form, digital reading is any kind of reading that takes place on a screen, as opposed to in print. From this perspective, three major design issues that may impact comprehension are screen size, paging vs. scrolling, and screen luminosity. Regarding size, a common intuition is that reading on a small screen, such as on a smartphone, would lead to lower comprehension. However, research on this issue is inconclusive, with research finding both null as well as negative effects favoring larger screens (Haverkamp et al., 2022). Regarding scrolling, meta-analytical evidence shows a tendency to favor paging over scrolling (Delgado et al., 2018). For example, undergraduate students read a long expository digital text, those who read the text using paging tended to show higher integrative comprehension than those using scrolling, and showed more instances of strategic backtracking to revise previous sections of the text (Haverkamp et al., 2022). Finally, regarding the effects of screen luminosity, Benedetto et al. (2013) found that among a group of adult readers, those who read a novel on a liquid crystal display (like an iPad) showed higher visual fatigue than those reading on an e-ink device (i.e. an e-reader) or in print. When it comes to comprehension, few studies have shown that low levels of luminosity (i.e. 50 lux) induce lower comprehension than higher levels (i.e. 500–12000 lux) (e.g. Wang & Lin, 2016).

Internet reading

Reading on the Internet presents different challenges than interacting with plain digital texts, some of which have been the focus of studies on effective interface designs. Once students go on the Internet, a great number of digital texts are readily accessible. Accordingly, they are responsible for selecting and potentially integrating a manageable subset of texts, usually via search engine results pages (SERPs). Few studies have shown that young students tend to base their selection decisions on giving more importance to superficial cues, such as the position of the result or typographical cues, than to the relevance of the webpage (Salmerón et al., 2018). As a consequence of inefficient navigation decisions, readers can easily lose track of what they are reading, a feeling termed "getting lost in hyperspace" (Theng & Thimbleby, 1998). To prevent this, webpages can incorporate graphical overviews, also termed navigational overviews, concept maps, or digital knowledge maps (see Amadieu & Salmerón, 2014), of the linked pages and their underlying structure to scaffold readers' comprehension and maximize their navigation coherence. According to Fesel et al. (2018), the effectiveness of graphical overviews depends on the complexity of the underlying hyperlink structure. While overviews can be beneficial for hierarchical structures, they may not be useful to support more complex networked structures. Another challenge of Internet reading is that it contains a great deal of dubious or false information, and readers must critically evaluate the information to avoid incorrect information. Recent research efforts are aimed at designing scenarios for increasing readers' skepticism toward misinformation, for instance, by providing warnings about possible misinformation on social media before reading (Scharrer et al., 2022).

Multimodal digital reading

Multimodal digital texts incorporate not only written information but also spoken or visual information in the form of pictures, graphs, animations, or videos. Few models describe how textual, pictorial, and auditory information are processed through separate channels, potentially resulting in a richer and more accessible mental representation than if only one channel is used (e.g. Mayer, 2005). However, the integration of information from different modalities is a demanding process requiring efficient use of cognitive capacity. Accordingly, the benefits of multimedia digital texts seem to rely on a careful design of the material that supports readers' attempts to integrate information from different modalities. In a recent meta-analysis, Noetel et al. (2022) identified 11 design principles that supported comprehension or learning (Table 3.1). The largest benefits, with medium to high effect sizes, were found for captioning second-language videos, temporal/spatial contiguity, and signaling. Other multimodal principles also provided positive jet small-size effects. Additionally, the efficacy of multimedia principles was more salient for more complex materials, as well as in system-paced environments than self-paced ones (e.g., websites).

TABLE 3.1 Design principles to support comprehension and learning of multimedia digital texts.

Multimedia principles	Definition	Effect size g [95% CI]
Captioning second-language videos	Provide captioning when presenting videos to non-native readers.	0.99 [0.60, 1.38]
Temporal/spatial contiguity	Presenting related multimodal material in the same place or at the same time.	0.74 [0.67, 0.82]
Signaling	Using design cues to guide students' attention toward more relevant information.	0.43 [0.35, 0.50]
Modality	Pictures must be complemented with audio rather than with text.	0.38 [0.33, 0.43]
Animation	Meaningful procedures must be displayed by means of animated, dynamic graphics, rather than with static images.	0.35 [0.29, 0.42]
Coherence/removing seductive details	Avoid content that could distract learners from the core content required for the reading task).	0.34 [0.30, 0.38]
Anthropomorphic	Human features added to graphics.	0.33 [0.23, 0.44]
Segmentation	Breaking a multimedia text into meaningful groups.	0.33 [0.18, 0.48]
Personalization	Adapting language to be either simpler, more polite, or more related to the reader.	0.23 [0.12, 0.33]
Pedagogical agents	An artificial tutor that guides the reader.	0.19 [0.12, 0.26]
Verbal redundancy	Including textual words in narrated audio (but not adding spoken words to written text).	0.15 [0.08, 0.22]
	Overall pooled effect size.	0.38 [0.27, 0.49]

Interactive digital reading

Interactive digital texts incorporate features that users can act upon, including hotspots (i.e. elements within the text that when being tapped initiate sounds, simple animations, and dialogue/sounds from the characters), digital glossaries, questions, or other type of tasks with feedback, collaborative annotations tools, or hyperlinks. Accordingly, interactively digital texts can provide a rich set of features that can accommodate different students' needs. However, those features can act as affordances or as constraints for comprehension. Recent meta-analyses by Furenes et al. (2021) and Clinton-Lisell et al. (2022) synthesize empirical research analyzing the effects of some interactive features on vocabulary and comprehension in children's narrative books and interactive digital textbooks, respectively. Furenes et al. (2021) concluded that the design of the features is critical, as those that support students' attempts to focus on the text's gist tend to improve comprehension, while those that distract them from the main points tend to have detrimental effects. This last point is clearly exemplified by hotspots, which can easily attract children's attention. When their design is aligned with the history plot, such as when a sound is coherent with the hidden character's intentions, they can support children's attempts to build a coherent representation of the story. If not, they can detract children's attention from the story, resulting in impoverished comprehension. Hyperlinks can also be a useful interactive element. Delgado et al. (2020) explored their utility when encountering conflicting information and dealing with multiple information sources in order to prevent readers from losing track of the text being read. In their meta-analysis, Clinton-Lisell et al. (2022) found a medium-sized positive effect of several interactive digital tools on comprehension, including questions, glossaries, and collaborative annotation tools. However, most of the included studies that showed positive effects had multiple interactive features, which makes it difficult to identify the most effective ones. The authors noticed that a critical issue in most studies was the extent to which students actually used the interactive features provided to them. Accordingly, they concluded, systems could be designed in which readers are obliged to respond to hints and prompts before continuing reading. Nevertheless, such logic contrasts with the adaptive nature of interactive digital texts, that is, to provide readers with the autonomy to decide if and when to use the affordances offered by the text to support their comprehension.

Feedback as a digital self-regulation tool

Being able to self-regulate digital reading is a big challenge. A great deal of research has studied how to support self-regulation and comprehension by means of system feedback (e.g. Swart et al., 2022). Feedback targeting text comprehension is defined as the "individualized information in response to readers' answer to comprehension questions about the text they read" (Swart et al., 2022, p. 3). Compared to classical feedback, digital systems can effectively provide more adaptive feedback based on the interpretation of students' states, for instance, using non-intrusive methodologies such as eye-tracking (Mills et al., 2021). Feedback can take various forms and, if we focus on the content of the message, there is a consensus to differentiate three types of feedback (Narciss, 2008; Shute, 2008): (1) *Knowledge of Response* (KR) or *Verification* contains information on the accuracy of the answers (e.g., Correct/Incorrect, 7.5/10, right answer); (2) *Knowledge of Correct Response* (KCR) provides the student with the expected response pattern (e.g., The solution is X, You should have said X) and (3) *Elaborated Feedback*

(EF) may include, in addition to KR or KCR, explanations of mistakes in the response, examples, hints or recommendations for improving the response, etc. According to different meta-analyses (van der Kleij et al., 2015; Wisniewski et al., 2019), EF is the most effective as it can help readers to fill the gap between their current level of text comprehension and the desirable level of understanding (i.e. a complete and coherent mental representation of information). That is, when readers get feedback with information about their current level of comprehension, they are able to activate monitoring processes that are essential for self-regulating their comprehension process (ter Beek et al., 2018) and, in turn, comprehension (Mañá et al., 2017). Recently, Swart et al. (2022) found that comprehension-focused feedback had a moderate positive effect on the use of reading strategies when reading a new text, as well as positively predicting final reading comprehension. Moreover, regarding the timing, they concluded that providing feedback during reading is likely to be more effective than after reading in teaching reading strategies that the learner can carry over into further reading. Therefore, considering that digital reading increases the reader's interaction and need for self-regulation, providing tailored EF during the reading process is a great instructional tool in digital reading (Kabudi et al., 2021).

As we know, digital systems have the advantage of being able to record the reading process (i.e. reading time, reading sequence, and links clicked) as well as the final performance and use this information to provide personalized feedback messages. However, designing effective feedback is not an easy task, especially in computerized environments where written feedback tends to be processed superficially (Timmers & Veldkamp, 2011). How can we design effective feedback in digital learning environments? According to ter Beek et al. (2018), effective feedback should help readers pay attention to both the cognitive and affective components of self-regulated learning. That is, messages should focus both on the strategies used or the ones that could be used to solve the task, and on motivational processes to protect the will to learn. Also, Panadero & Lipnevich (2022) state the need to adapt the information to the cognitive, motivational, emotional, and self-regulatory reactions of the learner. Despite these evidences, Maier & Klotz (2022) in a recent review have found that computerized feedback messages are more frequently adapted to student's current knowledge (i.e. task performance, incorrect exercises, or misconceptions) and less frequently to progress measures or to student's trait variables (e.g. attitudes or goal orientation). Accordingly, they also found that personalized feedback aims mainly to raise student's overall performance (62% of the studies reviewed), followed by engagement or motivation (29%) and self-regulated learning (9%). Altogether, it shows that the potential of digital reading environments for adapting feedback is not being fully exploited. This is represented by the few existing studies about feedback targeting motivational and self-regulated processes. For instance,

De Sixte et al. (2020) compared the impact of EF and the additional implementation of motivational elements (i.e. warm elaborated feedback -WEF) on the reading strategies of young students. Post-feedback behavior was measured as the rereading of relevant text information. Although both types of feedback showed more information rereading than a control group, readers who received WEF showed almost 50% more rereading than those who only received EF.

In summary, the evidence shows that the effectiveness of feedback depends on tailoring messages to the cognitive and motivational characteristics of the learner, although it seems that more research is needed related to tailoring to emotional and motivational characteristics in digital learning environments. As we shall review next, other relevant students' characteristics may moderate the effects of design features of digital texts.

Individual differences and the design of digital texts

Leu et al. (2015) point out in a review on individual differences in digital reading that we are unable to simply apply what we know about the effects of individual differences on reading and learning with printed texts to digital learning environments. Accordingly, in recent years there has been growing research interest in investigating how several individual differences specifically influence digital reading abilities and related activities (Afflerbach, 2015; Cho et al., 2021). As Coiro (2021) suggests, that it is important to clarify how these variables interact with one another, with texts, and with other features of the learning environments to influence performance on a particular digital reading activity. Although we do not have enough space to conduct an exhaustive review of the issue, we would like to highlight some of the main readers' characteristics that should be considered when designing effective digital learning environments. We focus on students' print-reading skills, gender, prior knowledge, motivational competencies, and different cognitive and metacognitive levels in digital reading, including a small mention of the case of students with learning disabilities.

The first and strongest predictor of digital reading comprehension is its close analogous: print reading comprehension (e.g., Cho & Afflerbach, 2017; Coiro, 2011; Leu et al., 2015). In general, readers who do better with print text comprehension are more likely to also do better comprehending digital texts than readers who have difficulties in comprehending printed texts (Kanniainen et al., 2019).

Secondly, regarding gender, the classic gap in print reading comprehension that has systematically favored girls in the last decades seems to be maintained when reading takes place in digital media. As an example of this trend, in all countries and economies that participated in PISA 2018, girls significantly outperformed boys in digital reading – by almost 30 score points, on average across OECD countries (OECD, 2019). Another example of such a consistent gender gap can be found in the study of Forzani (2018), in which within a large sample of seventh-grade students, girls outperformed boys in their ability to do online research and digital reading comprehension.

Thirdly, there is consensus that students' prior knowledge (PK) of a reading topic is a major contributor to reading comprehension in printed texts (e.g. McNamara & Magliano, 2009). On the issue at hand, several studies have shown that differences in PK also appear to be important during digital reading. For instance, Forzani (2018) encountered that students with greater PK and print reading comprehension ability can better evaluate online information compared with those with less PK. However, Coiro (2011) found that domain PK did not significantly contribute to predicting online research and comprehension performance among 13-year-old students when offline reading comprehension ability was controlled. Using other types of digital activities, specifically hypertext reading, Salmerón et al. (2005) showed that the benefit of PK only emerged when readers faced more challenging reading conditions (in this case, low coherence of the texts). In sum, results suggest that in a digital reading environment, higher levels of PK are associated with better reading comprehension, especially the benefit of challenging coherence gaps, which readers must complete with their own experiences. Nevertheless, due to the heterogeneity in digital reading activities and processes, more research is needed to establish the precise role of domain knowledge in digital reading.

Fourth, several studies have focused their interest on how motivational competencies play a role in reading comprehension. For instance, Cho et al. (2021) examined how individual differences, home-school resources, and instructional support could predict the digital reading comprehension of primary school students. They conducted multilevel regressions with two levels (student and school) using US datasets from (e)PIRLS 2016. Results at the student level indicated that the participating fourth graders' digital reading comprehension was predicted by their proficiency in print reading comprehension in conjunction with differences in student motivational differences (e.g. reader self-concept) and home resources. At the school level, however, neither digital resources nor instructional support were significant predictors of students' digital reading comprehension.

Finally, a large part of the studies on digital reading have focused their efforts on examining how readers process digital texts, trying to establish the cognitive and metacognitive processes that determine individual differences in students' digital reading performance and competence. According to Coiro (2021), these studies can be synthesized in five main categories that would explain such differences: the ability to attend to and remember information, monitor and self-regulate one's understanding, critically evaluate information for different purposes, integrate and synthesize information, and deeply process information.

In addition, these studies have led some researchers to investigate how these differences in cognitive and metacognitive processes emerge in some special populations of readers. Understandably, children with learning disabilities, such as those with dyslexia, ADHD, or intellectual disabilities, often have constraints with these skills, and may experience difficulties reading and understanding texts presented digitally (Ben-Yehudah et al., 2018). As an example of this area of study, Salmerón et al. (2016) investigated how adults with mild intellectual disabilities select web pages from the Internet. Contrary to their expectations, the results revealed that participants were able to select relevant and trustworthy web pages of familiar topics, although they also found that they needed more support when searching for information about less familiar topics.

From a different perspective, research has also analyzed how the affordances of digital learning environments can support populations who struggle in traditional print-reading environments. For example, several studies have shown the effectiveness of computer-assisted instruction in helping children at risk for dyslexia to develop pre-reading and basic reading skills (Torgesen et al., 2010) and for improving the level of reading comprehension of students with attention deficit disorders (Solomonidou et al., 2004), or intellectual disabilities (Snyder & Huber, 2019). Another example of the affordances of the digital environment is the flexibility of digital texts to customize the display and adjust it to help the learner. For instance, struggling readers can control font size and line spacing (Schneps et al., 2013), and readers with attentional difficulties could better focus their attention on reading in digital media with the help of multimedia elements (Shaw & Lewis, 2005). In sum, considering individual differences while designing digital reading environments can help to boost students' potential and mitigate their limitations.

A future of hybrid text scenarios

As we discussed earlier in this chapter, recent empirical evidence emphasizes the risks of a full transition from paper to digital reading in educational settings (e.g. Clinton, 2019; Delgado et al., 2018). As we have seen, careful design of digital reading environments can leverage students' comprehension and learning. However, at the moment, print reading still offers affordances for comprehension that should not be discarded, and that could be integrated with digital reading environments to create powerful hybrid scenarios.

The first affordance of in-print reading is its capacity to promote higher-focused reading. In a survey of 429 university students from several countries, including the USA, Japan, Germany, Slovakia, and India, Baron et al. (2017) found that the majority of participants (approx. 92%) found it easier to concentrate when reading in print rather than on screens. When indicating what they liked least of both media, 21% of the negative comments about digital texts concerned distraction or disorientation. One could argue that part of this distraction comes from system notifications that could be easily eliminated in designing digital reading environments. However, distraction can also come from students' interaction habits with digital screens. In their survey, Baron et al. (2017) found that students reported that they were more likely to multitask when reading on screen than in print. As multitasking during reading has negative consequences for comprehension (see Clinton-Lisell, 2021 for a meta-analysis), we can conclude that part of the screen reading disadvantage comes from such detrimental habits. In sum, teachers and instructors could introduce in-print reading as a way to train students to stay focused during reading.

A second affordance of in-print reading is that it is well-designed for reflective, long-form reading. As recently pointed out by van der Weel and Mangen (2022), in promoting digital reading environments we face the risk of reinterpreting our notion of text comprehension as mainly the primary outcome of processing digital texts, neglecting other facets of text comprehension such as long-form reading, which can be better promoted by printed texts. To avoid such oversimplification, we encourage educational settings to promote hybrid scenarios where digital and printed texts are used to support different reading comprehension processes. Teachers and instructors are encouraged to reflect on the pedagogical needs imposed by the topic to be learned and the tasks to be performed, and to select the best format for each purpose. Digital texts should be particularly recommended when the topic may benefit from a multimedia presentation; when learning about socio-scientific controversies, as the Internet facilitates students with quick and easy access to multiple perspectives of complex topics; or when the digital environment includes a well-designed feedback system. Printed options, or at least plain digital texts (as in e-readers), would be better suited for supporting the comprehension of long texts, and tasks that may require high-level comprehension processes, such as a final paper assignment.

Conclusion

As discussed in this chapter, digital reading environment designs should take into account several aspects related to digital text reading. For instance, features such as screen characteristics closer to print reading had better outcomes in reading performance and experience. To avoid students getting "lost in the hyperspace" we can scaffold their navigation skills, by providing navigational overviews or concept maps. However, how can we do it on complex networked structures? Research is needed to explore possible tools addressing this issue. Also, based on the poor abilities of readers to accurately assess credibility and source quality, we highlight the need to teach strategies so students become more efficient in detecting unreliable source-based information. Interactive elements could foster digital reading, as their design is aligned to fit students' meaning-construction efforts. However, because of their great variety, meta-analytic research is needed to analyze the contribution of specific interactive elements to digital reading. Regarding individual characteristics, self-regulation skills are essential to self-monitor readers' own processes. One beneficial tool is the EF that includes motivational aspects, which can be personally adapted in digital reading environments.

We advocate for a progressive digital transition based on evidence, acknowledging the advantages of digital but also print reading. Teachers and educators need to properly identify which media suits better for the task demands and skills required of the students. For instance, studying during long periods in print reading can be more adequate, while digital reading multimedia and the elements from interactive digital texts can enhance the processes required in searching and integrating information from different sources. We highlight the continuously changing nature of digital reading as technology and innovations keep growing. Accordingly, researchers and educators must keep in mind that the scientific field of digital reading still faces more uncertainties than truths, particularly when it comes to relevant aspects such as the role of individual differences, which potentially provide a large source of variability.

Evidence-based practice recommendations

Use multimedia design principles when creating multimodal digital texts.

Use interactive features that are well aligned with the gist of digital texts.

Implement EF that accounts for students' cognitive, motivational, and behavioral characteristics.

Consider hybrid in-print and digital systems that best match the reading purpose and task.

Take advantage of digital adaptability according to individual differences and needs.

Acknowledgments

Funding for this work was provided by Grant PID2023-152565OB-I00 funded by MCIN/AEI/10.13039/501100011033, from the Spanish Ministry of Science and Innovation.

Note

1 We use the term *scenario* as a synonym of *environment*, since we present here scientific evidences that have employed digital reading settings in which they measured different skills and variables. This meaning is the same that PISA reports use to describe their tests, the definition comes from authors O'Reilly & Sabatini (2013):

A scenario-based assessment mimics the way an individual interacts and uses literacy source material in a more authentic way than in traditional, decontextualized assessments. It presents students with realistic problems and issues to solve, and it involves the use of both basic and higher-level reading and reasoning skills.

References

Afflerbach, P. (2015). An overview of individual differences in reading: Research, policy, and practice. In P. Afflerbach (Ed.), *Handbook of individual differences in reading: Reader, text, and context* (pp. 19–30). Routledge. https://doi.org/10.4324/9780203075562

Amadieu, F., & Salmerón, L. (2014). Concept maps for comprehension and navigation of hypertexts. In D. Ifenthaler & R. Hanewald (Eds.), *Digital knowledge maps in education: Technology-enhanced support for teachers and learners* (pp. 41–59). Springer Science + Business Media. https://doi.org/10.1007/978-1-4614-3178-7_3

Baron, N. S., Calixte, R. M., & Havewala, M. (2017). The persistence of print among university students: An exploratory study. *Telematics and Informatics, 34*(5), 590–604. https://doi.org/10.1016/j.tele.2016.11.008

Benedetto, S., Drai-Zerbib, V., Pedrotti, M., Tissier, G., & Baccino, T. (2013). E-readers and visual fatigue. *PloS One, 8*(12), e83676. https://doi.org/10.1371/journal.pone.0083676

Ben-Yehudah, G., Hautala, J., Padeliadu, S., Antoniou, F., Petrová, Z., Leppänen, P., & Barzillai, M. (2018). Affordances and challenges of digital reading for individuals with different learning profiles. M. Barzillai, J. Thomson, S. Schroeder, & P. van der Broek (Eds.), *Learning to read in a digital world* (pp. 121–140). John Benjamins.

Cho, B.Y., & Afflerbach, P. (2017). An evolving perspective of constructively responsive reading comprehension strategies in multilayered digital text environments. In S. E. Israel (Ed.), *Handbook of research on reading comprehension* (pp. 109–134). The Guilford Press.

Cho, B. Y., Hwang, H., & Jang, B. G. (2021). Predicting fourth grade digital reading comprehension: A secondary data analysis of (e) PIRLS 2016. *International Journal of Educational Research, 105*, 101696. https://doi.org/10.1016/j.ijer.2020.101696

Clinton, V. (2019). Reading from paper compared to screens: A systematic review and meta-analysis. *Journal of Research in Reading, 42*(2), 288–325. https://doi.org/10.1111/1467-9817.12269

Clinton-Lisell, V. (2021). Stop multitasking and just read: Meta-analyses of multitasking's effects on reading performance and reading time. *Journal of Research in Reading, 44*(4), 787–816. https://doi.org/10.1111/1467-9817.12372

Clinton-Lisell, V., Seipel, B., Gilpin, S., & Litzinger, C. (2022). Interactive features of E-texts' effects on learning: A systematic review and meta-analysis. *Interactive Learning Environments*, 1–16. https://doi.org/10.1080/10494820.2021.1943453

Coiro, J. (2011). Predicting reading comprehension on the Internet: Contributions of offline reading skills, online reading skills, and prior knowledge. *Journal of Literacy Research*, *43*(4), 352–392. https://doi.org/10.1177%2F10862 96X11421979

Coiro, J. (2021). Toward a multifaceted heuristic of digital reading to inform assessment, research, practice, and policy. *Reading Research Quarterly*, *56*(1), 9–31. https://doi.org/10.1002/rrq.302

De Sixte, R., Mañá, A., Ávila, V., & Sánchez, E. (2020). Warm elaborated feedback. Exploring its benefits on post-feedback behaviour. *Educational Psychology*, *40*(9), 1094–1112. https://doi.org/10.1080/01443410.2019.1687853

Delgado, P., Stang-Lund, E., Salmerón, L., & Bråten, I. (2020). To click or not to click: Investigating conflict detection and sourcing in a multiple document hypertext environment. *Reading and Writing*, *33*, 2049–2072. https://doi.org/10.1007/s11145-020-10030-8

Delgado, P., Vargas, C., Ackerman, R., & Salmerón, L. (2018). Don't throw away your printed books: A meta-analysis on the effects of reading media on reading comprehension. *Educational Research Review*, *25*, 23–38. https://doi.org/10.1016/j.edurev.2018.09.003

Fesel, S. S., Segers, E., & Verhoeven, L. (2018). Individual variation in children's reading comprehension across digital text types. *Journal of Research in Reading*, *41*(1), 106–121. https://onlinelibrary.wiley.com/doi/full/10.1111/jcal.12243

Forzani, E. (2018). How well can students evaluate online science information? Contributions of prior knowledge, gender, socioeconomic status, and offline reading ability. *Reading Research Quarterly*, *53*(4), 385–390. https://psycnet.apa.org/doi/10.1002/rrq.218

Furenes, M. I., Kucirkova, N., & Bus, A. G. (2021). A comparison of children's reading on paper versus screen: A meta-analysis. *Review of Educational Research*, *91*(4), 483–517. https://doi.org/10.3102/0034654321998074

Haverkamp, Y. E., Bråten, I., Latini, N., & Salmerón, L. (2022). Is it the size, the movement, or both? Investigating effects of screen size and text movement on processing, understanding, and motivation when students read informational text. *Reading and Writing*, 1–20. https://doi.org/10.1007/s11145-022-10328-9

Kabudi, T., Pappas, I., & Olsen, D. H. (2021). AI-enabled adaptive learning systems: A systematic mapping of the literature. *Computers and Education: Artificial Intelligence*, *2*, 100017. https://doi.org/10.1016/j.caeai.2021.100017

Kanniainen, L., Kiili, C., Tolvanen, A., Aro, M., & Leppänen, P. H. (2019). Literacy skills and online research and comprehension: Struggling readers face difficulties online. *Reading and Writing*, *32*(9), 2201–2222. https://doi.org/10.1007/s11145-019-09944-9

Kong, Y., Seo, Y. S., & Zhai, L. (2018). Comparison of reading comprehension on screen and on paper: A metaanalysis. *Computers & Education*, *123*, 138–149. https://doi.org/10.1016/j.compedu.2018.05.005

Leu, D. J., Kiili, C., & Forzani, E. (2015). Individual differences in the new literacies of online research and comprehension. In P. Afflerbach (Ed.), *Handbook of individual differences in reading: Reader, text, and context* (pp. 277–290). Routledge.

Maier, U., & Klotz, C. (2022). Personalized feedback in digital learning environments: Classification framework and literature review. *Computers and Education: Artificial Intelligence*, 100080. https://doi.org/10.1016/j.caeai.2022.100080

Mañá, A., Vidal-Abarca, E., & Salmerón, L. (2017). Effect of delay on search decisions in a task-oriented reading environment. *Metacognition and Learning*, 12(1), 113–130. https://doi.org/10.1007/s11409-016-9162-x

Mayer, R. E. (2005). Cognitive theory of multimedia learning. In R. E. Mayer (Ed.), *The Cambridge handbook of multimedia learning* (pp. 31–48). Cambridge University Press. https://doi.org/10.1017/CBO9780511816819.004

Mills, C., Gregg, J., Bixler, R., & D'Mello, S. K. (2021). Eye-mind reader: An intelligent reading interface that promotes long-term comprehension by detecting and responding to mind wandering. *Human-Computer Interaction*, 36, 306–332. https://doi.org/10.1080/07370024.2020.1716762

Noetel, M., Griffith, S., Delaney, O., Harris, N. R., Sanders, T., Parker, P., del Pozo, B., & Lonsdale, C. (2022). Multimedia design for learning: An overview of reviews with meta-meta-analysis. *Review of Educational Research*, 92(3), 413–454. https://doi.org/10.3102/00346543211052329

O'Reilly, T., & Sabatini, J. (2013). *Reading for understanding: How performance moderators and scenarios impact assessment design*. ETS Research Report RR-13-31, http://www.ets.org/Media/Research/pdf/RR-13-31.pdf

OECD (2019). *PISA 2018 results (volume II): Where all students can succeed*. PISA, OECD Publishing. https://doi.org/10.1787/b5fd1b8f-en

Panadero, E., & Lipnevich, A. A. (2022). A review of feedback models and typologies: Towards an integrative model of feedback elements. *Educational Research Review*, 35, 100416. https://doi.org/10.1016/j.edurev.2021.100416

Salmerón, L., Cañas, J. J., Kintsch, W., & Fajardo, I. (2005). Reading strategies and hypertext comprehension. *Discourse Processes*, 40(3), 171–191. https://doi.org/10.1207/s15326950dp4003_1

Salmerón, L., Gómez, M., & Fajardo, I. (2016). How students with intellectual disabilities evaluate recommendations from internet forums. *Reading and Writing*, 29(8), 1653–1675. https://doi.org/10.1007/s11145-016-9621-4

Salmerón, L., Kammerer, Y., & Delgado, P. (2018). Non-academic multiple source use on the Internet. In J. L. Braasch, I. Bråten, & M. T. McCrudden (Eds.), *Handbook of multiple source use* (pp. 285–302). Routledge.

Salmerón, L., Vargas, C., Delgado, P., & Baron, N. (2022). Relation between digital tool practices in the language arts classroom and reading comprehension scores. *Reading and Writing*. https://doi.org/10.1007/s11145-022-10295-1

Scharrer, L., Pape, V. & Stadtler, M. (2022): Watch out: Fake! How warning labels affect laypeople's evaluation of simplified scientific misinformation. *Discourse Processes*, 1–16. https://doi.org/10.1080/0163853X.2022.2096364

Schneps, M. H., Thomson, J. M., Sonnert, G., Pomplun, M., Chen, C., & Heffner-Wong, A. (2013). Shorter lines facilitate reading in those who struggle. *PloS One*, 8(8), e71161. https://doi.org/10.1371/journal.pone.0071161

Shaw, R., & Lewis, V. (2005). The impact of computer-mediated and traditional academic task presentation on the performance and behaviour of children with ADHD. *Journal of Research in Special Educational Needs*, 5(2), 47–54. https://doi.org/10.1111/J.1471-3802.2005.00041.x

Shute, V. J. (2008). Focus on formative feedback. *Review of Educational Research*, 78(1), 153–189. https://doi.org/10.3102%2F0034654307313795

Snyder, S., & Huber, H. (2019). Computer assisted instruction to teach academic content to students with intellectual disability: A review of the literature. *American*

Journal on Intellectual and Developmental Disabilities, 124(4), 374–390. https://doi.org/10.1352/1944-7558-124.4.374

Solomonidou, C., Garagouni-Areou, F., & Zafiropoulou, M. (2004). Information and communication technologies (ICT) and pupils with attention deficit hyperactivity disorder (ADHD) symptoms: Do the software and the instruction method affect their behavior? *Journal of Educational Multimedia and Hypermedia*, 13(2), 109–128. https://www.learntechlib.org/primary/p/12868/

Swart, E. K., Nielen, T. M., & Sikkema-de Jong, M. T. (2022). Does feedback targeting text comprehension trigger the use of reading strategies or changes in readers' attitudes? A meta-analysis. *Journal of Research in Reading*. https://doi.org/10.1111/1467-9817.12389

ter Beek, M., Brummer, L., Donker, A. S., & Opdenakker, M. C. J. (2018). Supporting secondary school students' reading comprehension in computer environments: A systematic review. *Journal of Computer Assisted Learning*, 34(5), 557–566. https://doi.org/10.1111/jcal.12260

Theng, Y. L., & Thimbleby, H. W. (1998). Addressing design and usability issues in hypertext and on the World Wide Web by re-examining the "Lost in Hyperspace" problem. *Journal of Universal Computer Science*, 4(11), 839–855.

Timmers, C. F., & Veldkamp, B. P. (2011). Attention paid to feedback provided by a computer-based assessment for learning on information literacy. *Computers & Education*, 56(3), 923–930. https://doi.org/10.1016/j.compedu.2010.11.007

Torgesen, J. K., Wagner, R. K., Rashotte, C. A., Herron, J., & Lindamood, P. (2010). Computer-assisted instruction to prevent early reading difficulties in students at risk for dyslexia: Outcomes from two instructional approaches. *Annals of Dyslexia*, 60(1), 40–56. https://doi.org/10.1007/s11881-009-0032-y

van der Kleij, F. M., Feskens, R. C. W. & Eggen, T. J. H. M. (2015). Effects of feedback in a computer-based learning environment on students' learning outcomes: A meta-analysis. *Review of Educational Research*, 85(4), 475–511. https://doi.org/10.3102%2F0034654314564881

van der Weel, A., & Mangen, A. (2022). Textual reading in digitised classrooms: Reflections on reading beyond the internet. *International Journal of Educational Research*, 115, 102036. https://doi.org/10.1016/j.ijer.2022.102036

Wang, A. H., & Lin, K. C. (2016). Effects of display type and ambient illuminance on the comprehension performance of young and elderly readers. *Journal of Industrial and Production Engineering*, 33(7), 443–449. https://doi.org/10.1080/21681015.2016.1156033

McNamara, D. S., & Magliano, J. (2009). Toward a comprehensive model of comprehension. *Psychology of Learning and Motivation*, 51, 297–384. https://doi.org/10.1016/S0079-7421(09)51009-2

Narciss, S. (2008). Feedback strategies for interactive learning tasks. In J. M. Spector, M. D. Merrill, J. van Merriënboer, & M. P. Driscoll (Eds.), *Handbook of research on educational communications and technology* (pp. 125–144). Erlbaum.

Wisniewski, B., Zierer, K., & Hattie, J. (2019). The power of feedback revisited: A meta-analysis of educational feedback research. *Frontiers in Psychology*, 10, 487662. https://doi.org/10.3389/fpsyg.2019.03087

4

GEOGEBRA, A COMPREHENSIVE TOOL FOR LEARNING MATHEMATICS

Robert Weinhandl, Edith Lindenbauer, Stefanie Schallert-Vallaster, Julia Pirklbauer and Markus Hohenwarter

Introduction

Some experts (e.g., Lavicza et al., 2022) argue that more and more technologies are integrated into learning mathematics, while other experts (e.g., Clark-Wilson et al., 2020) state that the integration of technologies into school learning of mathematics is slow. However, almost all experts agree that modern technologies are essential for learning mathematics in our digital era. In this context, Weinhandl et al. (2022) emphasize that learning mathematics can benefit from using technologies and that using technologies is already integrated into many curricula and policy documents. However, according to Sinclair's (2020) summary, learning mathematics using modern technologies is also a complex process. For example, research findings on the use of technology in teaching often only show small positive effects on students' learning achievement (Drijvers et al., 2016). Furthermore, there are some studies (e.g., Odell et al., 2020) that even show that using technologies could have a negative impact on students' learning performance. To make the best use of the potential of technologies in the context of learning mathematics and to minimize any negative aspects, research and research-based development of learning environments are needed. To develop appropriate approaches and tools for the complex system of learning mathematics in technology-rich and technology-enhanced learning environments, the Research Centre at Johannes Kepler University's School of Education and the GeoGebra Development Centre are jointly exploring how technologies could facilitate learning mathematics in our digital era (Lavicza et al., 2022). Through this collaboration of scientific and technological research in recent years, GeoGebra has evolved from a dynamic geometry software to a

DOI: 10.4324/9781003386131-6

modular mathematics system, in which different mathematics-specific but also subject-independent apps are bundled and connected. Hereby, GeoGebra can be used as a tool for learning mathematics from the primary level (e.g., Korenova, 2017; Žilinskiene & Demirbilek, 2015) to the tertiary level (Alessio et al., 2019). In this chapter, we present how, in line with current research, the new GeoGebra apps, GeoGebra Notes, and GeoGebra Classroom, together with modern approaches to learning, e.g., flipped education, should be designed to support learning mathematics. When selecting the studies for our chapter, we mainly considered those studies that focus on teachers' or students' needs in relation to using technologies for learning mathematics because we consider these aspects to be essential for developing technology-enhanced learning environments.

GeoGebra Notes

GeoGebra Notes was initially developed as whiteboard software to enable users to combine pen functionalities and interactive GeoGebra applications in one software package (Ahrer et al., 2020; Hohenwarter & Hofstätter, 2017). However, according to Ahrer et al. (2020) and Weinhandl et al. (2021a), GeoGebra Notes can also be used on pads or laptops by students and teachers in addition to the whiteboard approach (see Figure 4.1). When GeoGebra Notes is used on pads or laptops, one of the aims is to make it easier for students and teachers to use handwriting, texts, videos, or other file formats as well as GeoGebra applications in one software package and to interactively connect the individual elements within GeoGebra Notes (Ahrer et al., 2020; Hohenwarter & Hofstätter, 2017; Weinhandl et al., 2021a).

GeoGebra Notes can be used as a student or teacher tool in many ways. Teachers can use GeoGebra Notes to prepare lessons, or teachers and students can use GeoGebra Notes to document lesson content and share lesson documentation (Ahrer et al., 2020). The time horizon for this approach of

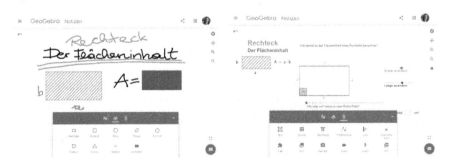

FIGURE 4.1 Using GeoGebra Notes to enable students to use handwriting and GeoGebra tools in one environment.

using GeoGebra Notes ranges from one or a few lessons in class and related teacher preparation and follow-up as well as student homework. However, GeoGebra Notes can also be used in a longer time horizon. According to Haas et al. (2020), teachers can also use GeoGebra Notes as a classroom management technology. This form of using GeoGebra Notes has proven to be a fruitful approach during COVID-19-related distance learning and should also be transferred to a post-COVID-19 period, especially when students learn mathematics independently outside classrooms. Using GeoGebra Notes when learning mathematics outside classrooms should make it easier for teachers to manage and keep track of students' assignments.

Like the feature described above, GeoGebra Notes can also be used as an ePortfolio (a portfolio in which students demonstrate their efforts, the development of their competencies, skills, and achievements using, photos, videos, or other ICT tools, as well as self-reflection) software according to Weinhandl et al. (2021a) and Weinhandl et al. (2021b). One advantage of using GeoGebra Notes as ePortfolio software is that the individual elements of the respective ePortfolios can be dynamically linked. Dynamically connecting the individual components of a GeoGebra Notes portfolio means that students can represent mathematical facts as functions, tables, graphs, or in a computer algebra system, and the different representations of the mathematical facts are connected. Interactively connecting different representations of the mathematical facts means that when, for example, the parameters of a function are changed, the values of the connected table and graph change automatically and simultaneously (see Figure 4.2).

According to Weinhandl et al. (2021a), this interactivity of GeoGebra Notes allows ePortfolios to remain dynamic even after the students have completed them, which is an advantage compared to other software solutions such as WordPress or Weebly, where the students' finished ePortfolio is mostly a static product.

Another advantage of using GeoGebra Notes as mathematical ePortfolio software is, according to Weinhandl et al. (2019) and Weinhandl et al. (2021a),

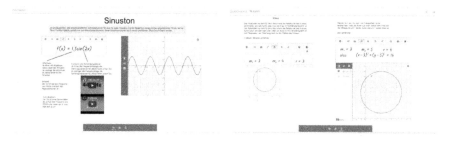

FIGURE 4.2   Take-outs from student work when GeoGebra Notes was used as ePortfolio software.

that non-mathematics-specific elements such as images, PDF files, or whole web pages can easily be integrated into the GeoGebra Notes environment. Integrating such information sources should make it easier for students to embed real-world questions or problems into the ePortfolio.

A benefit of GeoGebra Notes is that it is browser-based software, so there are almost no technical barriers to using GeoGebra Notes (Ahrer et al., 2020; Hohenwarter & Hofstätter, 2017; Weinhandl et al., 2021b), and thus GeoGebra Notes can be used both in classrooms and outside of schools for learning mathematics (Weinhandl et al., 2021a; Weinhandl et al., 2021b). The combination of browser-based whiteboard software that students can also use on pads and notebooks means that there are no graphical or layout restrictions when using GeoGebra Notes as an ePortfolio, as is the case with Mahara (Weinhandl et al., 2019, 2021a).

In summary, GeoGebra Notes is a digital tool that enables teachers and students to use handwriting, digital documents, and mathematical apps in one environment and to connect the different elements of the environment. GeoGebra Notes can be used to prepare and document individual lessons but can also be used as a classroom management technology or ePortfolio over a long period of time. One aspect of using GeoGebra Notes as classroom management technology or ePortfolio software is that viewers of learning artefacts can interact with the material presented. Interacting with the material means that viewers of GeoGebra Notes pages can change elements, such as parameters of a function, and thereby adapt the GeoGebra Notes page to their own concerns.

GeoGebra Classroom

GeoGebra Classroom is a virtual platform that enables teachers to assign interactive and engaging tasks to students. Furthermore, teachers can monitor their students' progress, as they get live updates of students working on a specific task (GeoGebra, 2022a). Due to these functionalities, GeoGebra Classroom could also be used for formative assessment. For example, it enables the implementation of interactive materials as described in Section 4.4. Through GeoGebra Classroom, teachers can collect and analyze students' answers and thus diagnose their conceptions in the respective mathematical field. Based on this analysis, teachers could design lesson plans for different student groups integrating digital materials and distributing them in GeoGebra Classroom (Lindenbauer & Lavicza, 2021; Zöchbauer et al., 2021).

Initially, GeoGebra Classroom was developed for face-to-face discussions in classrooms (Zöchbauer & Hohenwarter, 2020). Nevertheless, it can be used for teaching and learning online. During distance learning, caused by the COVID-19 pandemic, teachers used GeoGebra Classroom in

FIGURE 4.3 GeoGebra activity with interactive elements (GeoGebra app and question element) and "CREATE LESSON" button.

Source: Activity: https://www.geogebra.org/m/s5sz5qtt.

combination with a video system as a working tool and as a homework submission tool (Wolfinger, 2021).

For assigning tasks to students through GeoGebra Classroom, teachers first need a GeoGebra activity, which is an interactive worksheet that includes different elements (e.g., text, videos, GeoGebra apps, images, and questions). The activity can either be created by the teacher or it is also possible to use activities that are made by the GeoGebra community, as there are more than one million existing free-to-use GeoGebra resources (GeoGebra, 2022b).

After finding an activity, the teacher has to create a lesson by clicking the "CREATE LESSON" button in the top right corner of the activity, to share the activity with the students in GeoGebra Classroom (Figure 4.3).

Before the teacher is redirected to the Lesson Overview page, there is the possibility to enter a name for the lesson and decide whether the students should be able to view the correct answers for multiple-choice and open questions. If this option is enabled, students have three attempts to answer a multiple-choice question. They will get feedback after every check, and if they do not manage to answer the question correctly, they can view the correct answer after the third unsuccessful attempt. For open questions, students will be able to view a possible answer after the first attempt.

On the Lesson Overview page, the teacher needs to invite the students to join the lesson. This can either be done with the lesson code, which appears in the teacher's view, or the teacher can simply send the provided link to the

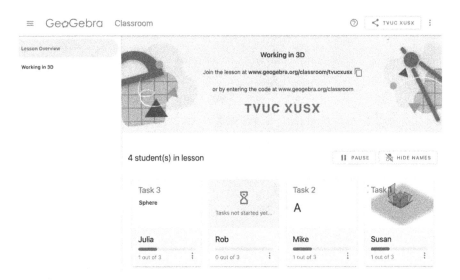

FIGURE 4.4   Lesson Overview page, where teachers get an overview of all students.

students. If the students have to join with the code, they can enter it at https://www.geogebra.org/classroom. Students can either join as a guest or they can join with their GeoGebra account. If they join with an account, they can access their work after closing the browser window again, which is not possible if they only join as a guest.

The Lesson Overview is the place where teachers see how many students have joined the lesson and if they have already started working. Furthermore, teachers see how many tasks the students have already started and on which task they are working at the moment. To get more insights, teachers can click on a student card, to see all answers of the selected student at one glance (Figure 4.4).

Beside the overview of single students, teachers can get an overview of the tasks too. In the Task Overview, teachers see the original activity they shared with their students and how many students have started each task. By selecting "DETAILS" teachers can see the answers to the corresponding task of all students. They can also see the progress of the students, as the answers are updated in real time (Figure 4.5).

For GeoGebra apps and open questions, teachers can see small thumbnail pictures of the students' work. The answers to multiple-choice questions are shown in the form of a bar chart (Figure 4.6).

Teachers can interrupt the work of the students at any time by clicking the "PAUSE" button. In this case, students are not able to continue working. They get the information that the lesson is paused and that they have to wait for their teacher to resume the lesson. For classroom discussions, teachers

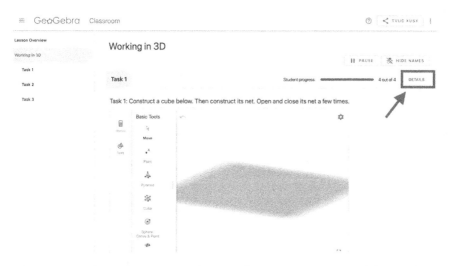

FIGURE 4.5   Task Overview page, where teachers get an overview of the students' progress for each task.

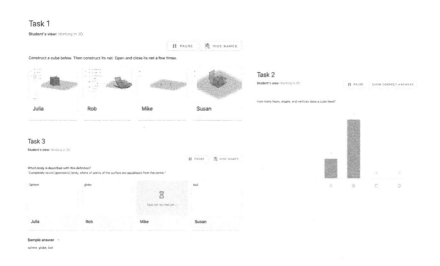

FIGURE 4.6   Task view for GeoGebra apps, multiple-choice questions, and open questions.

can hide the students' names to prevent students from feeling embarrassed while presenting all answers to the entire class (GeoGebra, 2022a).

In addition to the ability to hand out interactive tasks to students, GeoGebra Classroom also offers the possibility to provide interactive whiteboards, as GeoGebra Notes can be inserted into the GeoGebra activities.

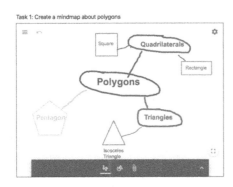
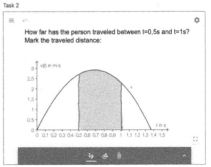

FIGURE 4.7 Pre-made files and mind maps in GeoGebra Classroom.

As already mentioned in the previous section, with GeoGebra Notes teachers have lots of options, as they can provide students with pre-made files or an empty whiteboard where students can write some handwritten notes, draw sketches, create mind maps, etc. (Wolfinger et al., 2022) (Figure 4.7).

In summary, GeoGebra Classroom is a tool that allows teachers to distribute interactive materials and monitor students' progress in real-time. It can be used in regular classes as well as for homework, distance learning, or flipped approaches (see Section 4.5). The next section points out what needs to be considered when creating such interactive materials by discussing concrete examples from the field of functions.

Interactive Resources in the Field of Functional Thinking

In this section, we focus on the important topic of functional relationships as an example to outline the potential and problems of interactive materials in mathematics education. Furthermore, various students' problems and problematic conceptions have been widely investigated, for instance, graph-as-picture error (Janvier, 1981), slope-height confusion (Clement, 1985), illusion of linearity (De Bock et al., 2002), or students' conflicting concept images and concept definitions (Vinner & Dreyfus, 1989). The development of dynamic mathematics software (DMS) such as GeoGebra enables us to examine multiple, dynamically linked representations in which changing one representation immediately affects the other(s) and thus supports students' development of functional thinking (Lichti & Roth, 2018) as the cognitive load is reduced from the necessity of imagining the representations to just comparing them.

During a qualitative study – conducted with 28 students of two Austrian grade 7 classes representing a broad range of different achievement levels (Lindenbauer, 2018) – we designed several interactive, GeoGebra-based

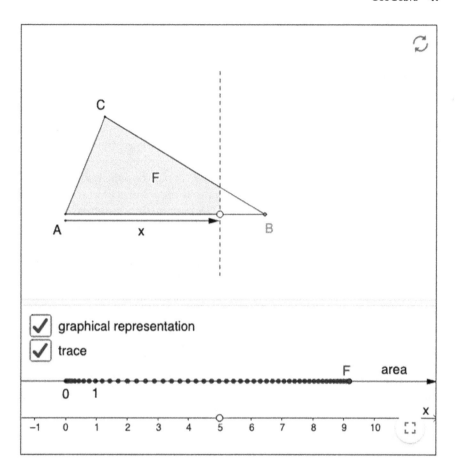

FIGURE 4.8   Interactive material 'Triangle dynagraph'.
Source: https://www.geogebra.org/m/wrVPlwHE.

materials based on examples of students' problems outlined in the literature, to support students in translating between representations of functional relationships. Figure 4.8 illustrates a typical example of the interactive materials designed for this study. Each material consists of an interactive GeoGebra applet, which visualizes an iconic situational model (i.e., a visualized simplified model of a real situation) and a graphical representation of a specific functional relationship – either utilizing Cartesian coordinates or dynagraphs (see Figure 4.8). Dynamically linked and interactive representations together with tasks that accompany the digital materials should engage students in examining connections between both representations in various ways and thus foster students' functional thinking (for an English version of the digital materials see https://www.geogebra.org/m/ftqpETqJ).

The qualitative results indicate that successfully influencing student conceptions using such interactive materials appears to depend on students' prior conceptions, and the level of complexity of student perceptions (i.e., consciously observing a feature of interactive material and further considering or interpreting it in a mathematical manner) is an essential factor in the learning process. The results indicate an intention-reality discrepancy that occurs between mathematical ideas intended by interactive materials and students' perceptions or interpretations – two activities influenced by students' prior knowledge and mathematical understanding. According to Prediger (2005), one cause for erroneous problem-solving could be divergent students' attention focus. Also, Trouche (2005) outlines the influence of students' perceptions on their learning processes. In the case of transfers between iconic situational and graphical representation, two highly visual representations, students particularly appear to focus on the visual or structural features of these representations even if they are mathematically not relevant (e.g., patterns of the graph in trace mode). Such features seem to significantly influence students' perceptions and thus their learning processes. Therefore, how to draw students' attention to those features relevant to mathematical understanding and how to discuss and reflect students' interpretations (Lindenbauer, 2018, 2020) is an issue to consider when integrating interactive materials into teaching.

Goldenberg et al. (1992) utilize another way to represent functional relationships in their software dynagraph, which uses two parallel axes (with or without scaling) as a coordinate system instead of two perpendicular axes. The authors outline the potential of dynagraph representations for analyzing functions in a qualitative way and for examining the covariational aspect of a function (i.e., how varying the argument changes the function value and vice versa), thus adding a dynamic perspective to static graphs in Cartesian coordinates (Goldenberg et al., 1992). Figure 4.8 presents interactive materials visualizing the representational transfer between an iconic situational model and a dynagraph (Lindenbauer, 2018, 2020).

According to Lindenbauer (2018, 2019), dynagraph representations provide easy access for students to graphical representations of functional relationships because students appear to be able to intuitively interpret them as they highlight the covariational aspect of functions probably because the dot representing the function value actually 'moves' on the upper axis when students change the argument. Furthermore, this representation emphasizes specific characteristics of functions such as inflection points, fixed points, or extrema. In summary, dynagraphs potentially scaffold the transfer from situational models to representations utilizing Cartesian coordinates.

Changing the focus from the advantages and disadvantages of specific interactive materials to considerations on how to integrate them practically into regular teaching, Lindenbauer and Lavicza (2021) suggest the design of a formative assessment (FA) tool focusing on the task underlying the interactive material presented in Figure 4.8 addressing a graph-as-picture error. Implementation with GeoGebra Classroom is recommended as it enables teachers to save student responses for FA (see section 4.3). The suggested FA tool consists of a GeoGebra Book that aims at (i) diagnosing and (ii) enhancing students' conceptions regarding this task (see https://www.geogebra.org/m/wxqmqjxb). The first step is a diagnostic task: students are asked to interpret a functional dependency presented in a situational model, choose the correct function graph via a single-choice item, and additionally describe their underlying considerations. The student responses saved in GeoGebra can now be analyzed and thus enable diagnosing and discussing students' conceptions. Such design of the diagnostic tool should support key FA strategies by providing feedback to students by the teacher and activating students individually (Black & Wiliam, 2009). Based on the diagnosis results, teachers can divide students into groups and provide them with specific lesson plans adapted to the needs of each group including variations of an interactive material to enhance their conceptual understanding. The presented GeoGebra Book consists of three differentiated lesson plans for students who (i) struggle to understand the presented situation, (ii) struggle with translating functional dependencies into Cartesian coordinates, or (iii) students with only minor difficulties. In particular, lesson plans (i) and (ii) integrate interactive material using dynagraph representations for scaffolding the representational transfer (for more details see Lindenbauer & Lavicza, 2021). The following FA key strategies outlined by Black and Wiliam (2009) should be supported: engineering classroom and peer discussions, providing feedback for the students, and activating students as owners of their learning.

The next section outlines a contemporary setting for learning and teaching mathematics in which GeoGebra Classroom can also be utilized in an effective way for social learning and self-assessment.

Combining GeoGebra with Flipped Approaches

In the following, we will discuss how GeoGebra could be combined with a contemporary way of teaching and learning mathematics, namely flipped classroom as well as flipped learning approaches. First, we will address flipped classrooms and then flipped learning. In flipped classroom scenarios, information-transmission teaching is mostly outsourced as homework to free up in-class time for active and social learning activities (Abeysekera & Dawson, 2015). Digital technologies such as GeoGebra do not necessarily have to be utilized in flipped settings, but they could enhance mathematics learning by providing additional possibilities, which will be described with the following examples. Hidayat et al. (2021) investigated students' engagement in a flipped multivariable calculus class. In this study, the learners were asked to prepare before class by using videos, PowerPoint slides, and assignments, followed by a question-and-answer session in class. During class, students should also model a given problem with GeoGebra by themselves, where knowledge on using GeoGebra as DMS is needed. Most of the participating students agreed that the use of GeoGebra for tackling the problem fostered deeper mathematical understanding. A recent quasi-experimental study (Ishartono et al., 2022) regarding flipped classrooms showed that GeoGebra can enhance mathematics learning out-of-class. In the experimental group, learners should deal with a GeoGebra worksheet including investigative questions pre-class, which improved their self-regulated learning ability. Using a case-study approach, Cevikbas and Kaiser (2020) thoroughly investigated a teacher flipping two of their mathematics classes where GeoGebra was implemented in class as well as out-of-class. For example, the investigated teacher used the gained in-class time to let students grasp the relationship between exponential and logarithmic functions with a GeoGebra worksheet. In a GeoGebra worksheet, a GeoGebra applet, which is a dynamic object, is accompanied by investigative questions, tasks, or explanations for learners (Hohenwarter & Preiner, 2007). While the learners were dealing with the GeoGebra worksheet, the teacher (Cevikbas & Kaiser, 2020) tried to foster students' mathematical understanding, the teacher was able to offer support with the students' needs.

Social constructivism (Vygotsky, 1978) is one of the underlying concepts of flipped approaches as learners gain knowledge through social interaction with their colleagues and teachers. By letting students in flipped classroom environments work in groups on GeoGebra activities, GeoGebra can be implemented as a social learning activity in mathematics education (Yurniwati & Utomo, 2020; Salas-Rueda, 2021). For FA, GeoGebra Classroom could be applied in flipped settings. Especially, GeoGebra Classroom could be used to orchestrate classroom discussions by monitoring students' progress, but more research is needed (Schallert-Vallaster & Lavicza, 2021).

Flipped learning can be seen as the further development of flipped classrooms. However, flipping a class is not a necessary preliminary stage of flipped learning (Flipped Learning Network, 2014). In contrast to flipped classroom scenarios, teachers do not lead the learning process by, for example, dividing out-of-class and in-class phases in flipped learning environments. Hence, flipped learning is a more student-driven approach where learners can choose the learning space, materials, and sometimes even objectives themselves. To facilitate flipped learning, educators should integrate the following four pillars into their practice: flexible environment, learning culture, intentional content, and professional educator (Flipped Learning Network, 2014). For each pillar, an example concerning GeoGebra will be described in the following.

The first pillar, a flexible environment, is characterized by letting the learners decide where and how they want to learn. In terms of using digital technologies in flipped settings, students can decide which tools to use themselves. Weinhandl et al. (2020a) investigated key elements for students when learning mathematics in a flipped learning scenario. In this design-based research study, GeoGebra was suggested to be used for modelling real-world problems and solving them mathematically, but students were not forced to use GeoGebra to do so. Analyzing interviews and written feedback from students following grounded theory approaches revealed that flexibility is one crucial element for students in flipped mathematics scenarios.

The second pillar, learning culture, refers to shifting from a teacher-centred learning approach to one that is more student-centred. To document the learning process in a flipped learning environment, students could utilize GeoGebra Notes as ePortfolio software, which was investigated in a recent study focusing on mathematics education (Weinhandl et al., 2021a).

Intentional content is the third flipped learning pillar which stays for the importance of curating relevant materials. A study (Weinhandl et al., 2020b) about synthesizing flipped learning with GeoGebra in mathematics education showed that various GeoGebra activities on one mathematical concept should be provided to prevent repetitive task completion.

In flipped learning scenarios, teachers should act as professional educators by providing learners with feedback and scaffolding when needed. GeoGebra Classroom could be a helpful tool to observe students' mathematics learning process. Additionally, learners could profit from technology-supported feedback and self-assess their learning with GeoGebra (Weinhandl et al., 2020b).

To sum up, GeoGebra can be a useful software package for flipped mathematics education. Pre-made GeoGebra materials can support teachers' lesson planning process for flipped environments as the activities can be implemented in class as well as out-of-class and enable learners to explore mathematical concepts (Schallert-Vallaster & Lavicza, 2021).

Conclusions and Outlook

GeoGebra tools (apps, Notes, and Classroom) provide diverse opportunities for mathematics teaching and learning. On the one hand, their functionalities may change methods and classroom management and thus enable more student-centred approaches such as flipped learning or FA, which also foster collaboration among students. On the other hand, the potential use of GeoGebra outlined in this chapter relates to mathematical use or content-specific themes such as functional thinking. In this sense, it covers all didactical functionalities outlined by Drijvers (2019): (i) GeoGebra can serve as a tool for doing mathematics, and (ii) this software can support learning mathematics with digital materials aiming either at developing mathematical concepts or practising skills.

As shown in a design-based research study (Weinhandl et al., 2020b), GeoGebra can serve as a single-source learning environment in flipped mathematics scenarios. By using GeoGebra as a comprehensive tool for flipped mathematics education, GeoGebra Notes (see Section 4.2) can be used as ePortfolio software to let students document their learning process. Furthermore, GeoGebra Classroom (see Section 4.3) can be utilized to orchestrate classroom discussions and monitor students' learning processes to support learners when needed. This tool of GeoGebra can be integrated into a FA setting for diagnosing and enhancing students' conceptions by utilizing interactive materials (see Section 4.4). Furthermore, teachers can implement pre-made materials in class or as homework in flipped settings.

Technological development and digitalization in education policies lead to an increased and widened use of digital tools and materials and teaching and learning mathematics in a diverse student population. Different requirements based on student's age, school type, etc. will probably entail further development of digital tools for particular student groups' needs. GeoGebra with its characteristics as a modular and comprehensive mathematics system offers opportunities for adaptations to such specific requirements also in the future and thus encompasses the need for further research.

Currently, various aspects are being examined – or planned to be – in this context. Concerning the GeoGebra Classroom, research is being conducted to determine how this tool should develop in the future. For example, the usage in practice is being examined to find out where difficulties still exist and which features would support the students and teachers further (Zöchbauer et al., 2021; Wolfinger, 2021). Another GeoGebra-related project that aims at designing high-quality digital materials will entail implementation research from students' and teachers' perspectives, for example, on how to support teachers in integrating interactive materials into teaching or how to implement such materials fruitfully into FA with GeoGebra Classroom.

Evidence-Based Practice Recommendations

- GeoGebra can be seen as a comprehensive tool for learning mathematics, as all didactical functionalities outlined by Drijvers (2019) are covered, for example, when combining physical and digital modelling.
- For flipped mathematics education, GeoGebra can serve with features like GeoGebra Notes and GeoGebra Classroom as a single-source learning environment.
- Digital materials can enhance students' conceptual development through multiple-linked interactive representations when carefully implemented in teaching.

References

Abeysekera, L., & Dawson, P. (2015). Motivation and cognitive load in the flipped classroom: Definition, rationale and a call for research. *Higher Education Research & Development, 34*(1), 1–14. https://doi.org/10.1080/07294360.2014.934336

Ahrer, J. M., Wolfinger, J., Hofstätter, A., & Hohenwarter, M. (2020). *Digitale Dokumentation von Schüler/-innenarbeit mit GeoGebra Notizen.* Universitätsbibliothek Dortmund.

Alessio, F. G., Demeio, L., & Telloni, A. I. (2019). A formative path in tertiary education through GeoGebra supporting the students' learning assessment and awareness. *International Journal for Technology in Mathematics Education, 26*(4), 191–203.

Black, P., & Wiliam, D. (2009). Developing the theory of formative assessment. *Educational Assessment, Evaluation and Accountability, 21*(1), 5–31. https://doi.org/10.1007/s11092-008-9068-5

Cevikbas, M., & Kaiser, G. (2020). Flipped classroom as a reform-oriented approach to teaching mathematics. *ZDM*, 1–15. https://doi.org/10.1007/s11858-020-01191-5

Clark-Wilson, A., Robutti, O., & Thomas, M. (2020). Teaching with digital technology. *ZDM Mathematics Education, 52*(7), 1223–1242. https://doi.org/10.1007/s11858-020-01196-0

Clement, J. (1985). Misconceptions in graphing. *Proceedings of the 9th Conference of the International Group for the Psychology of Mathematics Education, 1*, 369–375. http://people.umass.edu/~clement/pdf/MisconceptionsinGraphing.pdf

De Bock, D., Van Dooren, W., Janssens, D., & Verschaffel, L. (2002). Improper use of linear reasoning: An in-depth study of the nature and the irresistibility of secondary school students' errors. *Educational Studies in Mathematics, 50*(3), 311–334.

Drijvers, P. (2019). Head in the clouds, feet on the ground – A realistic view on using digital tools in mathematics education. In A. Büchter, M. Glade, R. Herold-Blasius, M. Klinger, F. Schacht, & P. Scherer (Eds.), *Vielfältige Zugänge zum Mathematikunterricht* (pp. 163–176). Springer Fachmedien Wiesbaden. https://doi.org/10.1007/978-3-658-24292-3_12

Drijvers, P., Ball, L., Barzel, B., Heid, M. K., Cao, Y., & Maschietto, M. (2016). *Uses of technology in lower secondary education.* Springer International Publishing. https://doi.org/10.1007/978-3-319-33666-4

Flipped Learning Network (2014). The four pillars of F-L-I-P. Retrieved from www.flippedlearning.org/definition

GeoGebra. (2022a). *Learn GeoGebra Classroom.* https://www.geogebra.org/m/hncrgruu

GeoGebra. (2022b). *Learn how to use resources.* https://www.geogebra.org/m/rgecrznx

Goldenberg, P., Lewis, P., & O'Keefe, J. (1992). Dynamic representation and the development of a process understanding of function. In G. Harel & E. Dubinsky (Eds.), *The concept of function: Aspects of epistemology and pedagogy* (pp. 235–260). Mathematical Association of America.

Haas, B., Kreis, Y., & Lavicza, Z. (2020). Connecting the real world to mathematical models in elementary schools in Luxemburg. *Proceedings of the British Society for Research into Learning Mathematics, 40*(2), 1–6.

Hidayat, D., Khabibah, S., & Artiono, R. (2021). Students: Engagement through flipped classroom using Geogebra task in multivariable calculus class. In *International Joint Conference on Science and Engineering 2021 (IJCSE 2021)* (pp. 551–554). Atlantis Press.

Hohenwarter, M., & Hofstätter, A. (2017). Entwicklung einer Online Tafelsoftware auf Basis von GeoGebra. In U. Kortenkamp & A. Kuzle (Hrsg.), *Beiträge zum Mathematikunterricht* (pp. 453–456). WTM-Verlag.

Hohenwarter, M., & Preiner, J. (2007). Creating Mathlets with open source tools. *The Journal of Online Mathematics and Its Applications, 7*, 1–29.

Ishartono, N., Nurcahyo, A., Waluyo, M., Prayitno, H. J., & Hanifah, M. (2022). Integrating GeoGebra into the flipped learning approach to improve students' self-regulated learning during the covid-19 pandemic. *Journal on Mathematics Education, 13*(1), 69–86. http://doi.org/10.22342/jme.v13i1

Janvier, C. (1981). Use of situations in mathematics education. *Educational Studies in Mathematics, 12*(1), 113–122. https://doi.org/10.1007/BF00386049

Korenova, L. (2017). GeoGebra in teaching of primary school mathematics. *International Journal for Technology in Mathematics Education, 24*(3), 155–160.

Lavicza, Z., Weinhandl, R., Prodromou, T., Anđić, B., Lieban, D., Hohenwarter, M., Fenyvesi, K., Brownell, C., & Diego-Mantecón, J. M. (2022). Developing and evaluating educational innovations for STEAM education in rapidly changing digital technology environments. *Sustainability, 14*(12), 7237. https://doi.org/10.3390/su14127237

Lichti, M., & Roth, J. (2018). How to foster functional thinking in learning environments using computer-based simulations or real materials. *Journal for STEM Education Research, 1*(1–2), 148–172. https://doi.org/10.1007/s41979-018-0007-1

Lindenbauer, E. (2018). *Students' conceptions and effects of dynamic materials regarding functional thinking* (Doctoral dissertation). Johannes Kepler Universität Linz.

Lindenbauer, E. (2019). Investigating students' use of dynamic materials addressing conceptions related to functional thinking. In U. T. Jankvist, M. van den Heuvel-Panhuizen, & M. Veldhuis (Eds.), *Proceedings of the 11th Congress of the European Society for Research in Mathematics Education* (pp. 2876–2883). Freudenthal Group & Freudenthal Institute, Utrecht University and ERME.

Lindenbauer, E. (2020). Interactive worksheets assisting students' functional thinking conceptions in lower secondary education. *Mathematica Didactica, 43*(1), 1–23.

Lindenbauer, E., & Lavicza, Z. (2021). From research to practice: Diagnosing and enhancing students' conceptions in a formative assessment tool utilizing digital worksheets in functional thinking. *International Journal of Technology in Mathematics Education, 28*(3), 133–141. https://doi.org/10.1564/tme

Odell, B., Cutumisu, M., & Gierl, M. (2020). A scoping review of the relationship between students' ICT and performance in mathematics and science in the PISA data. *Social Psychology of Education, 23*(6), 1449–1481. https://doi.org/10.1007/s11218-020-09591-x

Prediger, S. (2005). "Auch will ich Lernprozesse beobachten um besser Mathematik zu verstehen". Didaktische Rekonstruktion als mathematikdidaktischer Forschungsansatz zur Restrukturierung von Mathematik. *Mathematica Didactica, 28*(2), 23–47.

Salas-Rueda, R. A. (2021). Students' perceptions of the use of the flipped classroom during the educational process of linear functions. *Culture and Education, 33*(3), 431–454. https://doi.org/10.1080/11356405.2021.1949109

Schallert-Vallaster, S., & Lavicza, Z. (2021). Investigating mathematics teachers' intended use of GeoGebra in inquiry-based flipped classroom scenarios. *International Journal for Technology in Mathematics Education, 28*(3), 117–123.

Sinclair, N. (2020). On teaching and learning mathematics-technologies. In *STEM teachers and teaching in the digital era* (pp. 91–107). Springer. https://doi. org/10.1007/978-3-030-29396-3_6

Trouche, L. (2005). An instrumental approach to mathematics learning in symbolic calculator environments. In D. Guin, K. Ruthven, & L. Trouche (Eds.), *The didactical challenge of symbolic calculators: Turning a computional device into a mathematical instrument* (pp. 137–162). Springer. https://doi. org/10.1007/0-387-23435-7_7

Vinner, S., & Dreyfus, T. (1989). Images and definitions for the concept of function. *Journal for Research in Mathematics Education*, 20(4), 356–366. https:// doi.org/10.5951/jresematheduc.20.4.0356

Vygotsky, L. S. (1978). *Mind in society: The development of higher psychological processes*. Harvard University Press.

Weinhandl, R., Hohenwarter, M., Lavicza, Z., & Houghton, T. (2021a). Using GeoGebra Notes to dynamically organise digital learning resources and enhance students' mathematics skills. *International Journal for Technology in Mathematics Education*, 28(3), 171–181.

Weinhandl, R., Lavicza, Z., Hohenwarter, M., & Schallert, S. (2020b). Enhancing flipped mathematics education by utilising GeoGebra. *International Journal of Education in Mathematics, Science and Technology*, 8(1), 1–15. https://doi. org/10.46328/ijemst.v8i1.832

Weinhandl, R., Lavicza, Z., Houghton, T., & Hohenwarter, M. (2021b). A look over students' shoulders when learning mathematics in home-schooling. *International Journal of Mathematical Education in Science and Technology*, 1–21. https://doi. org/10.1080/0020739X.2021.1912423

Weinhandl, R., Lavicza, Z., & Schallert, S. (2020a). Towards flipped learning in upper secondary mathematics education. *Journal of Mathematics Education*, 5(1), 1–15. https://doi.org/10.31327/jme.v5i1.1114

Weinhandl, R., Mayerhofer, M., Houghton, T., Lavicza, Z., Eichmair, M., & Hohenwarter, M. (2022). Personas characterising secondary school mathematics students: Development and applications to educational technology. *Education Sciences*, 12(7), 447. https://doi.org/10.3390/educsci12070447

Weinhandl, R., Schallert, S., & Lavicza, Z. (2019). Merging flipped learning approaches and learning with ePortfolios in secondary mathematics education. In Evangelia Triantafyllou (Ed.), *Gaming elements and educational data analysis in the learning design of the flipped classroom* (pp. 5–24). Aalborg Universitetsforlag.

Wolfinger, J. (2021). *Einsatz von GeoGebra Classroom im sekundären und tertiären Bildungsbereich in Österreich* (Master's thesis, Johannes Kepler University).

Wolfinger, J., Weinhandl, R., & Hohenwarter, M. (2022). Using GeoGebra Classroom for remote learning. In *GeoGebra in research and innovation in mathematics education*. Benemérita Universidad Autónoma de Puebla Facultad de Ciencias Físico Matemáticas.

Yurniwati, Y., & Utomo, E. (2020). Problem-based learning flipped classroom design for developing higher-order thinking skills during the COVID-19 pandemic in geometry domain. *Journal of Physics: Conference Series*. https://doi. org/10.1088/1742-6596/1663/1/012057

Žilinskiene, I., & Demirbilek, M. (2015). Use of GeoGebra in primary math education in Lithuania: An exploratory study from teachers' perspective. *Informatics in Education*, 14(1), 127–142. https://doi.org/10.15388/infedu.2015.08

Zöchbauer, J., & Hohenwarter, M. (2020). Developing a live lesson feature for GeoGebra for teaching and learning mathematics. In *Proceedings of the 14th International Conference on Technology in Mathematics Teaching – ICTMT14: Essen, Germany, 22nd to 25th of July 2019* (pp. 144–145). https://doi.org/10.17185/duepublico/70734

Zöchbauer, J., Hohenwarter, M., & Lavicza, Z. (2021). Evaluating GeoGebra Classroom with usability and user experience methods for further development. *International Journal for Technology in Mathematics Education, 28*(3), 183–191.

PART III
Learning with Digital Videos

5

DYNAMIC VISUALIZATIONS

How to Overcome Challenges and Seize Opportunities

Martin Merkt and Markus Huff

Dynamic Visualizations: Setting the Scope for the Chapter

Dynamic visualizations such as videos and animations are ubiquitous on platforms such as YouTube. Next to videos that are produced for an entertainment purpose, a substantial number of media on these platforms also serve an educational purpose and are thus relevant for both formal and informal learning settings (Navarrete et al., 2021; Rat für kulturelle Bildung, 2019; Smith et al., 2018). In this chapter, we discuss the application of various design principles for multimedia learning materials to the specifics of dynamic visualizations. For this purpose, we use a broad definition of dynamic visualizations, which includes all kinds of external visual representations that provide dynamic information in either the auditory or the pictorial track. Whereas this broad definition covers dynamic media that allow for user interactions such as stopping the presentation or fast forward/rewind, it does not cover interactive computer simulations or data visualizations that require learners' continuous input in order to visualize change and are otherwise static. Thus, the representations covered in this chapter range from narrated slides (e.g., Merkt & Schwan, 2017) to photorealistic videos (e.g., Merkt et al., 2020). Whereas we do not propose that all of these different types of dynamic visualizations are the same, we do assume that there are some general challenges and opportunities that should be considered when designing dynamic visualizations. In the following, we will briefly describe these challenges and opportunities associated with using dynamic visualizations as learning materials (Section 5.2). In Section 5.3, we will briefly outline the theoretical underpinnings for the design principles (segmenting principle, signaling principle, instructors) described

DOI: 10.4324/9781003386131-8

in Section 5.4. Finally, the level of realism of dynamic visualizations is described as a potential boundary condition with regard to the effectiveness of the described design principle (Section 5.5), before we offer some final conclusions in Section 5.6.

Dynamic Visualizations: Are They Suitable for Learning?

The effectiveness of dynamic visualizations as learning materials should not be taken for granted. Notably, one of the main challenges for using dynamic visualizations in learning scenarios is associated with one of their features that is often named as an important cause for their popularity: i.e., the purported ease of comprehension (Rat für kulturelle Bildung, 2019). In an early study contrasting video-based learning materials (as an example of dynamic visualizations) with text-based learning materials, Salomon (1984) observed that learners perceived video-based learning materials to be easier than text-based learning materials. This perceived easiness was associated with less invested mental effort in the processing of video-based learning materials compared to text-based learning materials, so videos resulted in suboptimal learning outcomes as reflected in inference questions. In line with Salomon's findings, multiple studies replicated suboptimal learning outcomes with videos compared to text-based learning materials (e.g., DeFleur et al., 1992; Furnham et al., 1990; Gunter et al., 1984). However, most of these studies presented dynamic visualizations in a non-interactive broadcast mode, whereas the texts could be read in a self-paced fashion (see Merkt et al., 2011).

Thus, despite these previous findings, it may be worth considering dynamic visualizations as learning materials because various meta-analyses demonstrated that dynamic visualizations resulted in superior learning outcomes than content-equivalent static visualizations (Berney & Betrancourt, 2016; Höffler & Leutner, 2007; Ploetzner et al., 2020). Whereas all of these analyses found small (to medium) overall effects in favor of dynamic visualizations, both Höffler and Leutner (2007), as well as Ploetzner et al. (2020), come to the conclusion that dynamic visualizations are best suited for learning, if the displayed changes over time (including the sequence of the changes) are central to the learning goal. If this is the case, the contents of the dynamic visualization correspond to the learners' desired mental representation of the learning materials, which should also include information about the sequence of changes over time. In this specific case, dynamic visualizations depicting changes over time meet the requirements of the congruence principle (Tversky et al., 2002) because the characteristics of the external representation are aligned with the desired features of the learners' mental representation.

Theoretical Underpinnings

After establishing that dynamic visualizations are suitable for imparting knowledge even though there are some fundamental challenges associated with their use, we will now provide some basic principles for the optimal design of dynamic visualizations. For this purpose, this chapter describes the basic assumptions of the Cognitive Load Theory (CLT, Sweller et al., 1998, 2019), the Cognitive Theory of Multimedia Learning (CTML, Mayer, 2020), and the Cognitive-Affective-Social Theory of Learning in Digital Environments (CASTLE, Schneider et al., 2022) as the theoretical underpinnings for the principles presented in Section 5.4.

Cognitive Load Theory

The CLT (Sweller et al., 1998, 2019) is one of the most influential theories addressing the cognitive aspects of learning. Building on the assumption that learners' cognitive resources in working memory are limited (Miller, 1956), CLT postulates that learning materials should be designed to efficiently use these limited resources to avoid cognitive overload. Initially, CLT distinguished between three different sources of cognitive load: intrinsic (ICL), extraneous (ECL), and germane cognitive load (GCL) (Sweller et al., 1998). ICL is related to the complexity and difficulty of the learning materials and, thus, mostly determined by the contents that are presented in the learning materials. In contrast, ECL is related to the processing cost that is associated with the design of the learning materials and is thus subject to influences of instructional design decisions. Finally, GCL was introduced as a third source of cognitive load, which is associated with learners' deliberate elaboration processes while making sense of the learning materials. However, this initial definition of GCL was altered in a more recent version of CLT, in that GCL is no longer defined as an independent source of CL but rather as a shift of learners' attention from extraneous processing toward the elaboration of the learning contents (Sweller et al., 2019). Independent of the classification of GCL as an independent source of cognitive load (Sweller et al., 1998) or as a shift of attention toward the elaboration of the learning contents (Sweller et al., 2019), the central implications of CLT remain the same. In particular, designers of instructional materials should try to avoid design characteristics that induce high levels of ECL and rather use design principles that reduce ECL so that learners have sufficient cognitive resources to elaborate the learning materials. Otherwise, high levels of ECL in combination with difficult learning materials (as reflected in higher levels of ICL) could result in cognitive overload and, thus, suboptimal learning outcomes.

Cognitive Theory of Multimedia Learning

Comparable to CLT, the CTML (Mayer, 2020) also builds on the basic assumption that learners' cognitive resources in working memory are limited (*limited capacity assumption*) and should thus be efficiently used in order to optimize learning outcomes. According to CTML, instructional designers can use the fact that there are two different channels for auditory/verbal and visual/pictorial information (*dual-channels assumption*). First, the multimedia principle (Mayer, 2020) states that providing information both as text and picture results in a dual coding advantage over providing text alone (Paivio, 1986). Second, since the cognitive resources of these two channels are independent, one can make the best use of learners' cognitive resources if the learning materials are provided as a combination of auditory and visual information. Thus, providing spoken text and pictures is preferable over providing written text and pictures, especially for longer textual inputs (modality principle).

While processing the learning materials, learners actively select, organize, and integrate the auditory and visual information into a comprehensive mental representation, which is stored for later retrieval in long-term memory (*active processing assumption*). These processes may be supported by designing the learning materials to facilitate the selection, organization, and integration of relevant pieces of information. Regarding the selection and organization of information, learners may be supported by cues and signals that highlight relevant information and relations between different pieces of information (signaling principle). Additionally, a temporal and spatial alignment of related pieces of information should facilitate the integration of information (spatial and temporal contiguity principle, Bauhoff et al., 2012; Mayer, 2020).

Cognitive-Affective-Social Theory of Learning in Digital Environments

Whereas the CTML is continuously extended to cover more social aspects of learning (e.g., the personalization principle), its focus remains on the cognitive aspects of learning. In recent years, building on the theoretical underpinnings of CTML, theories were extended to cover the affective and social aspects of the learning process. Most recently, building on theories such as the Cognitive Affective Theory of Learning with Media (CATML, Moreno, 2006) and the Computers-As-Social-Actors paradigm (Nass et al., 1994), Schneider et al. (2022) proposed an extension of the CTML that highlights the importance of social cues in digital learning environments. In line with Social Agency Theory (Mayer, 2014), Schneider et al. (2022) postulate that even in individual learning settings, digital learning environments include social cues that may activate social schemata and thus trigger social processes (activation hypothesis). In turn, these social processes may influence how learners process information on a cognitive level (i.e., selection, organization, integration, and retrieval) (cognitive influence hypothesis). Importantly, CASTLE postulates that the strength of the social cues and, thus, the activation of social schemata varies with the characteristics of the media (social cue strength hypothesis). More specifically, the addition of pictures (e.g., the face of an instructor) and dynamic information (e.g., the human voice of an instructor; visible human mimics and gestures) may increase social responses by providing stronger social cues (Schneider et al., 2022).

Implications for Learning with Dynamic Visualizations

In this section, we have briefly described various theories relevant to learning with digital media. Whereas these theories cover a broad spectrum of different learning materials, the implications proposed here will focus on the application of the basic assumptions of these theories to the specifics of dynamic visualizations. Most importantly, the broad scope of this chapter encloses all external visual representations that provide either auditory or visual information dynamically, meaning that information is likely to be transient and replaced by other pieces of information during the reception process. Thus, learners need to pay continuous attention to new pieces of information while still selecting, organizing, and integrating information in working memory. Given learners' limited cognitive resources, it is evident that the dynamic presentation of transient information increases the risk of cognitive overload (transitory information effect, Leahy & Sweller, 2011), especially for learning contents that are rich in complexity. Thus, learners may be forced to process information superficially to avoid missing any new information. To overcome this challenge, implementing opportunities for user interactions is a promising approach (Merkt et al., 2011; Schwan & Riempp, 2004). In Section 5.4.1, we will describe the segmenting principle (Mayer, 2020) as one opportunity to overcome the challenges associated with the processing of transient information.

In addition, the transient presentation of dynamic information constrains the learners' time for selecting, organizing, and integrating relevant pieces of information in the learning materials because these processes need to occur in a system-determined timeframe. Thus, it is important to efficiently guide learners' attention to relevant pieces of information in dynamic visualizations, more so because dynamic visualizations may contain multiple moving elements that compete for the learners' visual attention, especially at the onset of new movements (Abrams & Christ, 2003). Section 5.4.2 will describe the signaling principle as one approach toward guiding learners' attention to relevant pieces of information.

Finally, dynamic visualizations allow for the inclusion of strong social cues into the learning materials (Schneider et al., 2022). In this regard, an instructor who presents the learning materials in the videos may constitute a strong social cue that may affect the learning outcomes. In Section 5.4.3, we will briefly summarize the state of research concerned with the effects of the presence of a human instructor in dynamic visualizations.

Principles for the Design of Dynamic Visualizations

Segmenting Principle

To address the challenge associated with the transience of information in dynamic visualizations (also see transitory information effect, Leahy & Sweller, 2011), the CTML proposes to provide learners with segmented dynamic visualizations that stop at pre-defined breakpoints in the learning materials (segmenting principle, Mayer, 2020). Multiple studies provide empirical support for the segmenting principle, as reflected in a meta-analysis by Rey et al. (2019), who observed that segmenting improved both retention and transfer with small to medium effect sizes. Whereas the definition of the segmenting principle explicitly includes the learners as the agents to continue the dynamic presentation after it was stopped at pre-determined positions (Mayer, 2020), some studies also show positive effects of system-paced segmenting in that the animation automatically continues after a pre-defined amount of time (Spanjers et al., 2012). Spanjers et al. (2012) even found that segmenting an animation with darkened screens without actual pauses may reduce self-reported mental effort. It is evident that introducing darkened screens without stopping the dynamic visualization does not reduce the need to continuously process new input. In recent years, research on the perception and processing of dynamic scenes (natural actions, motion pictures) has made great progress. It is based on the idea that humans segment the continuous stream of sensory information into meaningful units (Newtson & Engquist, 1976). Related theories, such as event segmentation theory (Zacks, 2020; Zacks & Swallow, 2007), describe how initial sensory information is first represented in working memory in the form of event models, and then represented in long-term memory as event schemas. Importantly, the processing of dynamic information is not continuous. Increased cognitive workload at the boundary of two meaningful units (Huff et al., 2012) is supposed to be related to higher memory performance (e.g., Huff et al., 2014; Meitz et al., 2020). Based on this research, it was argued that next to stopping the transient flow of information, providing learners with meaningful segments of the learning materials may also help them identify the meaningful structure of the contents (Merkt et al., 2018; Spanjers et al., 2010, 2012).

In their meta-analysis, Rey et al. (2019) distinguished between system-paced and learner-paced segmenting. Regarding the learning outcomes, they observed that system-paced segmenting positively affects both retention and transfer, whereas learner-paced segmenting only had a significant positive effect on transfer performance. Further, Rey et al. (2019) investigated the role of learners' prior knowledge as a moderator because, from a theoretical perspective, it could be assumed that segmenting is most effective for learners at risk for cognitive overload. In line with this reasoning, previous studies have already shown segmenting effects for learners with lower levels of working memory capacity (Lusk et al., 2009) and lower levels of prior knowledge (Spanjers et al., 2011). In contrast, there were no segmenting effects for learners with higher levels of working memory capacity and prior knowledge. However, contrary to theory and these empirical examples, Rey et al. (2019) found larger segmenting effects on retention for learners with higher levels of prior knowledge. This unexpected finding warrants future research on the moderating effects of prior knowledge on the segmenting principle (also see Mayer, 2020).

Including a pause button in dynamic visualizations is an alternative way to allow learners to control the transient flow of information. In a direct comparison of a dynamic visualization with learner-paced segmenting and the same dynamic visualization with a pause button, Hasler et al. (2007) observed that both ways of providing learner control improved learning of difficult content. Interestingly, these positive effects occurred, even though the learners' self-paced pauses were rather short in the segmenting condition (i.e., just above 2 seconds), and learners hardly made use of the pause button. The latter pattern was also observed in a more recent study in which giving learners the opportunity to make pauses in a medical simulation game positively affected learning outcomes, even though half the participants in the pause condition did not use the pause button (Lee et al., 2020). Taking a closer look at the development of cognitive load throughout the learning phase, Lee et al. (2020) observed an overall increase of cognitive load in the condition with a pause button, whereas cognitive load was reduced during the actual pauses. The reduction of cognitive load during the pauses can be interpreted as an indication that learners stop the simulation for a cognitive "break". However, the overall increase of cognitive load in the condition with an available pause button was interpreted as an indication that learners invest more mental effort to identify suitable breakpoints for pauses in the learning materials (Lee et al., 2020; also see Hasler et al., 2007). Corroborating the underlying assumptions that learners pause dynamic visualizations at difficult and meaningful breakpoints, Merkt et al. (2022) observed that the frequency of pauses on an educational video platform was increased at difficult positions and at meaningful structural breakpoints in the videos.

To sum up, there is ample evidence that providing learners with segmented learning materials and allowing them to stop the dynamic visualization with a pause button benefits learning by avoiding cognitive overload and increasing learners' awareness of the underlying structure of the learning materials.

Signaling Principle

To generate a comprehensive mental representation of the learning materials, it is essential that learners select the relevant information from the learning materials, organize the information, and integrate verbal and pictorial information with prior knowledge (Mayer, 2020). Whereas previous research has demonstrated that learners try to integrate auditory and visual information while processing dynamic information (Schüler & Merkt, 2021), the identification and integration of corresponding information may be complicated with the increasing complexity of the learning materials. To address the challenge of selecting relevant information in both static and dynamic visualizations, Mayer (2020) suggested the signaling principle, meaning that relevant information should be highlighted by verbal (e.g., headings, introductory sentences) and/or visual elements (e.g., arrows, blurring, color coding).

Two meta-analyses reported small to medium effects favoring signaled over non-signaled learning materials, both with regard to retention and transfer performance (Schneider et al., 2018) as well as comprehension and transfer performance (Richter et al., 2016). Both analyses addressed learners' prior knowledge, learner-control, and the transience of the learning materials as potential boundary conditions for signaling effects. With regard to prior knowledge, the two analyses come to different conclusions. Whereas Schneider et al. (2018) did not observe significant moderation effects of prior knowledge on retention and transfer, Richter et al. (2016) observed that positive signaling effects were only evident in learners with low to medium levels of prior knowledge, but not in learners with high levels of prior knowledge. Learner control as a moderator was concerned with providing system-paced or learner-paced learning materials. Whereas Schneider et al. (2018) did not find any evidence for learner control as a moderator of signaling effects, Richter et al. (2016) report tentative evidence from an exploratory analysis suggesting that signaling effects may be more pronounced in system-paced than in learner-paced materials. Finally, both analyses did not identify transience (static vs. dynamic presentations) as a boundary condition for signaling effects in multimedia learning materials.

Regarding the design of the signals, it is crucial to synchronize the signals to the relevant dynamics conveyed in the dynamic visualizations (Boucheix & Lowe, 2010; Boucheix et al., 2013). Next to visual signals such as spotlights (Jarodzka et al., 2012), salient colors (Jamet, 2014), or flashing relevant information when it is mentioned in the verbal narration (Jeung et al.,

1997), some studies demonstrated that referencing visual elements in the audio track successfully guides learners' attention to the referenced objects and in turn improves memory for visual details (Glaser & Schwan, 2015). Accordingly, the verbal facilitation effect describes that verbal information presented before an animation guides learners' attention to the most informative parts of the visual representation (Huff & Schwan, 2012). However, this latter effect may be limited to dynamic visualizations in which it is possible to unanimously refer to specific pieces of information using verbal references either immediately before or while the relevant visual information is depicted. In contrast, when a verbal description is presented after a visual animation, verbal overshadowing effects are likely to occur, negatively affecting memory for the visual pieces of the animation (Huff & Maurer, 2014; Huff & Schwan, 2008).

Instructors in Dynamic Visualizations

Whereas the segmenting and signaling principles aim at supporting learners to manage the cognitive demands of dynamic visualizations, the inclusion of a human instructor into the learning materials may be considered a source of distraction because it attracts learners' visual attention (Kizilcec et al., 2014; van Wermeskerken et al., 2018). However, in line with the basic assumptions of CASTLE (see Schneider et al., 2022), the inclusion of human-like or human instructors in educational materials may be considered a social cue that affects how learners process the dynamic visualizations.

With regard to animated pedagogical agents, Castro-Alonso et al. (2021) reported a small, but significant effect in favor of the inclusion of virtual pedagogical agents, which was only moderated by the dimensionality of the agents. In particular, there was a significant positive effect of pedagogical agents presented in 2D, whereas there was no significant effect of including a pedagogical agent in 3D. Other agent design characteristics, such as the agents' voice, gender, gesturing, eye gaze, facial expression, or motion, did not moderate the effects of human-like pedagogical agents.

With regard to the visibility of human instructors in educational materials, the systematic review by Henderson and Schroeder (2021) comes to the conclusion that there is no evidence against the inclusion of a visible human instructor because all of the studies included in the review article either report no significant effects or significant effects favoring the inclusion of a visible instructor into the learning materials. Whereas these findings are in line with the basic theoretical assumptions stating that adding social cues to the learning materials benefits learning, there still may be some boundary conditions for the inclusion of human instructors in the learning materials. In particular, some studies observed that learners spend a substantial amount of their learning time on visible human instructors (Kizilcec et al., 2014;

van Wermeskerken et al., 2018). Whereas these two studies did not observe negative effects of instructor presence on learning outcomes, a recent study using multiple short clips with rather dense information observed negative effects of a visible human instructor's talking head on objective learning outcomes, while the clips including a talking head were rated more favorably (Sondermann & Merkt, 2023). In light of this latter observation, it may be worthwhile to consider a strategic presentation of talking heads that makes use of the positive effect of talking heads on learners' ratings of the learning materials, while at the same time avoiding potentially negative effects on the learning outcomes. This may be achieved by providing talking heads only in sections of the video that provide visually irrelevant information, while avoiding talking heads in visually relevant sections of the video. In this regard, it should be noted that such a strategic presentation may increase the saliency of talking heads because the reappearance of the face repeatedly attracts learners' attention (see Kizilcec et al., 2015).

The Role of Realism in Dynamic Visualizations

This chapter uses a broad definition of dynamic visualizations to derive some theoretically and empirically based principles that inform the design of dynamic visualizations. It is evident that there are differences between narrated slides as encountered in lecture recordings, animated learning materials as encountered in virtual environments, and photo-realistic visualizations as encountered in educational videos. However, from our perspective, the underlying cognitive and social implications of the media characteristics described in this chapter should operate similarly across different types of dynamic visualizations. For example, the transient flow of information adds additional processing requirements to both virtual and photo-realistic learning materials. Nevertheless, differences between different types of dynamic visualizations may serve as boundary conditions for the principles described in the previous section.

In particular, the above examples of dynamic visualizations differ regarding the level of realism, which can be defined as the similarity of a visual depiction to its real-world referent (Imhof et al., 2011). Even though technology enables the creation of animations that are hardly discernable from reality, it is still feasible to assume that most computer-generated animations to date are characterized by lower levels of realism than photo-realistic recordings in educational videos. Overall, evidence regarding the effects of realism in dynamic visualizations is rather mixed. For example, in a meta-analysis, Höffler and Leutner (2007) found larger effects in favor of dynamic over static representations when the visuals were photo-realistic, whereas the effects were smaller when the visuals were computer-generated. However, the authors note that this difference in effect sizes may be confounded with the role of the animations because all the included studies using photo-realistic video-based animations were representational. In contrast, some of the studies using computer-based animations also used animations for decorative purposes. Adding to the reservations about the reliability of this finding, Imhof et al. (2011) did not find an effect of animations' level of realism on learning. In contrast, Scheiter et al. (2009) even observed negative effects of realistic animations. These heterogeneous findings imply that there is no general advantage of either photo-realistic or computer-based animations. Instead, it may be necessary to adapt the level of realism of the dynamic visualizations to the learning goal and the specifics of the learning contents. In particular, adding more realistic details to dynamic visualizations may increase the complexity of the learning materials, so learners need more support from design principles such as segmenting and signaling in order to avoid cognitive overload. In this regard, further research is necessary to identify how dynamic visualizations should be presented to best fit the requirements of specific learning situations.

Conclusion

In this chapter, we discussed three different design principles for designing dynamic visualizations, which were grounded in cognitive and affective theories of learning with media (e.g., Mayer, 2020; Schneider et al., 2022). Whereas findings from basic cognitive research, meta-analyses, and systematic reviews suggest that providing dynamic visualizations in a segmented way (Rey et al., 2019), using signals to highlight relevant pieces of information (Richter et al., 2016; Schneider et al., 2018), and including human-like (Castro-Alonso et al., 2021) or human (Henderson & Schroeder, 2021) instructors facilitate rather than hamper learning (but see Sondermann & Merkt, 2023), there may be boundary conditions such as prior knowledge or the complexity of the learning materials that qualify the effectiveness of the described principles. These boundary conditions should be thoroughly investigated in future research.

Evidence-Based Practice Recommendations

- Dynamic visualizations can be particularly useful when the presented learning material needs to display changes over time.
- Theory and research suggest that segmenting dynamic visualizations and signaling relevant information benefit learning.
- Regarding the inclusion of a human instructor, there are inconclusive theoretical assumptions and empirical evidence.

- Whether or not and under which conditions dynamic visualizations should display information in a realistic and possibly complex manner is not yet clear based on current research findings.

References

Abrams, R. A., & Christ, S. E. (2003). Motion onset captures attention. *Psychological Science, 14*(5), 427–432. https://doi.org/10.1111/1467-9280.01458

Bauhoff, V., Huff, M., & Schwan, S. (2012). Distance matters: Spatial contiguity effects as trade-off between gaze switches and memory load. *Applied Cognitive Psychology, 26*(6), 863–871. https://doi.org/10.1002/acp.2887

Berney, S., & Betrancourt, M. (2016). Does animation enhance learning? A meta-analysis. *Computers & Education, 101*, 150–167. https://doi.org/10.1016/j.compedu.2016.06.005

Boucheix, J., & Lowe, R. K. (2010). An eye tracking comparison of external pointing cues and internal continuous cues in learning with complex animations. *Learning and Instruction, 20*(2), 123–135. https://doi.org/10.1016/j.learninstruc.2009.02.015

Boucheix, J., Lowe, R. K., Putri, D. K., & Groff, J. (2013). Cueing animations: Dynamic signaling aids information extraction and comprehension. *Learning and Instruction, 25*, 71–84. https://doi.org/10.1016/j.learninstruc.2012.11.005

Castro-Alonso, J. C., Wong, R. M., Adesope, O. O., & Paas, F. (2021). Effectiveness of multimedia pedagogical agents predicted by diverse theories: A meta-analysis. *Educational Psychology Review, 33*(3), 989–1015. https://doi.org/10.1007/s10648-020-09587-1

DeFleur, M. L., Davenport, L., Cronin, M., & DeFleur, M. (1992). Audience recall of news stories presented by newspaper, computer, television and radio. *Journalism Quarterly, 69*(4), 1010–1022. https://doi.org/10.1177/107769909206900419

Furnham, A., Gunter, B., & Green, A. (1990). Remembering science: The recall of factual information as a function of the presentation mode. *Applied Cognitive Psychology, 4*(3), 203–212. https://doi.org/10.1002/acp.2350040305

Glaser, M., & Schwan, S. (2015). Explaining pictures: How verbal cues influence processing of pictorial learning material. *Journal of Educational Psychology, 107*(4), 1006–1018. https://doi.org/10.1037/edu0000044

Gunter, B., Furnham, A. F., & Gietson, G. (1984). Memory for the news as a function of the channel of communication. *Human Learning: Journal of Practical Research & Applications, 3*(4), 265–271.

Hasler, B. S., Kersten, B., & Sweller, J. (2007). Learner control, cognitive load and instructional animation. *Applied Cognitive Psychology, 21*(6), 713–729. https://doi.org/10.1002/acp.1345

Henderson, M. L., & Schroeder, N. L. (2021). A systematic review of instructor presence in instructional videos: Effects on learning and affect. *Computers and Education Open, 2*, 100059. https://doi.org/10.1016/j.caeo.2021.100059

Höffler, T. N., & Leutner, D. (2007). Instructional animation versus static pictures: A meta-analysis. *Learning and Instruction, 17*(6), 722–738. https://doi.org/10.1016/j.learninstruc.2007.09.013

Huff, M., & Maurer, A. E. (2014). Post-learning verbal information changes visual and motor memory for hand-manipulative tasks. *Applied Cognitive Psychology, 28*(5), 772–779. https://doi.org/10.1002/acp.3047

Huff, M., Meitz, T. G. K., & Papenmeier, F. (2014). Changes in situation models modulate processes of event perception in audiovisual narratives. *Journal of Experimental Psychology: Learning, Memory, and Cognition, 40*(5), 1377–1388. https://doi.org/10.1037/a0036780

Huff, M., Papenmeier, F., & Zacks, J. M. (2012). Visual target detection is impaired at event boundaries. *Visual Cognition, 20*(7), 848–864. https://doi.org/10.1080/1 3506285.2012.705359

Huff, M., & Schwan, S. (2008). Verbalizing events: Overshadowing or facilitation? *Memory & Cognition, 36*(2), 392–402. https://doi.org/10.3758/mc.36.2.392

Huff, M., & Schwan, S. (2012). The verbal facilitation effect in learning to tie nautical knots. *Learning and Instruction, 22*(5), 376–385. https://doi.org/10.1016/j. learninstruc.2012.03.001

Imhof, B., Scheiter, K., & Gerjets, P. (2011). Learning about locomotion patterns from visualizations: Effects of presentation format and realism. *Computers & Education, 57*(3), 1961–1970. https://doi.org/10.1016/j.compedu.2011.05.004

Jamet, E. (2014). An eye-tracking study of cueing effects in multimedia learning. *Computers in Human Behavior, 32*, 47–53. https://doi.org/10.1016/j.chb. 2013.11.013

Jarodzka, H., Balslev, T., Holmqvist, K., Nyström, M., Scheiter, K., Gerjets, P., & Eika, B. (2012). Conveying clinical reasoning based on visual observation via eye-movement modeling examples. *Instructional Science, 40*(5), 813–827. https://doi. org/10.1007/s11251-012-9218-5

Jeung, H., Chandler, P., & Sweller, J. (1997). The role of visual indicators in dual sensory mode instruction. *Educational Psychology, 17*(3), 329–345. https://doi. org/10.1080/0144341970170307

Kizilcec, R. F., Bailenson, J. N., & Gomez, C. J. (2015). The instructor's face in video instruction: Evidence from two large-scale field studies. *Journal of Educational Psychology, 107*(3), 724–739. https://doi.org/10.1037/edu0000013

Kizilcec, R. F., Papadopoulos, K., & Sritanyaratana, L. (2014). Showing face in video instruction. In M. Jones, P. Palanque, A. Schmidt, & T. Grossman (Eds.), *Proceedings of the SIGCHI Conference on Human Factors in Computing Systems* (pp. 2095–2102). ACM. https://doi.org/10.1145/2556288.2557207

Leahy, W., & Sweller, J. (2011). Cognitive load theory, modality of presentation and the transient information effect. *Applied Cognitive Psychology, 25*(6), 943–951. https://doi.org/10.1002/acp.1787

Lee, J. Y., Donkers, J., Jarodzka, H., Sellenraad, G., & van Merriënboer, J. (2020). Different effects of pausing on cognitive load in a medical simulation game. *Computers in Human Behavior, 110*, 106385. https://doi.org/10.1016/j.chb. 2020.106385

Lusk, D. L., Evans, A. D., Jeffrey, T. R., Palmer, K. R., Wikstrom, C. S., & Doolittle, P. E. (2009). Multimedia learning and individual differences: Mediating the effects of working memory capacity with segmentation. *British Journal of Educational Technology, 40*(4), 636–651. https://doi.org/10.1111/j.1467-8535.2008.00848.x

Mayer, R. (2014). Principles based on social cues in multimedia learning: Personalization, voice, image, and embodiment principles. In R. Mayer (Ed.), *The Cambridge handbook of multimedia learning* (pp. 345–368). Cambridge: Cambridge University Press. https://doi.org/10.1017/CBO9781139547369.017

Mayer, R. (2020). *Multimedia learning* (3rd ed.). Cambridge: Cambridge University Press. https://doi.org/10.1017/9781316941355

Meitz, T. G. K., Meyerhoff, H. S., & Huff, M. (2020). Event related message processing: Perceiving and remembering changes in films with and without soundtrack. *Media Psychology*, *23*(5), 733–763. https://doi.org/10.1080/15213269.2019.163 6660

Merkt, M., Ballmann, A., Felfeli, J., & Schwan, S. (2018). Pauses in educational videos: testing the transience explanation against the structuring explanation. *Computers in Human Behavior*, *89*, 399–410. https://doi.org/10.1016/j.chb.2018.01.013

Merkt, M., Hoppe, A., Bruns, G., Ewerth, R., & Huff, M. (2022). Pushing the button: Why do learners pause online videos? *Computers & Education*, *176*, 104355. https://doi.org/10.1016/j.compedu.2021.104355

Merkt, M., Lux, S., Hoogerheide, V., van Gog, T. & Schwan, S. (2020). A change of scenery: Does the setting of an instructional video affect learning? *Journal of Educational Psychology*, *112*(6), 1273–1283. https://doi.org/10.1037/edu0000414

Merkt, M. & Schwan, S. (2017). What you see is what you remember? Depictions of historical figures influence memory for historical facts. *Learning and Instruction*, *52*, 112–121. https://doi.org/10.1016/j.learninstruc.2017.05.004

Merkt, M., Weigand, S., Heier, A., & Schwan, S. (2011). Learning with videos vs. learning with print: The role of interactive features. *Learning and Instruction*, *21*(6), 687–704. https://doi.org/10.1016/j.learninstruc.2011.03.004

Miller, G. A. (1956). The magical number seven, plus or minus two: Some limits on our capacity for processing information. *Psychological Review*, *63*(2), 81–97. https://doi.org/10.1037/h0043158

Moreno, R. (2006). Learning in high-tech and multimedia environments. *Current Directions in Psychological Science*, *15*(2), 63–67. https://doi.org/10.1111/j.0963-7214.2006.00408.x

Nass, C., Steuer, J., & Tauber, E. R. (1994). Computers are social actors. In B. Adelson, S. Dumais, & J. Olson (Eds.), *Proceedings of the SIGCHI Conference on Human Factors in Computing Systems Celebrating Interdependence – CHI '94* (pp. 72–78). ACM Press. https://doi.org/10.1145/191666.191703

Navarrete, E., Hoppe, A., & Ewerth, R. (2021). A review on recent advances in video-based learning research: Video features, interaction, tools, and technologies. *Proceedings of the CIKM 2021 Workshops co-located with 30th ACM International Conference on Information and Knowledge Management (CIKM 2021)*. http://ceur-ws.org/Vol-3052/paper7.pdf

Newtson, D., & Engquist, G. (1976). The perceptual organization of ongoing behavior. *Journal of Experimental Social Psychology*, *12*(5), 436–450. https://doi.org/10.1016/0022-1031(76)90076-7

Paivio, A. (1986). *Mental representations: A dual-coding approach*. New York: Oxford University Press. https://doi.org/10.1093/acprof:oso/9780195066661.001.0001

Ploetzner, R., Berney, S., & Bétrancourt, M. (2020). A review of learning demands in instructional animations: The educational effectiveness of animations unfolds if the features of change need to be learned. *Journal of Computer Assisted Learning*, *36*(6), 838–860. https://doi.org/10.1111/jcal.12476

Rat für kulturelle Bildung (2019). *Jugend/YouTube/Kulturelle Bildung*. https://www.rat-kulturelle-bildung.de/fileadmin/user_upload/pdf/Studie_YouTube_Webversion_final_2.pdf

Rey, G. D., Beege, M., Nebel, S., Wirzberger, M., Schmitt, T. H., & Schneider, S. (2019). A meta-analysis of the segmenting effect. *Educational Psychology Review*, *31*(2), 389–419. https://doi.org/10.1007/s10648-018-9456-4

Richter, J., Scheiter, K., & Eitel, A. (2016). Signaling text-picture relations in multimedia learning: A comprehensive meta-analysis. *Educational Research Review*, *17*, 19–36. https://doi.org/10.1016/j.edurev.2015.12.003

Salomon, G. (1984). Television is "easy" and print is "tough": The differential investment of mental effort in learning as a function of perceptions and attributions. *Journal of Educational Psychology*, *76*(4), 647–658. https://doi.org/10.1037/0022-0663.76.4.647

Scheiter, K., Gerjets, P., Huk, T., Imhof, B., & Kammerer, Y. (2009). The effects of realism in learning with dynamic visualizations. *Learning and Instruction*, *19*(6), 481–494. https://doi.org/10.1016/j.learninstruc.2008.08.001

Schneider, S., Beege, M., Nebel, S., & Rey, G. D. (2018). A meta-analysis of how signaling affects learning with media. *Educational Research Review*, *23*, 1–24. https://doi.org/10.1016/j.edurev.2017.11.001

Schneider, S., Beege, M., Nebel, S., Schnaubert, L., & Rey, G. D. (2022). The cognitive-affective-social theory of learning in digital environments (CASTLE). *Educational Psychology Review*, *34*(1), 1–38. https://doi.org/10.1007/s10648-021-09626-5

Schüler, A., & Merkt, M. (2021). Investigating text-picture integration in videos with the multimedia contradiction paradigm. *Journal of Computer Assisted Learning*, *37*(3), 718–734. https://doi.org/10.1111/jcal.12518

Schwan, S., & Riempp, R. (2004). The cognitive benefits of interactive videos: Learning to tie nautical knots. *Learning and Instruction*, *14*(3), 293–305. https://doi.org/10.1016/j.learninstruc.2004.06.005

Smith, A., Toor, S., & van Kessel, P. (2018). Many turn to YouTube for children's content, news, how-to lessons. *Pew Research Centre*. https://www.pewresearch.org/internet/2018/11/07/many-turn-to-youtube-for-childrens-content-news-how-to-lessons/

Sondermann, C., & Merkt, M. (2023). Like it or learn from it: Effects of talking heads in educational videos. *Computers & Education*, *193*, 104675. https://doi.org/10.1016/j.compedu.2022.104675

Spanjers, I. E., van Gog, T., & van Merriënboer, J. G. (2010). A theoretical analysis of how segmentation of dynamic visualizations optimizes students' learning. *Educational Psychology Review*, *22*(4), 411–423. https://doi.org/10.1007/s10648-010-9135-6

Spanjers, I. E., van Gog, T., Wouters, P., & van Merriënboer, J. J. G. (2012). Explaining the segmentation effect in learning from animations: The role of pausing and temporal cueing. *Computers & Education*, *59*(2), 274–280. https://doi.org/10.1016/j.compedu.2011.12.024

Spanjers, I. E., Wouters, P., van Gog, T., & van Merriënboer, J. G. (2011). An expertise reversal effect of segmentation in learning from animated worked-out examples. *Computers in Human Behavior*, *27*(1), 46–52. https://doi.org/10.1016/j.chb.2010.05.011

Sweller, J., van Merriënboer, J. J. G., & Paas, F. (1998). Cognitive architecture and instructional design. *Educational Psychology Review* 10(3), 251–296. https://doi.org/10.1023/A:1022193728205

Sweller, J., van Merriënboer, J. J. G., & Paas, F. (2019). Cognitive architecture and instructional design: 20 years later. *Educational Psychology Review, 31*(2), 261–292. https://doi.org/10.1007/s10648-019-09465-5

Tversky, B., Morrison, J. B., & Betrancourt, M. (2002). Animation: can it facilitate? *International Journal of Human-Computer Studies, 57*(4), 247–262.

van Wermeskerken, M., Ravensbergen, S., & van Gog, T. (2018). Effects of instructor presence in video modeling examples on attention and learning. *Computers in Human Behavior, 89,* 430–438. https://doi.org/10.1016/j.chb.2017.11.038

Zacks, J. M. (2020). Event Perception and Memory. *Annual Review of Psychology, 71*(1), 165–191. https://doi.org/10.1146/annurev-psych-010419-051101

Zacks, J. M., & Swallow, K. M. (2007). Event Segmentation. *Current Directions in Psychological Science, 16*(2), 80–84. https://doi.org/10.1111/j.1467-8721.2007.00480.x

6

SIX EVIDENCE-INFORMED TIPS ON HOW TO OPTIMIZE LEARNING FROM INSTRUCTIONAL VIDEOS

Vincent Hoogerheide and Stoo Sepp

Since the inception of the motion picture, innovators have envisioned great things for its application in education. In 1922, Thomas A. Edison wrote: "I believe that the motion picture is destined to revolutionize our educational system and that in a few years, it will supplant largely, if not entirely, the use of textbooks." Back then, motion pictures failed to make a big impact on the world of education (Mayer et al., 2020). A century after Edison made his bold prediction, the medium of video has become immensely popular at all levels of education (Bétrancourt & Benetos, 2018; de Koning et al., 2018). Video plays a pivotal role in people's informal learning, in part thanks to popular websites such as YouTube. Video also plays a key role in formal education, as instructional video (IV) is a major component of new approaches such as massive open online courses and flipped classrooms. The widespread use of video learning is enabled by major technological advances on both the hardware side (e.g., the widespread availability of internet and mobile devices with a recording function) and the software side (e.g., free apps that allow for easy video recording and editing). Importantly, the popularity of video learning increased in recent years because of the COVID-19 pandemic, which forced a lot of institutions to resort to online education (Sepp et al., 2022).

The increasing popularity of video learning has inspired researchers across the globe to examine how to design IVs and support learning from IVs, and meta-analytic evidence indicates that studying instructional videos improves students' learning and motivation within both a flipped classroom and a regular classroom context (e.g., Cheng et al., 2018; Lin & Yu, 2023). Traditionally, there have been two main research traditions, inspired by either social-cognitive or cognitive theories (Hoogerheide & Roelle, 2020). Firstly, research inspired by Bandura's social learning theory (Bandura,

DOI: 10.4324/9781003386131-9

1986), which asserts the importance of learning from others in a social setting through observation, imitation, and an emotional connection, has primarily examined the effects of video modelling examples. Video modelling examples are how-to demonstration videos in which a person – the (role) *model*, which can be a peer, expert, or teacher – shows and explains which steps are necessary for completing a task or solving a problem, such as how to repair a faulty electrical circuit or how to solve a mathematical equation (for a recent review, see Van Gog et al., 2019). Secondly, research has been informed by cognitive theories such as Mayer's cognitive theory of multimedia learning (Mayer, 2020), which investigates learning in multimedia environments and with multimedia materials, and Sweller's cognitive load theory (Sweller et al., 2019), which explores the generalized effects of various instructional interventions predicated on the limitations of human cognitive architecture. Within this cognitive tradition, many researchers have explored the effects of different types of multimedia learning material, many of which qualify as IVs, such as video lectures (i.e., relatively lengthy recordings of lectures) or knowledge clips (i.e., relatively brief videos in which a concept is explained). In these videos, the explanations are provided by an *instructor*.

Although these two bodies of IV research both use carefully designed experiments to examine the effects of IV on learning outcomes, such as retention (i.e., remembering information), comprehension (i.e., understanding information), and transfer (i.e., using information in new contexts), they tend to act largely in isolation and until recently did not refer to each other much. This is likely because they (traditionally) rely on different theories and focus on different types of IV. The main aim of this chapter is to draw on these two key bodies of research to provide an overview of evidence-informed principles on how to optimize people's learning from IV. Such an integrated overview is missing yet could provide educational practitioners and developers of IV with important information on how to design and support learning from IV. Moreover, this overview could stimulate cross-pollination across the two different research traditions. Below, we detail six guidelines.

Tip #1: Only Present Information Relevant to Learning

When creating IVs, educators and educational content developers may wonder what details they should include in the video. Research inspired by cognitive theories has shown that if the aim is to optimize learning, IVs should only include information that is relevant to the instructional goal (for a meta-analysis, see Sundarajan & Adesope, 2020). For instance, Harp and Mayer (1997, 1998) found that including additional 'seductive' text and images that were not related to the instructional goal with the intention of making the video more engaging had a negative effect on learners' retention and transfer test scores. While observed in both single and multi-modality learning materials, this *seductive details principle* is particularly pronounced for learners with lower working memory capacity, likely in part because they attend to seductive details more frequently (Sanchez & Wiley, 2006).

Even information that is related to the instructional goal can hinder learning. For instance, presenting the same information in two different modalities (e.g., text and image) can impair learning relative to only presenting that information in a single modality (i.e., the redundancy principle; Kalyuga et al., 2004; for meta-analytic evidence, see Adesope & Nesbit, 2012). In multimedia lessons, a spectrum can exist between full redundancy and non-redundancy. Students learn more when verbal explanations deviate slightly from on-screen text when compared to verbatim explanations (Yue et al., 2013). Additionally, higher test scores result when text explanations are presented in summary form, when contrasted with full explanations (Mayer et al., 2001), while in both contexts, no redundancy is most advantageous. Other findings indicate that adding subtitles to an IV can impair learning (Mayer et al., 2020) – even when the instructor's narration is muted (Tarchi et al., 2021) – because learners are presented with two sources of visual information. That said, subtitles can be beneficial for those with different abilities (e.g., D/deaf or hard of hearing learners) and for those learning a new language, because in these situations, the subtitles are not redundant but necessary for understanding the instructional message (Mayer, 2020).

In sum, when creating IVs, creators should be mindful of what information is required for their audience to understand what is being presented. Importantly, this required information depends on the complexity of the task: A text that is self-explanatory because it presents a simple idea (e.g., the red balloon flies up into the sky) might not require any additional explanatory text or supporting imagery to illustrate this idea. For more complex tasks, such as sequential problem-solving or mechanical processes, if the IV is not self-explanatory, the thoughtful integration of additional supporting text, audio, or visual materials, such as diagrams and images, would likely support learners' understanding (Sweller et al., 2019).

Tip #2: Provide Cues to Direct Attention

While learning from IV has many advantages relative to more traditional ways of learning such as books, an important downside of video learning is that key information (e.g., a picture or a piece of written text) that is there one moment might be gone shortly afterwards. This transience of information means that it is crucial that learners pay attention to the right information at the right time (e.g., the visual information that the instructor/model is referring to in the narration; Singh et al., 2012). Indeed, in both research traditions, ample research has shown that including cues in an IV to direct attention to key information can guide learners' attention and help them learn more from the video (Castro-Alonso et al., 2021; Mayer et al., 2020; for meta-analytic evidence, see Schneider et al., 2018).

For instance, an effective strategy for written text (e.g., on a presentation slide or a whiteboard) is to highlight key terms with a different colour, as studies have shown that changing the colour of key terms in written text to red improved learners' retention of the learning material (e.g., Moreno & Abercrombi, 2010). Other studies have shown that highlighting or shading key areas of a diagram referred to in the oral explanations improved learners' retention and problem-solving transfer (De Koning et al., 2018, 2010; Ozcelik et al., 2010). The most prevalent way of cueing in IVs is to have the presenter gesture or gaze at the relevant material, which has been shown to help learners attend to the relevant material and thereby improve their learning (e.g., Ouwehand et al., 2015; Wang et al., 2020; see also tip #4). Hence, when creating IVs, any cueing of elements in a picture or text should be purposeful and guide learners' attention towards key terms or relationships between concepts.

In addition to cues in videos, learners can guide their own attention. Recent research on the relationship between human movement and learning has identified a *tracing principle*, which postulates that learning improves when learners are asked to trace along key areas of anatomy diagrams or geometry problems. Indeed, studies have found that, relative to a control condition that does not trace, those who engaged in tracing attained higher retention and transfer scores on a posttest (Ginns et al., 2020; Ginns & King, 2021). The described learning gains are usually observed when learners perform tracing gestures while studying visuospatial materials such as diagrams and mathematics problems, which can serve as a means to direct attention towards key elements or shapes in a diagram. For those creating IVs that include such materials, encouraging learners to pause and trace along diagrams can be beneficial for learning.

Tip #3: Segment and Pause (Longer) Videos

A key challenge for educators and educational content developers is to prevent learners' information processing systems from becoming overloaded when they study IVs. It is unfortunately rather easy for IVs to overload this system, because: (1) videos typically present auditory and visual information while the processing capacity for both types of information in our working memory is very limited, (2) the auditory and visual information are often both transient, which places an additional burden on working memory, and (3) a lot of videos are rather long while our attentional capabilities are limited (Mayer & Fiorella, 2021). Consequently, the effectiveness of (longer and more complex) IVs can be suboptimal, as learners might struggle to engage in the necessary cognitive processes that would allow them to make sense of the presented material.

Two strategies that can help prevent this cognitive overload and increase retention and transfer are system-paced and learner-paced segmentation (for a meta-analysis, see Rey et al., 2019). System-paced segmentation refers to when videos are presented in smaller 'chunks', either by providing separated short videos (as opposed to a single longer video) or by presenting a video that has built-in pauses or breaks. It is commonly argued that these breaks should occur at structural moments within a video, such as when there is a shift in the topic or when the video moves from one procedural step to the next, such as in a demonstration video (see Mura et al., 2013 for an example in practice). Learner-paced segmentation, on the other hand, describes when a video can be paused by the learner.

There are several explanations for how these strategies prevent cognitive overload (see e.g., Chen et al., 2017; Merkt et al., 2018; Rey et al., 2019). The 'structuring explanation' postulates that breaks at key moments help learners see the salience and make sense of the natural boundaries between events in a process or procedure. The 'transience explanation' argues that breaks in videos reduce the negative effects of video information being transient. It is also possible that breaks improve learning because they increase learning time or because they allow for the replenishment of limited working memory resources. Lastly, learner-initiated breaks might help learners to adapt the presentation pace to their own individual needs. Several tests of these explanations revealed mixed results (e.g., a well-designed experiment: Merkt et al., 2018; a meta-analysis: Rey et al., 2019), likely because there is some truth to most or all explanations.

Hence, when a video is long and complex for learners, it is important to ensure that there are breaks while studying. It is not entirely clear how long the breaks should be and whether it is best if those breaks are determined by an educator or designer of video material or whether learners should pause themselves (Merkt et al., 2018). Regardless, both giving learners access to interactive features that allow them to pause and replay parts of the video and encouraging them to use these features as they wish can enhance learning. This learner-paced segmentation is a type of self-management of cognitive resources, which in recent years has become a popular topic in research (e.g., Eitel et al., 2020). Interestingly, a recent study by Merkt et al. (2022) explored why learners pause videos, and they found that they primarily report doing so primarily at structural moments or when they have difficulty understanding the content of the video.

Tip #4: Show the Presenter in the Video

A key question for every video creator is, should the person who presents the information be on the screen or not? This question has been a focal point in both research lines in the past decade (Hoogerheide et al., 2014; Sepp et al.,

2022). From a social-cognitive perspective, one could argue that the presence of someone on the screen provides important social cues that help learners feel a social connection, which could improve learning (e.g., Beege et al., 2017). From a cognitive perspective, an important reason why someone on the screen could foster learning is that an instructor could help guide learners to the relevant information on the screen by gesturing or pointing, which we know can help students learn (cf. Tip #2). By contrast, one could argue that a person on the screen impairs learning because that person presents a source of split-attention, essentially drawing attention away from the learning materials (e.g., the slides). Indeed, people are real attention 'magnets', especially people's faces, and this is also true when studying IVs with a visible presenter (e.g., Van Wermeskerken & Van Gog, 2017).

The available evidence clearly shows that presenting someone on the screen does not impair learning relative to a voice-over with visual information (e.g., slides), regardless of whether that person presenting the information is a model in a video modelling example (e.g., Van Wermeskerken & Van Gog, 2017) or an instructor in a short knowledge clip (e.g., Wang et al., 2020) or video lecture (e.g., Kizilcec et al., 2015). Hence, there is basically no evidence for the "split-attention perspective". Several studies within both research traditions even found a positive effect on learning outcomes of showing an instructor on the screen (e.g., video examples: Van Gog et al., 2014; knowledge clips: Wang et al., 2020; for meta-analytic evidence, see Beege et al., 2023). Taken together, showing the presenter's body and face in an IV, especially at the start, might provide important social cues and thereby establish a social connection between the presenter and the learner (Sepp et al., 2022). For those learning online, this helps to establish social and instructor presence, important factors in ensuring effective communication online (Garrison et al., 1999).

When recording a video with a person on the screen, there are important boundary conditions to consider that influence how much people learn. For instance, it seems best to show the instructor from the front (rather than from the side), because people learn more from a video when an instructor addresses the audience directly, likely due to a stronger social connection (e.g., Beege et al., 2017). There is also evidence suggesting that learning improves when the person on the screen cues where the learner should look at key points in time, for instance by gesturing, pointing, or looking at the material (e.g., Mayer et al., 2020; see Tip #2). By contrast, mere "talking heads" that do not interact with the material at all might not improve learning (e.g., Kizilcec et al., 2015). Lastly, when recording video modelling examples for adolescents, research by Hoogerheide et al. (2016) suggests that people learn more from examples presented by an older model rather than a peer model, even if the content of the video is otherwise identical (i.e., same explanations and movements).

Tip #5: Show a Demonstration from a First-Person Perspective

When demonstrating procedural tasks showing a series of actions performed by a person (e.g., assembly tasks, repairing tasks, medical procedures), the perspective principle suggests that these videos should be filmed from the first-person perspective of the person demonstrating the task (Mayer et al., 2020; Sepp et al., 2022). This principle was first found with video modelling examples in a study by Fiorella et al. (2017). They showed university students in the United States and the Netherlands how to build an electrical circuit with a video recorded from the perspective of the model building it (i.e., first-person perspective) or the opposite perspective (i.e., third-person perspective). Across both samples, those who studied the first-person perspective video performed significantly better and somewhat faster on a posttest that required them to rebuild the circuit shown in the video. This effect was only found with a complex circuit, not with a relatively simple circuit. The most likely explanation is that converting information from the third-person perspective into one's own third-person perspective might impair memorization processes, because doing so is likely quite taxing for learners' cognitive systems (i.e., consumes valuable limited working memory resources).

Based on the described findings, it seems advised to show the demonstration from a first-person perspective, although future research will have to test this principle with other types of principles and tasks. Interestingly, follow-up research by Bouchiex and colleagues (2018) with a medical procedure (i.e., inserting a catheter) suggests that changing viewpoints when the task requires it (e.g., because the model's hand is blocking key information in the first-person perspective view) might further improve learning. Another important issue to note is that this finding is likely also relevant to other types of videos. For instance, even in video lectures, how-to demonstrations are common even if they do not make up the whole video.

Tip #6: Encourage Generative Learning Activities

One way to support learning from IVs is to have learners engage in generative learning, which is an overarching term for a wide range of activities that encourage learners to actively engage with the learning material, such as summarizing, explaining to oneself, teaching someone else, or answering practice questions. These generative learning activities are cognitively demanding yet often effective for learning, and can be used while studying or after studying an IV (Brod, 2021; Fiorella & Mayer, 2016).

In the cognitive tradition, early research revealed that writing down summary notes while viewing a lecture led to increased test performance when compared to not writing down summary notes (e.g., Peper & Mayer, 1978).

More recent research examined whether adding practice (quiz) questions in video lectures helped learners to remember the content of the video better, because decades of research have shown that retrieving information from memory promotes long-term retention (i.e., the retrieval practice/testing effect; for a recent review, see Yang et al., 2021). This so-called *interpolated testing* approach seems to enhance how much people learn from video lectures (e.g., Ying et al., 2016). Aside from the direct benefits of retrieval practice, interpolating practice questions in video lectures might also improve learning because practice questions reduce mind-wandering, which happens when an individual stops focusing on the content of the video and starts thinking about task-unrelated things. Mind-wandering is particularly common during video lectures because of their relatively long length and has been shown to impair learners' retention of the video content (Lindquist & McLean, 2011). Note that recently, research has started exploring whether other generative strategies such as drawing and explaining can help people learn more from IVs (Fiorella et al., 2019).

Video modelling example research has predominantly examined whether it is needed to alternate example study with practice problem-solving. Practice problems are essentially a form of practice testing (Van Gog & Sweller, 2015), because they only present the initial state (e.g., a tyre is flat) and goal state (e.g., the tyre is repaired), requiring learners to uncover the solution steps by themselves. Research has shown that novices (i.e., learners with low/no prior knowledge of the task) do not benefit much from repeatedly solving a practice problem, because they use ineffective strategies to uncover the solution steps; novices are much better off studying video modelling examples to first to learn (a part of) the solution procedure (e.g., Van Harsel et al., 2020). For learners with more prior knowledge, practice problem-solving does promote learning relative to example study, because more advanced learners no longer need the support provided by the examples (i.e., expertise-reversal principle; Kalyuga et al., 2003). Moreover, for novices, repeatedly studying video modelling examples seems to promote learning to a similar degree as studying example-problem pairs, in which an example study is always followed by a practice problem (e.g., Coppens et al., 2019). This finding is rather surprising in light of the cognitive research described above, and suggests that retrieval practice might not be as beneficial in the context of learning problem-solving skills from video modelling examples (Van Gog & Sweller, 2015).

Relatedly, recent studies suggest that the generative activity of *making* a video about learning material for someone else can also be a powerful way to learn (for reviews, see Lachner et al., 2022; for meta-analytic evidence, see Kobayashi, 2024; Ribosa & Duran, 2022). For instance, a recent study provided primary school children with a text on photosynthesis to take home over the weekend (Hoogerheide et al., 2019). The children were either instructed to study the text, to study and summarize the text, or to study and make a video about the text for a fellow student. After the weekend, children who made an IV performed significantly better on a knowledge test relative to those who only studied, while such an advantage was not found for the summarizing group. Moreover, making a video was perceived as more enjoyable than summarizing or studying. Future research will have to uncover which cognitive (e.g., explaining and/or retrieving information) and social mechanisms (e.g., imagining an audience) are responsible for this effect (Lachner et al., 2022).

Discussion

This chapter presented six tips for optimizing the effectiveness of learning from IVs, derived from decades of research inspired by social-cognitive or cognitive theories on the effects of studying IVs on learning outcomes. We hope that this overview stimulates cross-pollination across the different research traditions. For instance, the perspective principle has only been found with video modelling examples, so it is unclear whether the perspective is also an important factor with other types of IVs that could have a demonstration component, such as (longer) video lectures. Another example concerns generative learning, where video modelling example research has almost exclusively focused on the combination of video examples and practice problems (e.g., Van Harsel et al., 2020), while the cognitive research line has shown that other strategies that trigger different cognitive and metacognitive processes can also and perhaps even further improve learning from video (e.g., drawing or explaining/teaching; Fiorella et al., 2019).

Several limitations of this chapter should be addressed. Firstly, these tips only focus on optimizing people's *learning*, while in real-world classroom and study settings, there are many other factors that are important and can influence how much people learn, such as motivational and self-regulatory processes (for a similar argument, see De Bruin et al., 2020; Sepp et al., 2022). For example, it is not yet known how first- or third-person video presentations may affect motivation or self-regulation strategies. That said, following some of these tips could have additional benefits for learners' motivation and self-regulation. We know that increasing people's knowledge of a topic often positively affects aspects of student motivation such as (situational) interest (Rotgans & Schmidt, 2014) and that more knowledgeable learners are typically better at monitoring their understanding and regulating their study behaviour than less knowledgeable learners (Kruger & Dunning, 1999). For instance, a key advantage of generative learning activities is that these activities give learners important insights into what they do (not) know, thereby allowing them to make better study decisions than if they were to only passively study material (De Bruin et al., 2020; Lachner et al., 2022). Moreover, relative to passive study activities, generative activities can be more motivating (e.g., more enjoyable; Hoogerheide et al., 2019).

Secondly, although each tip can help improve the effectiveness of IV learning, it is important to note that 'merely' following these tips is not enough for a high-quality learning experience. A successful base for an IV is a well-designed and clear instructional message that sits at the right level of complexity and provides an appropriate level of support given the expertise of the learners (see Van Merriënboer & Kirschner, 2013). Moreover, the quality of the recording should be sufficient (e.g., adequate rate of speech, quality of visual and auditory information, no background noise); though it is likely not necessary or practically feasible for every video to be a Hollywood-level production. Importantly, there are other tips for optimizing the effectiveness of IVs that we did not cover, and these can be found in other reviews on video learning written from a cognitive perspective (e.g., De Koning et al., 2018; Fiorella & Mayer, 2018; Mayer et al., 2020) and in general instructional design guidelines for educational material that apply to learning from IVs (e.g., principles derived from cognitive theory of multimedia learning, Mayer, 2020; cognitive load theory, Sweller et al., 2019).

To conclude, we hope that this chapter inspires future research on this very important and timely topic and helps to improve the effectiveness of IVs in practice. Although future research is recommended to continue testing the generalizability of these six tips, each tip should in principle be robust and generalize across many different types of IVs, student age groups, and materials. Importantly, these tips should rarely, if ever, impair people's learning relative to not following these tips or common practices. Therefore, these tips can help educators, designers of educational material, and even learners themselves to improve retention and understanding of IV material. This increased knowledge should in turn help learners to transfer that knowledge and use it in new situations.

Evidence-Based Practice Recommendations

- We present six tips for optimizing the effect of instructional video [IV] on learning.
- IVs should only present information relevant to learning.
- Demonstration IVs should be recorded from a first-person perspective.
- IVs should show the presenter and cue attention to key visual elements.
- IVs should be enriched with generative learning activities such as practice questions.

References

Adesope, O. O., & Nesbit, J. C. (2012). Verbal redundancy in multimedia learning environments: A meta-analysis. *Journal of Educational Psychology*, 104(1), 250–263. https://doi.org/10.1037/a0026147

Bandura, A. (1986). *Social foundations of thought and action: A social cognitive theory*. Englewood Cliffs: Prentice Hall.

Beege, M., Schneider, S., Nebel, S., & Rey, G. D. (2017). Look into my eyes! Exploring the effect of addressing in educational videos. *Learning and Instruction*, *49*, 113e120. https://doi.org/10.1016/j.learninstruc.2017.01.004

Beege, M., Schroeder, N. L., Heidig, S., Daniel Rey, G., & Schneider, S. (2023). The instructor presence effect and its moderators in instructional video: A series of meta-analyses. *Educational Research Review*, *41*, 100564. https://doi.org/ 10.1016/j.edurev.2023.100564

Bétrancourt, M., & Benetos, K. (2018). Why and when does instructional video facilitate learning? A commentary to the special issue "developments and trends in learning with instructional video." *Computers in Human Behavior*, *89*, 471–475. https://doi.org/10.1016/j.chb.2018.08.035

Boucheix, J.-M., Gauthier, P., Fontaine, J., & Jaffeux, S. (2018). Mixed camera viewpoints improve learning medical hand procedure from video in nurse training? *Computers in Human Behavior*, *89*, 418–429. https://doi.org/10.1016/j. chb.2018.01.017

Brod, G. (2021). Generative learning: Which strategies for what age? *Educational Psychology Review*, *33*, 1295–1318. https://doi.org/10.1007/s10648-020-09571-9

Castro-Alonso, J. C., De Koning, B. B., Fiorella, L., & Paas, F. (2021). Five strategies for optimizing instructional materials: Instructor- and learner-managed cognitive load. *Educational Psychology Review*, *33*, 1–29. https://doi.org/10.1007/ s10648-021-09606-9

Chen, O., Castro-Alonso, J. C., Paas, F., & Sweller, J. (2017). Extending cognitive load theory to incorporate working memory resource depletion: Evidence from the spacing effect. *Educational Psychology Review*, *30*(2), 1–19. https://doi. org/10.1007/s10648-017-9426-2

Cheng, L., Ritzhaupt, A. D., & Antonenko, P. (2018). Effects of the flipped classroom instructional strategy on students' learning outcomes: A meta-analysis. *Educational Technology Research and Development*, *67*, 793–824. https://doi.org/10.1007/ s11423-018-9633-7

Coppens, L. C., Hoogerheide, V., Snippe, E. M., Flunger, B., & Van Gog, T. (2019). Effects of problem-example and example-problem pairs on gifted and nongifted primary school students' learning. *Instructional Science*, *47*, 279–297. https://doi. org/10.1007/s11251-019-09484-3

De Bruin, A. B. H., Roelle, J., Carpenter, S. K. et al. (2020). Synthesizing cognitive load and self-regulation theory: A theoretical framework and research agenda. *Educational Psychology Review*, *32*, 903–915. https://doi.org/10.1007/s10648- 020-09576-4

De Koning, B. B., Hoogerheide, V., & Boucheix, J.-M. (2018). Developments and trends in learning with instructional video. *Computers in Human Behavior*, *89*, 395–398. https://doi.org/10.1016/j.chb.2018.08.055

De Koning, B. B., Tabbers, H. K., Rikers, R. M. J. P., & Paas, F. (2010). Attention guidance in learning from a complex animation: Seeing is understanding? *Learning and Instruction*,*20*(2),111–122.https://doi.org/10.1016/j.learninstruc.2009.02.010

Eitel, A., Endres, T., & Renkl, A. (2020). Self-management as a bridge between cognitive load and self-regulated learning: The illustrative case of seductive details. *Educational Psychology Review*, *32*(4), 1073–1087. https://doi.org/10.1007/ s10648-020-09559-5

Fiorella, L., & Mayer, R. E. (2016). Eight ways to promote generative learning. *Educational Psychology Review*, *28*, 717–741. https://doi.org/10.1007/s10648- 015-9348-9

Fiorella, L., & Mayer, R. E. (2018). What works and doesn't work with instructional video. *Computers in Human Behavior, 89,* 465–470. https://doi.org/10.1016/j.chb.2018.07.015

Fiorella, L., Stull, A. T., Kuhlmann, S., & Mayer, R. E. (2019). Fostering generative learning from video lessons: Benefits of instructor-generated drawings and learner-generated explanations. *Journal of Educational Psychology, 112*(5), 895–906. https://doi.org/10.1037/edu0000408

Fiorella, L., Van Gog, T., Hoogerheide, V., & Mayer, R. E. (2017). It's all a matter of perspective: Viewing first–person video modeling examples promotes learning of an assembly task. *Journal of Educational Psychology, 109,* 653–665. https://doi.org/10.1037/edu0000161

Garrison, D. R., Anderson, T., & Archer, W. (1999). Critical inquiry in a text-based environment: Computer conferencing in higher education. *The Internet and Higher Education, 2*(2–3), 87–105. https://doi.org/10.1016/s1096-7516(00)00016-6

Ginns, P., Hu, F., & Bobis, J. (2020). Tracing enhances problem-solving transfer, but without effects on intrinsic or extraneous cognitive load. *Applied Cognitive Psychology, 34*(6). https://doi.org/10.1002/acp.3732

Ginns, P., & King, V. (2021). Pointing and tracing enhance computer-based learning. *Educational Technology Research and Development, 1–17*(69), 1387–1403. https://doi.org/10.1007/s11423-021-09997-0

Harp, S. F., & Mayer, R. E. (1997). The role of interest in learning from scientific text and illustrations: On the distinction between emotional interest and cognitive interest. *Journal of Educational Psychology, 89*(1), 92–102. https://doi.org/10.1037/0022-0663.89.1.92

Harp, S. F., & Mayer, R. E. (1998). How seductive details do their damage: A theory of cognitive interest in science learning. *Journal of Educational Psychology, 90*(3), 414–434. https://doi.org/10.1037/0022-0663.90.3.414

Hoogerheide, V., Loyens, S. M. M., & Van Gog, T. (2014). Comparing the effects of worked examples and modeling examples on learning. *Computers in Human Behavior, 41,* 80–91. https://doi.org/10.1016/j.chb.2014.09.013

Hoogerheide, V., & Roelle, J. (2020). Example-based learning: New theoretical perspectives and use-inspired advances to a contemporary instructional approach. *Applied Cognitive Psychology, 34,* 787–792. https://doi.org/10.1002/acp.3706

Hoogerheide, V., Van Wermeskerken, M., Loyens, S. M. M., & Van Gog, T. (2016). Learning from video modeling examples: Content kept equal, adults are more effective than peers. *Learning and Instruction, 44,* 22–30. https://doi.org/10.1016/j.learninstruc.2016.02.004

Hoogerheide, V., Visee, J., Lachner, A., & Van Gog, T. (2019). Generating an instructional video as homework activity is both effective and enjoyable. *Learning and Instruction, 64,* 101226. https://doi.org/10.1016/j.learninstruc.2019.101226

Kalyuga, S., Ayres, P., Chandler, P., & Sweller, J. (2003). The expertise reversal effect. *Educational Psychologist, 38,* 23–32. https://doi.org/10.1207/s15326985ep3801_4

Kalyuga, S., Chandler, P., & Sweller, J. (2004). When redundant on-screen text in multimedia technical instruction can interfere with learning. *Human Factors, 46,* 567–581. https://doi.org/10.1518/hfes.46.3.567.50405

Kizilcec, R. F., Bailenson, J. N., & Gomez, C. J. (2015). The instructor's face in video instruction: Evidence from two large-scale field studies. *Journal of Educational Psychology, 107,* 724–739. https://doi.org/10.1037/edu0000013

Kobayashi, K. (2024). Interactive learning effects of preparing to teach and teaching: A meta-analytic approach. *Educational Psychology Review*, *36*, 1–29. https://doi.org/10.1007/s10648-024-09871-4

Kruger, J., & Dunning, D. (1999). Unskilled and unaware of it: How difficulties in recognizing one's own incompetence lead to inflated self-assessments. *Journal of Personality and Social Psychology*, *77*, 1121–1134. https://doi.org/10.1037//0022-3514.77.6.1121

Lachner, A., Hoogerheide, V., Van Gog, T., & Renkl, A. (2022). Learning-by-teaching without audience presence or interaction: When and why does it work? *Educational Psychology Review*, *34*, 575–607. https://doi.org/10.1007/s10648-021-09643-4

Lin, Y., & Yu, Z. (2023). A meta-analysis evaluating the effectiveness of instructional video technologies. *Technology, Knowledge and Learning*. https://doi.org/10.1007/s10758-023-09669-3

Lindquist, S. I., & McLean, J. P. (2011). Daydreaming and its correlates in an educational environment. *Learning and Individual Differences*, *21*, 158e167. https://doi.org/10.1016/j.lindif.2010.12.006

Mayer, R. E. (2020). *Multimedia learning*. Cambridge University Press. https://doi.org/10.1017/9781316941355

Mayer, R. E., & Fiorella, L. (2021). Principles for managing essential processing in multimedia learning. In R. E. Mayer (Ed.), *The Cambridge handbook of multimedia learning* (3rd ed., pp. 243–260). Cambridge University Press. https://doi.org/10.1017/9781108894333.025

Mayer, R. E., Fiorella, L., & Stull, A. (2020). Five ways to increase the effectiveness of instructional video. *Educational Technology Research and Development*, *6*, 837–852. https://doi.org/10.1007/s11423-020-09749-6

Mayer, R. E., Heiser, J., & Lonn, S. (2001). Cognitive constraints on multimedia learning: When presenting more material results in less understanding. *Journal of Educational Psychology*, *93*(1), 187–198. https://doi.org/10.1037/0022-0663.93.1.187

Merkt, M., Ballmann, A., Felfeli, J., & Schwan, S. (2018). Pauses in educational videos: Testing the transience explanation against the structuring explanation. *Computers in Human Behavior*, *89*, 399–410. https://doi.org/10.1016/j.chb.2018.01.013

Merkt, M., Hoppe, A., Bruns, G., Ewerth, R., & Huff, M. (2022). Pushing the button: Why do learners pause online videos? *Computers & Education*, *176*, 104355. https://doi.org/10.1016/j.compedu.2021.104355

Moreno, R., & Abercrombi, S. (2010). Promoting awareness of learner diversity in prospective teachers: Signaling individual and group differences within virtual classroom cases. *Journal of Technology and Teacher Education*, *18*(1), 111–130.

Mura, K., Petersen, N., Huff, M., & Ghose, T. (2013). IBES: A tool for creating instructions based on event segmentation. *Frontiers in Psychology*, *4*, 994. https://doi.org/10.3389/fpsyg.2013.00994

Ouwehand, K., Van Gog, T., & Paas, F. (2015). Designing effective video-based modeling examples using gaze and gesture cues. *Educational Technology & Society*, *18*, 78–88. https://www.jstor.org/stable/jeductechsoci.18.4.78

Ozcelik, E., Arslan-Ari, I., & Cagiltay, K. (2010). Why does signaling enhance multimedia learning? Evidence from eye movements. *Computers in Human Behavior*, *26*(1), 110–117. https://doi.org/10.1016/j.chb.2009.09.001

Peper, R. J., & Mayer, R. E. (1978). Note taking as a generative activity. *Journal of Educational Psychology, 70,* 514–522. https://doi.org/10.1037/0022-0663.70.4.514

Rey, G. D., Beege, M., Nebel, S., Wirzberger, M., Schmitt, T. H., & Schneider, S. (2019). A meta-analysis of the segmenting effect. *Educational Psychology Review, 31*(2), 389–419. https://doi.org/10.1007/s10648-018-9456-4

Ribosa, J. & Duran, D. (2022). Do students learn what they teach when generating teaching materials for others? A meta-analysis through the lens of learning by teaching. *Educational Research Review, 37,* 100475. https://doi.org/10.1016/j.edurev.2022.100475

Rotgans, J. I., & Schmidt, H. G. (2014). Situational interest and learning: Thirst for knowledge. *Learning and Instruction, 32,* 37–50. https://doi.org/10.1016/j.edurev.2022.100475

Sanchez, C. A., & Wiley, J. (2006). An examination of the seductive details effect in terms of working memory capacity. *Memory & Cognition, 34*(2), 344–355. https://doi.org/10.3758/bf03193412

Schneider, S., Beege, M., Neubel, S., & Rey, G. D. (2018). A meta-analysis of how signaling affects learning with media. *Educational Research Review, 23,* 1–24. https://doi.org/10.1016/j.edurev.2017.11.001

Sepp, S., Wong, M., Hoogerheide, V., & Castro-Alonso, J. C. (2022). Shifting online: 12 tips for online teaching derived from contemporary educational psychology research. *Journal of Computer Assisted Learning, 38*(5), 1304–1320. https://doi.org/10.1111/jcal.12715

Singh, A., Marcus, N., & Ayres, P. (2012). The transient information effect: Investigating the impact of segmentation on spoken and written text. *Applied Cognitive Psychology, 26,* 848–853. https://doi.org/10.1002/acp.2885

Sundarajan, N., & Adesope, O. (2020). Keep it coherent: A meta-analysis of the seductive details effect. *Educational Psychology Review, 32,* 707–734. https://doi.org/10.1007/s10648-020-09522-4

Sweller, J., Van Merriënboer, J. J. G., & Paas, F. (2019). Cognitive architecture and instructional design: 20 years later. *Educational Psychology Review, 31*(2), 261–292. https://doi.org/10.1007/s10648-019-09465-5

Tarchi, C., Zaccoletti, S., & Mason, L. (2021). Learning from text, video, or subtitles: A comparative analysis. *Computers & Education, 160,* 104034. https://doi.org/10.1016/j.compedu.2020.104034

Van Gog, T., Rummel, N., & Renkl, A. (2019). Learning how to solve problems by studying examples. In J. Dunlosky & K. Rawson (Eds.), *The Cambridge handbook of cognition and education* (pp. 183–208). Cambridge University Press.

Van Gog, T., & Sweller, J., (2015). Not new, but nearly forgotten: The testing effect decreases or even disappears as the complexity of learning materials increases. *Educational Psychology Review, 27*(2), 247–264. https://doi.org/10.1007/s10648-015-9310-x

Van Gog, T., Verveer, I., & Verveer, L. (2014). Learning from video modeling examples: Effects of seeing the human model's face. *Computers & Education, 72,* 323–327. https://doi.org/10.1016/j.compedu.2013.12.004

Van Harsel, M., Hoogerheide, V., Verkoeijen, P., & Van Gog, T. (2020). Examples, practice problems, or both? Effects on motivation and learning in shorter and longer sequences. *Applied Cognitive Psychology, 34*(4), 793–812. https://doi.org/10.1002/acp.3649

Van Merriënboer, J. J. G., & Kirschner, P. A. (2013). *Ten steps to complex learning: A systematic approach to four-component instructional design* (2nd ed.). Taylor & Francis.

Van Wermeskerken, M., & Van Gog, T. (2017). Seeing the instructor's face and gaze in demonstration video examples affects attention allocation but not learning. *Computers & Education, 113*, 98–107. https://doi.org/10.1016/j.compedu.2017.05.013

Wang, J., Antonenko, P., & Dawson, K. (2020). Does visual attention to the instructor in online video affect learning and learner perceptions? An eye-tracking analysis. *Computers & Education, 146*, 103779. https://doi.org/10.1016/j.compedu.2019.103779

Yang, C., Luo, L., Vadillo, M. A., Yu, R., & Shanks, D. R. (2021). Testing (quizzing) boosts classroom learning: A systematic and meta-analytic review. *Psychological Bulletin, 147*(4), 399–435. https://doi.org/10.1037/bul0000309

Ying, H. G., Szpunar, K. K., & Schacter, D. L. (2016). Interpolated testing influences focused attention and improves integration of information during a video-recorded lecture. *Journal of Experimental Psychology: Applied, 22*(3), 305–318. https://doi.org/10.1037/xap0000087

Yue, C. L., Bjork, E. L., & Bjork, R. A. (2013). Reducing verbal redundancy in multimedia learning: An undesired desirable difficulty? *Journal of Educational Psychology, 105*(2), 266–277. https://doi.org/10.1037/a0031971

7
EYE MOVEMENT MODELING EXAMPLES

Tamara van Gog, Ellen Kok, Selina Emhardt,
Tim van Marlen and Halszka Jarodzka

Introduction

Learning by observing a good example is a very natural and powerful way of learning (Bandura, 1977; Sweller & Sweller, 2006), and a large body of experimental research in the lab, at schools, and in professional training contexts, has established the efficacy of example-based learning (for a review: Van Gog et al., 2019): replacing a substantial part of conventional practice tasks with worked examples or (video) modeling examples is often more effective (as evidenced by higher posttest performance) and efficient (i.e., requiring less investment of study time or mental effort) for novice learners.

Video modeling examples are widely used in (formal and informal) online learning environments nowadays. They can be designed in many different ways. For instance, the model can be visible in the video (e.g., next to a screen, Hoogerheide et al., 2016), only partly visible (e.g., hands manipulating objects, Fiorella et al., 2017), or not visible at all, when examples consist of screen recordings of the model performing a task on their computer screen (McLaren et al., 2016). Most video modeling examples also contain verbal explanations by the model of the solution steps they are demonstrating.

Eye movement modeling examples (EMME) can be seen as an enhanced or augmented version of screen-recording video modeling examples, in which eye-tracking technology is used to record and display the model's eye movements in the video example. So, students not only see the actions that the model is performing in the screen recording (e.g., typing, clicking, dragging, and dropping objects), but also a superimposed visualization of the model's eye movements. In such a visualization, it is indicated what is at the center of

DOI: 10.4324/9781003386131-10

the model's visual attention by means of a circle or dot, or by blurring out all other information (Figure 7.1; for an example EMME video in the domain of business process modeling, see https://www.youtube.com/watch?v=iqU_BxtKP80; Emhardt et al., 2022).

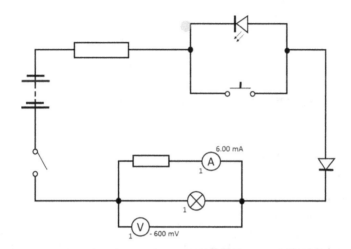

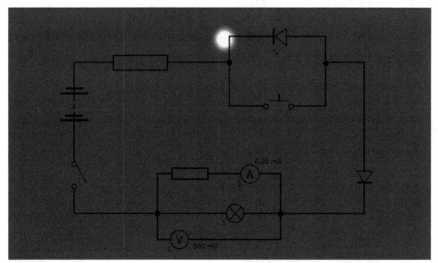

FIGURE 7.1 Screenshot based on materials used in Chisari et al. (2020).

Note: Screenshot based on materials used in Chisari et al. (2020). The EMME consisted of a static picture of an electronic circuit with verbal explanations of the model on how to troubleshoot the circuit (this was the only information present in the control condition), with the eye movements (fixations) of the model being visualized as a blue translucent dot (dot display, upper panel). An EMME can also be made by darkening or blurring non-attended areas and keeping fixated areas at regular color or resolution (spotlight display, lower panel; not used in Chisari et al.).

Thus, in EMME, students see where the model is looking at any given moment during task performance; they can see the task through the model's eyes, as it were. This can serve two important (not mutually exclusive) functions (Van Gog et al., 2009). First, visualizing the model's eye movements can synchronize the students' attention with the model's attention, thereby guiding students' attention to the relevant information at the relevant time. Second, it can make the perceptual and cognitive strategies that the model uses to tackle the task visible, which would otherwise not be observable to learners. As will become clear in the next sections, these functions seem to make EMME a useful tool for teaching a wide variety of learning tasks that have a strong visual component to them, such as problem-solving tasks, programming tasks, classification tasks, X-ray diagnosis, and study strategies.

Visualizing the Model's Eye Movements to Aid Comprehension and Learning

A precondition for the effectiveness of example-based learning is that the examples are well-designed (see Van Gog et al., 2019). To learn effectively from video modeling examples, learners must select the relevant visual and auditory information, organize it into a coherent representation, and integrate it with their prior knowledge (cf. Cognitive theory of multimedia learning, Mayer, 2022). Because information in videos is often transient, this means that learners will also need to select the right information at the right time, or it will not be available for further processing (i.e., organizing and integrating it), and learning will be hampered (Ayres & Paas, 2007).

Given the expertise difference between the model, who will typically have substantial expertise in performing the task, and the learners, who are typically new to it, it is unlikely that learners will be focusing on the relevant information (i.e., the information that the model is focusing on or referring to) at the right time. Individuals with high(er) levels of expertise on a task often attend to task-relevant information faster and relatively longer and pay less attention to task-irrelevant information than novices (Charness et al., 2001; Van Gog et al., 2005; Van Meeuwen et al., 2014; Wolff et al., 2016). This expertise effect has also been demonstrated *within* participants as a result of task experience (Blair et al., 2009; Haider & Frensch, 1999; Hegarty et al., 2010). The likely discrepancy in attention allocation between the expert model and the novice learner might make it hard for learners to attend to the relevant information at the right time when observing the video modeling example (Van Gog et al., 2009).

Unless, that is, the model's verbal explanation (if present, which it often is) would be sufficiently clear to rapidly guide learners' attention. This may not always be the case, however. Because learners are novices, they may not yet be familiar with some of the terminology the model is using, so they may not be able to timely locate the object or information that the model is referring to with a specific term (e.g., if the model is referring to a transistor when explaining how to troubleshoot an electrical circuit, this will not help learners to locate the relevant information if they do not know what the symbol for a transistor looks like). Another reason why the explanation might not help in timely locating information might lie in (verbal) ambiguity. This occurs, for instance, when there are multiple objects on the screen that a known term could refer to (e.g., even if a learner knows the symbol for a transistor, this is not necessarily useful in determining what the model is looking at and talking about when the circuit drawing would contain multiple transistors), or when the model uses unspecific language (e.g., 'this branch' when a circuit drawing contains multiple branches; Van Marlen et al., 2018, 2019).

Consequently, in regular screen-recording examples, learners may not always be able – both literally and figuratively speaking – to follow the model. If they cannot follow the demonstration and explanation, this could hamper their learning, because, as Bandura (1977) stated: 'people cannot learn much by observation unless they attend to, and perceive accurately, the significant features of the modelled behaviour' (p. 24). By visualizing the model's eye movements, a state of joint attention can be created, in which the learner attends to the same information as the model at the same time. This can be expected to reduce the extraneous cognitive load otherwise induced by searching for the relevant information (Ayres & Paas, 2007), making more working memory resources available for learning the demonstrated task.

Indeed, studies in which the effects on students' attention during the example study were measured, provide evidence that EMME can successfully synchronize the students' attention with the model's. For instance, in studies on learning to solve geometry problems, it was found that university students in the EMME condition located the information that the model was verbally referring to more often, looked at it faster, and looked at it longer than students in the regular example condition who did not see the model's eye movements (Van Marlen et al., 2016, 2018, Exp.1). Interestingly, this did not significantly affect learning outcomes of the university students, but a later study showed that the same EMME were effective for secondary education students, suggesting that whether or not the successful attention guidance is needed for successful learning may depend on learner characteristics such as prior knowledge (this mirrors findings on the effects of visual cues, such as color coding, highlighting, blurring, or adding arrows on learning from multimedia materials; Richter et al., 2016; Van Gog, 2022).

Using different types of analyses, other studies found that students in the EMME condition showed more coherent viewing behavior (scanpaths), as one would expect when they follow the model's eye movements. For instance, in a study on learning to classify fish locomotion patterns, Jarodzka et al. (2013) found that students who observed EMME had higher scanpath coherence during the example study compared to students who observed regular modeling examples without the model's eye movements, and also showed higher learning outcomes. In a classroom study in computer programming education, Bednarik et al. (2018) found that EMME-based interventions affected gaze following and resulted in improved problem-solving. Testing the connection more directly, using structural equation modeling, Chisari et al. (2020) showed that gaze following indeed seems to be the mechanism through which EMME affect learning: seeing the model's eye movements helped learners to look faster at referenced information, which was associated with higher learning outcomes.

Visualizing the Model's Eye Movements to Show Strategies: Making the Invisible Visible

Another affordance of EMME is that by displaying the model's eye movements, learners may also gain insight into the perceptual and cognitive strategies that the model is using, which would otherwise (in regular screen recordings) not be observable to them. There is quite some evidence that this can improve performance and learning.

In visual search tasks, there is quite some evidence that observing a (brief) visualization of a model's eye movements (without verbal explanations) improves the observer's performance on the same or a subsequent similar task when searching for errors on printed circuit boards (Nalanagula et al., 2006), errors in software code (Stein & Brennan, 2004), or when diagnosing medical images (Gegenfurtner et al., 2017; Litchfield et al., 2010; Seppänen and Gegenfurtner, 2012). In classification tasks, Jarodzka et al. (2013) found that students who had observed the EMME of an expert classifying fish locomotion patterns (with verbal explanations), not only looked along with the expert (i.e., higher scanpath coherence) *during* the example study compared to students in a regular video example condition, but also seemed to adopt a more effective viewing strategy (i.e., looking faster and longer at relevant information) on *subsequent*, novel fish locomotion videos in which the visualization of the expert's eye movements was no longer present (and this effect was stronger in the spotlight-EMME condition than in the dot-EMME condition; cf. Figure 7.1). Performance data showed they were also better able to interpret fish locomotion patterns in novel videos (although here, the dot-EMME condition seemed more effective than the spotlight-EMME condition).

Finally, EMME can also be effectively used to model study strategies. EMME (without verbal explanations) have been shown to enhance students' use of strategies for integrating digital hyperlinked texts (Salmerón & Llorens, 2018; ninth-graders), integrating digital documents by means of concept maps (García et al., 2021; sixth-graders), attending to the source information of webpages (Salmerón et al., 2020; undergraduates), and for integrating corresponding information from texts and pictures when learning from illustrated texts (seventh-graders: Mason et al., 2015, 2016, 2017; university: Scheiter et al., 2018). For instance, Mason et al. (2015, 2016, 2017) examined whether observing EMME prior to studying an illustrated text would enhance text–picture integration during later study. In the EMME, the model demonstrated how to integrate information from the text and picture by making transitions between certain terms in the text and the corresponding part of the picture. Compared to students who did not observe EMME (i.e., participants in the passive control group were only presented with the text without any other instructions), students in the EMME condition showed better text–picture integration while studying the (new) illustrated text and performed better on a text comprehension test.

We should note though, that while these studies highlight a very useful function of visualizing a model's eye movements to learners, most of the studies on visual search and study strategies did not have a very strong control condition (i.e., learners in this condition did not get any strategy information at all). So it is an open question whether the EMME would still be beneficial if the control condition would also have included some kind of modeling example as well, for instance, hearing the model think aloud while engaging in text–picture integration or X-ray diagnosis.

A Critical Look and a Look Ahead

As the previous sections have shown, EMME have proven effective for guiding students' attention and improving their learning of a variety of tasks, for students ranging from primary to tertiary education (see also the meta-analysis by Xie et al., 2021, and review by Emhardt et al., 2023). This is good news, as it shows that EMME can indeed successfully fulfill both functions (synchronizing attention with the model and making strategies visible) and thereby improve learning. However, the current body of literature is still relatively small and characterized by large differences among studies. As we will show in this section, there is a need for more systematic research on how EMME design characteristics, learning task characteristics, and learner characteristics, influence the effectiveness of EMME in terms of attention guidance and learning outcomes (Emhardt et al., 2023). Moreover, we should consider some fundamental open questions regarding the nature of eye movements as visual and social cues.

Design Characteristics

For instance, with regard to the design of EMME, as mentioned earlier, there are different ways of visualizing the expert's eye movements, but comparative studies in which different types of EMME are used are rare. The findings by Jarodzka et al. (2012, 2013) suggest that different types of gaze visualizations may be more or less effective for different types of outcome measures. Therefore, it would be interesting for future research to conduct systematic comparisons of which type of visualization is more effective for which type of task and which type of outcome measure.

Another question regarding design characteristics that has hardly been explored, is the question of how important it is that experts perform the task didactically (as is the case in most EMME studies; Emhardt et al., 2023). Is it necessary that they deliberately tailor their demonstration and explanation to a novice student audience, or can students also learn from the model's 'natural' performance (i.e., the way they would perform the task themselves, if they are not adapting their demonstration and explanation to their novice audience; e.g., Seppänen & Gegenfurtner, 2012)? It has been suggested that the expertise differences between the model and learner might on the one hand make natural performance hard to follow for students, while it could on the other hand help them abstract, which could benefit transfer (e.g., Hinds et al., 2001). Emhardt et al. (2020a) found that instructions to behave didactically do affect certain aspects of experts' viewing behavior, which might make it easier for students to follow the EMME. However, a study comparing the effects of EMME by naturally vs. didactically behaving models showed no differences in learning outcomes (Emhardt et al., submitted). Moreover, a recent review study showed that positive effects on learning were found both with natural and didactical model behavior in EMME (Emhardt et al., 2023).

Task Characteristics

With regard to learning task characteristics, it is interesting to note that initially, EMME seemed to be ineffective for step-wise problem-solving tasks (Van Gog et al., 2009; Van Marlen et al., 2016; Van Marlen et al., 2018, Exp. 1), in the sense that EMME did successfully guide students' attention during the example study, but this did not translate into higher learning outcomes (Van Marlen et al., 2016, 2018). This could point toward the role of task characteristics, because in step-wise problem-solving tasks, the model typically interacts with the task in other ways (e.g., by clicking) as well when solving each step, whereas in purely visual tasks like the classification of fish locomotion patterns (Jarodzka et al., 2013) or text–picture integration strategies (Mason et al., 2015), the model does not overtly interact with the information on the screen. Such potential influences of task characteristics would be worthwhile to further investigate.

Student Characteristics

However, the findings by Van Marlen et al. (2018, Exp. 2) suggest that the ineffectiveness of EMME for problem-solving tasks more likely resulted from student characteristics: EMME successfully guided university students' attention, but they did not need this attention guidance for learning to occur, whereas secondary education students did benefit from EMME. Therefore, an important question is which student characteristics (e.g., general ability, prior knowledge) might determine whether students actually need attentional guidance in order to optimize their learning.

Direct tests of the effects of prior knowledge are rare and led to mixed findings. For instance, in a study with EMME that aimed to foster text–picture integration strategies, Krebs et al. (2019) found that EMME were effective only for low prior knowledge learners, although in a subsequent study by the same authors with the same materials (Krebs et al., 2021), EMME were found to be effective for all learners. Chisari et al. (2020) directly manipulated prior knowledge by means of pre-training, yet found no significant effect of prior knowledge on learning from EMME. Other studies even showed more beneficial effects of EMME for participants with higher prior knowledge than for those with lower prior knowledge (Gegenfurtner et al., 2017; Scheiter et al., 2018). Indeed, the moderating effects of prior knowledge on the effectiveness of EMME failed to reach statistical significance in the meta-analyses of Xie et al. (2021) and Krebs et al. (2021).

As Krebs et al. (2021) point out, one potential explanation might lie in the different (and relative) definitions of prior knowledge used in different studies. Although one could argue that even if visualizing the model's eye movements does not help learning, it does not seem to hurt either (and can still benefit attention during the example study). Yet, research on the expertise reversal effect (Kalyuga, 2007) does suggest that instructional guidance can become redundant and actually start to hamper learning when students acquire more knowledge. So, another relevant question is whether there are student populations for whom EMME would become counterproductive and start to hamper learning (or whether this coincides with a level of prior knowledge at which they also do not need the examples at all anymore).

Modeling Study Strategies

With regard to EMME on study strategies, an interesting open question is whether students will also learn when to use the strategy when they are engaging in future study sessions. Thus far, students received EMME modeling the strategy on the same type of task they were to perform immediately afterward. So these studies show that students have learned *what* to do, but do not necessarily tell us whether students know *when to use* the modeled strategy. That would require a kind of transfer test at a later moment, where students are confronted with several tasks and have to recognize on which task they can apply the modeled strategy (or strategies).

Eye Movements vs. Other Visual Cues

And then there is a key question that will probably sound familiar to anyone who has conducted and presented EMME research: Why so complicated? Can't you just point out or highlight important information in the video? This question of whether the visualization of eye movements in EMME is 'just' a visual cue (on par with pointing with a mouse cursor, or other added visual cues like highlighting or arrows) or whether it is more than that, is an interesting issue to which there are several angles, none of which we currently know enough about.

It is important to note that there are some fundamental differences between displaying the model's eye movements and other types of visual cues. First, other types of visual cues have to be deliberately decided on, either by the model (pointing out information on the screen with the mouse cursor) or the instructional designer who adds visual cues to a recorded example (which also requires post-processing), whereas eye movements are just recorded (and displayed) continuously as they occur while the model is demonstrating the task. On the one hand, this makes the visualization of eye movements more 'noisy' than other visual cues. On the other hand, one is not dependent on an expert's deliberate decision about when students are likely no longer 'with' the model and need further attention guidance, which can be a benefit as task experts often find it difficult to estimate novices' prior knowledge and understanding of their explanations (e.g., Hinds, 1999; Hinds et al., 2001; Wittwer et al., 2008). Yet, the question of whether it matters for students' experiences and learning outcomes which approach is chosen, is an interesting one that has not received much attention thus far.

A study by Gallagher-Mitchell et al. (2018) compared the effects of observing a visualization of the model's eye movements ('gaze cursor') vs. mouse cursor. They found that viewing a gaze or mouse cursor during a simple number line estimation task both increased observers' later estimation performance compared to no attention guidance. In a study by Emhardt et al. (2022), novices studied examples of how to model business processes either with or without a gaze cursor and with or without a mouse cursor. The presence of the gaze cursor, mouse cursor, or both, had no significant effect on learning outcomes. However, Emhardt et al. also asked participants to self-report their experiences. Overall, participants responded positively to the gaze cursor, and participants who watched videos with the gaze cursor reported that they found it easier to follow the teacher, especially when the mouse cursor was not displayed in the video. Future research should address this question of whether other visual cues are equally or more effective than displaying the models' eye movements with other kinds of visual cues. It is possible that the answer might differ depending on whether the main function of the EMME is to guide attention, or to convey experts' (unconscious) visual strategies.

Second, another fundamental difference with other types of visual cues is the fact that the model's eye movements are an integral part of the modeled behavior, and as such, they are also a social cue rather than merely a visual cue. A prerequisite for the use of EMME is that learners can assign some meaning to these (moving) dots or circles, and interpret them in terms of another person's cognitive processes (cf. the eye-mind hypothesis, that the information we are looking at is also being processed, i.e., thought about, at that moment; Just & Carpenter, 1980), much in the same way that in real-world interactions, we automatically interpret other people's eye movements as indicative of their goals and intentions. Although research on this question is still in its infancy, there is some evidence that observers can, for instance, infer from displays of eye movements from another person what object they prefer (Foulsham & Lock, 2015), what instructions they were given when viewing a painting (Van Wermeskerken et al., 2018), and what multiple-choice answer they chose and how confident they were in their answer (Emhardt et al., 2020b).

An interesting study by Gobel et al. (2015) also suggests that a visual cue (dot) is interpreted and reacted to differently depending on whether students think it represents another person's gaze or not. Participants had to respond as fast as possible to the appearance of a target (a blue square) in one of four quadrants on the screen. Just before the appearance of the target shape, they were presented with a red dot in one of the four quadrants. Participants were led to believe either that this red dot was a computer-generated cue or that it represented the gaze location of a partner present on the other side of the room. When participants thought it was a gaze cue, it took them longer to respond to targets in locations that were (supposedly) already looked at by their partner (i.e., they seemed to rely on the other person having searched that part of the stimulus for the target). These findings may suggest that students may be more inclined to follow and attempt to interpret visualizations of the model's gaze than other types of visual cueing (even if those will also automatically draw students' attention). This could be an interesting avenue for future research, as we still know very little about how students experience and interpret the visualizations of the model's eye movements in EMME.

Social Processes

This social aspect of EMME also gives rise to the question of whether the (purported) social status of the model affects learning. Interestingly, in their second experiment, Gobel et al. (2015) found that the effect of taking longer to look at locations the 'partner' had already looked at was influenced by the purported social status; it only occurred when participants were led to believe the other person was high in social rank, not when they thought the other was low in social rank. The question of whether and how model characteristics affect students' feelings of self-efficacy and their learning outcomes has a long tradition in research on example-based learning (e.g., Bandura, 1977; Hoogerheide et al., 2016; Schunk et al., 1987). A few studies have started to explore this also for EMME, but so far, findings are mixed. Krebs et al. (2019) found that weaker learners seemed to benefit more from (purported) peer models than from (purported) highly competent models when learning text–picture integration strategies from EMME. However, in a later study (Krebs et al., 2021) the authors failed to replicate those findings. Van Marlen et al. (submitted) found no effects of purported expertise on learning from EMME on geometry problem-solving. They also asked students to rate the quality of the model's verbal explanations and found these to be high in both conditions (with no significant difference), which may suggest that the actual quality of the explanation (in terms of content and/or in terms of the expertise conveyed in the model's voice) is more critical for learning than the purported expertise of the model.

Conclusion

In sum, EMME serve two (not mutually exclusive) functions. Adding a visualization of the model's eye movements to video modeling examples can 1) synchronize the students' gaze with the model's gaze, which can aid the comprehension of the model's demonstration and explanation, and 2) give students insight into the perceptual or cognitive strategies the model uses to perform the task, which would otherwise not be observable for them. The studies discussed here provide evidence for these two functions, and taken together illustrate that EMME seem to be useful for teaching a wide variety of tasks that have a strong visual component to them, such as (geometry) problem-solving, programming, classification tasks, X-ray diagnosis, or text–picture integration strategies. Moreover, EMME can be used with a wide variety of learners, in primary, secondary, tertiary, and professional education. However, more systematic research on the effect of task, learner, and EMME-design characteristics is needed to get more insight into the conditions under which learning from EMME is most effective.

Evidence-Based Practice Recommendations

- Eye Movement Modeling Examples (EMME) show learners where a model who is demonstrating a task is looking.
- EMME are effective in guiding learners' attention.

- EMME also enhance learning outcomes, under certain conditions (e.g., for low prior knowledge learners).
- Design choices of EMME should correspond with particular learning goals and tasks.

Acknowledgment

During the realization of (the research reported in) this chapter, Ellen Kok, Selina Emhardt, and Tim van Marlen were supported by a grant from the Netherlands Initiative for Education Research (project 405-17-301) awarded to Tamara van Gog and Halszka Jarodzka.

References

Ayres, P., & Paas, F. (2007). Can the cognitive load approach make instructional animations more effective? *Applied Cognitive Psychology*, 21, 811–820. https://doi.org/10.1002/acp.1351

Bandura, A. (1977). *Social learning theory*. Prentice Hall.

Bednarik, R., Schulte, C., Budde, L., Heinemann, B., & Vrzakova, H. (2018). Eye-movement modeling examples in source code comprehension: A classroom study. In *Proceedings of the 18th Koli Calling International Conference on Computing Education Research* (pp. 22–25). ACM. https://doi.org/10.1145/3279720.3279722

Blair, M. R., Watson, M. R., & Meier, K. M. (2009). Errors, efficiency, and the interplay between attention and category learning. *Cognition*, 112, 330–336. https://doi.org/10.1016/j.cognition.2009.04.008

Charness, N., Reingold, E. M., Pomplun, M., & Stampe, D. M. (2001). The perceptual aspect of skilled performance in chess: Evidence from eye movements. *Memory & Cognition*, 29, 1146–1152. https://doi.org/10.3758/BF03206384

Chisari, L. B., Mockeviciute, A., Ruitenburg, S. K., Van Vemde, L., Kok, E. M., & Van Gog, T. (2020). Effects of prior knowledge and joint attention on learning from eye movement modeling examples. *Journal of Computer-Assisted Learning*, 36, 569–579. https://doi.org/10.1111/jcal.12428

Emhardt, S. N., Jarodzka, H., Brand-Gruwel, S., Drumm, C., Niehorster, D., & Van Gog, T. (2022). What is my teacher talking about? Effects of displaying the teacher's gaze and mouse cursor cues in video lectures on students' learning. *Journal of Cognitive Psychology*, 34, 846–864. https://doi.org/10.1080/20445911.2022.2080831

Emhardt, S. N., Kok, E. M., Jarodzka, H., Brand-Gruwel, S., Drumm, C., & Van Gog, T. (2020a). How experts adapt their gaze behavior when modeling a task to novices. *Cognitive Science*, 44, e12893. https://doi.org/10.1111/cogs.12893

Emhardt, S. N., Kok, E. M., Jarodzka, H., Brand-Gruwel, S., Drumm, C., & Van Gog, T. (submitted). *Effects of natural vs. didactic behavior of the expert model on novices' learning from eye movement modeling examples*. Manuscript submitted for publication.

Emhardt, S. N., Kok, E. M., Van Gog, T., Brandt-Gruwel, S., Van Marlen, T., & Jarodzka, H. (2023). Visualizing a task performer's gaze to foster observers' performance and learning: A systematic literature review on eye movement modeling examples. *Educational Psychology Review*, *35*, 23. https://doi.org/10.1007/s10648-023-09731-7

Emhardt, S. N., Van Wermeskerken, M., Scheiter, K., & Van Gog, T. (2020b). Inferring task performance and confidence from displays of eye movements. *Applied Cognitive Psychology*, *34*, 1430–1443. https://doi.org/10.1002/acp.3721

Fiorella, L., Van Gog, T., Hoogerheide, V., & Mayer, R. E. (2017). It's all a matter of perspective: Viewing first-person video modeling examples promotes learning of an assembly task. *Journal of Educational Psychology*, *109*, 653–665. https://doi.org/10.1037/edu0000161

Foulsham, T., & Lock, M. (2015). How the eyes tell lies: Social gaze during a preference task. *Cognitive Science*, *39*, 1704–1726. https://doi.org/10.1111/cogs.12211

Gallagher-Mitchell, T., Simms, V., & Litchfield, D. (2018). Learning from where "eye" remotely look or point: Impact on number line estimation error in adults. *Quarterly Journal of Experimental Psychology*, *71*(7), 1526–1534. https://doi.org/10.1080/17470218.2017.1335335

García, V., Amadieu, F., & Salmerón, L. (2021). Integrating digital documents by means of concept maps: testing an intervention program with eye-movements modelling examples. *Heliyon*, e08607. https://doi.org/10.1016/j.heliyon.2021.e08607

Gegenfurtner, A., Lehtinen, E., Jarodzka, H., & Säljö, R. (2017). Effects of eye movement modeling examples on adaptive expertise in medical image diagnosis. *Computers & Education*, *113*, 212–225. https://doi.org/10.1016/j.compedu.2017.06.001

Gobel, M. S., Kim, H. S., & Richardson, D. C. (2015). The dual function of social gaze. *Cognition*, *136*, 359–364. https://doi.org/10.1016/j.cognition.2014.11.040

Haider, H., & Frensch, P. A. (1999). Eye movement during skill acquisition: More evidence for the information-reduction hypothesis. *Journal of Experimental Psychology: Learning, Memory, and Cognition*, *25*, 172–190. https://doi.org/10.1037/0278-7393.25.1.172

Hegarty, M., Canham, M. S., & Fabrikant, S. I. (2010). Thinking about the weather: How display salience and knowledge affect performance in a graphic inference task. *Journal of Experimental Psychology: Learning, Memory, and Cognition*, *36*, 37–53. https://doi.org/10.1037/a0017683

Hinds, P. J. (1999). The curse of expertise: The effects of expertise and debiasing methods on prediction of novice performance. *Journal of Experimental Psychology: Applied*, *5*(2), 205–221. https://doi.org/10.1037/1076-898x.5.2.205

Hinds, P. J., Patterson, M., & Pfeffer, J. (2001). Bothered by abstraction: The effect of expertise on knowledge transfer and subsequent novice performance. *Journal of Applied Psychology*, *86*(6), 1232–1243. https://doi.org/10.1037/0021-9010.86.6.1232

Hoogerheide, V., Van Wermeskerken, M., Loyens, S., & Van Gog, T. (2016). Learning from video modeling examples: Content kept equal, adults are more effective models than peers. *Learning and Instruction*, *44*, 22–30. https://doi.org/10.1016/j.learninstruc.2016.02.004

Jarodzka, H., Balslev, T., Holmqvist, K. et al. (2012). Conveying clinical reasoning based on visual observation via eye-movement modelling examples. *Instructional Science*, *40*, 813–827. https://doi.org/10.1007/s11251-012-9218-5

Jarodzka, H., Van Gog, T., Dorr, M., Scheiter, K., & Gerjets, P. (2013). Learning to see: Guiding students' attention via a model's eye movements fosters learning. *Learning and Instruction*, *25*, 62–70. https://doi.org/10.1016/j.learninstruc.2012.11.004

Just, M. A., & Carpenter, P. A. (1980). A theory of reading: From eye fixations to comprehension. *Psychological Review*, *87*, 329–354. https://doi.org/10.1037/0033-295x.87.4.329

Kalyuga, S. (2007). Expertise reversal effect and its implications for learner-tailored instruction. *Educational Psychology Review*, *19*, 509–539. https://doi.org/10.1007/s10648-007-9054-3

Krebs, M. C., Schüler, A., & Scheiter, K. (2021). Do prior knowledge, model-observer similarity and social comparison influence the effectiveness of eye movement modeling examples for supporting multimedia learning? *Instructional Science*, *49*, 607–635. https://doi.org/10.1007/s11251-021-09552-7

Krebs, M.-C., Schüler, A., & Scheiter, K. (2019). Just follow my eyes: The influence of model-observer similarity on eye movement modeling examples. *Learning and Instruction*, *61*, 126–137. https://doi.org/10.1016/j.learninstruc.2018.10.005

Litchfield, D., Ball, L., Donovan, T., Manning, D., & Crawford, T. (2010). Viewing another person's eye movements improves identification of pulmonary nodules in chest X-ray inspection. *Journal of Experimental Psychology: Applied*, *16*, 251–262. https://doi.org/10.1037/a0020082

Mason, L., Pluchino, P., & Tornatora, M. C. (2015). Eye-movement modeling of integrative reading of an illustrated text: Effects on processing and learning. *Contemporary Educational Psychology*, *41*, 172–187. https://doi.org/10.1016/j.cedpsych.2015.01.004

Mason, L., Pluchino, P., & Tornatora, M. C. (2016). Using eye-tracking technology as an indirect instruction tool to improve text and picture processing and learning. *British Journal of Educational Technology*, *47*, 1083–1095. https://doi.org/10.1111/bjet.12271

Mason, L., Scheiter, K., & Tornatora, C. (2017). Using eye movements to model the sequence of textpicture processing for multimedia comprehension. *Journal of Computer Assisted Learning*, *33*, 443–460. https://doi.org/10.1111/jcal.12191

Mayer, R. E. (2022). The Cognitive Theory of Multimedia Learning. In R. E. Mayer & L. Fiorella (Eds.), *The Cambridge handbook of multimedia learning* (3rd rev. ed., pp. 57–72). Cambridge University Press. https://doi.org/10.1017/9781108894333.008

McLaren, B. M., Van Gog, T., Ganoe, C., Karabinos, M., & Yaron, D. (2016). The efficiency of worked examples compared to erroneous examples, tutored problem solving, and problem solving in computer-based learning environments. *Computers in Human Behavior*, *55*, 87–99. https://doi.org/10.1016/j.chb.2015.08.038

Nalanagula, D., Greenstein, J. S., & Gramopadhye, A. K. (2006). Evaluation of the effect of feedforward training displays of search strategy on visual search performance. *International Journal of Industrial Ergonomics*, *36*, 289–300. https://doi.org/10.1016/j.ergon.2005.11.008

Richter, J., Scheiter, K., & Eitel, A. (2016). Signaling text-picture relations in multimedia learning: A comprehensive meta-analysis. *Educational Research Review*, *17*, 19–36. https://doi.org/10.1016/j.edurev.2015.12.003

Salmerón, L., Delgado, P., & Mason, L. (2020). Using eye-movement modeling examples to improve critical reading of multiple webpages on a conflicting topic. *Journal of Computer Assisted Learning*, *36*, 1038–1051. https://doi.org/10.1111/jcal.12458

Salmerón, L., & Llorens, A. (2018). Instruction of digital reading strategies based on eye-movements modeling examples. *Journal of Educational Computing Research*, *57*(2), 343–359. https://doi.org/10.1177/0735633117751605

Scheiter, K., Schubert, C., & Schüler, A. (2018). Self-regulated learning from illustrated text: Eye movement modelling to support use and regulation of cognitive processes during learning from multimedia. *British Journal of Educational Technology, 88*, 80–94. https://doi.org/10.1111/bjep.12175

Schunk, D. H., Hanson, A. R., & Cox, P. D. (1987). Peer-model attributes and children's achievement behaviors. *Journal of Educational Psychology, 79*, 54–61. https://doi.org/10.1037/0022-0663.79.1.54

Seppänen, M., & Gegenfurtner, A. (2012). Seeing through a teacher's eyes improves students' imaging interpretation. *Medical Education, 46*, 1113–1114. https://doi.org/10.1111/medu.12041

Stein, R., & Brennan, S. E. (2004). Another person's eye gaze as a cue in solving programming problems. *Proceedings of the 6th International Conference on Multimodal Interfaces*, pp. 9–15. http://doi.acm.org/10.1145/1027933.1027936

Sweller, J. & Sweller, S. (2006). Natural information processing systems. *Evolutionary Psychology, 4*, 434–458. https://doi.org/10.1177/147470490600400135

Van Gog, T. (2022). The signaling (or cueing) principle in multimedia learning. In R. E. Mayer & L. Fiorella (Eds.), *The Cambridge handbook of multimedia learning* (3rd rev. ed., pp. 221–230). Cambridge University Press. https://doi.org/10.1017/9781108894333.022

Van Gog, T., Jarodzka, H., Scheiter, K., Gerjets, P., & Paas, F. (2009). Attention guidance during example study via the model's eye movements. *Computers in Human Behavior, 25*, 785–791. https://doi.org/10.1016/j.chb.2009.02.007

Van Gog, T., Paas, F., & Van Merriënboer, J. J. G. (2005). Uncovering expertise-related differences in troubleshooting performance: Combining eye movement and concurrent verbal protocol data. *Applied Cognitive Psychology, 19*, 205–221. https://doi.org/10.1002/acp.1112

Van Gog, T., Rummel, N., & Renkl, A. (2019). Learning how to solve problems by studying examples. In J. Dunlosky & K. Rawson (Eds.), *The Cambridge handbook of cognition and education* (pp. 183–208). Cambridge University Press. https://doi.org/10.1017/9781108235631.009

Van Marlen, T., Van Wermeskerken, M., Jarodzka, H., & Van Gog, T. (2016). Showing a model's eye movements in examples does not improve learning of problem-solving tasks. *Computers in Human Behavior, 65*, 448–459. https://doi.org/10.1016/j.chb.2016.08.041

Van Marlen, T., Van Wermeskerken, M, Jarodzka, H., & Van Gog, T. (2018). Effectiveness of Eye Movement Modeling Examples in problem solving: The role of verbal ambiguity and prior knowledge. *Learning and Instruction, 58*, 273–284. https://doi.org/10.1016/j.learninstruc.2018.07.005

Van Marlen, T., Van Wermeskerken, M., Jarodzka, H., & Van Gog, T. (submitted). *Does the purported expertise of a model influence the effectiveness of eye movement modeling examples?* Manuscript submitted for publication.

Van Marlen, T., Van Wermeskerken, M., & Van Gog, T. (2019). Effects of visual complexity and ambiguity of verbal instructions on target identification. *Journal of Cognitive Psychology, 31*, 206–214. https://doi.org/10.1080/20445911.2018.1552700

Van Meeuwen, L. W., Jarodzka, H., Brand-Gruwel, S., Kirschner, P. A., De Bock, J. J. R. P., & Van Merriënboer, J. J. G. (2014). Identification of effective visual problem solving strategies in a complex visual domain. *Learning and Instruction, 32*, 10–21. https://doi.org/10.1016/j.learninstruc.2014.01.004

Van Wermeskerken, M., Litchfield, D., & Van Gog, T. (2018). What am I looking at? Interpreting dynamic and static gaze displays. *Cognitive Science*, 42, 220–252. https://doi.org/10.1111/cogs.12484

Wittwer, J., Nückles, M., & Renkl, A. (2008). Is underestimation less detrimental than overestimation? The impact of experts' beliefs about a layperson's knowledge on learning and question asking. *Instructional Science*, 36, 27–52. https://doi.org/10.1007/s11251-007-9021-x

Wolff, C. E., Jarodzka, H., Van den Bogert, N., & Boshuizen, H.P.A. (2016). Teacher vision: Expert and novice teachers' perception of problematic classroom management scenes. *Instructional Science*, 44, 243–265. https://doi.org/10.1007/s11251-016-9367-z

Xie, H., Zhao, T., Deng, S., Peng, J., Wang, F., & Zhou, Z. (2021). Using eye movement modelling examples to guide visual attention and foster cognitive performance: A meta-analysis. *Journal of Computer Assisted Learning*, 37(4), 1194–1206. https://doi.org/10.1111/jcal.12568

PART IV

Learning from Simulated Realities

8
LEARNING WITH PEDAGOGICAL AGENTS IN DIGITAL ENVIRONMENTS

Maik Beege, Steve Nebel, Günter Daniel Rey and Sascha Schneider

Introduction

Pedagogical Agents: Definition and Implementation

Because of the ongoing digitalization and, in particular, during the COVID-19 pandemic, instructional interactions are moving from classical classroom environments to digital learning spaces. Consequently, the social exchange between learner and instructor diminished, which might result in hindered communication and learning (Burgoon et al., 2000). To counteract this, designers can implement real or fictitious social entities in digital learning environments. These virtual characters are defined as pedagogical agents (PAs). PAs are computer-generated or designed characters that serve instructional or conversational purposes in educational settings (Veletsianos & Russell, 2013; Martha & Santoso, 2019). Consequently, pedagogical agent is a collective term, summarizing the classical definition of PAs (characters that facilitate learning) and conversational agents (characters with artificial intelligence to respond to user's inputs; Weber et al., 2021). PAs can be implemented in a variety of different ways. PAs can be comic-like figures (e.g., Girard & Johnson, 2010), animated figures based on actual humans (e.g., Baylor & Kim, 2004), and actual humans that are filmed and implemented in learning environments (e.g., Wang & Antonenko, 2017). Furthermore, even voice-based or text-based support without an explicitly visible entity can be referred to as PA (e.g., Pareto et al., 2011). Whereas 2D PAs were mostly used in the past (e.g., Baylor & Kim, 2009), technological advantages led to an increased design and use of animated 3D agents (e.g., Liew et al., 2016). Research is conducted by considering visual presence,

DOI: 10.4324/9781003386131-12

age, appeal, gender, ethnicity, facial expression, first impression, movement (i.e., gestures), performance, cueing, nonverbal cues, as well as verbal characteristics (emotion, affection, empathy, wording). The choice of the PA design often depends on the context and purpose of use. PAs are used in formal instructional contexts (e.g., laboratory experiments and online learning environments; Mayer et al., 2003) and informal contexts (e.g., digital guides in museums; Lane et al., 2013). These various possibilities outline that the design and implementation of PAs require software expertise and time. Consequently, there is a legitimate question as to whether this investment is worthwhile at all. Within this chapter, the question will be discussed whether PAs are generally conducive to learning and which design features and frameworks have to be considered.

Do Pedagogical Agents Foster Learning?

Diverse theoretical implications, methodological issues, and the lack of control groups in empirical studies raised concern regarding the effectiveness of PAs during their early development (Heidig & Clarebout, 2011). Since then, meta-analyses (Schroeder et al., 2013; Castro-Alonso et al., 2021) have provided more information on whether PA's are supporting learning or not. Their conclusions are calculated with 75 individual effects resulting from experiments with over 5.000 participants. Results indicate a significant positive effect of the presence of PAs on learning with small effect sizes ($g = 0.19$ & $g = 0.20$). The most recent meta-analysis (Davis et al., 2022) further outlined that PAs are effective regardless of the testing format (multiple-choice questions: $g = 0.24$; transfer: $g = 0.35$; cued recall: $g = 0.29$; free recall: $g = 0.29$). However, meta-analyses from Schroeder et al. (2013) and Castro-Alonso et al. (2021) found important moderators for the effect of PAs on learning. Analyses revealed individual scenarios with stronger effects. For instance, PA's communication through on-screen text (e.g., Kim & Wei, 2011) resulted in moderate effects ($g = 0.51$). Sometimes, only specific variations, such as two-dimensional agents (e.g., Baylor & Kim, 2009), reached significance ($g = 0.38$) whereas other implementations, such as three-dimensional agents (e.g., Liew et al., 2016), did not ($g = 0.11$, n.s.). Overall, the calculations seem to reveal a preferable instructional design with static agents (e.g., Beege et al., 2017; $g = 0.37$), showing static facial features (e.g., Fountoukidou et al., 2019; $g = 42$), using supportive methods, such as gestures (e.g., Li et al., 2019; $g = 0.26$). In addition, learners should have at least some prior knowledge ($g = 0.31$), although it should be noted that the inhomogeneous reporting of prior knowledge within the primary studies is a major limitation of the corresponding analysis. In addition, some comparison groups within the moderation analysis are not yet sufficiently filled, making the analysis very challenging, if not impossible at all. For instance, an effect for humanized and non-humanized was found, but could not be compared to real human PA's as only one study investigates such a scenario. Despite this, and other still unexplored aspects of PA's, the overall learning influence appears to be positive and stable, and most of the smaller social features (e.g., voice variant or facial expression) seem to be less important. Two major implications can be drawn: First, the implementation of PAs is conducive to learning, but general effect sizes were rather small. Second, moderating effects and specific design features and principles should be considered and discussed regarding general multimedia learning theories to specify the effects of PA implementation on learning.

Design Principles

Cognitive Design Principles

PAs can promote cognitive processes in learning in different ways, but they can also potentially impair them. According to the Cognitive Load Theory (CLT; Sweller et al., 2019), cognitive resources are limited, and learning irrelevant loads should be minimized. Since PAs tie up cognitive resources, the implementation of PAs is viewed critically in the light of CLT. For example, the so-called split-attention effect should be mentioned, which states that the separation of related information sources (here: the presented learning materials and the PA) requires mental integration (e.g., Sweller & Chandler, 1994), which subsequently impairs learning performance. It is also conceivable that PAs can unintentionally appear as so-called seductive details, i.e., as interesting adjuncts that are irrelevant or unimportant to the learning topic (e.g., Harp & Mayer, 1998). The learning performance of learners can be impaired by these seductive details (e.g., Rey, 2012; Sundararajan & Adesope, 2020). For example, PAs could distract the learners' attention or, in general, lead to an overload of the learners' working memory due to the additional visual information. In this context, the presence principle (or image principle) can also be mentioned, which postulates that learners do not learn better if a PA is physically present as an image on the screen (Mayer et al., 2003).

Yet, specific design principles of PAs can also promote cognitive processes relevant to learning. PAs can perform pointing gestures, which can serve as signaling to emphasize relevant information in the learning materials. For example, in a study by Johnson et al. (2015), relevant information was either visually signaled or not signaled in multiple external representations. In one of several experimental conditions, pointing gestures from a PA were used for this purpose. It was found that the prior knowledge of the learners moderated the effects of the two experimental factors signaling (visual signaling, no visual signaling) and visibility of the PA (visual PA presence, no visual PA presence). Low-skill learners benefited from signaling and PAs, while high-skill learners performed better without PAs. An eye-tracking experiment by Li et al. (2019) showed that a PA with specific pointing gestures (e.g., pointing gestures to very specific diagram components mentioned in a narrative about neural transmission) attracts more attention to task-relevant elements than a PA with general pointing gestures, a PA with non-pointing gestures, and a PA without gestures. Retention and transfer performances measured immediately and one week later were also higher in the group receiving a PA with specific pointing gestures than in the other experimental conditions. In addition, PAs can also appear as teachers and thus take on teaching functions (Heidig & Clarebout, 2011). It is conceivable that these teaching functions as guidance should continuously be weakened in the course of the learning process following the guidance-fading effect (e.g., Renkl, 2012). This effect states that guidance should be reduced with increasing knowledge or skill level of the learner and that this fading effect leads to better learning performance than without fading guidance.

Emotional/Motivational Design Principles

Since PAs are suitable for performing or showing authentic emotional cues (Adamo et al., 2021), the emotional and motivational impacts of PAs on learning should be further discussed. Emotions play an important role during learning since cognitive processing and emotional experience are inseparably connected (LeDoux & Brown, 2017; Pekrun & Stephens, 2010). According to the Cognitive Affective Theory of Learning with Media (CATLM; Moreno, 2006) and the Integrated Cognitive Affective Model of Learning with Multimedia (ICALM; Plass & Kaplan, 2015), emotional as well as motivational processing can affect learning, but concrete implications were not specified. A more detailed insight is provided by the emotional design hypothesis (Park et al., 2015). On the one hand, emotional experiences can be conducive (emotion as a facilitator) to learning. In particular, a positive activation (inducing emotions with positive valence and high arousal) could foster motivation and is associated with enhanced mental effort in learning scenarios (Plass & Kalyuga, 2019; Schneider et al., 2019). Additionally, positive emotions can facilitate the perceived autonomy of learners (Pekrun, 2000). Enhanced autonomy is associated with various benefits on motivation and effort investment, and recent research outlined the positive effect of enhanced autonomy in learning with multimedia (Schneider, 2021). Consequently, the emotional, as well as motivational benefits of PAs, are inseparably connected. On the other hand, emotions might be obstructive (emotion as a suppressor) to learning. According to the CLT (Sweller et al., 2019), emotional processing can be viewed as an extraneous cognitive load since resources must be allocated to emotional processing. The resulting emotional regulation does not contribute to the learning goal and thus, should not be triggered (Ellis &

Ashbrook, 1988). In this vein, enhancing motivational processes and effort through emotional cues might not compensate for the negative effects of the additional processing (Park et al., 2011).

Technical advantages allow designers to create onscreen PAs that are suitable for expressing emotions. The affective animated PA system (Adamo et al., 2021) outlines that whole-body poses, specific arm/hand gestures, facial expressions, speech, and motion dynamics can transport emotional information. The positivity hypothesis states that people can recognize whether an instructor is displaying emotions even if the instructor is a computer-generated PA (equivalence principle; Horovitz & Mayer, 2021). Further, Lawson et al. (2021) found that emotions in the voice were independently rated correctly if PAs were visible or not. Nevertheless, the accuracy of emotional recognition and perceived intensity depends on the animation style of the PA (Meyer, 2021), while emotions of an actual human being are detected with higher accuracy than emotions of an animated PA (Horovitz & Mayer, 2021). Consequently, emotional as well as motivational benefits might be particularly relevant considering recent technological developments since detailed, high-quality, motion-animated PAs can be generated with accessible software.

Even if the emotions displayed by PAs are detected correctly by the learner, the question remains whether PAs who shows or performs emotional cues fosters learning. The emotional response theory outlines that instructor communication and student behavior are mediated by the emotional responses of students to instructor messages (Mottet et al., 2006). Research pointed out that the positive emotional perception of a PA is related to the learner's engagement with the learning environment (Saariluoma & Jokinen, 2014). An often-used term in the field of research is the PAs perceived enthusiasm (stimulating, energetic, and motivating behavior; Keller et al., 2016). According to Liew et al. (2017), verbal as well as nonverbal enthusiastic cues in PA induce higher positive emotions in learners, which in turn, foster, intrinsic motivation, and learning outcomes. Moderator variables are linked to this effect (e.g., the mental load of the learner; Beege et al., 2020), but several studies found positive relations between the enthusiasm of the PA for learning, in particular, to voice characteristics (Guo et al., 2014).

Besides voice characteristics, PAs can be explicitly designed to give motivational support, for example by providing positive feedback, emotional support, or fostering self-efficacy (Kizilkaya & Askar, 2008; Osman & Lee, 2014). Particularly concerning the effects on motivational processes, PAs can have special potential. In line with the results regarding (Heidig et al., 2015) learners receiving effective PAs might continue to engage with the material over a longer time. Studies on PAs rarely examine long-term effects, whereas in practice it is precisely this long-term use that is important. In a recent literature review (Dai et al., 2022), the authors outlined that few studies found long-term effects of PAs on learning performance, indicating that PAs can motivate learners to engage with the material longer and more intensively. These long-term motivational benefits might counteract short-term impairments in learning success that result from the cognitive strains caused by implemented PAs (e.g., seductive detail effect; Rey 2012). Motivating agents often use multiple design features like short, motivating sentences, emotional voice features (as discussed above), and learner-like characteristics (Baylor & Kim, 2005). In contrast to mentors or instructors, motivating PAs should have similar attributes considering the learner to support self-efficacy (for a review, see: Kim & Baylor, 2016). The instructional delivery, through a human-like voice with appropriate and relevant emotional expressions, is also a key motivational design feature (Baylor, 2011), highlighting the inseparability of emotions and motivational benefits.

Social Design Principles

The Cognitive-Affective-Social Theory of Learning in digital Environments (CASTLE; Schneider et al., 2021) postulates that activating social schemata in long-term memory through social cues can foster learning. These social processes can either directly influence the selection, organization, and integration of information into new mental models, or indirectly affect learning by triggering emotional, motivational, or meta-cognitive processes. A PA resembles such a social cue in digital learning materials. The more a PA is designed to trigger such a social schema, the more it can be used to facilitate learning. Recent research focuses not only on the examination of how such a PA can elicit social processes (e.g., Lin et al., 2020), but also on the examination of different design aspects, for example, how professional the agent looks (Kim & Baylor, 2016), what age and gender the agent has (e.g., Beege et al., 2017), which stereotypes are elicited by the choice of one specific agent (Veletsianos, 2010), and how might the sex appeal of the agent affect perception (Wang & Yeh, 2013). Based on the concept of anthropomorphism, which is described as all attributions of human characteristics to non-human artifacts, a phylogenetic similarity of PAs to humans can trigger social processes (Eddy et al., 1993), leading to higher learning outcomes (e.g., Schneider et al., 2018; for a meta-analysis, see Brom et al., 2018). Also, movements performed by PAs, such as gestures or mimics, were found to trigger a social schema (e.g., Davis, 2018). Gestures, for example, can draw the learner's attention directly to the lecturer (and therefore directly to speech; see Wakefield et al., 2018) and, thus, can support learning (the embodiment principle; Glenberg, 2010; Fiorella & Mayer, 2021).

Besides the visual appearance, verbal cues were examined under the premise of a social cue hypothesis. Here, research focused on how the speech of a pedagogical agent can act as a cue for perceived verbal competency (Kim et al., 2006), verbal motivation (Domagk, 2010), or the instructional role (Baylor & Kim, 2005). Based on the voice principle, explaining that a human voice with a normal intonation leads to higher learning performance than a computer-synthesized voice (Fiorella & Mayer, 2021). Voice prosody influences social perception as well as learning outcomes, in particular for non-native speakers (Davis et al., 2019). Audio tracks provide social cues (Nass & Gong, 2000) about the emotional state and personality of the speakers, their social and racial affiliation, and gender (for a review see; Edwards et al., 2019). Especially preferences for different voices can have a tremendous effect on learning independent of the cultural background of learners (Ahn & Moore, 2011). In addition, a high-quality voice (made with a highly refined speech engine) leads to higher credibility and commitment ratings compared to a low-quality voice (Chiou et al., 2020). Recent research further highlights the importance of voice quality on perceived trust in an online learning environment, showing that a high-quality voice increases the perception of trust (Craig et al., 2019). However, perceived trust does not appear to have a strong influence on learning outcomes (Schroeder et al., 2021). In line with the personalization principle (Fiorella & Mayer, 2021), which states that directly addressing learners in a conversational style increases learning compared to a formal style, the content of a PA's verbal message can also form a social cue. Based on this principle, also dialects (e.g., Rey & Steib, 2013), sociolects (e.g., Schneider et al., 2015a), or politeness (e.g., Schneider et al., 2015b) in utterances were found to positively affect learning. Overall, both the visual appearance and movements as well as verbal utterances of PAs can serve as a social cue eliciting social processes, which impact cognitive processes.

Conclusions

Considering the discussed design effects, it is difficult to postulate a general recommendation for implementing PAs in digital learning environments. According to effects based on cognitive frameworks (e.g., CLT; Sweller et al., 2019), PAs are not generally beneficial for learning (presence principle). In fact, including PAs could even suppress learning since PAs can be seen as seductive details. Consequently, PAs should be included with caution, and the concrete design and use of design features might determine if PAs are beneficial for learning or not. Moreno (2005) already pointed out that PAs may be effective for learning due to their pedagogy rather than merely their appearance. Thus, the question should not be whether to use a PA or not, but rather how to design PAs in an instructional effective manner. Consequently, different design principles can be used that trigger beneficial cognitive, affective, motivational, and social processes. To briefly summarize, the cognitive architecture of the learner should be considered. For example, the learner can be supported by providing cognitive guidance or highlighting important information.

Furthermore, PAs can positively activate learners through various techniques. Emotional activation is further associated with motivational benefits during learning. Finally, it can be beneficial to strengthen the social context of the learning situation. Some design principles are associated with multiple learning-relevant processes and research is needed for a detailed investigation of individual design features and resulting processes as well as potential interaction to get a comprehensive picture of learning with and from PAs.

In conclusion, there is a bright scope for future research. There are only a few studies that investigated several instructional roles of PAs (Martha & Santoso, 2019). For example, PAs as modeling examples or test administrators are rarely investigated but might be highly relevant when demonstrating physical processes, and cultural conventions or providing retrieval cues. Schroeder and Gotch (2015) already pointed out that primary studies with carefully planned and reported experiments should be carried out. In the past years, progress has been made. For example, primary studies, as well as meta-analyses, worked out the positive effects of different kinds of gestures or enthusiasm in the PA's voice (Davis, 2018; Liew et al., 2017). Nevertheless, there are still design features that have not been thoroughly investigated. In particular, design features depending on the target group of the instructional intervention should be considered. Studies already outlined different preferences for the design of the PA in dependence on learner characteristics (Girard & Johnson, 2010). Finally, the cost-effectiveness of PAs should be considered. Technological advantages simplify the production of various PAs, but production and implication are still time-consuming (or even cost-intensive). Design effects with low to medium effect sizes do still have practical importance, but designers should consider moderators and conditions under which the implementation is worthwhile. Researchers and designers should be aware that easy-to-implement design changes (i.e., use of pre-designed figures, animation through the webcam, manipulation of voice when recording the instructional information) might have higher cost-effectiveness than hard-to-implement changes (i.e., creation of a new PAs with image editors, animating detailed mimics of human-like PAs).

Evidence-Based Practice Recommendations

- The pedagogy and not the mere appearance of PAs is crucial for learning.
- The effectiveness of PAs for learning is predicted through multimedia learning theories.
- Cognitive, affective, motivational, as well as social processes should be considered when designing PAs.
- Future research should focus on diverse instructional roles, specific design features, and learner-relevant variables in light of technological advantages.

References

Adamo, N., Benes, B., Mayer, R. E., Lei, X., Wang, Z., Meyer, Z., & Lawson, A. (2021). Multimodal affective pedagogical agents for different types of learners. In D. Russo, T. Ahram, W. Karwowski, G. Di Bucchianico, & R. Taiar (Eds.), *Intelligent human systems integration 2021. IHSI 2021.* Advances in Intelligent Systems and Computing (Vol. 1322). Springer. https://doi.org/10.1007/978-3-030-68017-6_33

Ahn, J., & Moore, D. (2011). The relationship between students' accent perception and accented voice instructions and its effect on students' achievement in an interactive multimedia environment. *Journal of Educational Multimedia and Hypermedia, 20*(4), 319–335. Association for the Advancement of Computing in Education (AACE). Retrieved June 28, 2022 from https://www.learntechlib.org/primary/p/37520/

Baylor, A. L. (2011). The design of motivational agents and avatars. *Educational Technology Research and Development, 59*(2), 291–300. https://doi.org/10.1007/s11423-011-9196-3

Baylor, A. L., & Kim, S. (2009). Designing nonverbal communication for pedagogical agents: When less is more. *Computers in Human Behavior, 25*(2), 450–457. https://doi.org/10.1016/j.chb.2008.10.008

Baylor, A.L., & Kim, Y. (2004). Pedagogical agent design: The impact of agent realism, gender, ethnicity, and instructional role. In J. C. Lester, R. M. Vicari, & F. Paraguaçu (Eds.), *Intelligent tutoring systems. ITS 2004.* Lecture Notes in Computer Science (Vol. 3220). Springer. https://doi.org/10.1007/978-3-540-30139-4_56

Baylor, A. L., & Kim, Y. (2005). Simulating instructional roles through pedagogical agents. *International Journal of Artificial Intelligence in Education, 15*(2), 95–115. https://doi.org/10.1007/s40593-015-0055-y

Beege, M., Schneider, S., Nebel, S., Mittangk, J., & Rey, G. D. (2017). Ageism–age coherence within learning material fosters learning. *Computers in Human Behavior, 75*, 510–519. https://doi.org/10.1016/j.chb.2017.05.042

Beege, M., Schneider, S., Nebel, S., & Rey, G. D. (2020). Does the effect of enthusiasm in a pedagogical Agent's voice depend on mental load in the learner's working memory? *Computers in Human Behavior, 112*, 106483. https://doi.org/10.1016/j.chb.2020.106483

Brom, C., Starkova, T., & D'Mello, S. K. (2018). How effective is emotional design? A meta-analysis on facial anthropomorphisms and pleasant colors during multimedia learning. *Educational Research Review, 25*, 100–119. https://doi.org/10.1016/j.edurev.2018.09.004

Burgoon, J. K., Bonito, J. A., Bengtsson, B., Cederberg, C., Lundeberg, M., & Allspach, L. (2000). Interactivity in human–computer interaction: A study of credibility, understanding, and influence. *Computers in Human Behavior, 16*(6), 553–574. https://doi.org/10.1016/S0747-5632(00)00029-7

Castro-Alonso, J. C., Wong, R. M., Adesope, O. O., & Paas, F. (2021). Effectiveness of multi-media pedagogical agents predicted by diverse theories: A meta-analysis. *Educational Psychology Review, 33*(3), 989–1015. https://doi.org/10.1007/s10648-020-09587-1

Chiou, E. K., Schroeder, N. L., & Craig, S. D. (2020). How we trust, perceive, and learn from virtual humans: The influence of voice quality. *Computers & Education, 146*, 103756. https://doi.org/10.1016/j.compedu.2019.103756

Craig, S. D., Chiou, E. K., & Schroeder, N. L. (2019, November). The impact of virtual human voice on learner trust. In *Proceedings of the human factors and ergonomics society annual meeting* (Vol. 63, No. 1, pp. 2272–2276). SAGE Publications.

Dai, L., Jung, M. M., Postma, M., & Louwerse, M. M. (2022). A systematic review of pedagogical agent research: Similarities, differences and unexplored aspects. *Computers & Education*, 104607. https://doi.org/10.1016/j.eswa.2012.01.138

Davis, R. O. (2018). The impact of pedagogical agent gesturing in multimedia learning environments: A meta-analysis. *Educational Research Review*, 24, 193–209. https://doi.org/10.1016/j.edurev.2018.05.002

Davis, R. O., Park, T., & Vincent, J. (2022). A meta-analytic review on embodied pedagogical agent design and testing formats. *Journal of Educational Computing Research*. https://doi.org/10.1177/07356331221100556

Davis, R. O., Vincent, J., & Park, T. (2019). Reconsidering the voice principle with non-native language speakers. *Computers & Education*, 140, 103605. https://doi.org/10.1016/j.compedu.2019.103605

Domagk, S. (2010). Do pedagogical agents facilitate learner motivation and learning outcomes?: The role of the appeal of agent's appearance and voice. *Journal of Media Psychology: Theories, Methods, and Applications*, 22(2), 84–97. https://doi.org/10.1027/1864-1105/a000011

Eddy, T. J., Gallup Jr., G. G., & Povinelli, D. J. (1993). Attribution of cognitive states to animals: Anthropomorphism in comparative perspective. *Journal of Social Issues*, 49(1), 87–101. https://doi.org/10.1111/j.1540-4560.1993.tb00910.x

Edwards, C., Edwards, A., Stoll, B., Lin, X., Massey, N., & Edwards, C. (2019). Evaluations of an artificial intelligence instructor's voice: Social identity theory in human-robot interactions. *Computers in Human Behavior*, 90, 357–362. https://doi.org/10.1016/j.chb.2018.08.027

Ellis, H. C., & Ashbrook, P. W. (1988). Resource allocation model of the effects of depressed mood states. In K. Fiedler & J. Forgas (Eds.), *Affect, cognition and social behaviour* (pp. 25–43). Toronto: Hogrefe.

Fiorella, L., & Mayer, R. (2021). Principles based on social cues in multimedia learning: Personalization, voice, image, and embodiment principles. In R. Mayer & L. Fiorella (Eds.), *The Cambridge handbook of multimedia learning*. Cambridge Handbooks in Psychology (pp. 277–285). Cambridge University Press. https://doi.org/10.1017/9781108894333.029

Fountoukidou, S., Ham, J., Matzat, U., & Midden, C. (2019). Effects of an artificial agent as a behavioral model on motivational and learning outcomes. *Computers in Human Behavior*, 97, 84–93. https://doi.org/10.1016/j.chb.2019.03.013

Girard, S., & Johnson, H. (2010). What do children favor as embodied pedagogical agents? In V. Aleven, J. Kay, & J. Mostow (Eds.), *Intelligent tutoring systems. ITS 2010*. Lecture Notes in Computer Science (Vol. 6094). Springer. https://doi.org/10.1007/978-3-642-13388-6_35

Glenberg, A. M. (2010). Embodiment as a unifying perspective for psychology. *Wiley Interdisciplinary Reviews: Cognitive Science*, 1(4), 586–596. https://doi.org/10.1002/wcs.55

Guo, P. J., Kim, J., & Rubin, R. (2014). How video production affects student engagement: An empirical study of MOOC videos. In *Proceedings of the first ACM Conference on Learning @ Scale Conference* (pp. 41–50). ACM. https://doi.org/10.1145/2556325.2566239

Harp, S. F., & Mayer, R. E. (1998). How seductive details do their damage: A theory of cognitive interest in science learning. *Journal of Educational Psychology, 90*(3), 414–434. https://doi.org/10.1037/0022-0663.90.3.414

Heidig, S., & Clarebout, G. (2011). Do pedagogical agents make a difference to student motiva-tion and learning? *Educational Research Review, 6*(1), 27–54. https://doi.org/10.1016/j.edurev.2010.07.004

Heidig, S., Müller, J., & Reichelt, M. (2015). Emotional design in multimedia learning: Differentiation on relevant design features and their effects on emotions and learning. *Computers in Human Behavior, 44*, 81–95. https://doi.org/10.1016/j.chb.2014.11.009

Horovitz, T., & Mayer, R. E. (2021). Learning with human and virtual instructors who display happy or bored emotions in video lectures. *Computers in Human Behavior, 119*, 106724. https://doi.org/10.1016/j.chb.2021.106724

Johnson, A., Ozogul, G. and Reisslein, M. (2015). Supporting multimedia learning with visual signalling and animated pedagogical agent: Moderating effects of prior knowledge. *Journal of Computer Assisted Learning, 31*(2), 97–115. https://doi.org/10.1111/jcal.12078

Keller, M. M., Hoy, A. W., Goetz, T., & Frenzel, A. C. (2016). Teacher enthusiasm: Reviewing and redefining a complex construct. *Educational Psychology Review, 28*, 743–769. https://doi.org/10.1007/s10648-015-9354-y

Kim, Y., & Baylor, A. L. (2016). Research-based design of pedagogical agent roles: A review, progress, and recommendations. *International Journal of Artificial Intelligence in Education, 26*(1), 160–169. https://doi.org/10.1007/s40593-015-0055-y

Kim, Y., Baylor, A. L., & PALS Group. (2006). Pedagogical agents as learning companions: The role of agent competency and type of interaction. *Educational Technology Research and Development, 54*, 223–243. https://doi.org/10.1007/s11423-006-8805-z

Kim, Y., & Wei, Q. (2011). The impact of learner attributes and learner choice in an agent-based environment. *Computers & Education, 56*(2), 505–514. https://doi.org/10.1016/j.compedu.2010.09.016

Kizilkaya, G., & Askar, P. (2008). The effect of an embedded pedagogical agent on the students' science achievement. *Interactive Technology and Smart Education, 5*(4), 208–216. https://doi.org/10.1108/17415650810930893

Lane, H. C., Cahill, C., Foutz, S., Auerbach, D., Noren, D., Lussenhop, C., & Swartout, W. (2013, July). The effects of a pedagogical agent for informal science education on learner behaviors and self-efficacy. In H. C. Lane, K. Yacef, J. Mostow, & P. Pavlik (Eds.), *Artificial intelligence in education. AIED 2013.* Lecture Notes in Computer Science (pp. 309–318). Springer. https://doi.org/10.1007/978-3-642-39112-5_32

Lawson, A. P., Mayer, R. E., Adamo-Villani, N., Benes, B., Lei, X., & Cheng, J. (2021). Do learners recognize and relate to the emotions displayed by virtual instructors? *International Journal of Artificial Intelligence in Education, 31*(1), 134–153. https://doi.org/10.1007/s40593-021-00238-2

LeDoux, J. E., & Brown, R. (2017). A higher-order theory of emotional consciousness. *Proceedings of the National Academy of Sciences, 114*(10), 2016–2025. https://doi.org/10.1073/pnas.1619316114

Li, W., Wang, F., Mayer, R. E., & Liu, H. (2019). Getting the point: Which kinds of gestures by pedagogical agents improve multimedia learning? *Journal of Educational Psychology, 111*(8), 1382–1395. https://doi.org/10.1037/edu0000352

Liew, T., Azan Mat Zin, N., Sahari, N., & Tan, S. M. (2016). The effects of a pedagogical agent's smiling expression on the learner's emotions and motivation in a virtual learning environment. *International Review of Research in Open and Distributed Learning: IRRODL, 17*(5), 248–266. https://doi.org/10.19173/irrodl.v17i5.2350

Liew, T. W., Zin, N. A. M., & Sahari, N. (2017). Exploring the affective, motivational and cognitive effects of pedagogical agent enthusiasm in a multimedia learning environment. *Human-Centric Computing and Information Sciences, 7*(1), 1–21. https://doi.org/10.1186/s13673-017-0089-2

Lin, L., Ginns, P., Wang, T., & Zhang, P. (2020). Using a pedagogical agent to deliver conversational style instruction: What benefits can you obtain? *Computers & Education, 143*, 103658. https://doi.org/10.1016/j.compedu.2019.103658

Martha, A. S. D., & Santoso, H. B. (2019). The design and impact of the pedagogical agent: A systematic literature review. *Journal of Educators Online, 16*(1). https://doi.org/10.9743/jeo.2019.16.1.8

Mayer, R. E., Dow, G. T., & Mayer, S. (2003). Multimedia learning in an interactive self-explaining environment: What works in the design of agent-based microworlds? *Journal of Educational Psychology, 95*(4), 806–812. https://doi.org/10.1037/0022-0663.95.4.806

Meyer, Z. R. (2021). *Bodily expression of emotions in animated pedagogical agents* (Doctoral dissertation, Purdue University Graduate School).

Moreno, R. (2005). Multimedia learning with animated pedagogical agents. In R. Mayer (Ed.), *The Cambridge handbook of multimedia learning* (pp. 507–523). Cambridge University Press. https://doi.org/10.1017/CBO9780511816819.032

Moreno, R. (2006). Learning in high-tech and multimedia environments. *Current Directions in Psychological Science, 15*, 63–67. https://doi.org/10.1111/j.0963-7214.2006.00408.x

Mottet, T. P., Frymier, A. B., & Beebe, S. A. (2006). Theorizing about instructional communication. In T. P. Mottet, V. P. Richmond, & J. C. McCroskey (Eds.), *Handbook of instructional communication: Rhetorical and relational perspectives* (pp. 255–282). Allyn & Bacon.

Nass, C., & Gong, L. (2000). Speech interfaces from an evolutionary perspective. *Communications of the ACM, 43*, 36–43. https://doi.org/10.1145/348941.348976

Osman, K., & Lee, T. T. (2014). Impact of interactive multimedia module with pedagogical agents on students' understanding and motivation in the learning of electrochemistry. *International Journal of Science and Mathematics Education, 12*(2), 395–421. https://doi.org/10.1007/s10763-013-9407-y

Pareto, L., Arvemo, T., Dahl, Y., Haake, M., Gulz, A. (2011). A teachable-agent arithmetic game's effects on mathematics understanding, attitude and self-efficacy. In G. Biswas, S. Bull, J. Kay, & A. Mitrovic (Eds.), *Artificial intelligence in education. AIED 2011*. Lecture Notes in Computer Science (Vol. 6738). Springer. https://doi.org/10.1007/978-3-642-21869-9_33

Park, B., Knörzer, L., Plass, J. L., & Brünken, R. (2015). Emotional design and positive emotions in multimedia learning: An eyetracking study on the use of anthropomorphisms. *Computers & Education, 86*, 30–42. https://doi.org/10.1016/j.compedu.2015.02.016

Park, B., Moreno, R., Seufert, T., & Brünken, R. (2011). Does cognitive load moderate the seductive details effect? A multimedia study. *Computers in Human Behavior*, 27(1), 5–10. https://doi.org/10.1016/j.chb.2010.05.006

Pekrun, R. (2000). A social-cognitive, control-value theory of achievement emotions. In J. Heckhausen (Ed.), *Advances in psychology, 131. Motivational psychology of human development: Developing motivation and motivating development* (pp. 143–163). Elsevier Science. https://doi.org/10.1016/S0166-4115(00)80010-2

Pekrun, R., & Stephens, E. J. (2010). Achievement emotions: A control-value approach. *Social and Personality Psychology Compass*, 4(4), 238–255. https://doi.org/10.1111/j.1751-9004.2010.00259.x

Plass, J. L., & Kalyuga, S. (2019). Four ways of considering emotion in cognitive load theory. *Educational Psychology Review*, 31, 339–359. https://doi.org/10.1007/s10648-019-09473-5

Plass, J. L., & Kaplan, U. (2015). Emotional design in digital media for learning. In S. Tettegah & M. Gartmeier (Eds.), *Emotions, technology, design, and learning* (pp. 131–162). Elsevier. https://doi.org/10.1016/B978-0-12-801856-9.00007-4

Renkl, A. (2012). Guidance-fading effect. In N. M. Seel (Ed.), *Encyclopedia of the sciences of learning* (pp. 1400–1402). Springer. https://doi.org/10.1007/978-1-4419-1428-6_335

Rey, G. D. (2012). A review of research and a meta-analysis of the seductive detail effect. *Educational Research Review*, 7(3), 216–237. https://doi.org/10.1016/j.edurev.2012.05.003

Rey, G. D., & Steib, N. (2013). The personalization effect in multimedia learning: The influence of dialect. *Computers in Human Behavior*, 29(5), 2022–2028. https://doi.org/10.1016/j.chb.2013.04.003

Saariluoma, P., & Jokinen, J. P. (2014). Emotional dimensions of user experience: A user psychological analysis. *International Journal of Human-Computer Interaction*, 30(4), 303–320. https://doi.org/10.1080/10447318.2013.858460

Schneider, S. (2021). Are there never too many choice options? The effect of increasing the number of choice options on learning with digital media. *Human Behavior and Emerging Technologies*, 3(5), 759–775. https://doi.org/10.1002/hbe2.295

Schneider, S., Beege, M., Nebel, S., Schnaubert, L., & Rey, G. D. (2021). The cognitive-affective-social theory of learning in digital environments (CASTLE). *Educational Psychology Review*, 38, 1–38. https://doi.org/10.1007/s10648-021-09626-5

Schneider, S., Nebel, S., Beege, M., & Rey, G. D. (2018). Anthropomorphism in decorative pictures: Benefit or harm for learning? *Journal of Educational Psychology*, 110(2), 218–232. https://doi.org/10.1037/edu0000207

Schneider, S., Nebel, S., Pradel, S., & Rey, G. D. (2015a). Introducing the familiarity mechanism: A unified explanatory approach for the personalization effect and the examination of youth slang in multimedia learning. *Computers in Human Behavior*, 43, 129–138. https://doi.org/10.1016/j.chb.2014.10.052

Schneider, S., Nebel, S., Pradel, S., & Rey, G. D. (2015b). Mind your Ps and Qs! How polite instructions affect learning with multimedia. *Computers in Human Behavior*, 51, 546–555. https://doi.org/10.1016/j.chb.2015.05.025

Schneider, S., Wirzberger, M., & Rey, G. D. (2019). The moderating role of arousal on the seductive detail effect in a multimedia learning setting. *Applied Cognitive Psychology*, 33(1), 71–84. https://doi.org/10.1002/acp.3473

Schroeder, N. L., Adesope, O. O., & Gilbert, R. B. (2013). How effective are pedagogical agents for learning? A meta-analytic review. *Journal of Educational Computing Research*, *49*(1), 1–39. https://doi.org/10.2190/EC.49.1.a

Schroeder, N. L., Chiou, E. K., & Craig, S. D. (2021). Trust influences perceptions of virtual humans, but not necessarily learning. *Computers & Education*, *160*, 104039. https://doi.org/10.1016/j.compedu.2020.104039

Schroeder, N. L., & Gotch, C. M. (2015). Persisting issues in pedagogical agent research. *Journal of Educational Computing Research*, *53*(2), 183–204. https://doi.org/10.1177/0735633115597625

Sundararajan, N., & Adesope, O. (2020). Keep it coherent: A meta-analysis of the seductive details effect. *Educational Psychology Review*, *32*(3), 707–734. https://doi.org/10.1007/s10648-020-09522-4

Sweller, J., & Chandler, P. (1994). Why some material is difficult to learn. *Cognition and Instruction*, *12*(3), 185–233. https://doi.org/10.1207/s1532690xci1203_1

Sweller, J., van Merriënboer, J. J., & Paas, F. (2019). Cognitive architecture and instructional design: 20 years later. *Educational Psychology Review*, *31*(2), 261–292. https://doi.org/10.1007/s10648-019-09465-5

Veletsianos, G. (2010). Contextually relevant pedagogical agents: Visual appearance, stereotypes, and first impressions and their impact on learning. *Computers & Education*, *55*(2), 576–585. https://doi.org/10.1016/j.compedu.2010.02.019

Veletsianos, G., & Russell, G. S. (2013). Pedagogical agents. In J. M. Spector, M. D. Merrill, J. Elen, & M. J. Bishop (Eds.), *Handbook of research on educational communication and technology* (pp. 759–769). Springer Science + Business. https://doi.org/10.1007/978-1-4614-3185-5_61

Wakefield, E., Novack, M. A., Congdon, E. L., Franconeri, S., & Goldin-Meadow, S. (2018). Gesture helps learners learn, but not merely by guiding their visual attention. *Developmental Science*, *21*, e12664. https://doi.org/10.1111/desc.12664

Wang, C. C., & Yeh, W. J. (2013). Avatars with sex appeal as pedagogical agents: Attractiveness, trustworthiness, expertise, and gender differences. *Journal of Educational Computing Research*, *48*(4), 403–429. https://doi.org/10.2190/EC.48.4.a

Wang, J., & Antonenko, P. D. (2017). Instructor presence in instructional video: Effects on visual attention, recall, and perceived learning. *Computers in Human Behavior*, *71*, 79–89. https://doi.org/10.1016/j.chb.2017.01.049

Weber, F., Wambsganss, T., Rüttimann, D., & Söllner, M. (2021). Pedagogical agents for interactive learning: A taxonomy of conversational agents in education. In *Forty-Second International Conference on Information Systems (ICIS)*, Austin, Texas, (pp. 1–17).

9
DESIGNING EFFECTIVE IMMERSIVE VIRTUAL REALITY LEARNING ENVIRONMENTS

Gustav Bøg Petersen and Guido Makransky

Introduction

What does the future of education look like? Some researchers anticipate that the next iteration of the internet, the *Metaverse*, may reshape learning (Pimentel et al., 2022). This virtual world, accessible through technology, will consist of unique environments designed to entertain, socialize, educate, and so forth (Pimentel et al., 2022). However, the relationship between education and technology has historically been turbulent. Although unquenchable *EdTech* optimists have made claims throughout the years that educational information and communication technology will transform education, such technologies have not lived up to these expectations (Sanders & George, 2017). For a potential solution to this rhetoric-reality gap, consider the stance that Pimentel and colleagues take in their report on learning in the Metaverse: "Understanding the strengths and weaknesses of XR [extended reality, including augmented, mixed, and virtual reality] will allow for thoughtful reflection on how we use these tools for specific learning goals and contexts" (Pimentel et al., 2022, p. 10). In other words, there is a need to carefully consider how we can leverage the strengths of XR for certain educational aims and not view it as an all-encompassing, educational silver bullet. This chapter deals with how to design effective immersive virtual reality (VR) learning environments (hereinafter referred to as iVLEs) from an educational psychological perspective. By *effective* iVLEs, we mean theory- and research-based 3D virtual environments that have the capability to stimulate learning. We refer to iVLEs as environments that can be accessed using immersive VR systems and are *actively* manipulated (note that this precludes video-based learning material).

DOI: 10.4324/9781003386131-13

We start by defining immersive VR and introducing its unique characteristics. Afterward, we introduce existing theories and principles of learning in immersive VR environments. This is followed by an iVLE design framework, which is a theory- and research-based model that can be used to guide the development of immersive VR learning content.

Defining Immersive VR

According to (Mikropoulos & Natsis, 2011, p. 769) VR refers to a "mosaic of technologies that support the creation of synthetic, highly interactive three dimensional (3D) spatial environments that represent real or non-real situations." Slater (2009) defines immersion as a function of the valid actions that are possible within a VR system, i.e., actions that we are accustomed to performing in physical reality in order to perceive. As an example, consider a virtual environment delivered via an immersive VR system that uses a head-mounted display (HMD), haptic gloves, and earphones: Users of such an environment would be able to walk around each other, give each other high fives, and have conversations with each other while experiencing corresponding changes to the rendered images, haptic feedback in one's hands, and auditory changes depending on location (Slater et al., 2022). This can be contrasted with a non-immersive system, such as a desktop display (sometimes referred to as desktop VR), where turning one's head would simply result in physical reality coming into view, and navigation, rather, happens as a function of keyboard presses or joysticks (Slater, 2009). For simplicity, then, we refer to immersive VR as VR systems that incorporate an HMD, and contrast this with non-immersive systems such as desktop displays.

As of writing, several meta-analyses and systematic reviews of the available body of research on iVLEs have been published. Looking at learning outcomes, most meta-analyses and reviews find a small effect size in favor of immersive VR when compared to control conditions such as desktop VR or traditional lectures (Coban et al., 2022; Parong, 2022; Wu et al., 2020). However, authors who focused only on K-6 education recently reported an exception to this pattern; here, a large effect in favor of immersive VR was found (Villena-Taranilla et al., 2022). It should be noted that media comparisons can be problematic, as differences could be attributed to uncontrolled aspects of the content or instructional strategy rather than the medium (Clark, 1983). Additionally, Wu and colleagues reported that a non-trivial amount of the reviewed studies (26%) showed negative effects of immersive VR on learning, thereby underscoring the importance of the careful instructional design of iVLEs (Wu et al., 2020). Finally, in a systematic review of immersive VR applications for higher education, Radianti et al. (2020) outlined how immersive VR is most frequently used to teach procedural-practical knowledge, declarative knowledge, and analytical and problem-solving skills.

For long, researchers have been interested in the unique characteristics of immersive VR and how these can be leveraged for educational purposes. When surveying these characteristics, authors mention immersion (previously defined), interaction, and embodiment as the main characteristics of immersive VR (Johnson-Glenberg, 2018; Makransky & Petersen, 2021; Scavarelli et al., 2021). Interaction means that the virtual learning environment is responsive to the actions of the learner (as opposed to being static; Moreno & Mayer, 2007). Embodiment refers to the technological setup through which the learner's body is substituted by a virtual body, using head-tracking, motion capture, haptic feedback, etc. (Slater, 2017). In the following section, we present a select few theories and principles of immersive learning that describe how these unique VR characteristics lead to learning through psychological processes.

Theories and Principles of Immersive Learning

Several theories that focus on immersive learning currently exist. These can be traced to the constructivist view of learning as well as embodied cognition and situated cognition. Constructivism is an approach to learning that holds that knowledge is constructed by the learner (O'Donnell, 2012). Embodied cognition is a theory of cognition that emphasizes the central role of the body in constraining, regulating, and shaping the nature of mental activity (Foglia & Wilson, 2013). Situated cognition is the perspective that knowledge and learning are inseparable from the setting in which they occur (Wilson, 1993). This means that learning is bound to the particular iVLE in which it occurs. In this section, we introduce the Cognitive Affective Model of Immersive Learning (CAMIL), the Cognitive-Affective-Social Theory of Learning in digital Environments (CASTLE), and the Immersion Principle in Multimedia Learning (IPML). These theories can be used collectively to understand the processes associated with learning in iVLEs, and how VR's unique characteristics (i.e., immersion, interaction, and embodiment) influence learning through identified psychological factors such as presence, enjoyment, and interest.

The Cognitive Affective Model of Immersive Learning (CAMIL)

The CAMIL is a research-based theoretical model that describes the variables that play a role in learning with iVLEs (Makransky & Petersen, 2021; Petersen et al., 2022). Rather than focusing on the learning content of iVLEs, the CAMIL focuses on the psychological variables that are at play during the process of learning with iVLEs, with presence and agency being the most central ones (Makransky & Petersen, 2021). According to the CAMIL, situational interest, intrinsic motivation, self-efficacy, embodiment, cognitive load, and self-regulation are integral psychological factors during learning with iVLEs. The implications for instructional design based on CAMIL are that iVLEs should be designed to enhance the presence and agency felt by the learner, as these two factors predict the aforementioned variables (Makransky & Petersen, 2021). Moreover, the model suggests designing iVLEs according to the evidence-based instructional design principles proposed in the Cognitive Theory of Multimedia Learning (CTML) in order to ensure effective use of the learner's limited working memory capacity.

The Immersion Principle in Multimedia Learning (IPML)

The IPML is a recently coined multimedia learning principle that describes the mechanisms by which immersion positively impacts learning (Makransky, 2022; Makransky & Mayer, 2022). According to this principle, immersion only improves learning when the iVLE involves instructional design principles or generative learning strategies that either facilitate the features that make iVLEs unique, or mitigate the limitations of such learning environments (Makransky & Mayer, 2022). This principle is based on several value-added studies that demonstrate how incorporating instructional design principles leads to better learning, as well as media comparison studies showing that generative learning strategies can be more effective in iVLEs compared to less immersive environments (Makransky & Mayer, 2022). In an empirical study, Makransky and Mayer (2022) demonstrate how immersion impacts immediate and long-term retention via presence, enjoyment, and interest, thereby supporting the aforementioned CAMIL.

The Cognitive-Affective-Social Theory of Learning in digital Environments (CASTLE)

Building on prior interactive learning environments research (Moreno & Mayer, 2007), CASTLE is based on a perceived gap in the multimedia learning literature regarding the influence of social processes in digital learning environments (Schneider et al., 2022). The theory assumes the social mediation hypothesis as a basic foundation: "Social processes triggered by social cues mediate the cognitive processing of information when learning with digital materials" (Schneider et al., 2022, p. 8). CASTLE consists of five sub-hypotheses, which are listed in the following. The first hypothesis (the Activation Hypothesis) posits that social cues activate social schemata in long-term memory. This, in turn, enables social processes to influence all of the cognitive processes involved in learning (Cognitive Influence Hypothesis). Furthermore, these social processes may influence or be influenced by affective, motivational, and/or metacognitive processes (Interaction Hypothesis). The fourth hypothesis, the Schema Influence Hypothesis, posits that the magnitude of social schemata activation depends on the number and strength of social cues provided in the learning environment (as well as the level of development of social schemata). The final hypothesis (Social Cue Strength Hypothesis) states that social cues are easier integrated into multimodal learning environments than single modal environments (Schneider et al., 2022). Hence, the implications of CASTLE are that social processes affect individual learning with digital learning material.

iVLE Design Framework

Figure 9.1 illustrates an iVLE design framework that is based on theories and research in the field of learning with iVLEs. Each of the four general recommendations that instructional designers should consider when developing iVLEs is presented at the top of Figure 9.1, and in order in the following sections.

Always Ask, "Why Immersive VR?"

The first question you always need to ask yourself before starting an iVLE design process is, "Why VR?" Not everything needs to be virtualized, and so far, several studies show that VR can have harmful effects on learning (Makransky et al., 2019; Parong & Mayer, 2018; Wu et al., 2020). What content, then, is appropriate for rendering in an HMD? Bailenson (2018) suggests that VR should be used for rendering situations where the real-life

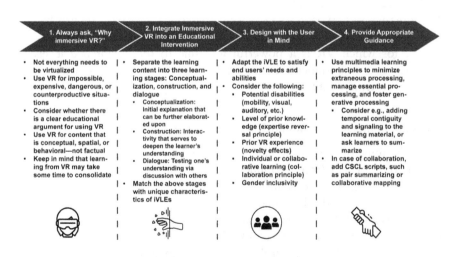

FIGURE 9.1 An illustration of the steps in the iVLE design framework.

Source: Icons (from left to right) created by Hilmy Abiyyu Asad, Victoruler, SBTS, and supalerk laipawat from NounProject.com CC BY 3.0.

counterpart would be impossible, expensive, dangerous, or counterproductive. This would, e.g., be the case in a maritime safety scenario (Makransky & Klingenberg, 2022), where the comparable real-life situation could involve death or serious injury, or a situation involving pipetting dangerous chemicals (Petersen et al., 2022).

Other scholars have suggested combining VR with traditional means of education (Parong & Mayer, 2018). E.g., it would comply with interest theory (Hidi & Renninger, 2006) to use VR at the onset of a lesson to spark interest in the subject matter and hereafter proceed with more traditional means of instruction. In that case, it can be argued that the content need not necessarily comply with Bailenson's aforementioned conditions of VR use, as the point would be to spark interest, which could be achieved merely by immersing the learner in a novel environment (Petersen et al., 2022). A rule of thumb that would make sense when dealing with iVLEs is to use them only if there is a clear educational argument for doing so.

Based on the revised version of Bloom's taxonomy, Makransky and Petersen (2021) suggest separating iVLE learning outcomes into factual knowledge, conceptual knowledge, procedural knowledge, and transfer. Research indicates that VR is not as effective as other media when it comes to teaching factual knowledge (Parong & Mayer, 2018). Rather, the technology is effective for conceptual and spatial knowledge (Baceviciute et al., 2022) as well as behavioral transfer (Makransky et al., 2019). In addition, Parong (2022) found that VR has a much larger effect on delayed assessments (median $d = .30$) compared to immediate assessments (median $d = .01$), suggesting that learning from VR might take some time to consolidate. We note that other types of iVLE learning outcomes also exist, such as behavior change (Plechatá et al., 2022) and perspective taking (Ventura et al., 2020), for which VR is a powerful tool due to the heightened levels of presence and embodiment. However, this chapter focuses on traditional, academic learning outcomes.

Integrate Immersive VR into an Educational Intervention

Once the topic of the lesson has been selected and it is determined that the lesson could benefit from an immersive VR component, the next step is to define how to integrate this into the educational intervention with the learning outcomes in mind. The framework proposed by Dalgarno and Lee (2010) constitutes a useful basis for selecting relevant learning activities. Here, they survey the learning affordances of 3D virtual environments that can be accessed via PC, taking a "technology first" approach (Dalgarno & Lee, 2010). In doing so, they identify representational fidelity and learner interaction as unique characteristics of 3D VLEs, whereas construction of identity, sense of presence, and co-presence are the result of these characteristics

(Dalgarno & Lee, 2010). Representational fidelity refers to the sensory fidelity of the environment (i.e., how the environment engages the visual, auditory, and haptic senses), whereas learner interaction refers to the embodiment afforded by 3D VLEs (Dalgarno & Lee, 2010). Note that these definitions overlap with the previously defined unique characteristics of immersive VR.

Following the identification of the unique characteristics of 3D VLEs, Dalgarno and Lee (2010) identify five learning affordances (i.e., learning tasks or activities) of such environments, which elicit the following learning benefits: 1) Spatial knowledge representation, 2) experiential learning, 3) engagement, 4) contextual learning, and 5) collaborative learning (Dalgarno & Lee, 2010). Here, 3D VLE characteristics and learning benefits should be understood as linked, such that greater fidelity, e.g., leads to a larger sense of presence, which leads to improved transfer (contextual learning). Dalgarno and Lee's framework can contribute to the design of iVLEs by outlining the learning outcomes that are well-suited to immersion, interaction, and embodiment. However, the model is unspecific with regard to how designers should approach the design of the learning tasks that may lead to these learning benefits. In addition, Fowler (2015) criticized the "technology first" perspective applied in Dalgarno and Lee's model, and, consequently, extended the model to emphasize pedagogical requirements at an early stage.

Fowler's enhanced model advises starting with a definition of the intended learning outcomes, which can be understood as a specification of what the learner is intended to know, understand, and be able to do at the end of the learning session (Fowler, 2015). The enhanced model incorporates an existing framework that categorizes learning into three fundamental stages (Mayes & Fowler, 1999), which can be matched with the technological characteristics of 3D VLEs specified by Dalgarno and Lee (i.e., representational fidelity and learner interaction). The first stage, conceptualization, refers to an initial explanation of the contents of the lesson that can be further elaborated upon at later stages. Evidence for the usefulness of conceptualization can be found in research showing that the pre-training principle enhances learning from VR lessons (i.e., people learn more deeply from a multimedia message when they are familiar with the names and characteristics of the main concepts beforehand; Meyer et al., 2019; Petersen et al., 2020). The second stage, construction, is characterized by interactivity related to the newly introduced concept, which serves to deepen the learner's understanding. This is consistent with the evidence-based ICAP framework, which posits that more active learning activities lead to deeper learning (Chi & Wylie, 2014). The third and final stage, dialogue, refers to testing one's understanding via discussion with other (person-controlled or computer-controlled) people (Fowler, 2015). Evidence for the usefulness of this final stage can be found in the generative learning literature, as, essentially, the dialogue stage is a generative activity similar to, e.g., learning by teaching (Fiorella &

Mayer, 2022b). As mentioned previously, research shows that generative learning activities can be particularly effective in iVLEs (Klingenberg et al., 2020; Makransky et al., 2021).

Fowler's Enhanced Model of Learning in 3D VLEs suggests a number of learning activities related to each of the three learning stages that, although they are quite general, can inspire iVLE design. We provide examples in the following and refer interested readers to a full exposition in Fowler (2015). For the conceptualization stage, narrated, dynamic visualization can convey initial information about the topic of the lesson. E.g., if the lesson is on animal cells, this initial step could display a 3D version of a cell with a narrated description of the name and function of each of its components. The construction stage could involve a clearly defined and engaging problem, which extends the initially introduced concept and involves the learner's input and decisions. If we continue with the animal cells lesson, the learner(s) could, e.g., be tasked with undergoing miniaturization and discovering how viruses enter our cells and replicate; this would deepen the learner's understanding of the cell and its functions. Finally, a relevant activity for the dialogue stage could be a prompt to summarize or discuss the learning material. In the animal cell example, a natural extension from the prior stage would be to prompt the learner to create a written or oral explanation of the process of viral entry and replication.

As presented above, the conceptualization, construction, and dialogue stages (and their associated learning activities) are broad enough to apply to learning interventions delivered via other means than immersive VR. However, as noted in Bower (2008), it is important to match learning tasks with learning technologies. For developing iVLEs, this means that learning tasks should be integrated with the high levels of immersion, interaction, and embodiment offered by immersive VR systems. E.g., 3D objects intended to convey initial information about the subject matter should behave in a way that is meaningful in terms of perception in addition to being responsive to the actions of the learner, and the learner should be represented by a virtual body.

Design with the User in Mind

Simultaneously to creating a preliminary outline of the learning activities, it is necessary to consider the people who will be engaging in those activities. "If the user can't use it, it doesn't work." This quote by human-computer interaction and user experience expert, Dr. Susan M. Dray, illustrates the importance of considering end users' needs and abilities: If the product is not usable for the people it is intended for, it has no real value whatsoever. This notion also applies to the design of iVLEs, where it is paramount to consider the learners who are intended to benefit from the learning environment.

Below, we review different characteristics that can have a large impact on the effectiveness of iVLEs.

The first thing we suggest to consider is whether the learners have any disabilities that need to be taken into consideration in the design of iVLEs. This can be regarded as *ethics by design*, where ethical aspects are integrated into the design process (Meacham & Shanley, 2022). Mott et al. (2019) suggest various ways that VR technologies can be designed to be accessible to people with disabilities. E.g., the learning material of iVLEs can be made accessible by enabling various representations of the same content (Mott et al., 2019): Closed captioning can allow people who are deaf to read the narrated material in a multimedia lesson, or color accessibility can allow people with color blindness to change the color combinations of elements in the iVLE. It is also conceivable that haptic rendering technologies will soon enable people who are blind to experience virtual 3D objects (Mott et al., 2019). Another significant area of accessibility for iVLEs is inclusive avatars. While learners with physical disabilities should not be forced to use any particular avatar, they should have the option to choose avatars that resemble their physical characteristics (Mott et al., 2019). Once the iVLE has been designed, it is possible to use the accessibility metric proposed by Thiel and Steed (2022), whereby five measures (Impulsiveness, Energy, Directness, Jerkiness, and Expansiveness) indicate the physical requirements of the simulation. In that way, impaired learners can judge whether they will be able to attend the virtual lesson.

Regardless of whether people have disabilities or not, it is important to consider the level of prior knowledge the learners possess. It is quite intuitive that learning interventions have a limited impact on people who already know the subject matter in advance. However, what if the learners possess domain expertise and want to learn new, advanced information within that domain? According to the expertise reversal principle in multimedia learning, there is an interaction effect between guided multimedia instruction and expertise, such that guidance benefits novices but harms experts (Kalyuga, 2022). In this context, guidance can be understood as the incorporation of instructional design principles derived from CTML. The expertise reversal happens as a consequence of the extra cognitive resources expended on processing the guidance rather than the learning material (Kalyuga, 2022). Therefore, assessments of prior knowledge are key in designing iVLEs. In reality, any learning intervention involving iVLEs will most likely involve people with different levels of expertise. A practicable solution would therefore be to design VLEs such that guidance can be added and removed according to the learner's needs.

In the same way as assessing prior knowledge is essential, it is also highly relevant to examine the learners' prior VR experience. Many authors cite research participants' lack of VR experience as a potential threat to internal validity due to the probable existence of novelty effects (i.e., people may pay special attention to media that are novel to them; Clark, 1983). A recent longitudinal VR study by Han et al. (2022) underscores the importance of being accustomed to VR technology in order to benefit from it, as all measures in the study, such as presence and enjoyment, increased over time. In terms of iVLE design, this implies that learners should have the option to become familiar with VR technology before trying the principal lesson. One way to achieve this would be to add an optional playground or tutorial at the beginning of the simulation, which displays basic VR functionality.

iVLE designers should also consider whether the learning environment is intended for individual learning or collaborative learning. In the case of computer-supported collaborative learning (CSCL), we suggest designing the environment according to the collaboration principle in multimedia learning: Collaborative learning is effective to the extent that the advantages associated with sharing the burden of information processing outweigh the costs associated with coordinating and regulating the group work (Janssen et al., 2022). The authors of the collaboration principle suggest a set of design guidelines focused on the learner, the team, the task, and the technological setup. We review the task and technological setup guidelines here, as those are most relevant for the development of iVLEs. We refer interested readers to Janssen et al. (2022) for a full exposition. When it comes to the learning tasks in collaborative learning environments, these should be sufficiently complex to justify the added mental effort caused by the group work (Janssen et al., 2022). This means that the level of difficulty of the lesson needs to be raised if the aim is collaboration. Moreover, the tasks should be designed to induce interdependence between group members; i.e., realization of the learning goals should be dependent on the input of each learner (Janssen et al., 2022). Finally, regarding the technological setup, collaboration scripts, scaffolds, and awareness tools can be used to facilitate effective collaboration (Janssen et al., 2022).

A final important factor to keep in mind when designing an iVLE is that of gender inclusivity. A recent book by journalist Caroline Criado Perez, *Invisible Women: Exposing Data Bias in a World Designed for Men*, draws attention to the fact that much of the modern world is built around men, putting women at a disadvantage, e.g., when it comes to car safety or smartphone use. According to the 2021 Developer Survey conducted by *Stack Overflow*, roughly nine out of ten software developers define themselves as men (Stack Overflow, 2021). Consequently, there is a risk that iVLEs unintentionally appeal mostly to men due to the fact that the majority of developers are men. To our knowledge, gender differences related to learning with iVLEs are an underexplored area. However, some studies find that women are more susceptible than men to discomfort or simulator sickness during the use of immersive VR (Grassini & Laumann, 2020). Stanney et al. (2020)

investigated the drivers of gender-based differences in the experience of simulator sickness and found that interpupillary distance non-fit was the main driver of those differences. Consequently, gender-inclusive design is an important aspect of iVLE development as well as VR hardware design.

Provide Appropriate Guidance

The final part of the iVLE design framework involves adding appropriate guidance to the lesson. We deliberately included this step as the final one, as the level and nature of the guidance will depend on the characteristics of the intended learners, such as their level of expertise or whether it is a single-player or multiplayer scenario.

Keeping the aforementioned expertise reversal principle in mind, if the learners are novices with regard to the learning topic, many of the principles proposed in CTML will be crucial for minimizing extraneous processing, managing essential processing, and fostering generative processing (Mayer, 2022). This, e.g., includes the temporal contiguity principle (i.e., better learning is achieved when words and corresponding graphics appear simultaneously rather than consecutively; Fiorella & Mayer, 2022a). Moreover, research shows that summarizing (Parong & Mayer, 2018) and signaling (Albus et al., 2021) are effective techniques in VR.

If the iVLE is designed to be used by multiple users, it is important to provide guidance in the form of CSCL scripts: Instructional prompts designed to elicit collaborative activities that promote deep learning (Vogel et al., 2017). This could, e.g., involve pair summarizing where two learners (listener and recaller) engage in summarizing, feedback, and joint elaboration, taking turns being the listener and recaller (King, 2007). The collaborative mapping principle would also be a useful collaborative feature whereby learners co-create a concept map (Adesope et al., 2022).

Worked Example

In the following, we discuss a worked example intended to illustrate how the iVLE design framework could apply to an existing immersive VR learning experience. Specifically, we employ a collaborative generative activity version of The Body VR: Journey Inside a Cell (The Body VR, 2016), which has been used in prior immersive VR research (Petersen et al., 2023), and teaches about the function and structural layout of cells.

Always Ask, "Why Immersive VR?"

First, we need to determine whether the topic of the lesson is suitable for teaching in immersive VR. Recall that this depends on the educational argument, and whether it would be impossible, expensive, dangerous, or counterproductive to receive the same lesson in real life. Since it would be impossible to be miniaturized and travel to the inside of a cell in real life, the topic of the lesson is suitable for immersive VR. It could also be argued that experiencing cells firsthand would be an excellent trigger for student interest.

Integrate Immersive VR into an Educational Intervention

Next, we need to determine the intended learning outcomes, separate the learning content into conceptualization, construction, and dialogue stages, determine suitable learning activities for each stage, and match these with the unique characteristics of immersive VR. The overall intended learning outcome is an understanding of the function and structural layout of cells. In the conceptualization stage, we want to provide a basic foundation of knowledge about cells. This can be achieved by sending learners on a narrated tour through the human body while showing them 3D models of the different cell parts and explaining their basic functionality. In the construction stage, we want to expose the learners to a clearly defined and interactive task that extends their initial understanding. This can be achieved by prompting students to construct a 3D model of a cell, placing the cell parts in their correct location, as well as asking students to explore how viruses enter our cells and replicate by simulating a virus attack step by step. In the dialogue stage, we want the learners to test their understanding via discussion with others. This can be achieved by prompting learners to explain the learning material to another learner in VR who provides feedback on potential errors or omissions. Finally, we want to make sure that the learning tasks build on immersion, interaction, and embodiment. E.g., the learner should be able to pick up cell parts and watch how the images change based on the angle of view. Moreover, the learner should be represented by a virtual body of their own choice.

Design with the User in Mind

Next, we need to adapt the iVLE to the people who are intended to learn from it. E.g., in the case of hearing-impaired learners, an option to include subtitles along with the narrations should be available. Moreover, we need to make sure the learning material is at a sufficient level of difficulty, which depends on the learners' prior knowledge—if the iVLE is intended for collaborative learning, the tasks might need to be made more challenging. If the learners have limited VR experience, a VR tutorial is necessary. Finally, it is paramount to make sure that the iVLE is gender-inclusive, and does not accidentally appeal mostly to one gender. In general, continual user testing is a practical method for ensuring that the iVLE is usable by the intended learners.

Provide Appropriate Guidance

Finally, we need to integrate appropriate guidance into the lesson, preferably such that it can be added or removed depending on the learners' level of expertise. One suggestion could be to add pre-training to the lesson, such that the learners are exposed to the names and characteristics of the main concepts beforehand (e.g., showing a cross section of a cell with labeled cell parts). Another suggestion would be to add cues to the lesson that guide the learners' attention to relevant elements in the learning material in accordance with the signaling principle.

Research Agenda

We conclude this chapter by briefly proposing a research agenda focused on the aspects of iVLE research we consider the most fruitful for the further development of the field. To begin with, an important next step for research on learning with immersive technology is to involve a broader range of learners. Much of the cited research in this chapter was conducted with university students residing in the Western World, otherwise known as Western, Educated, Industrialized, Rich, and Democratic (WEIRD) participants. However, as argued by Henrich et al. (2010), this poses a challenge to the understanding of human psychology and behavior since most of the world's population is not WEIRD. Until more diverse iVLE studies surface, we should be careful about making generalizations about how people learn from VR or similar immersive technologies. Makransky and Klingenberg (2022) recently carried out such a study with a non-WEIRD sample, and found evidence for the value of using immersive VR for safety training.

Collaborative learning with other people via avatars is another significant area of research for the near future due to the advent of the Metaverse. Currently, a limited amount of research has been done regarding collaboration in VR (see Han et al. (2022) for a literature review), and knowledge about collaborative learning in VR is scarce. Much is yet to be discovered regarding how VR technology can enable and, possibly, enhance CSCL via its unique affordances. According to the theoretical framework proposed by Kreijns (2013), social interaction influences individual and group learning in CSCL environments. Social interaction, in turn, is influenced by factors such as social presence and sociability, which VR can facilitate to a high degree, thereby suggesting a promising role for immersive VR in collaborative learning.

Evidence-Based Practice Recommendations

- As a tool for learning, immersive VR is suitable for conceptual and spatial knowledge outcomes as well as behavioral transfer—it is not ideal for learning factual knowledge.
- When designing a VR lesson, it is useful to divide it into three interconnected stages: conceptualization (overview of key concepts), construction (deepening of understanding), and dialogue (evaluating and consolidating understanding).
- VR learning activities should be designed such that they leverage the immersion, interaction, and embodiment offered by these systems.
- It is essential to build VR lessons with the learner and their specific needs and abilities in mind (e.g., disabilities or prior knowledge).
- Adding flexible guidance to VR lessons in the form of instructional design principles can accommodate learners with varying levels of expertise.

References

Adesope, O. O., Nesbit, J. C., & Sundararajan, N. (2022). The mapping principle in multimedia learning. In R. E. Mayer & L. Fiorella (Eds.), *The Cambridge handbook of multimedia learning* (3rd ed., pp. 351–359). Cambridge University Press.

Albus, P., Vogt, A., & Seufert, T. (2021). Signaling in virtual reality influences learning outcome and cognitive load. *Computers and Education, 166*. https://doi.org/10.1016/j.compedu.2021.104154

Baceviciute, S., Cordoba, A. L., Wismer, P., Jensen, T. V., Klausen, M., & Makransky, G. (2022). Investigating the value of immersive virtual reality tools for organizational training: An applied international study in the biotech industry. *Journal of Computer Assisted Learning, 38*(2), 470–487. https://doi.org/10.1111/jcal.12630

Bailenson, J. (2018). *Experience on demand: What virtual reality is, how it works, and what it can do.* Norton & Company.

Bower, M. (2008). Affordance analysis – matching learning tasks with learning technologies. *Educational Media International, 45*(1), 3–15. https://doi.org/10.1080/09523980701847115

Chi, M. T. H., & Wylie, R. (2014). The ICAP framework: Linking cognitive engagement to active learning outcomes. *Educational Psychologist, 49*(4), 219–243. https://doi.org/10.1080/00461520.2014.965823

Clark, R. E. (1983). Reconsidering research on learning from media. *Review of Educational Research, 53*(4), 445–459. https://doi.org/10.2307/1170217

Coban, M., Bolat, Y. I., & Goksu, I. (2022). The potential of immersive virtual reality to enhance learning: A meta-analysis. *Educational Research Review, 36*. https://doi.org/10.1016/j.edurev.2022.100452

Dalgarno, B., & Lee, M. J. W. (2010). What are the learning affordances of 3-D virtual environments? *British Journal of Educational Technology, 41*(1), 10–32. https://doi.org/10.1111/j.1467-8535.2009.01038.x

Fiorella, L., & Mayer, R. E. (2022a). Principles for reducing extraneous processing in multimedia learning. In R. E. Mayer & L. Fiorella (Eds.), *The Cambridge handbook of multimedia learning* (3rd ed., pp. 185–198). Cambridge University Press.

Fiorella, L., & Mayer, R. E. (2022b). The generative activity principle in multimedia learning. In R. E. Mayer & L. Fiorella (Eds.), *The Cambridge handbook of multimedia learning* (3rd ed., pp. 339–350). Cambridge University Press.

Foglia, L., & Wilson, R. A. (2013). Embodied cognition. *WIREs Cognitive Science*, 4, 319–325. https://doi.org/10.1002/wcs.1226

Fowler, C. (2015). Virtual reality and learning: Where is the pedagogy? *British Journal of Educational Technology*, 46(2), 412–422. https://doi.org/10.1111/bjet.12135

Grassini, S., & Laumann, K. (2020). Are modern head-mounted displays sexist? A systematic review on gender differences in HMD-mediated virtual reality. *Frontiers in Psychology*, 11. https://doi.org/10.3389/fpsyg.2020.01604

Han, E., Miller, M. R., Ram, N., Nowak, K. L., & Bailenson, J. N. (2022). Understanding group behavior in virtual reality: A large-scale, longitudinal study in the metaverse. *72nd Annual International Communication Association Conference*. https://ssrn.com/abstract=4110154

Henrich, J., Heine, S. J., & Norenzayan, A. (2010). Most people are not WEIRD. *Nature*, 466, 29. https://doi.org/10.1038/466029a

Hidi, S., & Renninger, K. A. (2006). The four-phase model of interest development. *Educational Psychologist*, 41(2), 111–127. https://doi.org/10.1207/s15326985ep4102_4

Janssen, J., Kirschner, F., & Kirschner, P. A. (2022). The collaboration principle in multimedia learning. In R. E. Mayer & L. Fiorella (Eds.), *The Cambridge handbook of multimedia learning* (3rd ed., pp. 304–312). Cambridge University Press.

Johnson-Glenberg, M. (2018). Immersive VR and education: Embodied design principles that include gesture and hand controls. *Frontiers in Robotics and AI*, 5(81), 1–19. https://doi.org/10.3389/frobt.2018.00081

Kalyuga, S. (2022). The expertise reversal principle in multimedia learning. In L. Fiorella & R. E. Mayer (Eds.), *The Cambridge handbook of multimedia learning* (3rd ed., pp. 171–182). Cambridge University Press. https://doi.org/10.1017/9781108894333.017

King, A. (2007). Scripting collaborative learning processes: A cognitive perspective. In F. Fischer, I. Kollar, H. Mandl, & J. M. Haake (Eds.), *Scripting computer-supported collaborative learning: Cognitive, computational and educational perspectives* (pp. 13–37). Springer. https://doi.org/10.1007/978-0-387-36949-5_2

Klingenberg, S., Jørgensen, M., Dandanell, G., Skriver, K., Mottelson, A., & Makransky, G. (2020). Investigating the effect of teaching as a general learning strategy when learning through desktop and immersive VR: A media and methods experiment. *British Journal of Educational Technology*, 51(6), 2115–2138.

Kreijns, K., Kirschner, P. A., & Vermeulen, M. (2013). Social aspects of CSCL environments: A research framework. *Educational Psychologist*, 48(4), 229–242. https://doi.org/10.1080/00461520.2012.750225

Makransky, G. (2022). The immersion principle in multimedia learning. In R. E. Mayer & L. Fiorella (Eds.), *The Cambridge handbook of multimedia learning* (3rd ed., pp. 296–303). Cambridge University Press.

Makransky, G., Andreasen, N. K., Baceviciute, S., & Mayer, R. E. (2021). Immersive virtual reality increases liking but not learning with a science simulation and generative learning strategies promote learning in immersive virtual reality. *Journal of Educational Psychology*, 113(4), 719–735. https://doi.org/10.1037/edu0000473

Makransky, G., Borre-Gude, S., & Mayer, R. E. (2019). Motivational and cognitive benefits of training in immersive virtual reality based on multiple assessments. *Journal of Computer Assisted Learning*, 35(6), 691–707.

Makransky, G., & Klingenberg, S. (2022). Virtual reality enhances safety training in the maritime industry: An organizational training experiment with a non-WEIRD sample. *Journal of Computer Assisted Learning, 38*(4), 1127–1140. https://doi. org/10.1111/jcal.12670

Makransky, G., & Mayer, R. E. (2022). Benefits of taking a virtual field trip in immersive virtual reality: Evidence for the immersion principle in multimedia learning. *Educational Psychology Review.* https://doi.org/10.1007/s10648-022-09675-4

Makransky, G., & Petersen, G. B. (2021). The cognitive affective model of immersive learning (CAMIL): A theoretical research-based model of learning in immersive virtual reality. *Educational Psychology Review.* https://doi.org/10.1007/s10648-020-09586-2

Makransky, G., Terkildsen, T. S., & Mayer, R. E. (2019). Adding immersive virtual reality to a science lab simulation causes more presence but less learning. *Learning and Instruction, 60,* 225–236. https://doi.org/10.1016/j.learninstruc.2017.12.007

Mayer, R. E. (2022). Cognitive theory of multimedia learning. In R. E. Mayer & L. Fiorella (Eds.), *The Cambridge handbook of multimedia learning* (3rd ed., pp. 57–72). Cambridge University Press.

Mayes, J. T., & Fowler, C. J. (1999). Learning technology and usability: A framework for understanding courseware. *Interacting with Computers, 11*(5), 485–497. https://doi.org/10.1016/S0953-5438(98)00065-4

Meacham, D., & Shanley, D. (2022). Getting real about ethics in virtual environments. *Striving for Social Harmony in XR.* https://www.youtube.com/watch?v= WFgDk5oqCoo

Meyer, O. A., Omdahl, M. K., & Makransky, G. (2019). Investigating the effect of pre-training when learning through immersive virtual reality and video: A media and methods experiment. *Computers & Education, 140,* 1–17. https://doi. org/10.1016/J.COMPEDU.2019.103603

Mikropoulos, T. A., & Natsis, A. (2011). Educational virtual environments: A ten-year review of empirical research (1999–2009). *Computers & Education, 56*(3), 769–780. https://doi.org/10.1016/j.compedu.2010.10.020

Moreno, R., & Mayer, R. (2007). Interactive multimodal learning environments. *Educational Psychology Review, 19,* 309–326. https://doi.org/10.1007/s10648-007-9047-2

Mott, M., Cutrell, E., Gonzalez Franco, M., Holz, C., Ofek, E., Stoakley, R., & Ringel Morris, M. (2019). Accessible by design: An opportunity for virtual reality. *Adjunct Proceedings of the 2019 IEEE International Symposium on Mixed and Augmented Reality, ISMAR-Adjunct 2019* (pp. 451–454). https://doi.org/10.1109/ISMAR-Adjunct.2019.00122

O'Donnell, A. M. (2012). Constructivism. In K. R. Harris, S. Graham, T. Urdan, C. B. McCormick, G. M. Sinatra, & J. Sweller (Eds.), *APA educational pyschology handbook, Vol. 1: Theories, constructs, and critical issues* (pp. 61–84). American Psychological Association. https://doi.org/10.1037/13273-000

Parong, J. (2022). Multimedia learning in virtual and mixed reality. In L. Fiorella & R. E. Mayer (Eds.), *The Cambridge handbook of multimedia learning* (3rd ed., pp. 498–509). Cambridge University Press. https://doi.org/10.1017/9781108894333.051

Parong, J., & Mayer, R. E. (2018). Learning science in immersive virtual reality. *Journal of Educational Psychology, 110*(6), 785–797. https://doi.org/10.1037/edu0000241

Petersen, G. B., Klingenberg, S., & Makransky, G. (2022). Pipetting in virtual reality can predict real-life pipetting performance. *Technology, Mind, and Behavior, 3*(3). https://doi.org/10.1037/tmb0000076

Petersen, G. B., Klingenberg, S., Mayer, R. E., & Makransky, G. (2020). The virtual field trip: Investigating how to optimize immersive virtual learning in climate change education. *British Journal of Educational Technology, 51*(6), 2098–2114. https://doi.org/10.1111/bjet.12991

Petersen, G. B., Petakis, G., & Makransky, G. (2022). A study of how immersion and interactivity drive VR learning. *Computers & Education, 179*, 1–16. https://doi.org/10.1016/j.compedu.2021.104429

Petersen, G. B., Stenberdt, V., Mayer, R. E., & Makransky, G. (2023). Collaborative generative learning activities in immersive virtual reality increase learning. *Computers & Education, 207*. https://doi.org/10.1016/j.compedu.2023.104931

Pimentel, D., Fauville, G., Frazier, K., McGivney, E., Rosas, S., & Woolsey, E. (2022). *An introduction to learning in the Metaverse*. Meridian Treehouse. https://www.meridiantreehouse.com/metaverse-education-guide

Plechatá, A., Morton, T., Perez-Cueto, F. J. A., & Makransky, G. (2022). A randomized trial testing the effectiveness of virtual reality as a tool for pro-environmental dietary change. *Scientific Reports*. https://doi.org/10.21203/rs.3.rs-1624509/v1

Radianti, J., Majchrzak, T. A., Fromm, J., & Wohlgenannt, I. (2020). A systematic review of immersive virtual reality applications for higher education: Design elements, lessons learned, and research agenda. *Computers & Education, 147*. https://doi.org/10.1016/j.compedu.2019.103778

Sanders, M., & George, A. (2017). Viewing the changing world of educational technology from a different perspective: Present realities, past lessons, and future possibilities. *Education and Information Technologies, 22*(6), 2915–2933. https://doi.org/10.1007/s10639-017-9604-3

Scavarelli, A., Arya, A., & Teather, R. J. (2021). Virtual reality and augmented reality in social learning spaces: A literature review. *Virtual Reality, 25*(1), 257–277. https://doi.org/10.1007/s10055-020-00444-8

Schneider, S., Beege, M., Nebel, S., Schnaubert, L., & Rey, G. D. (2022). The cognitive-affective-social theory of learning in digital environments (CASTLE). *Educational Psychology Review, 34*, 1–38. https://doi.org/10.1007/s10648-021-09626-5

Slater, M. (2009). Place illusion and plausibility can lead to realistic behaviour in immersive virtual environments. *Philosophical Transactions of the Royal Society B: Biological Sciences, 364*, 3549–3557. https://doi.org/10.1098/rstb.2009.0138

Slater, M. (2017). Implicit learning through embodiment in immersive virtual reality. In D. Liu, C. Dede, R. Huang, & J. Richards (Eds.), *Virtual, augmented, and mixed realities in education* (pp. 19–33). Springer. https://doi.org/10.1007/978-981-10-5490-7_2

Slater, M., Banakou, D., Beacco, A., Gallego, J., Macia-Varela, F., & Oliva, R. (2022). A separate reality: An update on place illusion and plausibility in virtual reality. *Frontiers in Virtual Reality, 3*. https://doi.org/10.3389/frvir.2022.914392

Stack Overflow. (2021). *2021 developer survey*. https://insights.stackoverflow.com/survey/2021#methodology-general

Stanney, K., Fidopiastis, C., & Foster, L. (2020). Virtual reality is sexist: But it does not have to be. *Frontiers in Robotics and AI, 7*(4). https://doi.org/10.3389/frobt.2020.00004

The Body VR. (2016). *The Body VR: Journey inside a cell – 360 gameplay*. https://www.youtube.com/watch?v=9zTsDXMyBEY

Thiel, F. J., & Steed, A. (2022). Developing an accessibility metric for VR games based on motion data captured under game conditions. *Frontiers in Virtual Reality, 3*. https://doi.org/10.3389/frvir.2022.909357

Ventura, S., Badenes-Ribera, L., Herrero, R., Cebolla, A., Galiana, L., & Banõs, R. (2020). Virtual reality as a medium to elicit empathy: A meta-analysis. *Cyberpsychology, Behavior, and Social Networking, 23*(10), 667–676. https://doi.org/10.1089/cyber.2019.0681

Villena-Taranilla, R., Tirado-Olivares, S., Cózar-Gutiérrez, R., & González-Calero, J. A. (2022). Effects of virtual reality on learning outcomes in K-6 education: A meta-analysis. *Educational Research Review, 35*. https://doi.org/10.1016/j.edurev.2022.100434

Vogel, F., Wecker, C., Kollar, I., & Fischer, F. (2017). Socio-cognitive scaffolding with computer-supported collaboration scripts: A meta-analysis. *Educational Psychology Review, 29*, 477–511. https://doi.org/10.1007/s10648-016-9361-7

Wilson, A. L. (1993). The promise of situated cognition. *New Directions for Adult and Continuing Education, 1993*(57), 71–79. https://doi.org/10.1002/ace.36719935709

Wu, B., Yu, X., & Gu, X. (2020). Effectiveness of immersive virtual reality using head-mounted displays on learning performance: A meta-analysis. *British Journal of Educational Technology, 51*(6), 1991–2005. https://doi.org/10.1111/bjet.13023

PART V

Game-Based and Sensor-Based Learning in Digital Environments

10

EFFECTIVENESS OF GAMIFICATION IN EDUCATION

Ruben Schlag, Michael Sailer, Daniel Tolks,
Manuel Ninaus and Maximilian Sailer

Gamification – using game elements to foster motivation

Motivation has long been identified as an essential factor in education. Among the aspects investigated in recent research on motivation in education are interest and intrinsic motivation (Wigfield et al., 2019). One way to reframe intrinsic motivation is to describe it as "fun" (Mitchell et al., 2020). While fun is difficult to define scientifically (Bisson & Luckner, 1996), the term is closely linked to games (Prensky, 2001). More precisely, certain characteristics of games can engage users by providing them with positive experiences (Prensky, 2001). This engagement can manifest as a mental state of intense concentration called "flow", during which players can achieve appreciable performance and pleasure (Csikszentmihalyi, 1992).

The video game industry in particular has displayed astonishing growth over the last 50 years. As such, the potential for video games to positively influence motivation and behavior has been of increasing interest in empirical research. Studies have shown that different aspects of video games affect users' motivation differently (Ryan et al., 2006). Accordingly, individual game elements have been used for decades as motivational affordances to enhance products and services (Hamari et al., 2014). While various terms have been used to describe this or similar processes (e.g., playfulness, gamefulness, gameful design, playful interaction design), "gamification" has been the most pervasive in recent empirical research. Deterding et al. (2011) define it as "the use of game design elements in non-game contexts" (p. 2), marking a keystone understanding of the concept. Gamification has since been deployed in various fields and disciplines such as business (Rocha et al., 2019) and tourism (Xu et al., 2017) or to promote well-being (Tolks et al., 2019).

DOI: 10.4324/9781003386131-15

However, the most common theme in recent gamification studies has been education (Kasurinen & Knutas, 2018). A list of commonly used game elements in education is provided in Section "Game elements used in education". Subsequently, a common theoretical framework of gamification application and research in education will be outlined (Section "Theoretical framework used in gamification (research)"). In order to reach conclusions about the effectiveness of gamification in education, the findings of several meta-analyses will be discussed in Section "Effects and moderating factors of gamification in education" before closing this chapter with practical implications.

Game elements used in education

Domain-specific taxonomies of game elements have been established (e.g., Bedwell et al., 2012 for education). However, only some of these elements have been implemented in educational settings. The nomenclature may vary, with terms like "game characteristic" (Prensky, 2001), "game design element" (Deterding et al., 2011) and "game attribute" (Bedwell et al., 2012). Following Landers (2015, see Section "Theory of gamified learning"), we will hereinafter use the term "game element". Below, we provide a collection of game elements that have been commonly used in education and examined in empirical research. This list is not meant to be exhaustive. We will also show how these elements might interlink in practice.

- **Points**
  Points are perhaps the simplest form of gamification. They constitute a basic form of immediate feedback to the user. Points might serve as a reward for completing tasks and illustrate progress in the learning process that might otherwise be difficult to grasp (Werbach & Hunter, 2012). As an extension of *point* systems, progress bars offer graphical information on learners' performance in relation to their previous accomplishments (Sailer et al., 2014). They can supplement *level-ups* by displaying certain thresholds of points or specific *quests* needed in order to advance. Reaching a certain number of points might award learners a *badge*. They can also act as a measure of social competition if the other learners' number of points is visible (*leaderboards*).
- **Leaderboards and rankings**
  Leaderboards and rankings allow the direct comparisons of learners' progress, representing a form of *competition*. This can be measured with *points*. There are absolute and relative types of leaderboards. The former type displays all users and their scores, while the latter only shows an individual user's score in relation to those directly above or below them (Ortiz-Rojas et al., 2019). Furthermore, leaderboards can be designed as public or anonymous. With public leaderboards, a higher position may lead to

increased motivation, while for anonymous ones, a higher position tends to be connected to better cognitive learning outcomes (Bai et al., 2021).

- **Badges and achievements**
Badges and achievements are (semi-)permanent measures of progress that commemorate passing a specific task or reaching a certain goal. Awards such as these are thought to resemble classic goal-setting (Groening & Binnewies, 2019); that is, they don't necessarily act as rewards on their own. Instead, they point learners in the correct direction, with the fun and interest of goal-seeking being central to these game elements. They are likely more effective when they are designed to occur in low quantities and are more difficult to obtain (Groening & Binnewies, 2019).

- **(Timed) Quests, missions, and tasks**
Quests, missions, and tasks are ways of reframing learning activities, which facilitate more personal experiences (Kim et al., 2018). Furthermore, a time limit might be placed on such activities, or additional content might be locked behind such tasks. Learners might also have to *collaborate* in order to complete a quest ("communal discovery"; Kim et al., 2018). Quests could also be framed diegetically (i.e., "in-universe") via *storytelling*. Successful and/or particularly quick completion of such a task might earn the learner a *badge*.

- **Avatars**
Avatars are a virtual representation of an individual learner (Kim et al., 2018). They can be premade characters or "copies" of the users (Kapp, 2012). They can serve as distinguishing features for learners and facilitate their swapping into another role (Werbach & Hunter, 2012). Avatars might be customizable in order to enhance their abilities or the learner's sense of identification with that avatar (Kim et al., 2018).

- **Storytelling**
The framing and context of the narrative can inject meaning into otherwise mundane scenarios and keep users engaged. It is especially useful when a real-world situation is perceived as boring and/or the narrative elements match personal interests. However, findings from the field of game-based learning suggest that the depth and complexity of narrative elements should be kept low (Clark et al., 2016).

- **Level-ups**
A level-up can be achieved by reaching certain thresholds of *points* or accomplishing certain *quests, missions, or tasks*. The ability to gain a level usually denotes an increase in power or skill. This can be viewed as an alternative to personal progression in the form of *badges*, instead providing a linear continuum that users can ascend. Adding powers or increasing attributes, as in computer games, isn't seamlessly transitioned into education. Nevertheless, level-ups need to provide some form of perceived benefit to be effective (Bai et al., 2020).

- **Competition and collaboration**
  Competition and collaboration can be seen as forms of interpersonal or social interaction (Bedwell et al., 2012). Competition means learners compete for *points, badges,* or *level*-ups, while collaboration occurs when peers work together to achieve a shared objective (Ho et al., 2021). Both forms of interaction may be combined when teams compete against each other. Teammates can promote conflict, competition, or cooperation (Kapp, 2012). Team-based learning can foster motivation and increased performance, with smaller groups being generally more effective (Swanson et al., 2017). A common level of knowledge is key to any competitive or collaborative task, especially for teams, and such tasks should be started simultaneously (Landers & Landers, 2015).

There has long been criticism leveled at the "pointlessness" of points and badges (Werbach & Hunter 2012, p. 70). Research has shown the ubiquity of PBLs in gamified education (Bai et al., 2020). This might be due to their simplicity and ease of implementation and is often called "pointification" (Subhash & Cudney, 2018). This is also exacerbated by the fact that PBLs are often constituent parts of more complex game elements. For example, in order to facilitate a leveling system, *points* are usually needed to show a current value that students must reach in order to gain a *level-up*. Applications such as online quiz tools often come "pre-loaded" with these mechanics, as well. For instance, Kahoot! incorporates *points, leaderboards,* and *timed challenges* in its design, among others. However, recent research has found varying effects of leaderboards, depending on their design and the learners' performance, for example (Bai et al., 2021). Altogether, evidence suggests a) the development and implementation of new game elements (Zainuddin et al., 2020) and b) moving the focus of future investigations to more substantial, less researched forms of gamification in education in order to advance the field. To that end, a solid theoretical foundation and evidence-based teaching practices are of paramount importance.

Theoretical framework used in gamification (research)

In a meta-review, Krath et al. (2021) identified 118 different theories used for empirical research on gamification and game-based learning. A collection of the most prevalent can be found in Table 10.1. While game-based learning also encompasses the use of full-fledged games, gamification draws on some of their elements instead, as previously mentioned. Their findings illustrate the variety of theories applied in gamification research and the pervasiveness of gamification across various domains.

There is currently no common or agreed-upon integrated theory of gamification. By the numbers, self-determination theory serves as the most

TABLE 10.1 Prevalent theories in research of gamification, serious games, and game-based learning by type of learning outcome

Affective and motivational outcomes	Behavioral outcomes	Cognitive outcomes
• Self-determination theory	• Technology acceptance model	• Experiential learning theory
• Flow theory	• Theory of planned behavior	• Constructivist learning theory
• ARCS model	• Reinforcement theory	• Cognitive load theory
• Goal-setting theory	• Transtheoretical model of behavior change	• Social cognitive theory
• Self-efficacy theory	• Theory of reasoned action	• Situated learning theory
• Social comparison theory	• Activity theory	• Sociocultural theory of cognitive development
• Achievement goal theory		• Social learning theory
		• Multimedia learning theory

Note: This table shows the most-used theories in research of gamification, serious games, and game-based learning relating to affective and motivational, behavioral, and cognitive learning outcomes. Excerpt reprinted with permission from "Revealing the theoretical basis of gamification: A systematic review and analysis of theory in research on gamification, serious games and game-based learning" by J. Krath, L. Schürmann, and H. F. O. von Korflesch, 2021, *Computers in Human Behavior, 125*, Article 106963.

important foundation of gamification research, being the most commonly used regarding affect and motivation (Krath et al., 2021). After elaborating on this key theory, we will highlight the two processes through which gamification can influence learning outcomes, according to Landers' theory of gamified learning (2015).

Self-determination theory

The connection between games and their potential to facilitate intrinsic motivation has long been made (Malone, 1981). Applying motivational elements to learning activities can affect the learning process positively (Cordova & Lepper, 1996). Since then, several studies have established a relationship between game elements and self-determination theory (Ryan & Deci, 2000; Mekler et al., 2017; Zainuddin et al., 2020). Three psychological needs that influence human behavior are defined by this theory: The need for autonomy, the need for competence, and the need for social relatedness (Ryan & Deci, 2000). For instance, teaching methods that support learners' autonomy can lead to increased effort applied to the learning process and can sustain

TABLE 10.2 Basic psychological needs according to self-determination theory and supporting game elements

Psychological need	Supporting game elements
Competence	• Points • Badges/achievements • Leaderboards/rankings • (Timed) Quests, missions, tasks • Level-ups
Autonomy	• Badges/achievements • (Timed) Quests, missions, tasks • Avatars • Storytelling
Social relatedness	• Badges/achievements • Leaderboards • Storytelling • Competition/collaboration

Note: This table shows three basic psychological needs that are matched with various gamification elements that can foster them. Adapted with permission from "Gamification als didaktisches Mittel in der Hochschulbildung" by D. Tolks and M. Sailer, 2021, *Digitalisierung in Studium und Lehre gemeinsam gestalten,* p. 517.

attention on the part of students (Baker & Goodboy, 2019). Self-determination is described as an active process. With this in mind, gamification can result in positive effects on learning (Ryan & Deci, 2000). Table 10.2 matches the game elements discussed in Section "Game elements used in education" with the basic psychological needs they can support (Sailer et al., 2017; Zainuddin et al., 2020).

As outlined, self-determination theory explains how learners' attitudes and behaviors might be positively influenced through the use of game elements. To further delineate how learning outcomes can be affected through gamification, the theory of gamified learning is showcased in the following section.

Theory of gamified learning

Drawing on the game element taxonomy of Bedwell et al. (2012), Landers (2015) introduced four components that describe the relationship between gamification and learning: (1) game elements, (2) instructional content, (3) behavior/attitude, and (4) learning outcomes. See Figure 10.1 for the processes in which gamification can affect learning outcomes.

By influencing behaviors and attitudes that, in turn, affect learning outcomes, gamification can improve existing instruction through a mediating

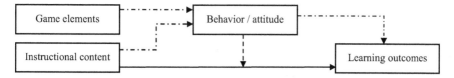

FIGURE 10.1   Theory of gamified learning.

Note: This figure shows the relationships between instructional content, learning outcomes, behavior/attitude, and game elements according to the theory of gamified learning. Directional arrows indicate theorized paths of causality. Dash–dot lines denote mediating processes. The dash line denotes a moderating process. The solid line denotes a direct influence. Adapted with permission from "Developing a theory of gamified learning: Linking serious games and gamification of learning" by R. N. Landers, 2015, *Simulation & Gaming*, *45*(6), p. 760.

process. This process has been supported empirically (Landers & Landers, 2015; Sailer & Sailer, 2020). Concurrently, behaviors and attitudes work as a moderating variable on the effect of instructional content on learning outcomes (Landers, 2015). This model illustrates that, in order for gamification in education to be effective, it cannot be separated from the instructional content. This is because learning outcomes are directly and causally influenced by effective learning materials and teaching tools. As a result, gamification cannot replace instruction. Instead, its goal is to further enhance instruction that is already effective by itself (Landers, 2015). This further means that, in order to evaluate gamified learning, research designs that deliberately target interactions between the variables described in Landers' model are needed.

To identify the beneficial behaviors that gamification can support, we draw on Chi and Wylie's (2014) taxonomy of learning activities. In the ICAP framework, they differentiate four modes of engagement: Interactive, constructive, active, and passive. Higher levels of student engagement are assumed to relate to higher levels of cognitive activity (Chi et al., 2018). It should be noted that, in practice, the design of constructive and interactive learning activities can be difficult (Ha et al., 2020). However, the motivating potential of game elements (Ryan et al., 2006) can be used to facilitate these higher modes of engagement. For example, interactive group discussions might be framed through storytelling and/or as timed, competitive missions. Meanwhile, the reward for the successful completion of the mission in the form of badges can be tied to especially fruitful collaboration. No matter the implementation, the instructional content should be relevant to the desired learning outcomes for this framework to be most effective (Chi & Wylie, 2014). This is in line with Landers' (2015) theory, as shown above. While the ICAP framework takes a probabilistic approach, in that higher levels of activity are *more likely* to lead to improved cognitive activity (Chi & Wylie, 2014), it illustrates how gamification can foster active learning (Prince, 2004).

Effects and moderating factors of gamification in education

The application and research of gamification have spanned widely across domains, with extensive theoretical approaches (see Section "Theoretical framework used in gamification (research)") and a defragmented knowledge base (Schmidt-Kraepelin et al., 2018). Still, the most pressing research issue currently is to collect evidence on the practical applications of gamification (Kasurinen & Knutas, 2018). Despite an overall maturation of gamification research (Nacke & Deterding, 2017), many questions remain. In order to shed light on the overall effects of gamification in education, we will discuss the results of four select, recent meta-analyses that also demonstrated moderating effects on gamification and learning (see Table 10.3). All of them showed significant, small to medium positive overall effects of gamification

TABLE 10.3 Selection of meta-analyses on the effects of gamification on learning, their focused learning outcome(s), and reported effect sizes of gamification on said learning outcomes

Meta-analysis	Focus	Effect(s) of gamification on learning outcomes
• Sailer and Homner (2020)	• Cognitive learning outcomes • Affective/motivational learning outcomes • Behavioral learning outcomes	• $g = 0.49$, 95% CI [.30, .69], $k = 19$, $N = 1686$ (cognitive outcomes) • $g = 0.36$, 95% CI [.18, .54], $k = 16$, $N = 2246$ (motivational outcomes) • $g = 0.25$, 95% CI [.04, .46], $k = 9$, $N = 951$ (behavioral outcomes)
• Bai et al. (2020)	• Cognitive learning outcomes • Learners' attitudes	• $g = 0.504$, 95% CI [.284–.723], $N = 3202$ (cognitive outcomes) • Attitudes were measured qualitatively
• Huang et al. (2020)	• Cognitive learning outcomes	• $g = 0.464$, 95% CI [.244, .684], $N = 3083$
• Ritzhaupt et al. (2021)	• Affective/motivational learning outcomes • Behavioral learning outcomes	• $g = 0.574$, 95% CI [.384, .764], $N = 1974$ (affective/motivational outcomes) • $g = 0.740$, 95% CI [.465, 1.014], $N = 1596$ (behavioral outcomes)

Note: This table names four recent meta-analyses on the effects of gamification on learning. Their respective focus on affective/motivational, behavioral, and/or cognitive learning outcomes is identified. Overall effect sizes of gamification on learning outcomes reported in each meta-analysis are provided.

or game elements on learning outcomes. This range of effect sizes aligns with the findings from other meta-analyses on the subject that either found no moderating effects or focused on only a few specific game elements (Yildirim & Şen, 2019; Vermeir et al., 2020; Kim & Castelli, 2021).

Sailer and Homner (2020) performed one of the first comprehensive meta-analyses on gamification and learning, differentiating between cognitive, affective/motivational, and behavioral learning outcomes. Bai et al. (2020) supplemented their investigation of gamification and cognitive learning outcomes with a synthesis of data from 32 qualitative studies. In contrast to the previous works, the related meta-analyses of Huang et al. (2020) and Ritzhaupt et al. (2021) focused on individual game elements and their effects on cognitive, affective/motivational, and behavioral learning outcomes, respectively. The selected works found contextual, situational, and methodological moderators that will be illustrated in the following section and are shown in Table 10.4. Afterwards, the analyses' results will be discussed.

TABLE 10.4 Moderating factors of gamification on learning

Meta-analysis	Significant moderating factors found (excerpt)
Sailer and Homner (2020)	• Inclusion of game fiction (in favor of presence for behavioral learning outcomes) • Social interaction (in favor of presence for behavioral learning outcomes) • Period of time (motivational learning outcomes) • Research context (cognitive learning outcomes) • Randomization (motivational learning outcomes)
Bai et al. (2020)	• Period of time
Huang et al. (2020)	• Leaderboards (in favor of absence) • Collaboration (in favor of presence) • Competition (in favor of absence) • Quests/missions/modules (in favor of presence) • Type of publication
Ritzhaupt et al. (2021)	• Competition (in favor of presence for effective learning outcomes) • Non-linear navigation (in favor of presence for behavioral learning outcomes) • Adaptivity/personalization (in favor of absence for behavioral learning outcomes) • Narrative/storytelling (in favor of absence for behavioral learning outcomes) • Publication bias

Note: This table lists all factors found by four recent analyses that significantly moderated the effect of gamification on affective/motivational, behavioral, and/or cognitive learning outcomes. Where applicable, it is mentioned whether the absence or presence of certain game elements was reported as more beneficial for learning outcomes.

Game elements and learning outcomes

Table 10.4 shows a list of the game characteristics that led to significant differences when present or absent. The following section will first elaborate on the results for cognitive, affective/motivational, and behavioral learning outcomes.

- Leaderboards

  For cognitive learning outcomes, Huang et al. (2020) found that the absence of leaderboards led to higher statistically significant effect sizes when compared to their presence.

- Storytelling

  The inclusion of game fiction was reported as bearing a significant, small positive effect on behavioral learning outcomes in contrast to a nonsignificant result of not including game fiction by Sailer and Homner (2020). In contrast, Ritzhaupt et al. (2021) found the absence of narrative/storytelling to be significantly more effective than its presence.

- Quests, missions, and tasks

  For cognitive learning outcomes, Huang et al. (2020) found that quests yielded the largest noted effect size for a game element.

- Competition and collaboration

  In Huang et al.'s (2020) sample, competition was employed more often than collaboration (21 vs. nine studies). Interestingly, studies that did not use competition reported higher statistically significant effect sizes on cognitive learning outcomes than those that did. Meanwhile, the use of collaboration led to the second highest reported effect size in this meta-analysis. Sailer and Homner (2020) coded social interaction as "none", "competitive", "collaborative", and "competitive-collaborative". For cognitive and affective/motivational learning outcomes, no significant differences were found. However, results showed that a combination of competition and collaboration was significantly more effective than no social interaction for behavioral learning outcomes. Ritzhaupt et al. (2021) did not find significant differences concerning the presence or absence of competition or collaboration for behavioral learning outcomes. However, the presence of competition led to the highest statistically significant effect size compared to its absence.

- Non-linear navigation

  Learners might follow a single, linear path toward an ultimate learning goal. When they are, instead, presented with multiple possible paths, Ritzhaupt et al. (2021) refer to it as non-linear navigation. They found that behavioral learning outcomes were positively and significantly influenced if non-linear navigation was not used.

- **Adaptivity and personalization**
  Adaptivity and personalization intend to provide learners with tailored options in gamified learning environments. For example, teacher scaffolding might be adjusted based on the learners' performance. Ritzhaupt et al. (2021) found the presence of this game element to be significantly detrimental to behavioral learning outcomes when compared to its absence. However, only a small number of studies investigated adaptivity and personalization, which impedes the capability of making design suggestions based on this finding.

Contextual, situational, and methodological moderators

- **Period of time**
  Gamification interventions can last for varying amounts of time, with different numbers of play/learning sessions. Sailer and Homner (2020) found that gamified learning instances lasting half a year or less were significantly more effective toward affective/emotional outcomes than those lasting one day or less. Contrasting these findings, Bai et al. (2020) noted that shorter gamified interventions had greater average effect sizes in their research.
- **Research context**
  For cognitive learning outcomes only, Sailer and Homner (2020) found that the effects in school settings were significantly higher than those in higher education or informal education settings. This might be explained by control groups in schools receiving traditional passive instruction, while those in higher education might have received mixed instruction.
- **Randomization**
  Quasi-experimental and experimental study designs differed significantly in Sailer and Homner's (2020) meta-analysis for affective/motivational and behavioral learning outcomes. This might hint at methodological rigor as a possible moderator of the effect size.
- **Type of publication**
  For Huang et al.'s (2020) sample, dissertations and theses reported overall negative effect sizes. In this way, they differed significantly from journal articles and conference proceedings that reported comparable positive effect sizes.
- **Publication bias**
  One outlier for both affective/motivational and behavioral learning outcomes resulted in a threat to the respective models in Ritzhaupt et al.'s (2021) analysis.

While some of the delineated results align, others do not. It is of note that the sampled studies varied between the meta-analyses, which might explain varying effect sizes. A second-order analysis would be helpful to more accurately and uniformly present a picture of gamification in education.

One point of conflict is the interaction of gamification and period of time. Is it better to have longer-lasting gamified interventions or shorter ones? One indication is provided by a longitudinal study (Rodrigues et al., 2022). Gamification has been reported to suffer from the novelty effect, meaning its perceived benefit decreases with time (Koivisto & Hamari, 2014). However, it may also benefit from the familiarization effect, according to Rodrigues et al., forming a U-curve. This means that after an initial downtrend, the declining effect of gamification is counteracted by learners becoming more familiar with the game elements and other aspects of the intervention. This process might take from two to six weeks. More longitudinal studies on the effects of gamified interventions are needed to further assess the long-term effects of gamified interventions.

Another point of contention relates to the effects of competition and collaboration. For example, the discussed findings show differences in cognitive vs. behavioral outcomes. Another meta-analysis on gamification and the impact of peer competition and collaboration found a moderating effect of competition on cognitive learning outcomes, but not of collaboration (Ho et al., 2021). This further adds to the inconsistency of the findings on this topic and points to the need for closer examinations. Bai et al. (2020) offered a possible explanation: In their qualitative synthesis, students reported feelings of jealousy or anxiety as one drawback of gamification. The latter might especially arise during competitive tasks. To this end, Rigby and Ryan (2011) distinguished between competition that is either constructive or destructive. The latter occurs when winning is perceived as more important than improving the skills of everyone involved. As a result, destructive competition can stifle feelings of social relatedness.

An aspect not touched upon by most analyses is that of difficulty. When learners perceive a task as too easy or too hard, their engagement may decrease (Baten et al., 2019). For example, gamified tasks or quizzes that are too difficult can lead to a decrease in feelings of competence (Sailer & Sailer, 2020). However, evidence suggests that by providing a task-related choice before learning, the negative effects of high-perceived task difficulty could be reduced (Schneider et al., 2022). Another way of handling difficulty is through the anchoring effect, in which learners who complete easier tasks at the start perceive subsequent, more difficult tasks as possible (Kim et al., 2018).

Building on the critique of pointification (see Section "Game elements used in education"), there mostly were no significant differences in the presence or absence of PBLs in gamified interventions. As a result, the authors unanimously argue for exploring and combining other game elements in education.

While differences in the effects of gamification are suspected between subject areas, there is not enough representation in all observed domains to gauge this interaction appropriately.

It is also of note that the coding of game elements varied between the meta-analyses. While some authors recorded the presence or absence of various game elements (e.g., Huang et al., 2020; Ritzhaupt et al., 2021), Sailer and Homner (2020) differentiated them further. Consequently, future research should be less about "either-or", and more about "how": For example, if storytelling elements are present, how relevant and deep are they to the learning experience (Clark et al., 2016)? These distinctions might help with more finely assessing the effects of game elements in education.

Most gamification implementations are adaptive systems and thus provide different feedback to different learners. This might result in different effects of game elements on different learners (e.g., Bai et al., 2021). Further, the interactions of individual differences (e.g., learners' prior knowledge or motives) with single game elements might influence the effects of gamification on different learners, as well. However, these differentiated effects and interactions have hardly been investigated in gamification research, as yet.

Evidence-based practice recommendations

- There is consistent evidence that the use of game elements (gamification) in education is an effective way of fostering cognitive, affective/motivational, and behavioral learning outcomes.
- According to Landers' (2015) theory of gamified learning, game elements influence attitudes and behavior that, in turn, affect the learning outcomes (mediating process). Additionally, attitudes and behavior act as moderators on the direct effect of instructional content on learning outcomes. This means that gamifying learning processes cannot remedy low-quality teaching methods, instead further enhancing well-designed instruction that can promote active learning.
- Gamification research uses a wide range of theoretical frameworks, with a focus on motivational aspects. Specific game elements have been shown to foster the psychological needs for autonomy, competence, and social relatedness. They should thus be used accordingly and combined to target all three of these needs.
- The use of points, badges, and leaderboards is so ubiquitous that there seem to be no significant differences, whether present or absent. As such, new game elements should be developed and implemented into gamified learning (Zainuddin et al., 2020) while providing elaborate feedback in the form of teacher scaffolding (Clark et al., 2016).

References

Bai, S., Hew, K. F., & Huang, B. (2020). Does gamification improve student learning outcome? Evidence from a meta-analysis and synthesis of qualitative data in educational contexts. *Educational Research Review*, 30, 100322. https://doi.org/10.1016/j.edurev.2020.100322

Bai, S., Hew, K. F., Sailer, M., & Jia, C. (2021). From top to bottom: How positions on different types of leaderboard may affect fully online student learning performance, intrinsic motivation, and course engagement. *Computers & Education*, 173, 104297. https://doi.org/10.1016/j.compedu.2021.104297

Baker, J. P., & Goodboy, A. K. (2019). The choice is yours: The effects of autonomy-supportive instruction on students' learning and communication. *Communication Education*, 68(1), 80–102. https://doi.org/10.1080/03634523.2018.1536793

Baten, E., Vansteenkiste, M., De Muynck, G.-J., De Poortere, E., & Desoete, A. (2019). How can the blow of math difficulty on elementaryschool children's motivational, cognitive, and affective experiences bedampened? The critical role of autonomy-supportive instructions. *Journal of Educational Psychology*, 112(18), 1490–1505. https://doi.org/10.1037/edu0000444

Bedwell, W. L., Pavlas, D., Heyne, K., Lazzara, E. H., & Salas, E. (2012). Toward a taxonomy linking game attributes to learning: An empirical study. *Simulation & Gaming*, 43(6), 729–760. https://doi.org/10.1177/1046878112439444

Bisson, C., & Luckner, J. (1996). Fun in learning: The pedagogical role of fun in adventure education. *Journal of Experiential Education*, 19(2), 108–112. https://doi.org/10.1177/105382599601900208

Chi, M.T. H., Adams, J., Bogusch, E. B., Bruchok, C., Kang, S., Lancaster, M., Levy, R., Li, N., McEldoon, K. L., Stump, G. S., Wylie, R., Xu, D., & Yaghmourian, D. L. (2018). Translating the ICAP theory of cognitive engagement into practice. *Cognitive Science*, 42(6), 1777–1832. https://doi.org/10.1111/cogs.12626

Chi, M. T. H., & Wylie, R. (2014). The ICAP framework: Linking cognitive engagement to active learning outcomes. *Educational Psychologist*, 59(4), 219–243. https://doi.org/10.1080/00461520.2014.965823

Clark, D. B., Tanner-Smith, E. E., & Killingsworth, S. S. (2016). Digital games, design, and learning: A systematic review and meta-analysis. *Review of Educational Research*, 86(1), 79–122. https://doi.org/10.3102/0034654315582065

Cordova, D. I., & Lepper, M. R. (1996). Intrinsic motivation and the process of learning: Beneficial effects of contextualization, personalization, and choice. *Journal of Educational Psychology*, 88(4), 715–730. https://doi.org/10.1037/0022-0663.88.4.715

Csikszentmihalyi, M. (1992). The flow experience and human psychology. In M. Csikszentmihalyi & I. S. Csikszentmihalyi (Eds.), *Optimal experience: Psychological studies of flow in consciousness* (pp. 16–35). Cambridge University Press.

Deterding, S., Dixon, D., Khaled, R., & Nacke, L. (2011). From game design elements to gamefulness: Defining gamification. In *Proceedings of the 15th international academic MindTrek conference: Envisioning future media environments* (pp. 9–15). Tampere: ACM.

Groening, C., & Binnewies, C. (2019). "Achievement unlocked!"–The impact of digital achievements as a gamification element on motivation and performance. *Computers in Human Behavior*, 97, 151–166. https://doi.org/10.1016/j.chb.2019.02.026

Ha, J., Su, M., Chi, M. T. H., & Cullicott, C. (2020). Misunderstandings of Teachers Applying ICAP Theory into Practice. In M. Gresalfi, & I. S. Horn (Eds.), *The Interdisciplinarity of the Learning Sciences, 14th International Conference of the Learning Sciences (ICLS) 2020, Volume 4* (pp. 2407–2408). Nashville, Tennessee: International Society of the Learning Sciences.

Hamari, J., Koivisto, J., & Sarsa, H. (2014). Does gamification work? A literature review of empirical studies on gamification. In R. H. Sprague Jr. (Ed.), *Proceedings of the 47th Annual Hawaii International Conference on System Sciences* (pp. 3025–3034). Washington, DC: IEEE. https://doi.org/10.1109/hicss.2014.377

Ho, J. C.-S., Hung, Y.-S., & Kwan, L. Y.-Y. (2021). The impact of peer competition and collaboration on gamified learning performance in educational settings: A meta-analytical study. *Education and Information Technologies, 27*, 3833–3866. https://doi.org/10.1007/s10639-021-10770-2

Huang, R., Ritzhaupt, A. D., Sommer, M., Zhu, J., Stephen, A., Valle, N., Hampton, J., & Li, J. (2020). The impact of gamification in educational settings on student learning outcomes: A meta-analysis. *Education Technology Research and Development, 68*, 1875–1901. https://doi.org/10.1007/s11423-020-09807-z

Kapp, K. M. (2012). *The gamification of learning and instruction: Game-based methods and strategies for training and education.* John Wiley & Sons.

Kasurinen, J., & Knutas, A. (2018). Publication trends in gamification: A systematic mapping study. *Computer Science Review, 27*, 33–44. https://doi.org/10.1016/j.cosrev.2017.10.003

Kim, J., & Castelli, D. M. (2021). Effects of gamification on behavioral change in education: A meta-analysis. *International Jourrnal of Environmental Research and Public Health, 18*(7), Article 3550. https://doi.org/10.3390/ijerph18073550

Kim, S., Song, K., Lockee, B., & Burton, J. (2018). *Gamification in learning and education. Enjoy learning like gaming.* Springer. https://doi.org/10.1007/978-3-319-47283-6

Koivisto, J., & Hamari, J. (2014). Demographic differences in perceived benefits from gamification. *Computers in Human Behavior, 35*, 179–188. https://doi.org/10.1016/j.chb.2014.03.007

Krath, J., Schürmann, L., & von Korflesch, H. F. O. (2021). Revealing the theoretical basis of gamification: A systematic review and analysis of theory in research on gamification, serious games and game-based learning. *Computers in Human Behavior, 125*, Article 106963. https://doi.org/10.1016/j.chb.2021.106963

Landers, R. N. (2015). Developing a theory of gamified learning: Linking serious games and gamification of learning. *Simulation & Gaming, 45*(6), 752–768. https://doi.org/10.1177/1046878114563660

Landers, R. N., & Landers, A. K. (2015). An empirical test of the theory of gamified learning: The effect of leaderboards on time-on-task and academic performance. *Simulation & Gaming, 45*(6), 769–785. https://doi.org/10.1177/1046878114563662

Malone, T. W. (1981). Toward a theory of intrinsically motivating instruction. *Cognitive Science, 5*(4), 333–369. https://doi.org/10.1207/s15516709cog0504_2

Mekler, E. D., Brühlmann, F., Tuch, A. N., & Opwis, K. (2017). Towards understanding the effects of individual gamification elements on intrinsic motivation and performance. *Computers in Human Behavior, 71*, 525–534. https://doi.org/10.1016/j.chb.2015.08.048

Mitchell, R., Schuster, L., & Jin, H. S. (2020). Gamification and the impact of extrinsic motivation on needs satisfaction: Making work fun? *Journal of Business Research, 106*, 323–330. https://doi.org/10.1016/j.jbusres.2018.11.022

Nacke, L. E., & Deterding, S. (2017). Editorial: The maturing of gamification research. *Computers in Human Behavior, 71*, 450–454. https://doi.org/10.1016/j.chb.2016.11.062

Ortiz-Rojas, M., Chiluiza, K., & Valcke, M. (2019). Gamification through leaderboards: An empirical study in engineering education. *Computer Applications in Engineering Education, 27*, 777–788. https://doi.org/10.1002/cae.12116

Prensky, M. (2001). Fun, play and games: What makes games engaging. In M. Prensky (Ed.), *Digital game-based learning* (pp. 05-1–05-31). McGraw-Hill.

Prince, M. (2004). Does active learning work? A review of the research. *Journal of Engineering Education, 93*, 223–231. https://doi.org/10.1002/j.2168-9830.2004.tb00809.x

Rigby, S., & Ryan, R. M. (2011). *Glued to games: How video games draw us in and hold us spellbound.* Praeger.

Ritzhaupt, A. D., Huang, R., Sommer, M., Zhu, J., Stephen, A., Valle, N., Hampton, J., & Li, J. (2021). A meta-analysis on the influence of gamification in formal educational settings on affective and behavioral outcomes. *Education Technology Research and Development 69*, 2493–2522. https://doi.org/10.1007/s11423-021-10036-1

Rocha, E. M., Pereira, G. M., & Pacheco, D. A. D. J. (2019). The role of the predictive gamification to increase the sales performance: A novel business approach. *Journal of Business & Industrial Marketing, 35*(5), 817–833. https://doi.org/10.1108/JBIM-01-2019-0005

Rodrigues, L., Pereira, F.D., Toda, A.M., Palomino, P. T., Pessoa, M., Carvalho, L. S. G., Fernandes, D., Oliveira, E. H. T., Cristea, A. I., & Isotani, S. (2022). Gamification suffers from the novelty effect but benefits from the familiarization effect: Findings from a longitudinal study. *International Journal of Educational Technology in Higher Education, 19*(13). https://doi.org/10.1186/s41239-021-00314-6

Ryan, R. M., & Deci, E. L. (2000). Self-determination theory and the facilitation of intrinsic motivation, social development, and well-being. *American Psychologist, 55*(1), 68–78. https://doi.org/10.1037/0003-066X.55.1.68

Ryan, R. M., Rigby, C. S., & Przybylski, A. (2006). The motivational pull of video games: A self-determination theory approach. *Motivation and Emotion, 30*(4), 344–360. https://doi.org/10.1007/s11031-006-9051-8

Sailer, M., Hense, J., Mandl, J., & Klevers, M. (2014). Psychological perspectives on motivation through gamification. *Interaction Design and Architecture Journal, 19*, 28–37.

Sailer, M., Hense, J. U., Mayr, S. K., & Mandl, H. (2017). How gamification motivates: An experimental study of the effects of specific game design elements on psychological need satisfaction. *Computers in Human Behavior, 69*(Supplement C), 371–380. https://doi.org/10.1016/j.chb.2016.12.033

Sailer, M., & Homner, L. (2020). The gamification of learning: A meta-analysis. *Educational Psychology Review, 32*(1), 77–112. https://doi.org/10.1007/s10648-019-09498-w

Sailer, M., & Sailer, M. (2020). Gamification of in-class activities in flipped classroom lectures. *British Journal of Educational Technology.* https://doi.org/10.1111/bjet.12948

Schmidt-Kraepelin, M., Thiebes, A., Baumsteiger, S., & Sunyaev, D. (2018). State of play: A citation network analysis of healthcare gamification studies. In *Research Papers, 173* (p. 1–17). *European Conference on Information Systems (ECIS2018),* Portsmouth. https://aisel.aisnet.org/ecis2018_rp/17

Schneider, S., Nebel, S. Meyer, S., & Rey, G. D. (2022). The interdependency of perceived task difficulty and the choice effect when learning with multimedia materials. *Journal of Educational Psychology, 114*(3), 443–461. https://doi.org/10.1037/edu0000686

Subhash, S., & Cudney, E. A. (2018). Gamified learning in higher education: A systematic review of the literature. *Computers in Human Behavior, 87,* 109–206. https://doi.org/10.1016/j.chb.2018.05.028

Swanson, E., McCulley, L. V., Osman, D. J., Scammacca Lewis, N., & Solis, M. (2017). The effect of team-based learning on content knowledge: A meta-analysis. *Active Learning in Higher Education, 20*(1), 39–50. https://doi.org/10.1177/1469787417731201

Tolks, D., & Sailer, M. (2021). Gamification als didaktisches Mittel in der Hochschulbildung. In *Digitalisierung in Studium und Lehre gemeinsam gestalten* (pp. 515–532). Hochschulforum Digitalisierung. https://doi.org/10.1007/978-3-658-32849-8_29

Tolks, D., Sailer, M., Dadaczynski, K., Lampert, C., Huberty, J., Paulus, P., & Horstmann, D. (2019). ONYA – the wellbeing game: How to use gamification to promote wellbeing. *Information, 10*(2):58. https://doi.org/10.3390/info10020058

Vermeir, J. F., White, M. J., Johnson, D., Crombez, G., & van Ryckeghem, D. M. L. (2020). The effects of gamification on computerized cognitive training: Systematic review and meta-analysis. *JMIR Serious Games, 8*(3), Article e18644. https://doi.org/10.2196/18644

Werbach, K., & Hunter, D. (2012). *For the win: How game thinking can revolutionize your business.* Wharton Digital Press.

Wigfield, A., Faust, L. T., Cambria, J., & Eccles, J. S. (2019). Motivation in education. In R. M. Ryan (Ed.), *The Oxford handbook of human motivation* (pp. 443–461). Oxford University Press.

Xu, F., Buhalis, D., & Weber, J. (2017). Serious games and the gamification of tourism. *Tourism Management, 60,* 244–256. https://doi.org/10.1016/j.tourman.2016.11.020

Yildirim, I., & Şen, S. (2019). The effects of gamification on students' academic achievement: A meta-analysis study. *Interactive Learning Environments, 29*(8), 1301–1318. https://doi.org/10.1080/10494820.2019.1636089

Zainuddin, Z., Chu, S. K. W., Shujahat, M., & Perera, C. J. (2020). The impact of gamification on learning and instruction: A systematic review of empirical evidence. *Educational Research Review, 30,* Article 100326. https://doi.org/10.1016/j.edurev.2020.100326

11

SENSORS AND WEARABLES

Byron Havard

Sensors and Wearables

The purpose of this chapter is to provide an overview of sensors and wearables and the potential benefits these devices may offer for enhancing learning and human performance through instructional and non-instructional interventions. These devices change the dynamics of how individuals acquire, store, and retrieve information, virtually eliminating the disconnect between humans and computers. Wearables include a variety of body-borne sensory, communication, and computational components that may be worn on the body, under, over, or within clothing (Havard & Podsiad, 2017).

To limit the scope of this review, only studies with a focus on sensor and wearable use on learning and human performance outcomes were included. Virtual reality (VR) headsets may be considered wearables. However, this designation blurs the lines between studies of wearables and VR. For this chapter, literature focusing on headset wearables for VR emphasis was not included. The vast majority of sensor and wearable literature focuses on the healthcare sector. Studies related to healthcare education are included, however, those related to health or fitness maintenance, exercise regimes, or lifestyle changes are only briefly addressed.

Current trends in commercially available wearables include smartwatches, headsets, smart jewelry, eyewear, and e-textiles. At the time of this writing, according to Vandrico (2024), the wearable technology market includes 431 devices commercially available devices, with 225 devices used for lifestyle applications and an average cost of $326 (USD). The accelerometer is currently considered the most popular component included. The database is constantly updated and has been available since 2008. However, this

DOI: 10.4324/9781003386131-16

database does not account for the vast number of noncommercial sensors and wearables evident in the research literature.

Research regarding the efficacy of wearables as a technology to enhance teaching and learning has increased extensively since the first documented wearable was introduced in the 1960s (Havard & Podsiad, 2017). Advances in wearable technology have progressed significantly over the past several decades. Researchers and educators are continually developing strategies for incorporating wearables into academic settings to enhance the learning environment. The body of research regarding wearables in educational settings has matured, however, the majority of the research literature is comprised of proof-of-concept studies with one-group posttest only designs. While the rigor of the current body of research regarding wearables is limited, a review of the recent focus of these studies provides insight into the potential for the enhancement of teaching and learning.

Studies of sensors and wearables and their influence on learning and performance support include a variety of learners, learning strategies, and learning environments. As an example of the various learners, Zhou et al. (2017) used an ankle wearable with individuals 65 years and older to measure their cognitive performance. Peppler et al. (2010) used a collaborative activity with individuals 7–8 years old using a wearable glove to mimic the collection of honey from a beehive. Wearables research has also included a variety of strategies for integration including task-based (de la Guía et al., 2016; Nederveen et al., 2019), project-based (Byrne et al., 2017; Kuhn et al., 2016), and game-based (Lindberg et al., 2016; Oh et al., 2018) learning strategies. Researchers have explored the integration of wearables in diverse learning environments including military (Divis et al., 2018), nursing (Gauttier, 2018), business (Schaule et al., 2018), and K-12 engineering (Ngai et al., 2010) environments.

A framework for learning outcomes can serve as a means to review publications encompassing the wide variety of sensors and wearables. A recognized taxonomy for educational objectives that categorizes learning outcomes as cognitive, affective, or psychomotor (Anderson et al., 2001) can serve as this framework. Each domain may be hierarchically organized by the level of outcome desired. The cognitive domain relates to intellectual skills, whereas attitudes are associated with the affective domain (Krathwohl et al., 1964). Physical movement and coordination outcomes are associated with the psychomotor skills domain (Harrow, 1972). Sensors and wearables have demonstrated efficacy in non-instructional interventions as well. These devices may also support and improve human performance in a variety of environments. For this review, sensor and wearable research has been loosely categorized as (a) cognitive and psychomotor, (b) affective, and (c) performance and disability support.

History

The first wearable computer is attributed to Thorp and Shannon in the 1960s with their roulette wheel predictor (Havard & Podsiad, 2017; Soni & Goodman, 2017). The roulette wheel predictor was a cigarette-sized wearable computer that was intended to predict where the ball would land. It was not until Thorp published the work and findings in 1966 that the device earned the title of the first wearable computer (McCann & Bryson, 2009). The Bell Helicopter Company experimented with a head-mounted display (HMD) camera-based augmented-reality systems in 1967. Within the same year, Hubert Upton created a wearable computer with an eyeglass-mounted display to aid in lip reading (Popat & Sharma, 2013). By the late 1970s, C. C. Collins developed a wearable head-mounted camera for the blind, Hewlett Packard designed an algebraic calculator watch, and Eudaemonic Enterprises created a wearable shoe computer to predict roulette wheels (Popat & Sharma, 2013).

In the early 1980s, Mann experimented with a backpack-mounted computer with smart glasses and a one-handed keying input device (Mann, 1996). Mann's photographically-mediated reality was an early attempt at augmented reality in a wearable device (Mann, 2014). By 1989, the smart glasses concept evolved into the commercially available Private Eye. Doug Platt introduced a hip-mounted computer incorporating the Private Eye and a palmtop keyboard in 1991 (Amft & Lukowitz, 2009; Rhodes, n.d.; Starner, 1994). Platt and Starner combined the functionality of the Private Eye and the Twiddler, a commercially available one-handed keyboard, into the first context-aware system in 1993. This design became the basis on which the Lizzy at the MIT Media Lab was established.

In 1991, students from Carnegie Mellon University's Engineering Design Research Center developed VuMan 1, a wearable computer to view blueprints (Bass et al., 1997). BBN Technologies produced the first wearable computer with GPS, the Pathfinder system, in the Fall of 1993 (Rhodes, n.d.). Feiner et al. (1993) presented a prototype augmented reality system called KARMA (Knowledge-based Augmented Reality for Maintenance Assistance). The system used an HMD to present and explain printer maintenance to the end-user. By the end of 1994, Lamming and Flynn (1994) developed "Forget-Me-Not," a wearable device that records interactions with people, places, and devices; Matias and Ruicci of the University of Toronto, built a wrist computer with a half-QWERTY keyboard (Matias et al., 1994); and Mann (1997) went on to develop the Wearable Wireless Webcam, a camera he used to transmit live images to the internet. Since the initial robust innovation in wearables at the MIT Media Lab, research and development have continued.

Cognitive and Psychomotor

Wearables have been integrated into a wide variety of contexts for the improvement of cognitive and psychomotor learning outcomes. Programmable electronic textiles (smart textiles) provide the basis for an authentic context for teaching engineering concepts across K-12 environments (Fogarty et al., 2016; Litts et al., 2017). Student understanding of functional circuits significantly increased through the use of electronic textiles in an introductory-level computer science high school course (Litts et al., 2017). High school students, ages 16–17, increased their abilities to design circuits and remix code (Litts et al., 2017). Middle and high school students from different communities collaborated on a wearable project called Engineering Brightness (Fogarty et al., 2016). Fogarty et al. (2016) used 3D printers to develop wearable wristwatches with solar-powered lights for children in underdeveloped countries to read at night without electricity (Fogarty et al., 2016). Students shared information about circuits, collaboratively planned and designed wearable wristwatches, and deepened their understanding of the technology, as well as its philanthropic impacts (Fogarty et al., 2016).

The integration of wearables to support composition and writing offers insight into potential strategies for future learning environments (Euteneuer, 2018; Wargo, 2018; Wood, 2018). Students in a first-year composition course explore the nature of wearables through a structured course framework (Wood, 2018). In defining "wearing" during this course, students delve into how they interact with wearables and how wearables influence their actions. Euteneuer (2018) suggests that a shift from computers to wearables offers educators an opportunity to enhance students' digital literacy. He proposes the term *conspicuous computing* where he encourages students to look beyond the remediated use of wearables as passive consumers to productive mediums. Students engage in gamified experiences combining Pokemon GO and Fitbit supporting creative composition Euteneuer (2018). Wearables can support writing at much earlier ages. Wargo (2018) for example explores how wearables and sounds in particular generated through their use can influence "literacy in action" for students 6–8 years old (p. 503).

Wearable technologies can facilitate learning through gaming (Lindberg et al., 2016; Rosales et al., 2015; Vasudevan et al., 2015). Lindberg et al. (2016) developed an exergame combining the use of a smartphone and wristband. Students learn the required physical education curriculum while playing Running Othello 2. Evaluation of the exergame with 61 third-grade students indicated learning was more efficient, and engagement increased for students compared to traditional methods (Lindberg et al., 2016). ARfract is a science museum-based immersive experience for learning light refraction concepts (Oh et al., 2018). Optical see-through augmented reality (AR) glasses are integrated into game-based and non-game-based simulations. Twenty participants, from 12 to 14 years of age, were paired in 10 mixed-gender dyads. A multiple choice and short answer item instrument regarding concepts of light refraction was administered before and after the immersive learning experience. Paired-sample t-test results revealed a significant increase in learning outcomes. The order of game/non-game experience did not significantly influence the results. Vasudevan et al. (2015) analyzed the impact of constructionist gaming on students' level of interest in computing. Researchers facilitated a four-month-long workshop with 12 middle school students and analyzed students' ability to creatively modify existing games (Vasudevan et al., 2015). Students used computational construction to design and create wearable glove controllers that coincide with the Flappy Birds computer game. Students' wearable controllers connect to a platform called MaKey MaKey (Vasudevan et al., 2015). Wearable Sounds, Statue, and FeetUp are wearable accessories created for use during free play with young children (Rosales et al., 2015). Three wearable accessories were piloted with 24 students enrolled in an after-school program. Examination of students' interactions during playtime while wearing the computational accessories revealed students express themselves creatively through play, sometimes creating new and alternative games to those suggested by the researchers (Rosales et al., 2015).

Affective

Affective learning outcomes may be represented by values, feelings, and self-efficacy (Krathwohl et al., 1964). Motivation, as a physiological state, was also included as an outcome in this review (Pintrich & Schunk, 2002). This review includes studies relating to wearable use in STEM and health education regarding affective and physiological learning outcomes. Google Glass was paired with a prototype app gPhysics that assists students in performing experiments regarding acoustics (Kuhn et al., 2016). A total of 46 high school students with a mean age of 13 years participated in one of three groups. The treatment group students used Google Glass and the gPhysics app. The two control groups used tablets and either the gPhysics app or a commercially available app SpectrumView. ANCOVA results revealed positive effects on wondering and curiosity for the treatment group. Merkouris et al. (2017), engaged 36 students ages 12–13 in block-based visual programming where the target platforms included wearables (Arduino Lilypad), robots (Lego Mindstorms), and computers. The wearable and robot platforms did not reveal a significant improvement in students' computational concept learning. However, students' emotions related to programming including happy, confident, interested, satisfied, and determined for both the wearable and robot platforms were higher than the computer platform. Nederveen et al. (2019)

explored the use of the first-person perspective (FPP) in pre-laboratory preparation. In this study, a GoPro camera was considered wearable in the creation of the FPP video instruction. Participants included 30 undergraduate students with a mean age of 20.7 (10 women and 20 men). Student enjoyment and task-specific self-efficacy regarding pre-laboratory preparation were significantly higher for the FPP treatment group compared to the text-only control group. Motivation to learn about computer science and self-efficacy in pursuing a career in computer science both significantly increased for 21 male and female treatment group students with a mean age of 16 exposed to a hackathon workshop. Team-based design challenges included prototyping a wearable fitness tracker and web app "BetaFit" and a multi-use wearable smart glove "EyeGlove" capable of heating and cooling, playing music, and making phone calls (Byrne et al., 2017). Researchers who work on the WearTec project investigated the use of electronic textiles with students in fourth through sixth grade (Barker et al., 2015). Students used the engineering design process to build electronic textiles and also engaged in computing, and the results revealed increased attitudes toward STEM, including motivation to learn, self-efficacy, and learning as a whole (Barker et al., 2015).

There are a considerable number of studies focused on the improvement of healthy lifestyle habits. The prevalence and focus of many commercially available wearables have possibly led to this abundance of research in this area. The integration of wearables in healthcare environments is prevalent and use is evident in physical activity tracking (Díaz et al., 2019), mental health treatment (Knight & Bidargaddi, 2018), and health monitoring (Van Til et al., 2019). The research in these areas is extensive and includes several meta-analyses and systematic reviews focused on sensor and wearable use to improve physical activity (Kirk et al., 2019; Yen & Chiu, 2019). Kirk et al. (2019) found significant increases in physical activity and time spent in moderate to vigorous physical activity through wearable use. Yen and Chiu (2019) identified significant decreases in body weight, waist circumference, and body mass index attributed to the use of wearables.

Several of these studies are described here and there are many more that can be found in the research literature. For example, wrist-worn activity trackers were used by 43 undergraduate students in a 12-week eHealth literacy course as a means to learn about personal health (Sobko & Brown, 2019). An ePortfolio component required participants to enter biometric data and reflect on their data in the context of eHealth. A significant difference was revealed in higher eHealth literacy scores on a pretest/posttest eHealth assessment. The ePortfolio was associated with positive learning and ease of use. Almusawi et al. (2021) analyzed 38 public school physical education teachers' semistructured interviews and identified eight themes relating to readiness to integrate wearables in physical education. However,

Kerner and Goodyear (2017) administered the Behavioral Regulation in Exercise Questionnaire II and the Psychological Need Satisfaction in Exercise Scale to 84 adolescents. The authors found that the 13- to 14-year-old participants' competence, autonomy, relatedness, and autonomous motivation decreased after eight weeks of Fitbit Charge use. A motivation significantly increased suggesting that wearables focused on healthy lifestyle habits may have contributed to negative motivational consequences. Exercise dependence and eating disorders may be exacerbated by fitness wearable use. Blackstone and Herrmann (2020) found that fitness wearables promote compensatory behaviors based on 327 female US college students with a mean age of 19.31. Results from the Exercise Dependence Scale and the Eating Pathology Symptom Inventory revealed both purging and restricting food were significant predictors of behavior when step and caloric output goals were not met.

Performance and Disability Support

Advances in technology, reducing the hardware size, and increasing computing speed and capability spurred advances in sensor and wearable learning environments as tools to support performance on the job (Amft, 2018; Gauttier, 2018; Liu, 2004; Minocha et al., 2018; Najjar et al., 1999). Researchers have started to incorporate wearables to enhance healthcare and nursing. Gauttier (2018) suggested that a wearable could provide job enhancements to nurses by monitoring their cognitive and physiological levels and providing medical information related to patient records and diseases. Amft (2018) identified specific ways that wearables could enhance digital health. Wearables could aid in the prevention and diagnostics of diseases (Amft, 2018). One example is using a wearable to identify risk factors associated with Alzheimer's disease (Pontoriero et al., 2018).

Sensors and wearables may also provide clinical support to doctors and nurses, monitor cognitive and physiological responses, and integrate wearable data and clinical data (Amft, 2018). Wearables not only provide a way for tracking information and data from patients but also can provide doctors and nurses with a way to maintain data records and patient information while on the go. Schaule et al. (2018) designed a system that utilized a wearable to identify times appropriate for interruptions at work based on a worker's physiological state. The wearable device, a smartwatch, tracked data such as the worker's heart rate and wrist movement. The system provided a red or green signal to co-workers, based on the worker's cognitive load, to indicate whether or not the worker could be interrupted (Schaule et al., 2018). This system provided a way to maintain work efficiency and minimize or postpone interruptions during high cognitive load times. Brewer et al. (2016) explored the influence of Google Glass and proprietary software on the accuracy of needle placement of 11 cardiothoracic students. The video was streamed in real-time by the student to the trainer, who offered placement directions. The needle placement error score fell significantly, and the students also reported the device was unobtrusive. Chaukos et al. (2018) integrated health trackers in Stress Management and Resiliency Training (SMART-R), a resiliency program to alleviate intern burnout. Participants included 73 medicine and 17 psychiatry interns at a large US teaching hospital. Individual adherence to wearing the trackers was inconsistent, and there was no significant difference in behavior between those who exhibited burnout and those who did not. The authors discuss improvements to the program and research design to improve on determining the effects of SMART-R and fitness tracker use to prevent burnout.

Sensors and wearables can aid students with both physical (Borthwick et al., 2015; Damopoulos & Kambourakis, 2019; Parton, 2017; ReWalk Robotics, 2014; Shilkrot et al., 2014) and learning disabilities (Alchalcabi et al., 2017; Garcia et al., 2013). ReWalk is the first, and only FDA-approved wearable exoskeleton designed to allow people with spinal cord injuries to stand and walk (ReWalk Robotics, 2014). The FingerReader is a finger-worn device that reads the text aloud as the wearer's finger runs across the words (Shilkrot et al., 2014). Originally designed for visually impaired people, this wearable device can be used by students who are auditory learners or are learning to read. Parton (2017) piloted a study using Glass Vision 3D, QR codes, and Google Glass with fifth-grade students who have hearing impairments. Students scan the codes with glasses, prompting an American Sign Language video to appear via AR (Parton, 2017). Students use gestures to access videos on the glasses, rather than using their voice because many students with hearing impairments are not comfortable with verbal language (Parton, 2017).

Accessing a computer may be cumbersome based on some disabilities. A variety of glass wearable devices are currently available, including Solos Smart Glasses, Raptor, and R-9 Smartglasses, in addition to Google Glass. Damopoulos and Kambourakis (2019) created Gauth, a system that establishes a communication channel between the computer and glass device through machine-readable codes, reducing the time required for authentication challenges. Wearables can also keep track of glucose levels for students with diabetes and monitor students with seizures (Borthwick et al., 2015). Garcia et al. (2013) describe wearable devices for children with ADHD. KITA is a toy that measures and assesses behavior and provides kinesiofeedback regarding the appropriateness of the behavior. WRISTWIT increases on-task behavior through suppression of undesired behavior related to attention and time, where positive feedback and rewards support the learning process in daily routines (Garcia et al., 2013). Alchalcabi et al. (2017) combined a serious game and the wearable EMOTIV headset to address the ability to focus for individuals with ADHD and ADD. Results of their experiment revealed a 10% increase in engagement and an 8% increase in focus using the wearable compared to the keyboard only. Williams and Gilbert (2020) reviewed 70 publications regarding wearable use for autism intervention. The majority of studies (45%) focused on social skills and facial emotion recognition, further marginalizing individuals with autism. The authors suggest future research should focus on wearable use as an assistive technology to enhance autonomy, competence, and connection.

Sensor and Wearable Acceptance

Many sensors and wearables, like those mentioned in this chapter, have not made it past the development stage due to certain limitations. Privacy is the main concern for wearable wearers and poses one of the biggest limitations across wearable literature (e.g., Amft, 2018; Perez & Zeadally, 2018; Seneviratne et al., 2017). Privacy issues include tracking and storing data not approved by the wearer (Perez & Zeadally, 2018). As an example, cloud service providers do not have to comply with Health Insurance Portability and Accountability Act (HIPAA) if the wearable's classification is not as a medical or healthcare wearable device (Perez & Zeadally, 2018). Therefore, wearer data could be shared with the cloud service providers and then shared externally. Perez and Zeadally (2018) suggested that the wearer could control privacy guidelines by allowing the selection of sharable data with the cloud service provider. Seneviratne et al. (2017) divided privacy threats into three categories: confidentiality, integrity, and availability. Attackers may access wearer data through wireless networks, alter the data without permission, and block the communication between the wearable and its receiver (e.g., smartphone; Seneviratne et al., 2017). Encryption and authorization protocols could mitigate the security threats that wearable devices face (Seneviratne et al., 2017). Jacobs et al. (2019) surveyed 1,273 employed adults in the US. The strongest predictors of willingness to use wearables were performance expectancy and safety climate. The highest acceptance of wearables in the work environment occurred when wearables were integrated for employee safety, while the lowest acceptance occurred when wearables were used for tracking employee information to improve productivity.

Several studies have investigated the influence of existing technology acceptance model factors on wearable use. Jacobs et al. (2019) surveyed 1,273 employed adults in the US. The strongest predictors of willingness to use wearables were performance expectancy and safety climate. The highest acceptance of wearables in the work environment occurred when wearables were integrated for employee safety, while the lowest acceptance occurred when wearables were used for tracking employee information to improve productivity. Arias-Oliva et al. (2021) surveyed 1,563 adults from seven different countries regarding UTAUT2 and TAM2 factors relating to wearable and insideable intention to use. Performance expectancy and hedonic motivation both had a significant and positive influence. Two studies including 572 (Al-Emran et al., 2020) and 679 (Al-Emran et al., 2021) university students, respectively, revealed perceived usefulness and perceived ease of use as significant predictors of smartwatch use for educational purposes.

Conclusion and Future Research

This chapter provided an overview of the potential benefits of sensor and wearable use to enhance learning and human performance through instructional and non-instructional interventions. A thorough review of the literature has revealed that measurable learning outcomes can be achieved through appropriate project-based, task-based, and game-based strategies (Havard & Podsiad, 2020). Non-instructional sensor and wearable interventions have demonstrated efficacy in enhancing job performance and disability support. However, goals should be established, even if sensors and wearables are used for support, creativity, and play. A desired outcome is more likely to result in effective use, even if the user chooses the goal (Byrne et al., 2017; Peppler et al., 2010; Rosales et al., 2015). Perhaps the most recognizable commercial trend in sensor and wearable use is related to health and fitness maintenance. Caution regarding the type of sensor or wearable and purpose should be considered where the desired outcome is healthy lifestyle habits, as compensatory behaviors may result (Blackstone & Herrmann, 2020).

While empirical research on the efficacy of sensors and wearables in educational environments is limited, great potential exists (Mann, 2014). Amft (2018) indicated that designers still need to address challenges related to wearable technology and compliance. More research and development are necessary to understand the full potential of sensors and wearables and overcome the challenges that still exist. Lee et al. (2019) offer a conceptual framework suggesting future research integrate cognitive and behavioral principles and systematic evaluations toward the development of evidence-based persuasive systems. As previously stated, formal research regarding the efficacy of wearables for learning and performance support is emerging, with the majority comprised of proof-of-concept studies. Future research should include valid and reliable instruments based on pretest/posttest research designs. A meta-analysis of wearables research in educational settings published between 2016 and 2019 initially included 171 potential studies (Havard & Podsiad, 2020). However, only 12 studies either reported or provided the necessary data to calculate effect sizes, revealing an overall weighted mean effect size for 20 outcomes (g = .6373, SE = .1622). Positive effects regarding learning outcomes in primary through post-secondary educational environments have been noted. While proof-of-concept studies are necessary to an extent, a trend toward continued rigorous research in adult learning environments is warranted.

Evidence-Based Practice Recommendations

- Project-based, task-based, and game-based strategies for sensor and wearable integration in learning environments lead to measurable learning outcomes.
- When integrating sensors and wearables for support, creativity, or play, a goal should be established, even if the user chooses the goal.
- Research regarding the influence of sensor and wearable use on learning outcomes should, at a minimum, include valid and reliable instruments based on pretest/posttest research designs.
- Fitness tracking sensors and wearables, while readily available and relatively easy to integrate, should be used with caution as there is a tendency for compensatory behavior.

References

Alchalcabi, A. E., Eddin, A. N., & Shirmohammadi, S. (2017). More attention, less deficit: Wearable EEG-based serious game for focus improvement. In *Proceedings of the 2017 IEEE 5th International Conference on Serious Games and Applications for Health (SeGAH)*. Perth, Australia: IEEE. https://doi.org/10.1109/SeGAH.2017.7939288

Al-Emran, M., Al-Maroof, R., Al-Sharafi, M. A., & Arpaci, I. (2020). What impacts learning with wearables? An integrated theoretical model. *Interactive Learning Environments*, ahead-of-print (ahead-of-print), 1–21. https://doi.org/10.1080/10494820.2020.1753216

Al-Emran, M., Granić, A., Al-Sharafi, M. A., Ameen, N., & Sarrab, M. (2021). Examining the roles of students' beliefs and security concerns for using smartwatches in higher education. *Journal of Enterprise Information Management*, 34(4), 1229–1251. https://doi.org/10.1108/JEIM-02-2020-0052

Almusawi, H. A., Durugbo, C. M., & Bugawa, A. M. (2021). Innovation in physical education: Teachers' perspectives on readiness for wearable technology integration. *Computers and Education*, 167, 104185. https://doi.org/10.1016/j.compedu.2021.104185

Amft, O. (2018). How wearable computing is shaping digital health. *IEEE Pervasive Computing*, 17(1), 92–98. https://doi.org/10.1109/MPRV.2018.011591067

Amft, O., & Lukowitz, P. (2009). From backpacks to smartphones: Past, present, and future of wearables. *IEEE Pervasive Computing*, 8(3), 8–13. https://doi.org/10.1109/MPRV.2009.44

Anderson, L. W., Krathwohl, D. R., Bloom, B. S., & Bloom, B. S. (2001). *A taxonomy for learning, teaching, and assessing: A revision of Bloom's taxonomy of educational objectives*. New York, NY: Longman.

Arias-Oliva, M., Pelegrín-Borondo, J., Murata, K., & Gauttier, S. (2021). Conventional vs. disruptive products: A wearables and insideables acceptance analysis: Understanding emerging technological products. *Technology Analysis & Strategic Management*. Advance online publication. https://doi.org/10.1080/09537325.2021.2013462

Barker, B., Melander, J., Grandgenett, N., & Nugent, G. (2015). Utilizing wearable technologies as a pathway to STEM. In D. Rutledge & D. Slykhuis (Eds.), *Proceedings of SITE 2015 – Society for Information Technology & Teacher Education International Conference* (pp. 1770–1776). Association for the Advancement of Computing in Education (AACE). Retrieved from https://www.learntechlib.org/p/150591/

Bass, L., Kasabach, C., Martin, R., Siewiorek, D., Smailagic, A., & Stivoric, J. (1997, March). The design of a wearable computer. *Proceedings of the ACM SIGCHI Conference on Human Factors in Computing Systems*, Atlanta, GA (pp. 139–146). https://sigchi.org

Blackstone, S. R., & Herrmann, L. K. (2020). Fitness wearables and exercise dependence in college women: Considerations for university health education specialists. *American Journal of Health Education*, 51(4), 225–233. https://doi.org/10.1080/19325037.2020.1767004

Borthwick, A. C., Anderson, C. L., Finsness, E. S., & Foulger, T. S. (2015). Special article personal wearable technologies in education: Value or villain? *Journal of Digital Learning in Teacher Education*, 31(3), 85–92. https://doi.org/10.1080/21532974.2015.1021982

Brewer, Z. E., Fann, H. C., Ogden, W. D., Burdon, T. A., & Sheikh, A. Y. (2016). Inheriting the learner's view: A Google glass-based wearable computing platform for improving surgical trainee performance. *Journal of Surgical Education*, 73(4), 682–688. https://doi.org/10.1016/j.jsurg.2016.02.005

Byrne, J. R., O'Sullivan, K., & Sullivan, K. (2017). An IoT and wearable technology hackathon for promoting careers in computer science. *IEEE Transactions on Education*, 60(1), 50–58. https://doi.org/10.1109/te.2016.2626252

Chaukos, D., Chad-Friedman, E., Mehta, D. H., Byerly, L., Celik, A., Mccoy, T. H., & Denninger, J. W. (2018). SMART-R: A prospective cohort study of a resilience curriculum for residents by residents. *Academic Psychiatry*, 42(1), 78–83. https://doi.org/10.1007/s40596-017-0808-z

Damopoulos, D., & Kambourakis, G. (2019). Hands-free one-time and continuous authentication using glass wearable devices. *Journal of Information Security and Applications*, 46, 138–150. https://doi.org/10.1016/j.jisa.2019.02.002

de la Guía, E., Camacho, V. L., Orozco-Barbosa, L., Luján, V. M. B., Penichet, V. M., & Pérez, M. L. (2016). Introducing IoT and wearable technologies into task-based language learning for young children. *IEEE Transactions on Learning Technologies*, 9(4), 366–378. https://doi.org/10.1109/TLT.2016.2557333

Díaz, A., Pérez, S., & López, D. M. (2019). Adaptation component based on wearable technology to support personalized tracking of physical activity in children. *Studies in Health Technology and Informatics*, 261, 115–121.

Divis, K., Anderson-Bergman, C., Abbott, R., Newton, V., & Emmanuel-Aviña, G. (2018). Physiological and cognitive factors related to human performance during the Grand Canyon rim-to-rim hike. *Journal of Human Performance in Extreme Environments*, 14(1), Article 5. https://doi.org/10.7771/2327-2937.1095

Euteneuer, J. (2018). Conspicuous computing: Gamified bodies, playful composition, and the monsters in your pocket. *Computers and Composition, 50*, 53–65. https://doi.org/10.1016/j.compcom.2018.07.001

Feiner, S., MacIntyre, B., & Seligmann, D. (1993). Knowledge-based augmented reality. *Communications of the ACM, 36*(7), 53–62. https://doi.org/10.1145/159544.159587

Fogarty, I., Winey, T., Howe, J., Hancox, G., & Whyley, D. (2016, March). Engineering brightness: Using STEM to brighten hearts and minds. In *Integrated STEM Education Conference (ISEC), 2016 IEEE* (pp. 5–12). IEEE. Retrieved from http://ieeexplore.ieee.org.ezproxy.lib.uwf.edu/stamp/stamp.jsp?tp=&arnumber=7457559

Garcia, J. J., de Bruyckere, H., Keyson, D. V., & Romero, N. (2013). Designing personal informatics for self-reflection and self-awareness: The case of children with attention deficit hyperactivity disorder. In J. C. Augusto, R. Wichert, R. Collier, D. Keyson, A. A. Salah, & A. H. Tan (Eds.), *Ambient intelligence*. Lecture Notes in Computer Science. Cham: Springer.

Gauttier, S. (2018, July). Hospital 5.0: Enhancing nurses with the use of wearables. *Proceedings of the 32nd International BCS Human Computer Interaction Conference*, Belfast, UK (pp. 1–5). https://doi.org/10.14236/ewic/HCI2018.78

Harrow, A. (1972). *A taxonomy of psychomotor domain: A guide for developing behavioral objectives.* New York, NY: Addison-Wesley Longman Ltd.

Havard, B., & Podsiad, M. (2017). Wearable computers. In T. Kidd & L. R. Morris (Eds.), *Handbook of instructional systems and technology* (pp. 356–365). Hershey, PA: IGI Global.

Havard, B. & Podsiad, M. (2020). A meta-analysis of wearables research in educational settings published 2016–2019. *Education Technology Research and Development, 68*(4), 1829–1854. https://doi.org/10.1007/s11423-020-09789-y

Jacobs, J. V., Hettinger, L. J., Huang, Y.-H., Jeffries, S., Lesch, M. F., Simmons, L. A., Verma, S. K., & Willetts, J. L. (2019). Employee acceptance of wearable technology in the workplace. *Applied Ergonomics, 78*, 148–156. https://doi.org/10.1016/j.apergo.2019.03.003

Kerner, C., & Goodyear, V. A. (2017). The motivational impact of wearable healthy lifestyle technologies: A self-determination perspective on fitbits with adolescents. *American Journal of Health Education, 48*(5), 287–297. https://doi.org/10.1080/19325037.2017.1343161

Kirk, M. A., Amiri, M., Pirbaglou, M., & Ritvo, P. (2019). Wearable technology and physical activity behavior change in adults with chronic cardiometabolic disease: A systematic review and meta-analysis. *American Journal of Health Promotion, 33*(5), 778–791. https://doi.org/10.1177/0890117118816278

Knight, A., & Bidargaddi, N. (2018). Commonly available activity tracker apps and wearables as a mental health outcome indicator: A prospective observational cohort study among young adults with psychological distress. *Journal of Affective Disorders, 236*, 31–36. https://doi.org/10.1016/j.jad.2018.04.099

Krathwohl, D. R., Bloom, B. S., & Masia, B. B. (1964). *Taxonomy of educational objectives: The classification of educational goals. Handbook II: Affective domain.* New York, NY: David McKay Co., Inc.

Kuhn, J., Lukowicz, P., Hirth, M., Poxrucker, A., Weppner, J., & Younas, J. (2016). gPhysics: Using smart glasses for head-centered, context-aware learning in physics experiments. *IEEE Transactions on Learning Technologies*, 9(4), 304–317. https://doi.org/10.1109/tlt.2016.2554115

Lamming, M., & Flynn, M. (1994). Forget-me-not: Intimate computing in support of human memory. *Proceedings of FRIEND21, 1994 International Symposium on Next Generation Human Interface*, Meguro Gajoen, Japan (pp. 125–128).

Lee, U., Han, K., Cho, H., Chung, K.-M., Hong, H., Lee, S.-J., Youngtae, N., Park, S., & Carroll, J. M. (2019). Intelligent positive computing with mobile, wearable, and IoT devices: Literature review and research directions. *Ad Hoc Networks, 83*, 8–24. https://doi.org/10.1016/j.adhoc.2018.08.021

Lindberg, R., Seo, J., & Laine, T. H. (2016). Enhancing physical education with exergames and wearable technology. *IEEE Transactions on Learning Technologies*, 9(4), 328–341. https://doi.org/10.1109/TLT.2016.2556671

Litts, B., Kafai, Y., Lui, D., Walker, J., & Widman, S. (2017). Stitching codeable circuits: High school students' learning about circuitry and coding with electronic textiles. *Journal of Science Education & Technology*, 26(5), 494–507. https://doi.org.ezproxy.lib.uwf.edu/10.1007/s10956-017-9694-0

Liu, D. (2004). Maintenance activities with wearables as training and performance aids. *Proceedings of the 2004 Conference of the Computer-Human Interaction Special Interest Group of the Human Factors and Ergonomics Society of Australia (OzCHI2004)*, Wollongong, NSW, (pp. 1–5).

Mann, S. (1996, November). 'Smart clothing': Wearable multimedia computing and 'personal imaging' to restore the technological balance between people and their environments. *ACM Multimedia, 96*, 163–174. Retrieved from http://www.nomads.usp.br

Mann, S. (1997, October). An historical account of the 'WearComp' and 'WearCam' inventions developed for applications in 'personal imaging'. *Proceedings of the First International Symposium on Wearables*, Cambridge, MA, (pp. 66–73). https://doi.org/10.1109/ISWC.1997.629921

Mann, S. (2014). Wearable computing. In M. Soegaard & R. F. Dam (Eds.), *The encyclopedia of human-computer interaction* (2nd ed.). Retrieved from https://www.interaction-design.org/literature/book/the-encyclopedia-of-human-computer-interaction-2nd-ed/wearable-computing

Matias, E., MacKenzie, I. S., & Buxton, W. (1994, April). Half-QWERTY: Typing with one hand using your two-handed skills. *Proceedings of the CHI '94 Conference on Human Factors in Computing Systems*, Boston, MA, (pp. 51–52).

McCann, J., & Bryson, D. (Eds.). (2009). *Smart clothes and wearable technology*. Sawston, Cambridge: Woodhead Publishing.

Merkouris, A., Chorianopoulos, K., & Kameas, A. (2017). Teaching programming in secondary education through embodied computing platforms. *ACM Transactions on Computing Education*, 17(2), 1–22. https://doi.org/10.1145/3025013

Minocha, S., Tudor, A. D., Banks, D., Holland, C., McNulty, C., Ail, R., Rohit, P. J., & Bowering, S. (2018). Role of digital health wearables in the wellbeing and quality of life of older people and careers. *Knowledge Exchange Seminar Series (KESS): Using Technology in Social Care*, Belfast, UK. http://oro.open.ac.uk/id/eprint/55887

Najjar, L., Thompson, C., & Ockerman, J. (1999). Using a wearable computer for continuous learning and support. *Mobile Networks & Applications*, 4(1), 69–74. https://doi.org/10.1023/A:1019126226904

Nederveen, J. P., Thomas, A. C. Q., & Parise, G. (2019). Examining the first-person perspective as appropriate prelaboratory preparation. *Advances in Physiology Education, 43*(3), 317–323. https://doi.org/10.1152/advan.00213.2018

Ngai, G., Chan, S. C. F., Ng, V. T. Y., Cheung, J. C. Y., Choy, S. S. S., Lau, W. W. Y., & Tse, J. T. P. (2010, April). i*CATch: A scalable plug-n-play wearable computing framework for novices and children. In *Proceedings of the SIGCHI Conference on Human Factors in Computing Systems*, Atlanta, GA (pp. 443–452). ACM. https://doi.org/10.1145/1753326.1753393

Oh, S., So, H.-J., & Gaydos, M. (2018). Hybrid augmented reality for participatory learning: The hidden efficacy of multi-user game-based simulation. *IEEE Transactions on Learning Technologies, 11*(1), 115–127. https://doi.org/10.1109/tlt.2017.2750673

Parton, B. S. (2017). Glass vision 3D: Digital discovery for the deaf. *TechTrends, 61*(2), 141–146. https://doi.org/10.1007/s11528-016-0090-z

Peppler, K., Danish, J., Zaitlen, B., Glosson, D., Jacobs, A., & Phelps, D. (2010, June). BeeSim: Leveraging wearable computers in participatory simulations with young children. In *Proceedings of the 9th International Conference on Interaction Design and Children*, Barcelona, Spain (pp. 246–249). ACM. https://doi.org/10.1145/1810543.1810582

Perez, A. J., & Zeadally, S. (2018). Privacy issues and solutions for consumer wearables. *IT Professional, 20*(4), 46–56. https://doi.org/10.1109/MITP.2017.265105905

Pintrich, P. R., & Schunk, D. H. (2002). *Motivation in education: Theory, research, and applications* (2nd ed.). Englewood Cliffs, NJ: Merrill, Prentice-Hall International.

Pontoriero, A. D., Charlton, P. H., & Alastruey, J. (2018). Alzheimer's disease: A step towards prognosis using smart wearables. *Multidisciplinary Digital Publishing Institute Proceedings, 4*(1), 8–14. https://doi.org/10.3390/ecsa-5-05742

Popat, K. A., & Sharma, P. (2013). Wearable computer applications: A future perspective. *International Journal of Engineering and Innovative Technology 3*, 213–217.

ReWalk Robotics. (2014). ReWalk motorized device helps people with disabilities to walk. Retrieved from https://www.disabled-world.com/assistivedevices/mobility/rewalk.php

Rhodes, B. (n.d.). A brief history of wearable computing. Retrieved from http://www.media.mit.edu/wearables/lizzy/timeline.html

Rosales, A., Sayago, S., & Blat, J. (2015). Beeping socks and chirping arm bands: wearables that foster free play. *Computer, 48*(6), 41–48. https://doi.org/10.1109/MC.2015.168

Schaule, F., Johanssen, J. O., Bruegge, B., & Loftness, V. (2018). Employing consumer wearables to detect office workers' cognitive load for interruption management. *Proceedings of the ACM on Interactive, Mobile, Wearable and Ubiquitous Technologies, 2*(1), Article 32. https://doi.org/10.1145/3191764

Seneviratne, S., Hu, Y., Nguyen, T., Lan, G., Khalifa, S., Thilakarathna, K., Mahbub, H., & Seneviratne, A. (2017). A survey of wearable devices and challenges. *IEEE Communications Surveys & Tutorials, 19*(4), 2573–2620. https://doi.org/10.1109/COMST.2017.2731979

Shilkrot, R., Huber, J., Liu, C., Maes, P., & Nanayakkara, S. C. (2014, April). FingerReader: A wearable device to support text reading on the go. *Proceedings of the CHI'14 Extended Abstracts on Human Factors in Computing Systems*, Ontario, CA (pp. 2359–2364). https://doi.org/10.1145/2559206.2581220

Sobko, T., & Brown, G. (2019). Reflecting on personal data in a health course: Integrating wearable technology and ePortfolio for eHealth. *Australasian Journal of Educational Technology, 35*(3). https://doi.org/10.14742/ajet.4027

Soni, J., & Goodman, R. (2017). *A mind at play: How Claude Shannon invented the information age.* New York, NY: Simon & Schuster.

Starner, T. (1994). The cyborgs are coming or the real personal computers. Retrieved from https://hd.media.mit.edu/tech-reports/TR-318-ABSTRACT.html

Van Til, K., McInnis, M. G., & Cochran, A. (2019). A comparative study of engagement in mobile and wearable health monitoring for bipolar disorder. *Bipolar Disorders.* https://doi.org/10.1111/bdi.12849

Vandrico. (2024). The wearables database. Retrieved from https://vandrico.com/wearables/list.html

Vasudevan, V., Kafai, Y., & Yang, L. (2015). Make, wear, play: Remix designs of wearable controllers for scratch games by middle school youth. In *Proceedings of the 14th International Conference on Interaction Design and Children* (pp. 339–342). ACM. https://doi.org/10.1145/2771839.2771911

Wargo, J. M. (2018). Writing with wearables? Young children's intra-active authoring and the sounds of emplaced invention. *Journal of Literacy Research, 50*(4), 502–523. https://doi.org/10.1177/1086296X18802880

Williams, R. M., & Gilbert, J. E. (2020). Perseverations of the academy: A survey of wearable technologies applied to autism intervention. *International Journal of Human-Computer Studies, 143*, 102485. https://doi.org/10.1016/j.ijhcs.2020.102485

Wood, S. A. (2018). Framing wearing: Genre, embodiment, and exploring wearable technology in the composition classroom. *Computers and Composition, 50*, 66–77. https://doi.org/10.1016/j.compcom.2018.07.004

Yen, H.-Y., & Chiu, H.-L. (2019). The effectiveness of wearable technologies as physical activity interventions in weight control: A systematic review and meta-analysis of randomized controlled trials. *Obesity Reviews, 10*, 1485. https://doi.org/10.1111/obr.12909

Zhou, B., Bahle, G., Fürg, L., Singh, M. S., Cruz, H. Z., & Lukowicz, P. (2017, March). Trainwear: A real-time assisted training feedback system with fabric wearable sensors. *Proceedings of the 2017 IEEE International Conference on Pervasive Computing and Communications Workshops (PerCom Workshops)*, Kona, HI (pp. 85–87). https://doi.org/10.1109/PERCOMW.2017.7917531

PART VI

Digital Learning in Social Contexts

12

COMPUTER-SUPPORTED COLLABORATIVE LEARNING

Ingo Kollar, Martin Greisel, Tugce Özbek, Laura Spang and Freydis Vogel

What Is Computer-Supported Collaborative Learning?

Computer-Supported Collaborative Learning (CSCL) is an umbrella term that can be applied to characterize a very broad range of instructional scenarios in which "peers interact [...] with each other for the purpose of learning and with the support of information and communication technologies" (Suthers, 2012, p. 719). Given the breadth of this definition, it is not surprising that CSCL can come in very different forms, both with respect to the specific instructional setting and with respect to the kinds of technologies that are used as support for collaborative learning (Cress et al., 2021). For example, while quite some CSCL studies focus on small groups such as dyads (e.g., Popov et al., 2017) or triads (e.g., Slof et al., 2016), others investigate CSCL in whole classrooms (e.g., Chan, 2011) or even in large-scale online communities that consist of thousands of learners (e.g., Halatchliyski et al., 2014). With respect to technology, studies range from using synchronous chat environments (e.g., Lee et al., 2015) and asynchronous discussion forums (De Wever et al., 2010) to computer simulations (e.g., Lui & Slotta, 2014), multitouch tables (Bause et al., 2018), or virtual (VR) or augmented reality (AR) technology (Enyedy & Yoon, 2021).

This vast variety of different CSCL approaches is accompanied by a multiplicity of (largely compatible) theoretical and methodological approaches. At the theoretical level, socio-cognitive theories (e.g., Fischer et al., 2013) intermingle with socio-cultural theories (e.g., Bereiter & Scardamalia, 2014) as well as with theories from philosophy (e.g., Stahl, 2021) or linguistics (Wegerif, 2006). Methodologically, experimental (Janssen & Kollar, 2021) as

DOI: 10.4324/9781003386131-18

well as non-experimental case study designs (Koschmann & Schwarz, 2021) and both quantitative and qualitative analysis methods (for an overview, see Hmelo-Silver & Jeong, 2021) are used to investigate a broad variety of research questions related to CSCL, often following a design-based research approach (Kali & Hoadley, 2021).

This variety of theoretical, methodological, and instructional approaches affects how this chapter summarizes meta-analytic evidence on the effectiveness of CSCL. First, unlike many other chapters in this volume, this chapter is not and cannot be restricted to just one specific digital medium. Instead, we try to present findings that cover a broad range of media and instructional settings. Second, in order to keep with the overall concept of this volume, we mostly restrict ourselves to meta-analytical findings that by nature build on quantitative, (quasi-)experimental research. Nevertheless, we do want to point out that there is a wealth of high-quality qualitative and mixed methods research on CSCL that has produced and still continues to produce important insights into the conditions and effects, and most importantly, into the processes that happen during CSCL and their importance for learning at the individual and the social level (see Uttamchandani & Lester, 2019).

Against this background, this chapter is structured as follows: In Section "The Overall Effectiveness of CSCL—Or: Why Should CSCL Be Effective in the First Place?", we provide theoretical reasons for why CSCL should be an effective learning method. Section "What Are the Effects of "CS" in CSCL?" turns to the available meta-analytical evidence, starting with studies that looked at the overall effects of CSCL (compared to more traditional ways of teaching and learning) on various learning outcomes. In Section "Enhancing the Effects of CSCL Through Scaffolding", we report meta-analytical evidence on the effects that computer support (in its various forms) has on the effectiveness of collaborative learning. This is followed by Section "What Learning Processes Are Crucial for the Effectiveness of CSCL?" that describes meta-analytical evidence on different scaffolding approaches in CSCL, as scaffolding appears to be one of the main topics of CSCL research that is covered with (quasi-)experimental design and quantitative methods (Kollar et al., 2018). In Section "Further Important Moderators for the Effectiveness of CSCL", we report on the (scarce) meta-analytical evidence regarding the question of which learning processes are likely to be responsible for the effects of CSCL on learning outcomes before we discuss important moderator variables that have an impact on the effectiveness of CSCL. The chapter ends with a summary of the meta-analytical evidence and a description of possible routes for further (meta-analytical) research on CSCL (Section "Limitations, Conclusions, and Avenues for Future Research").

The Overall Effectiveness of CSCL—Or: Why Should CSCL Be Effective in the First Place?

As mentioned previously, a broad range of theories postulate that CSCL has a high potential to facilitate learning processes and outcomes. From a socio-cognitive perspective, CSCL is assumed to be a context in which socio-cognitive conflicts are likely to unfold. Solving such socio-cognitive conflicts (e.g., when two learners disagree in their understanding of a scientific concept) is assumed to be associated with a restructuring of cognitive schemata in long-term memory (Weinberger et al., 2013). From a socio-cultural perspective, learners may provide each other with so-called zones of proximal development (ZPD). This refers to situations in which one learner helps another learner accomplish tasks that would otherwise be too difficult for them, for example by asking thought-provoking questions (see King, 2007).

In line with these theoretical considerations, existing meta-analyses report positive (albeit moderate) overall effects of CSCL on performance and learning. For example, a meta-analysis by Jeong et al. (2019) that investigated the effects of CSCL in STEM domains based on 316 outcomes from 143 studies with $N = 12.380$ students that compared CSCL with some kind of control group (ranging from individual learning with or without computers to traditional classrooms using little or no technology) yielded an overall effect of $g = 0.51$. Almost identical results were obtained by Talan (2021), who reported an average effect of CSCL on academic achievement of $g = 0.52$, based on 40 studies including $N = 3.474$ participants. Thus, the meta-analyses show that CSCL improves the effectiveness of learning arrangements moderately on average.

What Are the Effects of "CS" in CSCL?

Clearly, the effect sizes reported so far can only provide a very coarse-grained idea of the effectiveness of CSCL, as they are based on comparisons that do not differentiate between different kinds of CSCL, different instructional approaches, or different kinds of digital tools that are used to support collaboration. The question of what computer support actually adds to the effects of collaborative learning has however been investigated in several meta-analyses. Based on results from 71 studies with a total of $N = 11.286$ students, Chen et al. (2018) found collaborative learning with computer support to be significantly more effective than collaborative learning without computer support, with effect sizes ranging from $g = 0.45$ (for effects on knowledge) to $g = 0.89$ (for effects on group task performance). When only covering CSCL studies that used mobile computer support (e.g., mobile phones, handhelds, or wearables) and comparing its effect to groups that collaborated without computers, Sung et al. (2017) arrived at an effect size of $g = 0.47$ based on 11 studies. However, when comparing mobile to non-mobile computer support, further comparisons based on six studies showed that mobile computer support was only descriptively superior to non-mobile computer support ($g = 0.20$). Thus, the potential effects of mobile technologies to support CSCL are only small at best, compared to non-mobile CSCL.

Besides different devices, computers are used to support collaborative learning in very different instructional arrangements. The aforementioned study by Jeong et al. (2019) investigated whether the effectiveness of CSCL depends on the kind of computer support that was used in related studies (in the STEM context). Their results showed that CSCL seems to work best when it is realized in settings that use computer simulations to support learning ($g = 1.07$), followed by CSCL in integrated environments (i.e., environments that use multiple technological tools to support learning and collaboration; $g = 0.68$), and settings that make use of participatory technology (e.g., wikis; $g = 0.65$). At the lower end of the spectrum were settings that used immersive technologies ($g = 0.31$). Results from the meta-analysis of Chen et al. (2018) partially support this pattern: In their study, which used a slightly different typology of digital tools that have been used in CSCL research, the largest effects were found for settings that were based on learning with graphs or multimedia ($g = 0.67$ for knowledge; $g = 1.20$ for skills as dependent variable). Interestingly though, when certain tools are combined, the positive effect of CSCL may even disappear: According to Jeong et al. (2019), this is the case, for example, in CSCL settings that combine email with chat and video conferencing ($g = -0.02$). Whether students collaborate synchronously or asynchronously, however, does not seem to make a difference: For both modes of collaboration, Jeong et al. (2019) found almost identical effect sizes ($g = 0.51$ for synchronous collaboration, and $g = 0.50$ for asynchronous collaboration).

Thus, overall, computer support indeed seems to make collaborative learning more effective. This seems to be the case, especially when group task performance is used as a dependent variable. For (individual) knowledge acquisition, positive CSCL effects exist as well but are considerably smaller. Also, the kind of technology that is used to realize CSCL seems to matter: It seems that effects are larger when computers do not simply offer digital communication channels but are rather used to provide didactically designed tools such as simulations or integrated learning environments. Yet, the findings by Jeong et al. (2019) showing that CSCL that combines email with chat and videoconferencing does not yield positive effects point to caution when deciding what kinds of technologies to combine to support CSCL.

Enhancing the Effects of CSCL Through Scaffolding

As mentioned, a large part of the (quasi-)experimental CSCL research is concerned with the question of how learners can be scaffolded in CSCL contexts. Scaffolds enable students to solve tasks that are slightly above their current proficiency level and thereby help them acquire higher competence levels (Wood et al., 1976). In terms of CSCL, scaffolding is often directed toward helping students engage in discourse on a higher level, which in turn is assumed to be positively related to knowledge and skill acquisition.

In an attempt to estimate the effects of various kinds of CSCL scaffolds on learning outcomes, Chen et al. (2018) differentiated between four scaffolding strategies: (a) teacher's facilitation, in which guidance is provided by the teacher or instructor, (b) peer feedback and peer assessment, in which support is provided by peers, (c) role assignment, which may, for example, be done by describing and distributing activities that are associated with different roles during collaboration (De Wever & Strijbos, 2021), and (d) instruction and guidance, which refers to scaffolds intentionally designed beforehand to support student engagement in higher-order learning activities (e.g., through activity prompts). When it comes to fostering knowledge acquisition (defined as subject matter knowledge improvement), the effects of all these scaffolds are rather similar to each other, with moderate effect sizes around $g = 0.40$. With respect to skill acquisition (e.g., thinking skills and problem-solving skills), however, instruction and guidance have considerably larger effects ($g = 0.75$) than peer feedback and assessment ($g = 0.51$) and teacher facilitation ($g = 0.36$). Yet, when considering group task performance, teacher guidance has effects that are comparable to instruction and guidance (around $g = 0.50$–0.60), while peer feedback and assessment as well as role assignment have hardly any effects.

One scaffolding approach that has received particular attention in CSCL research is the collaboration script approach (Kollar et al., 2006). Collaboration scripts (or "CSCL scripts"; Vogel et al., 2022) are scaffolds that specify, sequence, and distribute learning activities and/or collaboration roles among the learners of a small group and thereby aim at supporting learners' knowledge and skill acquisition. For example, in a study by Weinberger et al. (2010), Educational Science students were asked to solve authentic problem cases with the aid of psychological theories in triads. In one condition, triads received a CSCL script that had the three group members take turns analyzing the cases and critiquing the case analyses of their fellow learners. For each of these tasks, they received prompts that helped them fill in their current role at a high level (e.g., when critiquing their fellow learners' analysis, one prompt was "What I did not understand in your analysis was…"). Results showed that learners from the scripted condition outperformed learners from an unscripted condition when analyzing a subsequent transfer case.

Similar evidence has been collected across a broad range of domains and tasks (e.g., Demetriadis et al., 2011; Gelmini-Hornsby et al., 2011; Noroozi et al., 2013; Rummel & Spada, 2005; Schwaighofer et al., 2017). In an attempt to aggregate these findings, Vogel et al. (2017) conducted a meta-analysis that tested the effects of CSCL scripts on (a) the acquisition of domain-specific knowledge (i.e., knowledge about the content that is discussed within groups), and (b) the acquisition of cross-domain skills such as argumentation skills or collaboration skills. Based on 22 articles with a total of N = 2.825 participants, they found a large positive effect on the acquisition of cross-domain skills (d = 0.95), and a small positive effect on the acquisition of domain knowledge (d = 0.20), which however increased to d = 0.30 when CSCL scripts were enhanced or combined with some sort of content-related support such as worked examples or content schemes.. Similar results were found by Radkowitsch et al. (2020), based on 53 studies in which N = 5.616 learners participated. Yet, the study by Radkowitsch et al. (2020) enhanced the previous analyses by not only considering cognitive but also motivational learning outcomes. They included motivational outcomes because of claims in the literature that scripting CSCL risks diminishing learners' autonomy regarding how to collaborate with each other. Based on self-determination theory (Ryan & Deci, 2000), low levels of perceived autonomy might undermine intrinsic motivation. The results of the meta-analysis by Radkowitsch et al. (2020), however, seem to imply that this concern is not warranted: Descriptively, they even found a small positive (albeit insignificant) effect of CSCL scripts on motivation (g = 0.13).

To sum up, meta-analytical evidence clearly shows that the effectiveness of CSCL can be significantly enhanced when additional scaffolds are introduced that structure within-group collaboration. This seems to be specifically true for the development of skills and to a lesser extent for the acquisition of domain-specific knowledge. Thereby, predefined and predesigned guidance such as the use of CSCL scripts seems to be particularly helpful, especially when it is combined with content-specific support.

What Learning Processes Are Crucial for the Effectiveness of CSCL?

As previously mentioned, the meta-analysis by Chen et al. (2018) reported a positive effect of CSCL on individual learning outcomes with an effect size of g = 0.45. Yet, the question is which processes are responsible for these effects. Unfortunately, though, this question has hardly been analyzed in meta-analyses on CSCL as of now (even though there are some primary studies on this issue showing that learners seem to learn more, the more they build on each other's contribution, e.g., through the development of counterarguments; see, for example, Vogel, et al., 2016).

One exception is a meta-analysis by Saqr et al. (2022). The authors aggregated the results of 19 studies with a total of N = 12.293 participants that gathered CSCL process data through Social Network Analysis (SNA) and looked at the extent to which different measures of centrality predict learning outcomes (which in most studies was measured via final course or task grade). SNA gives researchers the opportunity to identify interaction patterns between the members of a group, resulting in a network of nodes (representing members of the group) and connections between nodes that are getting thicker the more two group members interact with each other. At the statistical level, SNA produces a range of "centrality" indicators that reflect how crucial the individual group members were for communication within a group. For example, *degree centrality* represents the overall number of connections (of whatever type) one group member has to all other members of the group. Degree centrality can further be subdivided into *indegree centrality* (how often a group member was addressed by other group members) and *outdegree centrality* (how often a group member turned to each other group member). Results of this meta-analysis showed that the various centrality indicators were on average correlated with achievement by $r = 0.46$. This indicates that the more central group members are during CSCL, the higher their achievement.

To sum up, evidence both from primary studies as well as from meta-analyses indicates that CSCL leads to higher learning outcomes, the more the CSCL scenario triggers students to build on each others' contributions to the learning process. Yet, meta-analytical evidence on this topic is limited, as it hardly investigated how exactly groups and group members actually engage in collaboration during CSCL. Here, further research is clearly needed.

Further Important Moderators for the Effectiveness of CSCL

The previous sections already alluded to the fact that the effects of CSCL at least partially seem to be dependent on further variables, so-called *moderators*. As described, important moderators seem to be the kind of digital tool that is being used to realize CSCL (Jeong et al., 2019) as well as the dependent variables that are considered (Chen et al., 2018, Vogel et al., 2017). Thus, the overall mid-sized effects of CSCL from the studies by Jeong et al. (2019) and from Talan (2021) we reported earlier appear to be a rather coarse-grained approximation to predict the effectiveness of CSCL in a specific context. In the following, we list results from moderator analyses in the aforementioned studies that focus on (a) the educational levels of participants in CSCL studies, (b) the domain in which CSCL is realized, and (c) the intervention duration.

Educational level. The results of Talan (2021), Jeong et al. (2019), and Sung et al. (2017) consistently show that the effects of CSCL seem to be largest for secondary-level students ($g \approx 0.65$). Similar, but a bit lower effect sizes (roughly around $g = 0.50$) are reported for university students, at least by Talan (2021) as well as by Jeong et al. (2019). The latter additionally shows that graduate students seem to benefit more from CSCL than under-graduate students. The results by Sung et al. (2017) represent an interesting exception: In their meta-analysis, which is restricted to the comparison of *mobile* CSCL vs. collaboration without technology support, the average effect size for adult learners is only $g = 0.38$. A speculative interpretation might be that a considerable share of adult learners might lack thorough experiences with mobile learning settings, which might make mobile CSCL more challenging for these learners than for younger students. The fact that the meta-analysis by Sung et al. (2017) includes a fair share of primary studies from before 2010 might add to this interpretation, as using mobile technologies to support learning has only rather recently been taken up more broadly (before 2010, adult learners very likely had hardly any prior experiences with mobile learning, putting them into an even more disad-vantaged position).

Domain. Also, the domain in which CSCL is realized seems to have an impact on its effectiveness. Yet, available meta-analytical evidence does not appear to be conclusive: While Jeong et al. (2019) report the largest CSCL effects in the science domain ($g = 0.67$), in Talan's (2021) study, CSCL had the largest effects when being used in computer science ($g = 0.66$). In his study, the effects in the science domain were considerably lower ($g = 0.52$) than in Jeong et al. (2019). However, both studies agree more or less on the fact that CSCL seems to be less effective when used in the social sciences: For the domain of education, Jeong et al. (2019) report an effect size of $g = 0.39$, and Talan (2021) presents an overall effect size of $g = 0.43$ for the social sciences in general. Similar results are reported by Vogel et al. (2017) for the effectiveness of CSCL scripts, which appear to be higher when used in science than in the social sciences. Again, though, the analogous effect size reported by Sung et al. (2017) is considerably smaller ($g = 0.22$). A tentative explanation might be that social sciences students might have less experience with mobile learning and therefore struggle with such learning environments more than students from the sciences. Another idea might be that social sciences students are con-fronted with ill-defined problems more often than students from other domains. When they are supposed to work on such complex tasks while being required to use technology that they may be unfamiliar with, this might easily result in cognitive overload (Kirschner et al., 2018). Yet, whether this really is the case should be established by further studies.

Intervention duration. Both the results by Chen et al. (2018) and Sung et al. (2017) seem to imply that in order to be effective, CSCL interventions should not be too short, but also not take too much time: In Sung et al. (2017), the largest effects were found for interventions that lasted between one and four weeks ($g = 0.87$). Chen et al. (2018) report higher effect sizes for interventions with a duration of between one month and one semester

(g = 0.52) than for shorter (g = 0.36) or longer interventions (g = 0.40), at least when CSCL was compared to individualized computer-supported learning. Thus, to play out its potential, it seems advisable to give students the opportunity to collect plenty of experiences with CSCL, but also not overdo it so that students might become bored with the experience. In fact, some of the decrease in effect sizes in interventions with longer duration may actually hint at the existence of a novelty effect. Yet, further research is necessary to test this assumption.

Limitations, Conclusions, and Avenues for Future Research

Limiting this chapter to the summary of meta-analytical evidence on CSCL does not come without problems. Most importantly, it cannot cover empirical evidence that has not yet been a topic of meta-analytical research on CSCL. Thus, on the one hand, this chapter neither covers the rich body of CSCL research that exhibits a more qualitative (e.g., Hämäläinen & Arvaja, 2010) nor the results from publications that have their origins in the computer science community, which represents a significant contributor to research on CSCL as well (e.g., Villasclaras-Fernandéz et al., 2013). On the other hand, the sheer number of meta-analyses on CSCL is still small. In other words, many questions remain open, even though primary studies with (quasi-)experimental research designs exist, which however have not yet been merged in a meta-analytical way. For example, there is a considerable number of studies on group awareness tools (i.e., scaffolds that mirror results from pre-questionnaires or from automated interaction analyses back to the group; Schnaubert & Bodemer, 2022), the results of which have not yet undergone a meta-analysis. Thus, we recommend CSCL research to conduct further meta-analyses on important research questions, but also pledge for more narrative reviews that also cover the abundant results from non-(quasi-) experimental research on CSCL.

Despite these shortcomings, this chapter provides meta-analytical evidence that CSCL is an effective way to foster learning, with moderate effect sizes. We further showed that part of these effects can be attributed to the provision of computer support. In addition, we saw that using technology to not only give a forum for, but rather to *scaffold* collaboration increases the effects of CSCL even more, for example through the provision of CSCL scripts. All these effects, however, seem to be moderated by a range of variables, including both proximal ones such as the kind of dependent variables that are studied, and more distal ones such as the participants' educational level, the domain of study, or the intervention duration.

Against the background of this chapter, we see at least two avenues for future meta-analytical CSCL research: First, we must concede that even though first meta-analytical evidence on the effects of CSCL on learning

188 Designing Effective Digital Learning Environments

processes is available (see Saqr et al., 2022), more of such research is necessary. Most importantly, it is still unclear (a) how students' actual engagement in interactive activities *in general*, and (b) their engagement in *certain kinds* of interactive activities (such as negotiation or argumentation) relates to academic achievement (and possibly also non-cognitive learning outcomes). We therefore recommend future meta-analytical research on CSCL to aggregate findings from CSCL studies that provide in-depth analyses of learning processes, in order to increase our knowledge of which learning processes to target when designing CSCL. Second, along with the rise of Learning Analytics, more personalized and adaptive CSCL environments come within reach of educational practice. However, up to now, evidence of the effects of such adaptive CSCL environments is scarce. Instead, CSCL research in this area has mainly focused on the promises of Learning Analytics to support teacher behavior during CSCL (e.g., van Leeuwen et al., 2014; Rodriguez-Triana et al., 2015). As a more long-term goal, we hope to see more research that analyzes the actual effects of adaptive CSCL on learning, which might then eventually be summarized in a subsequent meta-analysis.

Evidence-Based Practice Recommendations

- CSCL can be an effective way to facilitate learning across different domains, age groups, and educational institutions.
- Using computer technology to scaffold collaboration can make collaborative learning more effective.
- Providing additional structure to CSCL, for example, through the provision of collaboration scripts, can enhance its effectiveness.
- CSCL is especially effective when learners are encouraged to frequently build on each other's contributions.
- New technologies are promising to make adaptive support for CSCL possible.

References

Bause, I., Brich, I. R., Wesslein, A.-K., & Hesse, F. W. (2018). Using technological functions on a multi-touch table and their affordances to counteract biases and foster collaborative problem solving. *International Journal of Computer-Supported Collaborative Learning*, 13(1), 7–33. https://doi.org/10.1007/s11412-018-9271-4

Bereiter, C., & Scardamalia, M. (2014). Knowledge building and knowledge creation: One concept, two hills to climb. In S. C. Tan, H. J. So, & J. Yeo (Eds.), *Knowledge creation in education* (pp. 35–52). Springer.

Chan, C. K. K. (2011). Bridging research and practice: Implementing and sustaining knowledge building in Hong Kong classrooms. *International Journal of Computer-Supported Collaborative Learning*, 6, 147–186. https://doi.org/10.1007/s11412-011-9121-0

Chen, J., Wang, M., Kirschner, P. A., & Tsai, C-C. (2018). The role of collaboration, computer use, learning environments, and supporting strategies in CSCL: A meta-analysis. *Review of Educational Research*, 88(6), 799–843. https://doi.org/10.3102/0034654318791584

Cress, U., Oshima, J., Rosé, C., & Wise, A. (2021). Foundations, processes, technologies, and methods: An overview of CSCL through its handbook. In U. Cress, J. Oshima, C. Rosé, & A. Wise (Eds.), *International handbook of computer-supported collaborative learning* (pp. 3–22). Springer.

De Wever, B., & Strijbos, B. (2021). Roles for structuring groups for collaboration. In U. Cress, J. Oshima, C. Rosé, & A. Wise (Eds.), *International handbook of computer-supported collaborative learning* (pp. 315–331). Springer.

De Wever, B., Van Keer, H., Schellens, T., & Valcke, M. (2010). Roles as a structuring tool in online discussion groups: The differential impact of different roles on social knowledge construction. *Computers in Human Behavior*, 26(4), 516–523. https://doi.org/10.1016/j.chb.2009.08.008

Demetriadis, S., Egerter, T., Hanisch, F., & Fischer, F. (2011). Peer review-based scripted collaboration to support domain-specific and domain-general knowledge acquisition in computer science. *Computer Science Education*, 21(1), 29–56. https://doi.org/10.1080/08993408.2010.539069

Enyedy, N., & Yoon, S. (2021). Immersive environments: Learning in augmented + virtual reality. In U. Cress, J. Oshima, C. Rosé, & A. Wise (Eds.), *International handbook of computer-supported collaborative learning* (pp. 389–405). Springer.

Fischer, F., Kollar, I., Stegmann, K., & Wecker, C. (2013). Towards a script theory of guidance in computer-supported collaborative learning. *Educational Psychologist*, 48(1), 56–66. https://doi.org/10.1080/00461520.2012.748005

Gelmini-Hornsby, G., Ainsworth, S., & O'Malley, C. (2011). Guided reciprocal questioning to support children's collaborative storytelling. *International Journal of Computer-Supported Collaborative Learning*, 6(4), 577–600. https://doi.org/10.1007/s11412-011-9129-5

Halatchliyski, I., Moskaliuk, J., Kimmerle, J., & Cress, U. (2014). Explaining authors' contribution to pivotal artifacts during mass collaboration in the Wikipedia's knowledge base. *International Journal of Computer-Supported Collaborative Learning*, 9, 97–115. https://doi.org/10.1007/s11412-013-9182-3

Hämäläinen, R., & Arvaja, M. (2010). Scripted collaboration and group-based variations in a higher education CSCL context. *Scandinavian Journal of Educational Research*, 53(1), 1–16. https://doi.org/10.1080/00313830802628281

Hmelo-Silver, C. E. & Jeong, H. (2021). An overview of CSCL methods. In U. Cress, C. Rosé, Wise, A. F. & J. Oshima (Eds.), *International handbook of Computer-Supported Collaborative Learning* (pp. 65–83). Springer.

Janssen, J., & Kollar, I. (2021). Experimental and quasi-experimental research in CSCL. In U. Cress, C. Rosé, A. Wise, & J. Oshima (Eds.), *International handbook of computer-supported collaborative learning* (pp. 497–515). Springer.

Jeong, H., Hmelo-Silver, C. E., & Jo, K. (2019). Ten years of computer-supported collaborative learning: A meta-analysis of CSCL in STEM education during 2005–2014. *Educational Research Review*, 28, Article 100284. https://doi.org/10.1016/j.edurev.2019.100284

Kali, Y., & Hoadley, C. (2021). Design-based research methods in CSCL: Calibrating our epistemologies and ontologies. In U. Cress, C. Rosé, A. Wise, & J. Oshima (Eds.),

International handbook of computer-supported collaborative learning (pp. 479–496). Springer.

King, A. (2007). Scripting collaborative learning processes: a cognitive perspective. In F. Fischer, I. Kollar, H. Mandl, & J. M. Haake (Eds.), *Scripting Computer-supported collaborative learning – Cognitive, educational, and computational perspectives* (pp. 13–37). Springer.

Kirschner, P. A., Sweller, J., Kirschner, F. & Zambrano, J. R. (2018). From cognitive load theory to collaborative cognitive load theory. *International Journal of Computer-Supported Collaborative Learning*, *13*, 213–233. https://doi.org/10.1007/s11412-018-9277-y

Kollar, I., Fischer, F., & Hesse, F. W. (2006). Collaboration scripts—A conceptual analysis. *Educational Psychology Review*, *18*(2), 159–185. https://doi.org/10.1007/s10648-006-9007-2

Kollar, I., Wecker, C., & Fischer, F. (2018). Scaffolding and scripting (computer-supported) collaborative learning. In F. Fischer, C. E. Hmelo-Silver, S. R. Goldman, & P. Reimann (Eds.), *International handbook of the learning sciences* (pp. 340–350). Routledge.

Koschmann, T., & Schwarz, B. B. (2021). Case studies in theory and practice. In U. Cress, C. Rosé, A. Wise, & J. Oshima (Eds.), *International handbook of computer-supported collaborative learning* (pp. 463–478). Springer.

Lee, A., O'Donnell, A. M., & Rogat T. K. (2015). Exploration of the cognitive regulatory sub-processes employed by groups characterized by socially shared and other-regulation in a CSCL context. *Computers in Human Behavior*, *52*, 617–627. https://doi.org/10.1016/j.chb.2014.11.072

Lui, M., & Slotta, J. D. (2014). Immersive simulations for smart classrooms: Exploring evolutionary concepts in secondary science. *Technology, Pedagogy and Education*, *23*(1), 57–80. https://doi.org/10.1080/1475939X.2013.838452

Noroozi, O., Teasley, S. D., Biemans, H. J. A., Weinberger, A., & Mulder, M. (2013). Facilitating learning in multidisciplinary groups with transactive CSCL scripts. *International Journal of Computer-Supported Collaborative Learning*, *8*(2), 189–223. https://doi.org/10.1007/s11412-012-9162-z

Popov, V., van Leeuwen, A., & Buis, S. C. A. (2017). Are you with me or not? Temporal synchronicity and transactivity during CSCL. *Journal of Computer-Assisted Learning*, *33*, 424–442. https://doi.org/10.1111/jcal.12185

Radkowitsch, A., Vogel, F., & Fischer, F. (2020). Good for learning, bad for motivation? A meta-analysis on the effects of computer-supported collaboration scripts. *International Journal of Computer-Supported Collaborative Learning*, *15*(1), 5–47. https://doi.org/10.1007/s11412-020-09316-4

Rodriguez-Triana, M. J., Martinez-Monés, A., Asensio-Pérez, J. I., & Dimitriadis, Y. (2015). Scripting and monitoring meet each other: Aligning learning analytics and learning design to support teachers in orchestrating CSCL situations. *British Journal of Educational Technology*, *46*(2), 330–343. https://doi.org/10.1111/bjet.12198

Rummel, N., & Spada, H. (2005). Learning to collaborate: An instructional approach to promoting collaborative problem solving in computer-mediated settings. The *Journal of the Learning Sciences*, *14*(2), 201–241. https://doi.org/10.1207/s15327809jls1402_2

Ryan, R. M., & Deci, E. L. (2000). Self-determination theory and the facilitation of intrinsic motivation, social development, and well-being. *American Psychologist*, *55*, 68–78. https://doi.org/10.1037/0003-066X.55.1.68

Saqr, M., Elmoazen, R., Tedre, M., Lopez-Pernas, S., & Hirsto, L. (2022). How well centrality measures capture student achievement in computer-supported collaborative learning? – A systematic review and meta-analysis. *Educational Research Review*, *35*, Article 100437 https://doi.org/10.1016/j.edurev.2022.100437

Schnaubert, L., & Bodemer, D. (2022). Group awareness and regulation in computer-supported collaborative learning. *International Journal of Computer-Supported Collaborative Learning*, *17*(1), 11–38. https://doi.org/10.1007/s11412-022-09361-1

Schwaighofer, M., Vogel, F., Kollar, I., Ufer, S., Strohmaier, A., Terwedow, I., Ottinger, S., Reiss, K., & Fischer, F. (2017). How to combine collaboration scripts and heuristic worked examples to foster mathematical argumentation – When working memory matters. *International Journal of Computer-Supported Collaborative Leaning*, *12*(3), 281–305. https://doi.org/10.1007/s11412-017-9260-z

Slof, B., Nijsdam, D., & Janssen, J. (2016). Do interpersonal skills and interpersonal perceptions predict student learning in CSCL-environments? *Computers & Education*, *97*, 49–60. https://doi.org/10.1016/j.compedu.2016.02.012

Stahl, G. (Ed.) (2021). *Theoretical investigations. Philosophical foundations of group cognition.* Springer.

Sung, Y.-T., Yang, J.-M., & Lee, H.-Y. (2017). The effects of mobile computer-supported collaborative learning: A meta-analysis and critical synthesis. *Review of Educational Research*, *87*(4), 768–805. https://doi.org/10.3102/0034654317704307

Suthers, D. D. (2012). Computer-supported collaborative learning. In N. M. Seel (Ed.), *Encyclopedia of the sciences of learning* (pp. 719–722). Springer.

Talan, T. (2021). The effect of computer-supported collaborative learning on academic achievement: A meta-analysis. *International Journal of Education in Mathematics, Science, and Technology (IJEMST)*, *9*(3), 426–488. https://doi.org/10.46328/ijemst.1243

Uttamchandani, S. & Lester, J. N. (2019). Qualitative approaches to language in CSCL. In U. Cress, J. Oshima, C. Rosé, & A. Wise (Eds.), *International handbook of computer-supported collaborative learning* (pp. 605–623). Springer.

Van Leeuwen, A., Janssen, J., Erkens, G., & Brekelmans, M. (2014). Supporting teachers in guiding collaborating students: Effects of learning analytics in CSCL. *Computers & Education*, *79*, 28–39. https://doi.org/10.1016/j.compedu.2014.07.007

Villasclaras-Fernandéz, E., Hernández-Leo, D., Asensio-Pérez, J. I., & Dimitriadis, V. (2013). Web Collage: An implementation of support for assessment design in CSCL macro-scripts. *Computers & Education*, *67*, 79—97. https://doi.org/10.1016/j.compedu.2013.03.002

Vogel, F., Kollar, I., Fischer, F., Reiss, K., & Ufer, S. (2022). Adaptable scaffolding of mathematical argumentation skills: The role of self-regulation when scaffolded with CSCL scripts and heuristic worked examples. *International Journal of Computer-Supported Collaborative Learning*, *17*(1), 39–64. https://doi.org/10.1007/s11412-022-09363-z

Vogel, F., Kollar, I., Ufer, S., Reichersdorfer, E., Reiss, K., & Fischer, F. (2016). Developing argumentation skills in mathematics through computer-supported collaborative learning: The role of transactivity. *Instructional Science*, *44*(5), 477–500. https://doi.org/10.1007/s11251-016-9380-2

Vogel, F., Wecker, C., Kollar, I., & Fischer, F. (2017). Socio-cognitive scaffolding with collaboration scripts: A meta-analysis. *Educational Psychology Review*, *29*(3), 477–511. https://doi.org/10.1007/s10648-016-9361-7

Wegerif, R. (2006). A dialogic understanding of the relationship between CSCL and teaching thinking skills. *International Journal of Computer-Supported Collaborative Learning, 1*, 143–157. https://doi.org/10.1007/s11412-006-6840-8

Weinberger, A., Marttunen, M., Laurinen, L., & Stegmann, K. (2013). Inducing socio-cognitive conflict in Finnish and German groups of online learners by CSCL script. *International Journal of Computer-Supported Collaborative Learning, 8*, 333–349. https://doi.org/10.1007/s11412-013-9173-4

Weinberger, A., Stegmann, K., & Fischer, F. (2010). Learning to argue online: Scripted groups surpass individuals (unscripted groups do not). *Computers in Human Behavior, 26*(4), 506–515. https://doi.org/10.1016/j.chb.2009.08.007

Wood, D., Bruner, J. S., & Ross, G. (1976). The role of tutoring in problem solving. *Child Psychology & Psychiatry & Allied Disciplines, 17*(2), 89–100. https://doi.org/10.1111/j.1469-7610.1976.tb00381.x

13

SOCIAL MEDIA IN CLASS

Problem or panacea?

Antoine van den Beemt

Introduction

The past decade saw a prevalence of social media and its educational use (Li & Wong, 2021). The importance of social media for young people often elicits teachers to explore the added value of social media, for example, as a language learning environment (Barrot, 2021), communication channel (Katz & Nandi, 2021), knowledge source (Garcia et al., 2022), or its effect on learning performance (Alshalawi, 2022). However, downsides of social media in classrooms reported by teachers include disturbance (Haşiloğlu et al., 2020), distraction (Dontre, 2021), and teachers' lack of technical pedagogical content knowledge to enrich teaching with social media (Van den Beemt & Diepstraten, 2016).

In 2020, a literature review analysed the educational use of social media at the levels of student, teacher, and school (Van den Beemt, et al., 2020). The results showed how difficult it was for teachers and schools to find a balance between possible negative aspects and educational benefits of social media in class. It would be relevant for research and education to explore what happened with research on the topic as a reflection of developments in educational practice. Therefore, this chapter aims to summarise insights from a review of over a decade of research (Van den Beemt et al., 2020) and recent case studies and literature reviews on social media in class. Is it still considered a problem, or do we see signs of a panacea?

Definitions of social media include a variety of appearances influenced by the characteristics that authors aim to highlight. For example, Carr and Hayes (2015) emphasise interaction and experienced value by defining social media as websites focused on communication "that allow users to

DOI: 10.4324/9781003386131-19

opportunistically interact and selectively self-present, either in real-time or asynchronously, with both broad and narrow audiences who derive value from user-generated content and the perception of interaction with others" (Carr & Hayes, 2015, p. 50). Five years later, Greenhow & Chapman (2020) added the importance of connections, while widening the applied technology: "[Social media are applications accessed over the Internet that] spotlight people's list of connections and feature the ability to view and traverse the connections of others" (Greenhow & Chapman, 2020, p. 342). For our purpose, it is relevant to note that the literature offers general definitions of social media, rather than conceptions connected to the educational context.

When these conceptions of social media are connected to education, literature reviews emphasise the pedagogical use of specific applications, such as wikis for learning skills and knowledge (Trocky & Buckley, 2016), Twitter for sharing information and building connections (Aydin, 2014), Facebook for teacher–student interactions (Chugh & Ruhi, 2018), or TikTok as a knowledge repository (Garcia et al., 2022). Some authors point out that social media were never developed for pedagogical uses and that they belong to students' leisure time (Balakrishnan, 2014; Bruneel et al., 2013). Others distinguish between the wish for a successful use of social media in education, and the oftentimes weak empirical evidence (e.g., Tess, 2013).

Conceptual model

This chapter takes the integrated perspective of three levels of curriculum consisting of (a) the intended curriculum – the formal ideal image; (b) the implemented curriculum – the operationalised version; and (c) the attained curriculum – the curriculum as experienced by learners (Van den Akker, 2003; Van den Beemt et al., 2020; see also Figure 13.1). This perspective allows us to explore hypotheses around conditions and outcomes in sub-areas, while at the same time considering the complexity of everyday educational practice.

Each of the three levels helps to point out direct and indirect factors. For instance, the intended curriculum especially plays out at the school level, where the educational vision and the policy on learning materials should include any tool or platform used in class, including social media (*cf.* Kirschner & Wopereis, 2003). Conditions in the implemented curriculum can be learning goals, pedagogy, and existing knowledge, skills, and values of teachers (Van Veen et al., 2012). In the attained curriculum, student characteristics play a role, such as preferences for types of interactive media (Van den Beemt et al., 2010), and knowledge, values, age, and gender (Kuiper et al., 2005).

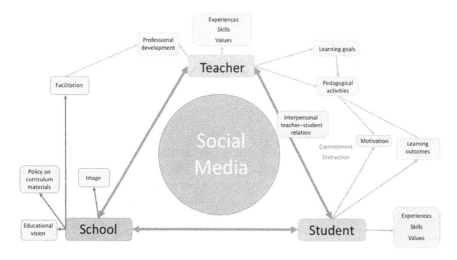

FIGURE 13.1 Conceptual model including three levels of curriculum and related factors.

Source: Based on Van den Beemt et al., 2020.

Below first, the main results of the earlier review are summarised and updated with new literature reviews and case studies. Then we focus on existing research challenges and points for future research. For detailed descriptions of research questions, methods, and results, please see Van den Beemt et al. (2020).

Review results

School

The main goals reported by school leaders were improved communication with the outside world and colleagues, motivating students, and improving transparency in communication and the assessment and evaluation of education (Cox & McLeod, 2014b). However, the obligational character was felt as a barrier: once you start communicating through social media, people expect you to continue (Cox & McLeod, 2014a). When schools used social media to improve their image, students reported to think more positively about teachers and their school (Neier & Zayer, 2015).

School leaders use social media to promote social learning and teacher professional development. However, work still exists to reduce fears among teachers about social media as a pedagogical tool, about insufficient support, and about lack of knowledge to find things out by themselves (Goktalay, 2013). Recent studies report hurdles including teachers' resistance to using social media, as well as the anxiety of participating in open online spaces (Acuyo, 2022). In multiple educational contexts, it is suggested that teachers with strong social media experience should be appointed to leadership roles to speed up the required changes (e.g., Katz & Nandi, 2021). Social networking for teachers, therefore, can become a source of administrative, collegial, and pedagogical support (Beard, 2005).

The role of social media in the intended curriculum at the school level appears under-represented in research results, compared to the teacher and student levels. Especially vision and policy as characteristics of leadership show only a few results in existing studies. The research agenda for social media in education therefore should pay more attention to questions about vision and attitude towards social media for school communication and as learning materials.

Teacher

Implementing social media in education implies new teacher roles and original approaches to teaching and learning (Hoyos, 2014). This requires training and re-training of teachers (Gan et al., 2015), which was shown to be a significant predictor of the integration of new online technologies in schools (Pan & Franklin, 2011). Suggested strategies for teacher training continue to include peer mentoring and experts showing technical possibilities (Cochrane & Narayan, 2012; Nyagadza & Mazuruse, 2021). The effect of peer mentoring might be strengthened if they already have experience with blended learning or ICT, because that experience correlates positively with the educational use of social media among teachers (Manca & Ranieri, 2016).

Studies on social media as a means for teacher professional development all concluded positive effects on teachers' competencies (Visser et al., 2014). Especially the possibility to reflect and respond instantaneously when working on their professional development was valued (Yuksel, 2013). The popularity of websites such as Facebook is reported to be increasing among teachers because these websites can be used to gain knowledge, receive feedback, and support while simultaneously sharing teachers' knowledge and expertise (Trust, 2012; Umameh, 2020; Verklan, 2021). It is, however, too early to conclude whether new platforms, such as TikTok, can work as a (nano)learning platform, despite the intent of a growing group of TikTokers to educate rather than entertain (Garcia et al., 2022).

From existing research, a long list of experienced barriers can be derived: teachers' lack of experience (Goktalay, 2013) and of knowledge about social media (Dickie & Meier, 2015), not knowing how to integrate social media into existing online learning environments (Sobaih et al., 2016), lack of infrastructure such as network access (Kamalodeen & Jameson-Charles, 2016), access (Balakrishnan, 2014) and time (Sobaih et al., 2016), worries about privacy and security (Dickie & Meier, 2015), distraction (Jiménez-Rodríguez et al., 2021), and ethics (Sobaih et al., 2016). Furthermore, teachers were afraid to lose control of attention in class (Sobaih et al., 2016). They also thought that social media belonged to students and that they should not interfere (Dickie & Meier, 2015).

It is suggested that teachers explore the educational benefits of social media, focusing on how they impact the teaching and learning processes (Froment et al., 2022). This highlights the need for research studies that analyse the relationship between teachers' social media activities and other variables at play in teaching and learning, such as student involvement, interest, and engagement. Social media can enrich teaching activities, making it crucially important to identify how they influence student learning. To bridge the "pedagogical gap", regular interactions with social media are important to enable teachers to better understand and teach with it (Jogezai et al., 2021; Otchie et al., 2022), and overcome reported difficulty differentiating between social and educational purposes (Mangundu, 2022; O'Connor et al., 2021). The main advice for teachers that can be derived from research is that they should try and use social media from the perspective of teaching and learning, and share their experiences and thoughts with colleagues.

Despite the ongoing call for attention to learning goals in instructional design (Merrill, 2002; Reigeluth, 2016), only a few studies discussed learning goals while using social media in class (e.g., Bicen & Uzunboylu, 2013; see also Li & Wong, 2021). These studies showed that teachers and students reported the importance of formulating and communicating learning goals related to the use of social media, however, without giving advice on how to define those goals.

The general reported advantage of social media was the combination of informal and formal learning (McCarthy, 2010), and the affordance to collaborate and support (e.g., Chen & Bryer, 2012) in authentic situations (Whittaker et al., 2014). This, in turn, prepares students for the future and enables them to develop knowledge (Yakin & Tinmaz, 2013) and (professional) identity (e.g., Kabilan, 2016).

Student

Many studies on social media examined variables related to students and their learning processes, most often with mixed bags of results. For example, a large number of studies found that social media increased students' motivation and engagement (e.g., Evans, 2013). Others reported no increase in student motivation (Welch & Bonnan-White, 2012), or even a decrease (Dyson et al., 2015). When students reported social media as being distracting in class, they showed less positive attitudes towards the educational use of social media (O'Bannon et al., 2013). However, perceiving social media in class as a distraction did not appear to stop students from using them (Shane-Simpson & Bakken, 2022). Apparently, the fear of missing out (FOMO) drives students' social media behaviour, where classes and study time only appear as obstacles to one's social desires (Shane-Simpson and Bakken, 2022).

Studies with an explicit focus on learning results in relation to social media as a learning tool, including a range of school-subjects, also showed a variety of results. Reported positive effects of Facebook and Twitter are, for instance, increased student engagement (Junco et al., 2011) and better grades (Wang, 2013). However, in many cases, students (González-Ramírez et al., 2015) and teachers (Bicen & Uzunboylu, 2013) only *thought* that learning results improved. Negative learning results were often related to the distraction of social media and to students' short attention spans (Gupta & Irwin, 2016; Li & Wong, 2021).

A noteworthy result is the use of social media, and especially Facebook, for writing lessons and language courses. Studies with a focus on writing and language showed increased results and interest among students when using social media as learning tools (Lee et al., 2016; Vikneswaran & Krish, 2015). These results were confirmed by a recent review focusing on language learning (Barrot, 2021), which suggested that high-profile platforms, such as Facebook, WhatsApp, and Twitter, attract the greatest attention from language learning scholars, because of their multiple and flexible communication affordances, geographical distribution, and large user base.

Next steps

Clear statements about conditions and outcomes regarding social media in education were hindered by ambiguous results and poor quality of studies (see also Li & Wong, 2021). Furthermore, existing research repeatedly focused on one single aspect of social media, without paying attention to the interrelatedness of factors on the levels of school, teacher/class, and student. Li and Wong (2021), in their review, added that social media were mainly used as a learning management system and for enhancing student engagement. Opportunities for education are the popularity of social media among students, the support of two-way communication, knowledge sharing, community building, and collaborative learning, which all enhance student learning experiences. However, recent reviews and case studies argue for clear evidence on learning results and attainment (e.g., Alshalawi, 2022; Barrot, 2021; Li & Wong, 2021). The results from the updated review can be summarised in practical advice and considerations that can help schools and teachers enrich their education with social media. As such, we contribute to knowledge and understanding about the educational use of social media in teaching and in supporting educational processes.

Barriers to the educational use of social media include teachers' need to develop social media knowledge and skills (Li & Wong, 2021), uncertainty about privacy and security (Dickie & Meier, 2015), lack of experience and a negative attitude towards social media (Goktalay, 2013), blurred boundaries between the public and private lives of students, and doubtful effectiveness for knowledge construction (Li & Wong, 2021). This is in line with earlier research about teachers' attitudes towards innovation (Thurlings et al., 2015) and about considerations for ICT use among teachers (Van den Beemt & Diepstraten, 2016). The barriers reported in our review suggest that much is to be gained by a systematic and profound elaboration upon the intended curriculum regarding social media. This implies developing a clear vision at the school level on the use of social media in class, translating this vision into policy and a didactical approach.

Based on the updated review results, educational practice still appears in need of development of social media skills of both teachers and students (Li & Wong, 2021), and also to consider diversity in experiences and values regarding social media (Manca et al., 2021). Furthermore, it is still debatable whether students' learning results can be improved by social media or not (Van & Underwood, 2021). Of course, learning results can be improved by enhanced interactions between students (Lai, 2016). However, it is not evident how social media contributes either positively or negatively. This is in part because academic outcomes can be improved by a multiplicity of factors and because much social and professional interaction in schools is still in the real space of the classroom. If this is true, and the barriers outweigh the benefits, should teachers then respond to the popularity of social media after all?

The need exists for future practice-based research in collaboration with teachers and students on effective educational uses of social media (Katz & Nandi, 2021; Li & Wong, 2021). Future research should attend to the complexity of interrelated factors, rather than focusing on a single aspect of social media. This can be done by taking into account the levels of intended, implemented, and attained curriculum, thus raising awareness of hidden positions and curriculum aspects (Van den Beemt et al., 2020). The relation between conditions and outcomes regarding social media in classrooms still needs to be clarified and confirmed. Furthermore, cause and effect should clearly and objectively be identified to determine the effectiveness of specific pedagogical uses of social media in classrooms. This implies mixed methods, including analyses of, for instance, learning results, rather than relying on self-reports and perception surveys. The context-dependency of studies also influences this obscurity: executed in a specific course, and in a specific educational culture.

While the use of social media in writing and language courses appeared most convincing (Barrot, 2021; Lee et al., 2016; Vikneswaran & Krish, 2015), other domains, such as STEM (McMillan & Day, 2020) or medical studies (Katz & Nandi, 2021), showed less convincing results, regarding pedagogical activities or learning results. The question of whether social media are a problem, or a panacea was difficult to answer from the initial review study. This was mainly the result of ambiguity in research outcomes, caused by a range of methods applied in a wide array of educational activities. Recent review studies show that the question is still difficult to answer, which diffuses well-considered and evidence-based choices for the pedagogical use of social media. The results suggest that the answer can be found in developing vision and policy at the school level. What do teachers and management see as educational value for social media? And what are the attitudes of teachers and students regarding social media? Take into account teacher professional development for and with social media. If social media are to be included in the curriculum, ensure a clear role following the institute's educational concept and didactical approach, for example, in supporting self-directed learning, communication, interaction, and knowledge development, all following clearly defined learning goals.

Evidence-based practice recommendations

For the school context:

- Apply social media to reach a broader audience and to increase transparency in internal and external communication.
- Include social media in policy on curriculum materials and educational vision, as this promotes the use of social media as a learning tool.
- Develop focused policy and support to diminish anxiety and resistance experienced by teachers. Facilitate teachers, especially in technical support and in time to work on their social media skills.

For teachers:

- Develop knowledge and skills within teacher teams, use experts, and peer learning.
- Scrutinise your own experiences, skills, and values regarding social media to understand barriers to the pedagogical use of this technology. Explore the possible educational benefits of social media.
- Facilitate students with clear, instruction-focused goals, while adapting to their social and educational needs. Effective learning goals are related to communication, sharing knowledge, and collaborative learning.
- Social media are suitable for social constructivist approaches to learning and self-directed learning. Central is active engagement with content, for instance, by producing digital content. The teacher's role is coaching.

- Purposeful teacher presence on social media, to support groups of students as an online community, can strengthen interpersonal teacher–student relations.

For students:

- Examine the status quo: not all students perceive social media as a tool for learning. Consider diversity in experience, skills, and values regarding social media.
- Students use social media to communicate rather than develop or share information.
- Learning results (i.e., grades) do not increase automatically by social media. Social media in the classroom can improve indirect learning outcomes, such as engagement, collaboration, communication, or motivation.
- Meta-cognitive skills are prerequisites for a focused use of social media. However, this use also increases self-directed learning skills.
- Not all students have sufficient social media knowledge and skills. Explain aspects of security and privacy.

References

Acuyo, A. (2022). Reviewing the literature on professional development for higher education tutors in the work-from-home era: Is it time to reconsider the integration of social media? *Education and Information Technologies, 27*(1), 89–113. https://doi.org/10.1007/s10639-021-10603-2

Alshalawi, A. S. (2022). Social media usage intensity and academic performance among undergraduate students in Saudi Arabia. *Contemporary Educational Technology, 14*(2), article number: ep361. https://doi.org/10.30935/cedtech/11711

Aydin, S. (2014). Twitter as an educational environment. *Turkish Online Journal of Distance Education, 15*, 10–21. https://doi.org/10.1111/j.1744-6171.2009.00208.x

Balakrishnan, V. (2014). Using social networks to enhance teaching and learning experiences in higher learning institutions. *Innovations in Education and Teaching International, 51*, 595–606. https://doi.org/10.1080/14703297.2013.863735

Barrot, J. S. (2021). Social media as a language learning environment: A systematic review of the literature (2008–2019). *Computer Assisted Language Learning*, 1–29. https://doi.org/10.1080/09588221.2021.1883673

Beard, K. W. (2005). Internet addiction: a review of current assessment techniques and potential assessment questions. *Cyber Psychology & Behavior, 8*(1), 7–14. https://doi.org/10.1089/cpb.2005.8.7

Bicen, H., & Uzunboylu, H. (2013). The use of social networking sites in education: A case study of Facebook. *Journal of Universal Computer Science, 19*, 658–671. https://doi.org/10.3217/jucs-019-05-0658

Bruneel, S., De Wit, K., Verhoeven, J., & Eelen, J. (2013). Facebook: When education meets privacy. *Interdisciplinary Journal of E-Learning and Learning Objects, 9*, 125–148. https://doi.org/10.28945/1868

Carr, C., & Hayes, R. (2015). Social media: Defining, developing, and divining. *Atlantic Journal of Communication, 23*, 46–65. https://doi.org/10.1080/1545687 0.2015.972282

Chen, B., & Bryer, T. (2012). Investigating instructional strategies for using social media in formal and informal learning. *The International Review of Research in Open and Distance Learning, 13*, 87–104. https://doi.org/10.19173/irrodl. v13i1.1027

Chugh, R., & Ruhi, U. (2018). Social media in higher education: A literature review of Facebook. *Education and Information Technologies, 23*(2), 605–616. https:// doi.org/10.1007/s10639-017-9621-2

Cochrane, T., & Narayan, V. (2012). Redesigning professional development: Reconceptualising teaching using social learning technologies. *Research in Learning Technology, 21*(3), 1–19. https://doi.org/10.3402/rlt.v21i0.19226

Cox, D., & McLeod, S. (2014a). Social media marketing and communications strategies for school superintendents. *Journal of Educational Administration, 52*, 850–868. https://doi.org/10.1108/JEA-11-2012-0117

Cox, D., & McLeod, S. (2014b). Social media strategies for school principals. *NASSP Bulletin, 98*, 5–25. https://doi.org/10.1177/0192636513510596

Dickie, V. A., & Meier, H. (2015). The Facebook tutor: Networking education. *Ubiquitous Learning, 8*(2), 1–12. https://doi.org/10.18848/1835-9795/CGP/ v08i02/40400

Dontre, A. J. (2021). The influence of technology on academic distraction: A review. *Human Behavior and Emerging Technologies, 3*(3), 379–390. https://doi. org/10.1002/hbe2.229

Dyson, B., Vickers, K., Turtle, J., Cowan, S., & Tassone, A. (2015). Evaluating the use of Facebook to increase student engagement and understanding in lecture-based classes. *Higher Education, 69*, 303–313. https://doi.org/10.1007/ s10734-014-9776-3

Evans, B. (2013). Enhancing undergraduate teaching and feedback using social media: An engineering case study. *Engineering Education, 8*(2), 44–53. https://doi. org/10.11120/ened.2013.00015

Froment, F., García-González, A. J., & Cabero-Almenara, J. (2022). The relationship of Twitter with teacher credibility and motivation in university students. *Comunicar, 30*(71), 131–142.

Gan, B., Menkhoff, T., & Smith, R. (2015). Enhancing students' learning process through interactive digital media: New opportunities for collaborative learning. *Computers in Human Behavior, 51*, 652–663. https://doi.org/10.1016/j. chb.2014.12.048

Garcia, M. B., Juanatas, I. C., & Juanatas, R. A. (2022, April). TikTok as a knowledge source for programming learners: A new form of nanolearning? In *2022 10th International Conference on Information and Education Technology (ICIET)* (pp. 219–223). IEEE.

Goktalay, S. (2013). Challenges facing higher education: Faculty's concerns about technologies of social media. *International Journal of Continuing Engineering Education and Life-Long Learning, 23*, 67–90. https://doi.org/10.1504/ IJCEELL.2013.051767

González-Ramírez, R., Gascó, J., & Taverner, J. (2015). Facebook in teaching: Strengths and weaknesses. *International Journal of Information and Learning Technology, 32*, 65–78. https://doi.org/10.1108/IJILT-09-2014-0021

Greenhow, C., & Chapman, A. (2020). Social distancing meet social media: Digital tools for connecting students, teachers, and citizens in an emergency. *Information and Learning Sciences*. https://doi.org/10.1108/ILS-04-2020-0134

Gupta, N., & Irwin, J. (2016). In-class distractions: The role of Facebook and the primary learning task. *Computers in Human Behavior*, *55*, 1165–1178. https://doi.org/10.1016/j.chb.2014.10.022

Haşiloğlu, M. A., Çalhan, H. S., & Ustaoğlu, M. E. (2020). Determining the views of the secondary school science teachers about the use of social media in education. *Journal of Science Education and Technology*, *29*(3), 346–354. https://doi.org/10.1007/s10956-020-09820-0

Hoyos, J. (2014). Social networking sites in the classroom: Unveiling new roles for teachers and new approaches to online course design. *Ikala*, *19*, 269–283.

Jiménez-Rodríguez, D., Belmonte García, M. T., Arcos García, J., & Castro-Luna, G. (2021). Development and validation of a social media questionnaire for nursing training: A pilot study. *IHealthcare*, *9*(3), 344. https://doi.org/10.3390/healthcare9030344

Jogezai, N. A., Baloch, F. A., Jaffar, M., Shah, T., Khilji, G. K., & Bashir, S. (2021). Teachers' attitudes towards social media (SM) use in online learning amid the COVID-19 pandemic: the effects of SM use by teachers and religious scholars during physical distancing. *Heliyon*, *7*(4). https://doi.org/10.1016/j.heliyon.2021.e06781

Junco, R., Heiberger, G., & Loken, E. (2011). The effect of Twitter on college student engagement and grades. *Journal of Computer Assisted Learning*, *27*, 119–132. https://doi.org/10.1111/j.1365-2729.2010.00387.x

Kabilan, M. (2016). Using Facebook as an e-portfolio in enhancing pre-service teachers' professional development. *Australasian Journal of Educational Technology*, *32*, 19–31.

Kamalodeen, J., & Jameson-Charles, M. (2016). A mixed methods research approach to exploring teacher participation in an online social networking website. *International Journal of Qualitative Methods*, *15*, 1–14. https://doi.org/10.1177/1609406915624578

Katz, M., & Nandi, N. (2021). Social media and medical education in the context of the COVID-19 pandemic: scoping review. *JMIR Medical Education*, *7*(2), article number: e25892. https://doi.org/10.2196/25892

Kirschner, P., & Wopereis, I. (2003). Mindtools for teacher communities: A European perspective. *Technology, Pedagogy and Education*, *12*, 105–124. https://doi.org/10.1080/14759390300200148

Kuiper, E., Volman, M., & Terwel, J. (2005). The web as an information resource in K–12 education: Strategies for supporting students in searching and processing information. *Review of Educational Research*, *75*, 285–328. doi:10.3102/00346543075003285

Lai, C. (2016). Training nursing students' communication skills with online video peer assessment. *Computers and Education*, *97*, 21–30. https://doi.org/10.1016/j.compedu.2016.02.017

Lee, J., Koo, Y., & Kim, M. (2016). Enhancing problem solving skills in science education with social media and an e-collaboration tool. *New Educational Review*, *43*, 248–259. https://doi.org/10.15804/tner.2016.43.1.21

Li, K. C., & Wong, B. T. M. (2021). The opportunities and challenges of social media in higher education: A literature review. *SN Computer Science*, *2*(6), 1–11. https://doi.org/10.1007/s42979-021-00857-5

Manca, S., Bocconi, S., & Gleason, B. (2021). "Think globally, act locally": A glocal approach to the development of social media literacy. *Computers & Education, 160*, 104025. https://doi.org/10.1016/j.compedu.2020.104025

Manca, S., & Ranieri, M. (2016). Facebook and the others: Potentials and obstacles of social media for teaching in higher education. *Computers and Education, 95*, 216–230. https://doi.org/10.1016/j.compedu.2016.01.012

Mangundu, J. (2022). Social media for teaching and learning: A technology acceptance model analysis of preservice teachers' perceptions during the COVID-19 pandemic. *International Journal of Learning, Teaching and Educational Research, 21*(5). https://doi.org/10.26803/ijlter.21.5.10

McCarthy, J. (2010). Blended learning environments: Using social networking sites to enhance the first year experience. *Australasian Journal of Educational Technology, 26*. https://doi.org/10.14742/ajet.1039

McMillan, M., & Day, J. (2020, September). Social media in STEM: Academic and student perspectives on social media as a teaching tool. In *Proceedings of the Australian Conference on Science and Mathematics Education* (p. 54).

Merrill, M. D. (2002). A pebble-in-the-pond model for instructional design. *Performance Improvement, 41*(7), 41–46.

Neier, S., & Zayer, L. (2015). Students' perceptions and experiences of social media in higher education. *Journal of Marketing Education, 37*, 133–143. https://doi.org/10.1177/0273475315583748

Nyagadza, B., & Mazuruse, G. (2021). Embracing public relations (PR) as survival panacea to private colleges' corporate image & corporate identity erosion. *Cogent Social Sciences, 7*(1), 1974179. https://doi.org/10.1080/23311886.2021.1974179

O'Bannon, B., Beard, J., & Britt, V. (2013). Using a Facebook group as an educational tool: Effects on student achievement. *Computers in the Schools, 30*, 229–247. https://doi.org/10.1080/07380569.2013.805972

O'Connor, S., Zhang, M., Honey, M., & Lee, J. J. (2021). Digital professionalism on social media: A narrative review of the medical, nursing, and allied health education literature. *International Journal of Medical Informatics, 153*. https://doi.org/10.1016/j.ijmedinf.2021.104514

Otchie, W., Bardone, E., & Pedaste, M. (2022). Bridging the pedagogical gap between operational and contextual affordances with social media. *Encyclopaideia, 26*(62), 57–80. https://doi.org/10.6092/issn.1825-8670/13223

Pan, S., & Franklin, T. (2011). In-service teachers' self-efficacy, professional development, and web 2.0 tools for integration. *New Horizons in Education, 59*(3), 28–40.

Reigeluth, C. M. (2016). The learner-centered paradigm of instruction. In *Issues in Technology, Learning, and Instructional Design* (pp. 147–154). Routledge.

Shane-Simpson, C., & Bakken, T. (2022). Students' fear of missing out predicts in-class social media use. *Teaching of Psychology*. https://doi.org/10.1177/00986283211060752

Sobaih, A., Moustafa, M., Ghandforoush, P., & Khan, M. (2016). To use or not to use? Social media in higher education in developing countries. *Computers in Human Behavior, 58*, 296–305. https://doi.org/10.1016/j.chb.2016.01.002

Tess, P. (2013). The role of social media in higher education classes (real and virtual): A literature review. *Computers in Human Behavior, 29*(5), 60–68. https://doi.org/10.1016/j.chb.2012.12.032

Thurlings, M., Evers, A., & Vermeulen, M. (2015). Towards a model of explaining teachers' innovative behaviour: A literature review. *Review of Educational Research*, *85*, 430–471. https://doi.org/10.3102/0034654314557949

Trocky, N., & Buckley, K. (2016). Evaluating the impact of wikis on student learning outcomes: An integrative review. *Journal of Professional Nursing*, *32*, 364–376. https://doi.org/10.1016/j.profnurs.2016.01.007

Trust, T. (2012). Professional learning networks designed for teacher learning. *Journal of Digital Learning in Teacher Education*, *28*, 133–138. https://doi.org/10.1080/2 1532974.2012.10784693

Umameh, M. A. (2020). *Mathematics teachers' appropriation of digital and non-digital resources and its impact on classroom practices*. Doctoral dissertation, University of Leeds.

Van den Akker, J. (2003). Curriculum perspectives: An introduction. In J. van den Akker, W. Kuiper, & U. Hameyer (Eds.), *Curriculum landscapes and trends* (pp. 1–10). Kluwer.

Van den Beemt, A., Akkerman, S., & Simons, P. R. J. (2010). Pathways in interactive media practices among young people. *Learning, Media and Technology*, *35*, 419–434. https://doi.org/10.1080/17439884.2010.531395

Van den Beemt, A., & Diepstraten, I. (2016). Teachers' perspectives on ICT: A learning ecology approach. *Computers and Education*, *92–93*, 161–170. https://doi.org/10.1016/j.compedu.2015.10.017

Van Den Beemt, A., Thurlings, M., & Willems, M. (2020). Towards an understanding of social media use in the classroom: A literature review. *Technology, Pedagogy and Education*, *29*(1), 35–55. https://doi.org/10.1080/1475939X.2019.1695657

Van, T. H. Q., & Underwood, J. (2021). Social networking platforms and classroom culture. *Polish Journal of Educational Studies*, *73*(1), 138–150. https://doi.org/10.2478/poljes-2021-0010

Van Veen, K., Zwart, R. C., & Meirink, J. A. (2012). What makes teacher professional development effective? A literature review. In M. Kooy & K. van Veen (Eds.), *Teacher learning that matters* (pp. 3–21). New York, NY: Routledge.

Verklan, M. (2021). *How principals can facilitate teacher technology use in the age of problematic adolescent social media use*. Masters thesis, City University of Seattle. http://hdl.handle.net/20.500.11803/1586

Vikneswaran, T., & Krish, P. (2015). Utilising social networking sites to improve writing: A case study with Chinese students in Malaysia. *Technology, Pedagogy and Education*, *25*, 287–300. https://doi.org/10.1080/1475939X.2015.1030441

Visser, R., Calvert Evering, L., & Barrett, D. (2014). Twitter for teachers: The implications of Twitter as a self-directed professional development tool for K–12 teachers. *Journal of Research on Technology in Education*, *46*, 396–413. https://doi.org/10.1080/15391523.2014.925694

Wang, J. (2013). What higher educational professionals need to know about today's students: Online social networks. *The Turkish Online Journal of Educational Technology*, *12*(3), 180–193.

Welch, B., & Bonnan-White, J. (2012). Twittering to increase student engagement in the university classroom. *Knowledge Management and E-Learning*, *4*, 325–345. https://doi.org/10.1080/09523987.2020.1848508

Whittaker, A. L., Howarth, G. S., & Lymn, K. A. (2014). Evaluation of Facebook to create an online learning community in an undergraduate animal science class.

Educational Media International, 51, 37–41. https://doi.org/10.1080/09523987. 2014.924664

Yakin, I., & Tinmaz, H. (2013). Using Twitter as an instructional tool: A case study in higher education. *The Turkish Online Journal of Educational Technology,* 12(4), 209–218. https://doi.org/10.1111/j.1365-2729.2010.00387.x

Yuksel, D. (2013). Technology use in reflective teaching: A practicum research project. *Anthropologist,* 16, 145–152. https://doi.org/10.1080/09720073.2013.1189 1343

14

CLICKERS FOR EFFECTIVE LEARNING AND INSTRUCTION

An examination of the effects of audience response systems in the classroom

Nathaniel J. Hunsu, Isaac D. Dunmoye and Taiwo R. Feyijimi

Introduction

In their Clickers study, Mayer et al. (2009) described a scenario that many instructors encounter with students in large classrooms. Instructors may ask questions in class to gauge students' understanding of the concepts being taught, encourage participation, or initiate discussions. More often than not, however, they only get back blank stares, and just a few students respond to such questions or participate during class discussions. Unfortunately, passivity and silence in class are counterproductive to most instructional goals (Joshi et al., 2021; Khan et al., 2019). Getting students to volunteer responses and engage in large classrooms can take time and effort. For one, many students would not respond in class for fear of being wrong and appearing stupid among their peers. However, little do they realize that they are not alone – many of their peers may not have answers to the question. Knowing they are not alone in their struggle may diminish hesitancy and get more students involved in co-constructing knowledge with their peers (Hunsu et al., 2016).

The fewer students participate in class, the less cognitively engaged with learning they tend to be, and the more prone they are to becoming distracted (Gupta & Irwin, 2016). Hence, improving student interaction is pertinent to enhancing the learning experience in the lecture classroom. As a result, instructors often look to instructional technologies to enhance their pedagogy and facilitate qualitative behavioral, social, and cognitive engagement in the classroom (Stevens et al., 2017). Clickers are one example of instructional technologies employed to enhance classroom participation (Keough, 2012). In subsequent sections of this chapter, we briefly describe what clickers are and highlight theoretical and empirical perspectives on clicker effects

DOI: 10.4324/9781003386131-20

in the classroom based on the literature. Finally, we offered some thoughts for instructors to consider about using clickers in their classrooms.

Clickers or audience response systems

Clickers or Audience Response System (ARS) have been used in various contexts to facilitate participation and interaction (Castillo-Manzano et al., 2016; Liu et al., 2017). Technology-savvy instructors who look to technology to aid instruction and curious adopters of instructional technologies have employed various clicker-based systems to promote student engagement with classroom learning activities. Over the years, ARS has evolved from being only a specialized handheld classroom device to including a variety of web-based audience response solutions (Shea, 2016). The ARS has been referred to by various terms, including student response systems, ARSs (Cain et al., 2009), personal response systems (Chan & Knight, 2010), and classroom response systems (Graeff et al., 2011). Traditionally, the ARS comprised a handheld transmitter–receiver device that fed electronic signals into a computer software program. A receiver unit receives and collates signals (student responses) from handheld devices (clickers). The responses are tabulated and displayed by a computer application for instructional use. Without clicker-based technology, instructors have traditionally asked students to raise their hands or paddles to answer questions during lectures (Mayer et al., 2009; Hunsu et al., 2016). However, raising a hand or a paddle to respond makes the respondent visible. Many students who are shy or reticent are less likely to participate in class under those conditions. By using clicker-based technology to seek a response, many students feel more comfortable participating anonymously in class (Mayer et al., 2009). The software end of an ARS provides a graphical summary of responses that can be viewed instantaneously by the instructor and students.

The handheld transmitter–receiver clicker system was an innovative student engagement tool for many years. However, with the advancement of several web-based alternatives in the last decade, handheld ARSs are now all but obsolete. However, web-based ARSs now leverage the versatility and ubiquity of mobile devices such as laptops, tablet computers, and smartphones to offer more real-time student participation in the classroom (Mader & Bry, 2019). In addition, these new platforms can accept a wider variety of student response types and thus can offer multiple response options. For example, the erstwhile handheld clicker devices could only handle pre-set response types (e.g., multiple choice and true/false) from quizzes. However, smartphones and mobile computing devices provide multiple input features that may allow students to type their thoughts, send emojis, or upload graphics in response to different types of in-class activities (González-Tato et al., 2013; Mader & Bry, 2019). Contemporary examples of web-based ARSs include user-friendly apps such as Socrative (Socrative.com), Poll Everywhere (polleverywhere.com), POPin (popinnow.com), and Mentimeter (Mentimeter.com) (McKenzie & Ziemann, 2020).

Theoretical support for clicker effective

The clicker research literature is replete with studies investigating the efficacy of ARSs in promoting different positive learning outcomes (Chien et al., 2016; Hunsu et al., 2016; Pfaller-Sadovsky et al., 2020). As such, there have been claims and counter-claims about their effectiveness in fostering engagement and learning. Studies that champion clickers and argue for their effectiveness draw on different theoretical perspectives to support or explain the 'clicker phenomenon.' The most basic explanation of the clicker effect draws on the behaviorist learning theory. According to this perspective, using clickers in class creates a stimuli-response interaction between students and instructional content (Naismith et al., 2004). For example, the instructor poses questions (stimuli that trigger participation). Students click in response to the stimuli – i.e., instructors. In addition, to the primary stimuli-response loop initiated between students and instructors, a computer program or web-based service tallies (aggregates) students' responses and displays the polls as charts. In turn, the instructor may use the tally to identify gaps and misconceptions in students' knowledge – to focus more instructional efforts on addressing such gaps or misconceptions (Caldwell, 2007; Cline et al., 2020). In addition to highlighting knowledge states, the clicker response tally *cum* display allows instructors to initiate classroom discussions around particular topics. For example, following a clicker activity, an instructor may structure small groups or whole class discussions toward honing problematic concepts and providing the class with real-time and targeted feedback (Hutain & Michinov, 2022; Papadopoulos et al., 2019).

The clicker phenomenon has also been explained through the perspectives of constructivist learning theories (Micheletto, 2011; Wood & Shirazi, 2020). For example, some studies invoke the generative learning theory (GLT) to explain the effect of using clickers on student participation and learning (Brod, 2021; Joshi et al., 2021). The GLT proposes that learning is a generative activity involving integrating new ideas into knowledge units already existing in the learner's prior knowledge (Fiorella & Mayer, 2016). The main emphasis of the GLT is being 'active' in learning. For meaningful learning to occur, students must actively engage in effortful activities that trigger prior knowledge and organize, reorganize, and integrate new ideas into their existing schemas (Osborne & Wittrock, 1983). In a nutshell, students must engage in activities that foster meaningful knowledge construction to learn with understanding.

As the preceding implies, the GLT provides a predictive and explanatory framework for understanding potential clicker effects on instruction and learning. For example, using clicker promotes a frequent use of questions and discussions – by the very nature of clicker-driven instruction. Such intermittent question-and-discussion sessions not only foster cognitive engagement but also increase the likelihood that instructors would discover and address misconceptions in learning in the classroom. Hence, instructors may use clickers in their classrooms to foster conceptual learning and understanding as they forge cognitive interactions between students and instructors (Hunsu et al., 2016).

The literature on student attention and engagement also explains clicker effects on learning. Some extant studies have suggested that student attention to lecture diminishes sufficiently after 20 minutes of lecture time (Burns, 1985). However, using clicker questions could provide opportunities to break lecture time and change students' focus to other instructional components designed to further entrench the subject of learning. Breaking lecture periods by introducing clicker questions at the end of pre-determined breaks can be an efficient way to let students recoup their attention and refocus on other details of instructional content during lecture time (Hunsu et al., 2016). Hence, instructors may utilize clickers or ARSs to address the challenges of keeping students actively and cognitively engaged, especially in vast classrooms. Using clickers in the classroom may positively impact student perceptions about the quality of their instruction and stimulate motivation to attend and be involved in class activities.

It can be challenging for instructors to engage most students in large classrooms with learning activities. In addition to being distracted and disengaged in class, some students refrain from overt participation in the classroom for fear of giving wrong answers or appearing incompetent before their peers (Barr, 2017). However, prior studies suggest that students participate more actively in clicker-based classrooms because they can answer anonymously and thus retain their dignity (Brady et al., 2020; Caldwell, 2007). Furthermore, when responses to clicker questions are aggregated, and an actual state of class knowledge is revealed, many students find out that they share the same struggles as their peers. Thus, they feel better about themselves and are more inclined to participate in peer discussions and knowledge co-construction.

Empirical support for clicker-based instruction

Positive empirical evidence: Over the last two decades, several comparative research studies have examined the effect of using clickers or related technologies on engagement pedagogies and fostering positive learning outcomes in small and large classrooms (Dong et al., 2017; Remón et al., 2017; Park & Farag, 2015). Many studies reported positive clicker effects on several non-cognitive and affective learning outcomes (e.g., participation, satisfaction, and perception of quality instruction). For example, Heaslip et al. (2014) examined the effect of using clickers on student engagement in large classes. They observed that the level of student interactivity in clicker classrooms increased significantly relative to non-clicker classrooms. Other studies reported that students' participation and engagement in classroom activities increased when clickers were integrated into the classrooms than when they were not (Dong et al., 2017; Keough, 2012; Matesic & Adams, 2008). In some studies, students who attended classrooms that used clickers attributed perceived improvements in their learning experiences to the use of clickers in the classrooms (Humphries & Whelan, 2009; Sprague & Dahl, 2010; Stagg & Lane, 2010). They felt that using clickers made class time less boring and created more opportunities to initiate peer discussions (McDonough & Foote, 2015). Clickers also engender prompt feedback during the discussions engendered by using clicker questions (Egelandsdal, & Krumsvik, 2017; Hedgcock & Rouwenhorst, 2014; Koppel & Berenson, 2009).

Beyond being effective in fostering non-cognitive outcomes, several past studies have claimed that clickers also benefit classroom learning. These claims are often backed by empirical evidence from comparative studies of clicker and non-clicker classrooms (Hunsu et al., 2016; Chien et al., 2016). For example, Mayer et al. (2009) explored how clickers promote student–instructor interaction in a large lecture class. Students who used clickers to stimulate questions and discussions during the lecture were compared to a non-clickers control group with in-class questions and discussions. In addition to enhancing student–instructor interaction in the large classroom, they also found that the students in a clicker group performed significantly higher than the non-clicker group on the students' final performances. In particular, the authors observed that students in the clicker classroom performed better than those in a non-clicker classroom that used a similar questioning technique as the clicker group ($d = 0.38$). Furthermore, the clicker group performed better than the control group that did not use a similar questioning pedagogy as the clicker group ($d = 0.40$). In addition, they observed that the non-clicker class group and the control group did not differ from each other.

Mayer et al. (2009) attributed their observations to the fact that using clickers in the classroom makes questions and discussions more frequent and deliberate. For example, Andre & Thieman (1988) posited that students perform better if they respond to adjunct questions after studying or reading a text than if they do not have to respond to any test. Furthermore, taking a test after reading a text or study improves memorization more than reading again, thereby increasing encoding variability (Rowland, 2014; Adesope et al., 2017). Finally, since clicker-facilitated instruction often punctuates lecture time and integrates questions into lecture delivery, the authors argued that the continual use of adjunct questions prompts students to engage in active cognitive processing that fosters meaningful learning (Mayer et al., 2009). Hence, clickers can be used masterfully to stimulate generative learning activities in the classroom.

In addition to using clickers to engender a testing or questioning effect in the classroom, other studies have examined the feedback effect that stems from using clicker questions and discussions. A study by Lantz and Stawiski (2014) showed that when feedback is given promptly, clicker questions improved students' memory of studied materials after two days better than no-clicker control groups. Brady et al. (2013) examined the effect of using clickers on metacognitive self-regulation in a large classroom relative to raising a paddle (a low-technology polling device) to answer questions during classroom time. They found that students in a clicker section performed better than those in a comparison group. Their study suggested that the use of clickers fostered metacognitive self-regulation, which had a formative influence on the learning process and led to better performance outcomes.

Negative empirical evidence: While several studies have reported empirical evidence that strongly favors using clickers in the classroom, others have also reported empirical evidence that was unfavorable to using clickers in the classroom. For example, some studies reported that the use of clickers did not provide students with opportunities to take notes, and students may even become less cognitively engaged – being distracted by another tech toy in the classroom (Bain & Przybyla, 2009; Carnaghan & Webb, 2007; Morse et al., 2010). In addition, Lincoln (2007) argued that clicker intervention had no tangible effect on high-achieving and the most underperforming students, nor were they effective in getting some poorly motivated students to participate in class activities. A few more studies also reported that using clickers negatively impacted attendance (Dunnett et al., 2011; MacArthur & Jones, 2008). Finally, Carnaghan and Webb (2007) argued that poor clicker implementation might leave students with a critical and unsatisfactory learning experience.

Resolving the conflicting perspectives about the effectiveness of clickers: Are clickers, or ARSs effective instructional aids, and how effective are they in fostering positive educational outcomes? As demonstrated in the preceding, some studies reported that clickers effectively foster different cognitive and non-cognitive learning outcomes. Contrariwise, the studies that found adverse clicker effects highlight the need for caution and thoughtful contemplation as instructors consider when and how to use ARS in their classrooms. A comparative meta-analysis of 53 clicker articles that compared the clicker vs. non-clicker classrooms showed that clicker effects ranged from very high to non-existent for different educational outcomes (Hunsu et al., 2016). Across 41 independent studies, we observed a small but positive effect of sustained using clickers on student achievement (Hedge's $g = 0.21$). However, clickers did not affect low-level cognitive activities such as recall or retention

TABLE 14.1 Effect Sizes of Clicker Use in the Classroom on Desirable Learning Outcomes

Education Outcome	Hedge's g	SE
Cognitive Outcomes		
Retention	–0.00	0.02
Knowledge Transfer	0.11	0.04
Mixed	0.21	0.03
Non-cognitive Outcomes		
Engagement and Participation	0.19	0.05
Self-efficacy	0.86	0.11
Attendance	0.21	0.07
Perception of Quality	0.24	0.06
Interest and Likeness	0.09	0.07

($g = 0$). According to our findings, clicker effects were most tangible for non-cognitive educational outcomes. Table 14.1 summarizes the perceived effects of clicker usage on cognitive and non-cognitive outcomes.

Overall, our meta-analysis revealed that the answer to the question of clicker effectiveness is nuanced. Whether clickers or ARS are effective depends on the context in which they are used, the purposes for which they are used, and how they are implemented. For example, using clicker questions rather than clickers without questioning techniques was advantageous (Hunsu et al., 2016; Sullivan, 2009; Yourstone et al., 2008). In essence, posing clicker-aided questions and the discussions that follow them may be the main factors contributing to the effective use of clickers in the classroom. To further strengthen this argument, we observed that clicker effects were most notable in classes with 20 or more students. However, the clicker effect diminished significantly beyond 50 students. One possible explanation for this observation is that instructors may have less oversight over student discussion as class size increases.

The technology media and learning debate

Clickers are likely beneficial in promoting positive learning outcomes. Nevertheless, some have argued against indiscriminate reliance on technology as a panacea for addressing every classroom malaise (Bain & Przybyla, 2009; Koppel & Berenson, 2009; Hunsu et al., 2016). In their classical debate on the influence of media and technology on learning, Clark and Kozma contended the significance of media and methods in learning. After reviewing several studies that explored the effectiveness of different media in fostering learning, Clark (1994) argued that no direct relationship between media use and learning could be established. Using a delivery vehicle analogy, Clark contended that technology media 'do not affect student achievement any more than the truck that delivers our groceries causes changes in our nutrition' (Clark, 1983, p. 445). Consequently, Clark's position on media emphasizes that the sentiment about how the effect of technology media on learning depends on methods – i.e., how teachers use them and how students interact with them – and not just on the technology.

On the contrary, Kozma views Clark's position on the matter as being overly reductionistic. He argued that Clark's view on technology and learning creates an 'unnecessary schism between media and method.' Kozma (1994) argued that media and method are often inseparable in the learning context. In his view, learning is not the product of a passive reception of instruction or information akin to grocery delivery and nutritional values. Instead, learning stems from constructive cognitive and social processes significantly impacted by the environment in which it occurs (Kozma, 1991). In Kozma's mind, media attributes provide affordances that shape or constrain instructional methods and influence how students interact with the learning process. Invariably, the effectiveness of media-mediated instruction on learning is influenced by instructional methods alone and media attributes and learner characteristics (Yang et al., 2014). Therefore, to understand the effects of media on learning and to channel such effects for instructional benefits, we must understand how they influence and are influenced by instructional methods and learner characteristics.

The *media and learning* debate has raged, waned, and morphed over the years. The major keynotes from the media debate are applicable in contextualizing potential clicker effects on learning performance, like any other instructional media. Based on the findings of most clicker studies in the literature, the use of ARS in classrooms can positively affect different cognitive and affective educational outcomes. However, how instructors use them can determine their effectiveness in learning and classroom dynamics. Strong indications suggest that poorly designed clicker instruction will frustrate the best instructional intention and be poorly received by students (Carnaghan & Webb, 2007). Hence, instructional designers and lesson planners can leverage the affordances of using clickers to ensure impactful instruction. The following section highlights some considerations for vitalizing clicker use to foster a positive learning experience.

Considerations for implementing effective clicker-based instruction

Clark's objection to the effect of media on learning and performance may have been clear-cut in the early 1990s. However, in the age of social media and sophisticated multi-media, such as the x-realities, the debate has to be more nuanced than ever. Nevertheless, whether using something as simple as a clicker or some head-mounted VR device, the most crucial consideration for adopters of instructional technologies is first 'to do no harm.' At best, poorly implemented tech facilities could be distracting or deleterious to learning at worst (Parong & Mayer, 2018). Alternatively, if well implemented, clickers and any other educational technology can facilitate conditions that motivate learning and foster the socio-cognitive processes that enhance learning and academic performance.

Instructors seeking to employ clickers in their classrooms would also be invested in successfully deploying them. As such, they may adopt some metrics or indicators to measure the success of their implementation. On the other hand, instructors who expect too much from using clickers may perform less than expected for some of the purposes for which they use them. Hence, expectations of successful clicker implementation should be realistic. Furthermore, evidence from clicker efficacy studies suggests that clickers may be more effective for engendering affective and non-cognitive outcomes of engagement and learning than promoting achievement outcomes. For example, clickers were highly effective in fostering non-cognitive educational outcomes such as self-efficacy (Hedge's $g = 0.86$) and perception of quality ($g = 0.24$). However, they were less effective in promoting learning and performance outcomes such as knowledge retention ($g = 0$) and knowledge transfer ($g = 0.11$; Hunsu et al., 2016). Hence, it is expedient for instructors to be realistic about what to expect from using clickers to facilitate different classroom objectives.

According to the literature, one of the most prevalent reasons why many instructors use ARSs in the classroom is to gain and maintain their students' attention, especially in large lecture classrooms. In this age of instant gratification, to keep most students' attention in a large classroom beyond 20 minutes is a feat. However, savvy instructors can include clicker time in lecture time to redirect students' attention toward pre-planned activities designed to complement the subject of their lesson (Bunce et al., 2010), after which their attention can be refocused on the lecture. Clicker breaks may serve as mental pauses during the lecture period. However, how instructors use these 'clicker breaks' is critical to realizing their instructional objective. By integrating clicker questions into the class period, instructors can break mental passivity and bolster student participation in cognitively engaging activities.

Instructors may integrate clicker questions at strategic points during the lecture to which students respond. Instructors may consider using such questions to achieve several instructional objectives. First, they may be used for formative assessments to gauge the state of class-group knowledge, identify problem areas, or pinpoint misconceptions that direct instruction failed to address (Caldwell, 2007; Cline et al., 2020). Based on the tally of students' responses, instructors may facilitate think-pair-share or other group discussions – to get students to talk about and resolve doubtful or problem concepts or ideas (Chen et al., 2016). However, clicker times may be more or less worthwhile based on the type of questions instructors choose to ask. Recall questions are helpful only if the goal is to check whether students remember the critical point from earlier reading or previous class (Lantz & Stawiski, 2014; Smith & Knight, 2020). Questions that spur students to critical thinking questions, scenarios, or application questions are better suited to initiate discussion, collaboration, and inquiry. Clicker applications can be configured to allow anonymous responses. Leveraging this feature, instructors may get more students to participate in certain instances if they can do so anonymously (Barr, 2017). Finally, instructors may consider using questions that seek students' perspectives on hot-button topics or self-assessment of learning to gain their participation in situations where many students may be reticent to participate (Stowell et al., 2010).

Instructors can use clicker questions to elicit more students' participation and initiate discussions. These capabilities may be viewed as instructional assets for classroom management, but they are also germane for promoting meaningful learning. The literature suggested that instructors can integrate clickers to channel students' attention to enhance cognitive processes during classroom instruction. To achieve this, however, they must intentionally plan clicker questions and the timing of clicker breaks during a lecture to realize this objective (Lantz & Stawiski, 2014). If discussions or activities follow clicker questions, instructors must be intentional about how they moderate such discussions or activities. For example, class and group sizes, type of topic, students' prior knowledge of a topic, and time availability are all factors that can affect the feasibility, extent, and quality of the post-clicker question activities (Hunsu et al., 2016). The number of clicker breaks within any lesson must also be contemplated. The use of clickers may provide an anonymity shield for students who are introverted, shy, or uncertain about themselves to get involved in class activities or to stake an uncomfortable opinion (Stowell et al., 2010). Hence, it is pertinent that the instructor facilitates a safe and respectful environment for post-clicker question discussions.

Some instructors use clickers in their classrooms to take students' attendance or to administer pop quizzes (Keough, 2012). Before the advancement of web-based clickers, each student in a classroom was assigned a clicker transmitter that they could use to 'register' their presence in class. They may also use them to respond to opinion polls or pop quizzes that instructors may be tied to attendance. Each device is unique to particular students and tracks their involvement in class over the semester. Many web-based ARSs that have sprung up recently can facilitate registering attendance (Mader & Bry, 2019).

Finally, it is worth mentioning that some instructors have negative views of clickers or related technologies for various reasons. Similarly, the time commitment to properly use clickers can deter some from considering clickers in their classrooms. For example, many undergraduate lesson periods are

50 minutes long. The time crunch that instructors may be up against and the additional prep time needed to set up clicker-based instruction could discourage some from considering using them in their classrooms. A natural conflict may arise between racing through the planned instructional curriculum and interjecting lecture time with clicker activities that may interrupt the available class period. While there are no easy ways to address this conflict, an instructor's teaching philosophy and curricular objective – whether to cover breadth or drill deep – might play a significant role in how they approach the issue. It is worth noting that clicker questions can sometimes help instructors identify course content that most students have already mastered and may not need to be taught again.

Conclusion

Instructors have looked to clickers or ARSs to enhance classroom management tasks such as monitoring attendance and student attention. They have also been used to promote activities that enhance meaningful cognitive engagement in the classroom. Clickers can be introduced into lecture time for better or for worse. Whether they turn out for better or worse depends on what they are used for and how they are used. In the preceding sections, we highlighted the theoretical perspective of learning and student engagement that suggests why and how clickers can be an excellent addition to planning and delivering effective instruction. We further described some empirical positions for and against clicker use in the classroom. By delineating these empirical perspectives, we showcased some potential and limitations of using clickers. Lastly, we highlighted a few things to consider when using clickers to get more done in the classroom. The perspectives and considerations in this chapter are a partial discussion of the subject matter. However, we hope they provide reasonable insights on using ARS technologies effectively to promote engagement and productive student interaction in the classroom.

Evidence-based practice recommendations

- **Consider using clickers for attendance and pop quizzes:** Instructors can use clickers to streamline administrative tasks such as taking attendance or administering pop quizzes. Web-based ARSs offer convenient features for tracking attendance and facilitating quizzes, relieving instructors of manual record-keeping and grading tasks. Integrating clickers into these routine activities can also reinforce student accountability and engagement.
- **Integrate clicker questions strategically during lecture time:** Incorporating clicker questions at strategic points during lectures promotes student engagement and participation. These questions can be used to formatively assess or gauge student understanding, identify misconceptions, and

stimulate discussion. By planning clicker breaks to complement the lecture content, instructors can break mental passivity and maintain student attention throughout the class period.

- **Use varied question types to stimulate cognitive engagement:** Clicker questions should not be solely recall questions. Instructors should use diverse question types that encourage critical thinking, application, and reflection. Clicker questions that prompt deeper cognitive processing are more likely to foster meaningful learning and enhance student engagement. Additionally, leveraging the anonymity feature of clickers can encourage participation from students who may be hesitant to speak up in class.
- **Facilitate post-clicker question discussions effectively:** After posing clicker questions, instructors should facilitate discussions or activities that allow students to explore and clarify concepts collaboratively. Factors such as class size, topic complexity, and students' prior knowledge should be considered when moderating post-clicker question activities. Creating a safe and respectful discussion environment is essential to ensuring active participation from all students.
- **Manage time effectively to balance instructional goals:** While incorporating clicker activities into the lesson plan, instructors should manage time effectively to balance instructional goals and class objectives. Recognizing the constraints of the class period and aligning clicker use with teaching philosophy and curricular objectives can help optimize the learning experience. Additionally, instructors should be mindful of the time commitment required for planning and executing clicker-based instruction, ensuring that it enhances rather than detracts from the overall educational outcomes.

By following these evidence-based practice recommendations, instructors can harness the potential of clickers to promote active learning, foster student engagement, and enhance the overall classroom experience.

References

Adesope, O. O., Trevisan, D. A., & Sundararajan, N. (2017). Rethinking the use of tests: A meta-analysis of practice testing. *Review of Educational Research*, 87(3), 659–701.

Andre, T., & Thieman, A. (1988). Level of adjunct question, types of feedback, and learning concepts by reading. *Contemporary Educational Psychology*, 13(3), 296–307.

Bain, L. Z., & Przybyla, J. (2009). The impact of student response systems on student behavior and performance in a management information systems course. *Issues in Information Systems*, 10(1), 1–12.

Barr, M. L. (2017). Encouraging college student active engagement in learning: Student response methods and anonymity. *Journal of Computer Assisted Learning*, 33(6), 621–632.

Brady, M., Rosenthal, J. L., Forest, C. P., & Hocevar, D. (2020). Anonymous versus public student feedback systems: metacognition and achievement with graduate learners. *Educational Technology Research and Development*, 68(6), 2853–2872.

Brady, M., Seli, H., & Rosenthal, J. (2013). "Clickers" and metacognition: A quasi-experimental comparative study about metacognitive self-regulation and use of electronic feedback devices. *Computers & Education*, 65, 56–63.

Brod, G. (2021). Generative learning: Which strategies for what age? *Educational Psychology Review*, 33(4), 1295–1318.

Bunce, D. M., Flens, E. A., & Neiles, K. Y. (2010). How long can students pay attention in class? A study of student attention decline using clickers. *Journal of Chemical Education*, 87(12), 1438–1443.

Burns, R. A. (1985, May). Information impact and factors affecting recall. In *Paper presented at Annual National Conference on Teaching Excellence and Conference of Administrators*, Austin, TX.

Cain, J., Black, E. P., & Rohr, J. (2009). An audience response system strategy to improve student motivation, attention, and feedback. *American Journal of Pharmaceutical Education*, 73(2), 1–7.

Caldwell J. E. (2007). Clickers in the large classroom: Current research and best-practice tips. *CBE Life Science Education*, 6(1), 9–20. https://doi.org/10.1187/cbe.06-12-0205

Carnaghan, C., & Webb, A. (2007). Investigating the effects of group response systems on student satisfaction, learning, and engagement in accounting education. *Issues in Accounting Education*, 22(3), 391–409.

Castillo-Manzano, J. I., Castro-Nuño, M., López-Valpuesta, L., Sanz-Díaz, M. T., & Yñiguez, R. (2016). Measuring the effect of ARS on academic performance: A global meta-analysis. *Computers & Education*, 96, 109–121.

Chan, E., & Knight, L. (2010). Clicking with your audience. *Communications in Information Literacy*, 4(2), 192–201.

Chen, H., Daito, M., & Lin, C. (2016). Effects of adding clickers to think-pair-share for learning English grammar. *Focus on the Learner*, 461–467.

Chien, Y. T., Chang, Y. H., & Chang, C. Y. (2016). Do we click in the right way? A meta-analytic review of clicker-integrated instruction. *Educational Research Review*, 17, 1–18.

Clark, R. (1994). Media will never influence learning. *Educational Technology Research & Development*, 42, 2, 21–29.

Clark, R. E. (1983). Reconsidering research on learning from media. *Review of Educational Research*, 53, 445–459. https://doi.org/10.3102/00346543053004445

Cline, K., Zullo, H., Huckaby, D. A. (2020). Addressing common errors and misconceptions in integral calculus with clickers and classroom voting. *Teaching Mathematics and its Applications: An International Journal of the IMA*, 39(2), 71–85.

Dong, J. J., Hwang, W. Y., Shadiev, R., & Chen, G. Y. (2017). Pausing the classroom lecture: The use of clickers to facilitate student engagement. *Active Learning in Higher Education*, 18(2), 157–172.

Dunnett, A. J., Shannahan, K. L., Shannahan, R. J., & Treholm, B. (2011). Exploring the impact of clicker technology in a small classroom setting on student class attendance and course performance. *Journal of the Academy of Business Education*, 12, 43–56.

Egelandsdal, K., & Krumsvik, R. J. (2017). Clickers and formative feedback at university lectures. *Education and Information Technologies, 22*(1), 55–74.

Fiorella, L., & Mayer, R. E. (2016). Eight ways to promote generative learning. *Educational Psychology Review, 28*(4), 717–741.

González-Tato, J., Llamas-Nistal, M., Caeiro-Rodríguez, M., & Mikic-Fonte, F. A. (2013). Web-based audience response system using the educational platform called BeA. *Journal of Research and Practice in Information Technology, 45*(3/4), 251–265.

Graeff, E. C., Vail, M., Maldonado, A., Lund, M., Galante, S., Tataronis, G. (2011). Click it: Assessment of classroom response systems in physician assistant education. *Journal of Allied Health, 40*(1), 1–5.

Gupta, N., & Irwin, J. D. (2016). In-class distractions: The role of Facebook and the primary learning task. *Computers in Human Behavior, 55*, 1165–1178.

Heaslip, G., Donovan, P., & Cullen, J. G. (2014). Student response systems and learner engagement in large classes. *Active Learning in Higher Education, 15*(1), 11–24.

Hedgcock, W. H., & Rouwenhorst, R. M. (2014). Clicking their way to success: Using student response systems as a tool for feedback. *Journal for Advancement of Marketing Education, 22*(2), 16–25.

Humphries, S. A., & Whelan, C. (2009). Effectiveness of interactive technology in business education. *Business Education Innovation Journal, 1*(2), 53–58.

Hunsu N. J., Adesope O., & Bayly D. J., (2016), A meta-analysis of the effects of audience response systems (clicker-based technologies) on cognition and affect. *Computers & Education, 94*, 102–119.

Hutain, J., & Michinov, N. (2022). Collective feedback based on quizzes in online learning: A "double-edged sword" effect on attitude to courses, emotions, and academic behaviors. *Interactive Learning Environments, 32*(5), 1–13.

Joshi, N., Lau, S. K., Pang, M. F., & Lau, S. S. Y. (2021). Clickers in class: Fostering higher cognitive thinking using conceptests in a large undergraduate class. *The Asia-Pacific Education Researcher, 30*(5), 375–394.

Keough, S. M. (2012). Clickers in the classroom: A review and a replication. *Journal of Management Education, 36*(6), 822–847.

Khan, A., Schoenborn, P., & Sharma, S. (2019). The use of clickers in instrumentation and control engineering education: A case study. *European Journal of Engineering Education, 44*(1–2), 271–282.

Koppel, N., & Berenson, M. (2009). Ask the audience e using clickers to enhance introductory business statistics courses. *Information Systems Education Journal, 7*(92), 1–18.

Kozma, R. B. (1991). Learning with media. *Review of Educational Research, 61*, 179–212. https://doi.org/10.3102/00346543061002179

Kozma, R. B. (1994). Will media influence learning, *ETR&D, 42*(2), 7–19.

Lantz M. E., & Stawiski A., (2014), Effectiveness of clickers: Effect of feedback and timing of questions on learning. *Computers in Human Behavior, 31*, 280–286.

Lincoln, D. (2007). Using student response pads ('clickers') in the principles of marketing classroom. In *Proceedings of the 2007 ANZMAC Conference* (pp. 3328–3333).

Liu, C., Chen, S., Chi, C., Chien, K.-P., & Chou, T.-L. (2017). The effects of clickers with different teaching strategies. *Journal of Educational Computing Research, 55*(5), 603–628. https://doi.org/10.1177/0735633116674213

MacArthur, J. R., & Jones, L. L. (2008). A review of literature reports of clickers applicable to college chemistry classrooms. *Chemistry Education Research and Practice, 9*(3), 187–195.

Mader, S., & Bry, F. (2019). Audience response systems reimagined. In M. Herzog, Z. Kubincová, P. Han, & M. Temperini (Eds.), *Advances in web-based learning – ICWL 2019. ICWL 2019.* Lecture Notes in Computer Science (Vol. 11841). Springer. https://doi.org/10.1007/978-3-030-35758-0_19

Matesic, M. A., & Adams, J. M. (2008). Provocation to learn – A study in the use of personal response systems in information literacy instruction. *Partnership: the Canadian Journal of Library and Information Practice and Research, 3*(1), 1–14.

Mayer, R. E., Stull, A., DeLeeuw, K., Almeroth, K., Bimber, B., Chun, D., et al. (2009). Clickers in college classrooms: fostering learning with questioning methods in large lecture classes. *Contemporary Educational Psychology, 34*(1), 51–57.

McDonough, K., & Foote, J. A. (2015). The impact of individual and shared clicker use on students' collaborative learning. *Computers & Education, 86*, 236–249.

McKenzie, M., & Ziemann, M. (2020). Assessment of the web-based audience response system Socrative for biomedical science revision classes. *International Journal of Educational Research Open, 1*, 100008.

Micheletto, M. J. (2011). Conducting a classroom mini-experiment using an audience response system: Demonstrating the isolation effect. *Journal of College Teaching & Learning (TLC), 8*(8), 1–14.

Morse, J., Ruggieri, M., & Whelan-Berry, K. (2010). Clicking our way to class discussion. *American Journal of Business Education, 3*(3), 99–108.

Naismith, L., Lonsdale, P., Vavoula, G., & Sharples, M. (2004). *Report 11: Literature review in mobile technologies and learning.* NESTA Futurelab.

Osborne, R. J., & Wittrock, M. C. (1983). Learning science: A generative process. *Science Education, 67*, 489–508.

Papadopoulos, P. M., Natsis, A., Obwegeser, N., & Weinberger, A. (2019). Enriching feedback in audience response systems: Analysis and implications of objective and subjective metrics on students' performance and attitudes. *Journal of computer assisted learning, 35*(2), 305–316.

Park, S., & Farag, D. (2015). Transforming the legal studies classroom: Clickers and engagement. *Journal of Legal Studies Education, 32*, 47.

Parong, J., & Mayer, R. E. (2018). Learning science in immersive virtual reality. *Journal of Educational Psychology, 110*(6), 785.

Pfaller-Sadovsky, N., Hurtado-Parrado, C., Cardillo, D., Medina, L. G., & Friedman, S. G. (2020). What's in a click? The efficacy of conditioned reinforcement in applied animal training: A systematic review and meta-analysis. *Animals, 10*(10), 1757.

Remón, J., Sebastián, V., Romero, E., & Arauzo, J. (2017). Effect of using smartphones as clickers and tablets as digital whiteboards on students' engagement and learning. *Active Learning in Higher Education, 18*(2), 173–187.

Rowland, C. A. (2014). The effect of testing versus restudy on retention: A meta-analytic review of the testing effect. *Psychological Bulletin, 140*(6), 1432.

Shea, K. M. (2016). Beyond clickers, next generation classroom response systems for organic chemistry. *Journal Chemical Education, 93*(5), 971–974.

Smith, M. K., & Knight, J. K. (2020). Clickers in the biology classroom: Strategies for writing and effectively implementing clicker questions that maximize student learning. In J. J. Mintzes & E. M. Walter (Eds.), *Active learning in college science* (pp. 141–158). Springer.

Sprague, E. W., & Dahl, D.W. (2010). Learning to click: an evaluation of the personal response system clicker technology in introductory marketing courses. *Journal of Marketing Education*, 32(1), 93–103.

Stagg, A., & Lane, M. (2010). Using clickers to support information literacy skills development and instruction in first-year business students. *Journal of Information Technology Education: Research*, 9(1), 197–215.

Stevens, N. T., McDermott, H., Boland, F., Pawlikowska, T., & Humphreys, H. (2017). A comparative study: do "clickers" increase student engagement in multi-disciplinary clinical microbiology teaching? *BMC Medical Education*, 17(1), 1–8.

Stowell, J. R., Oldham, T., & Bennett, D. (2010). Using student response systems ("clickers") to combat conformity and shyness. *Teaching of Psychology*, 37(2), 135–140.

Sullivan, R. (2009). Principles for constructing good clicker questions: Going beyond rote learning and stimulating active engagement with course content. *Journal of Educational Technology Systems*, 37(3), 335–347.

Wood, R., & Shirazi, S. (2020). A systematic review of audience response systems for teaching and learning in higher education: The student experience. *Computers & Education*, 153, 103896.

Yang, K., Wang, T., & Chiu, M. (2014). How technology fosters learning: inspiration from the "media debate". *Creative Education*, 5(12), Article ID: 47329.

Yourstone, S. A., Kraye, H. S., & Albaum, G. (2008). Classroom questioning with immediate electronic response: do clickers improve learning? *Decision Sciences Journal of Innovative Education*, 6(1), 75–88.

PART VII

Designing Digital Classrooms

15

EFFECTIVENESS OF FLIPPED CLASSROOMS

Marlene Wagner, Andreas Gegenfurtner and Detlef Urhahne

Definition of Flipped Classroom

Although the flipped classroom approach has attracted increasing attention among researchers in the past decade, there still exists no universally agreed definition or model (Abeysekera & Dawson, 2015; Geiger et al., 2019; Li et al., 2023; Strelan et al., 2020). Broadly speaking, a flipped or inverted classroom implies a change in learning activities in both space and time. "Events that have traditionally taken place *inside* the classroom now take place *outside* the classroom and vice versa" (Lage et al., 2000, p. 32). From this definition, however, it remains open which kinds of classroom and at-home activities are typically arranged in a flipped classroom. Some authors (e.g., Bishop & Verleger, 2013; DeLozier & Rhodes, 2017) provide a slightly narrower definition by characterising the flipped classroom approach by its course structure: individualised computer-based instruction outside the classroom and group-based interactive learning activities inside the classroom. This definition highlights that the use of instructional media outside the classroom and the utilisation of group-based learning activities inside the classroom are integral components of a flipped classroom. By moving instruction time out-of-class, more time is freed up for active learning in class and guidance by the teacher.

Since computer-based and face-to-face learning are combined, flipped classrooms are a special kind of blended learning (Cheng et al., 2019). Widespread disagreement, however, exists as to which medium must be used in the out-of-class learning part to be defined as a flipped classroom (Bernard, 2015; van Alten et al., 2019). While some authors specify that pre-class instructional videos are a key component of flipped classrooms

DOI: 10.4324/9781003386131-22

(e.g., Bishop & Verleger, 2013; Bredow et al., 2021; Cheng et al., 2019; Lo et al., 2017), others claim that any form of individualised computer-based instruction, e.g., open educational resources, can be utilised (e.g., Johnson et al., 2015). Other researchers (e.g., Abeysekera & Dawson, 2015; Akçayır & Akçayır, 2018; van Alten et al., 2019) even use a wider definition by proposing that neither instructional videos nor technology need to be integrated into flipped classrooms. Such a wide definition encompasses that assigning reading as homework and holding discussions in class would also be considered a flipped classroom (Bishop & Verleger, 2013). In a similar manner, it is not clear whether particular in-class activities have to be performed in order to be defined as a flipped classroom. Typically implemented in-class activities include quizzes, individual practices, small-group activities ("pair and share"), and student presentations (DeLozier & Rhodes, 2017; Lo & Hew, 2017). Bishop and Verleger (2013), however, highlighted that flipped classrooms necessitate group-based interactive learning activities in face-to-face lessons. With the spread of the COVID-19 pandemic, the so-called "fully online flipped classroom" (e.g., Lo & Hew, 2022) emerged, meaning that the "in-class" activities can also happen online by using web-based videoconferencing tools. These substantial differences in the implementation, however, present an obstacle to evaluating the effectiveness of flipped classrooms (DeLozier & Rhodes, 2017; Wright & Park, 2021).

Recently, a trend towards using the term "flipped learning" instead of "flipped classroom" has been noticed (e.g., Bredow et al., 2021; Cheng et al., 2020; Kapur et al., 2022). While most authors use these two terms synonymously, the Flipped Learning Network (2014), among others, argues that flipped classrooms can – but does not necessarily – result in flipped learning. They define flipped learning as

> a pedagogical approach in which direct instruction moves from the group learning space to the individual learning space, and the resulting group space is transformed into a dynamic, interactive learning environment where the educator guides students as they apply concepts and engage creatively in the subject matter.
>
> (The Flipped Learning Network, 2014, p. 1)

In this wide definition, at-home and in-class activities as well as the type of educational materials are not specified.

Since the aim of this book chapter is to provide a holistic overview of the flipped classroom approach and its effects, the flipped classroom is broadly defined as an instructional approach in which students study educational materials at home and complete homework assignments in class. Traditional classrooms, in contrast, are characterised by teacher-directed instruction and individual practice in class as well as homework assignments of tasks that could not be completed in class.

Theoretical Underpinnings of Flipped Classroom

Albeit there is no universal theoretical framework, the supposed effectiveness of flipped classrooms can be explained using different psychological and pedagogical theories. From a cognitive psychology perspective, the Cognitive Load Theory (e.g., Sweller, 2011) and the Cognitive Theory of Multimedia Learning (e.g., Mayer, 2022) provide reasonable explanatory approaches for the effectiveness of flipped classrooms. Cognitive Load Theory suggests that our working memory capacity is limited and that cognitive overload impedes learning (Sweller, 2011). It is assumed that flipped classrooms can have a positive impact on students' cognitive load since students can study the learning materials at their own pace, which should help them better manage their cognitive load and therefore improve learning (Abeysekera & Dawson, 2015). Empirical evidence for this assumption can be found in the study by Turan and Goktas (2016), in which students in the flipped classroom had higher achievement and lower cognitive load levels than students in the traditional classroom. The Cognitive Theory of Multimedia Learning proposes that multimedia learning environments (e.g., instructional videos), which are designed according to how the human mind works, lead to higher learning outcomes than those that are not designed in such a way (Mayer, 2022). Within the past three decades, a multitude of evidence-based principles for the design of multimedia learning environments have been established. The multimedia principle, for example, states that people learn better from a combination of words and pictures than from words alone. If these principles are considered (e.g., in the design of an instructional video), a positive effect on student achievement is assumed (Mayer, 2022).

From a motivational psychology perspective, Ryan and Deci's (2017) Self-Determination Theory offers a further explanation for the effectiveness of flipped classrooms. The theory suggests that human's basic psychological needs for competence, social relatedness, and autonomy need to be fulfilled in order to feel intrinsically motivated. It is assumed that flipped classrooms are more likely to promote the satisfaction of students' basic psychological needs and therefore enhance motivation and learning (Abeysekera & Dawson, 2015; Persky & McLaughlin, 2017). The basic need for competence is satisfied because students assume an active role both in the out-of-class and the in-class learning phase and (self-)assessments allow them to reflect on their strengths and weaknesses. The basic need for autonomy is fulfilled because students can learn on their own time and at their own pace in the out-of-class learning phase, and usually, a choice of activities is provided in the in-class learning phase. The basic need for social relatedness is satisfied because students typically work in small groups in the in-class learning phase and there are more social interactions among the students and between the students and the teacher (Abeysekera & Dawson, 2015; Persky & McLaughlin, 2017). These assumptions have been empirically supported by research undertaken by Sergis et al. (2018), who found statistically significant differences for all three dimensions between students in a flipped classroom setting and a traditional classroom setting.

Finally, Constructivist Learning Theory is an additional explanatory approach to the effectiveness of flipped classrooms. It proposes that students actively construct knowledge and skills and reorganise their understanding through interactions with their environment (Lee & Hannafin, 2016). Effective flipped classrooms require a systematic instructional design, including precisely defined learning objectives, appropriate forms of assessment, and activities that are aligned to accomplish the anticipated objectives (Persky & McLaughlin, 2017). The constructive alignment approach (Biggs, 1996) is a specific application of Constructivist Learning Theory, which can be used as a framework for designing and implementing a flipped classroom course (Persky & McLaughlin, 2017). Generally, it is recommended to start with simpler tasks in the out-of-class learning phase and continue with more complex tasks by means of active learning techniques in the in-class learning phase. One of the main advantages of the flipped classroom approach is that it frees up class time for a large variety of active learning techniques and problem-solving activities (DeLozier & Rhodes, 2017). Empirical research has shown that active learning, i.e., activities or discussion in class, better enhances student achievement compared to traditional lecturing (Freeman et al., 2014). These active learning techniques can also promote students' self-regulated learning (e.g., Hewitt et al., 2014), which in turn has a positive impact on student achievement (Dent & Koenka, 2016). However, self-regulated learning behaviour is also an important prerequisite for the effectiveness of flipped classrooms (van Alten et al., 2020b). To sum up, the theoretical underpinnings elaborated above suggest the assumption that flipped classrooms can be an effective learning approach.

Effectiveness of Flipped Classrooms in Different Educational Settings

In the past decade, a substantial amount of research has been conducted on the effectiveness of flipped classrooms in different educational settings. Myriad empirical studies investigated whether the flipped classroom approach has a positive impact on cognitive and affective student learning outcomes. The extensive body of research has already been synthesised in several meta-analyses (e.g., Cheng et al., 2019; Låg & Sæle, 2019; Lo et al., 2017; Strelan et al., 2020; van Alten et al., 2019; Wagner et al., 2021) as well as second-order meta-analyses (e.g., Hew et al., 2021; Kapur et al., 2022). Such meta-analyses provide valuable information on "what works" in education and lay the foundation for evidence-based practice (Knogler et al., 2022). However, Hew et al. (2021) found that prior meta-analyses on flipped classroom effectiveness had methodological flaws, which limits the credibility of results to a certain extent and warrants the need for more high-quality meta-analytic studies. Below, a brief overview of meta-analytic evidence for the effectiveness of flipped classrooms in school and higher education is provided.[1] We mainly refer to meta-analyses that are frequently cited and published in high-ranking journals. A major focus is placed on cognitive student outcomes, i.e., students' academic achievement.

In their second-order meta-analysis, Hew et al. (2021) identified a total of 17 meta-analyses, which investigated the effects of the flipped classroom on cognitive student outcomes. According to their synthesis, all meta-analyses drew the conclusion that flipped classrooms enhance students' cognitive learning outcomes. Overall average effect sizes ranged from 0.19 to 1.13; however, the two largest effect sizes (1.06 and 1.13) were derived from studies conducted exclusively with Chinese nursing students and are therefore not representative. Kapur et al. (2022) identified 46 meta-analyses and found a mean effect of 0.69 with an even broader range of 0.19 to 2.29 and a substantial standard error of 0.12. In general, previous meta-analyses documented small to medium effect sizes for the effectiveness of flipped classrooms in different educational settings.

The vast majority of empirical studies were conducted in the context of higher education, while studies in school education are less common. The meta-analysis by Wagner et al. (2021) focused solely on flipped classroom studies in secondary education and identified 25 articles. The meta-analytic results for the effect size "treatment" supported the effectiveness of flipped classrooms on student achievement in comparison to traditional instruction ($d = 0.42$). In some of the other meta-analyses, sub-group analyses were performed for the population of school students. Cheng et al. (2019), for example, found a mean effect size of $g = 0.22$ ($k = 12$): flipped classroom students significantly outperformed students in the traditional classroom. Van Alten et al. (2019) yielded a mean effect size of $g = 0.18$ ($k = 11$) for secondary school students, Låg and Sæle (2019) a mean effect size of $g = 0.45$ ($k = 20$) and Strelan et al. (2020) an even higher mean effect size of $g = 0.64$ ($k = 21$) for this population.

For the context of higher education, mean effect sizes ranged from $g = 0.21$ ($k = 39$) (Cheng et al., 2019) to $g = 0.39$ ($k = 114$, all studies including those in secondary education) (van Alten et al., 2019) to $g = 0.48$ ($k = 174$) (Strelan et al., 2020). The most recent and extensive meta-analysis for the context of higher education was conducted by Bredow et al. (2021) and identified a mean effect size of $g = 0.39$ ($k = 282$) for overall academic performance.

However, they found significant differences between the three different academic performance outcomes. Effect sizes for academic and professional skills ($g = 0.53$) were significantly higher than for foundational knowledge ($g = 0.34$) and higher-order thinking ($g = 0.20$). Based on these findings, a flipped classroom appears to be an effective approach, which can be deployed both in school and higher education.

Previous meta-analyses also investigated the impact of different moderators on flipped classroom effectiveness. The two most common statistical methods to identify moderators are meta-regression and hierarchical subgrouping of studies. One major problem of moderator analyses is the low statistical power due to a smaller amount of studies (Schmidt, 2017). The results of moderator analyses should therefore be interpreted carefully and considered as patterns that need further investigation (van Alten et al., 2019). Moderator variables in previous flipped classroom meta-analyses included educational context (e.g., subject discipline, country, educational level), study design (e.g., implementation duration, sample size, instructor equivalence), publication characteristics (e.g., publication type, publication year), and flipped classroom design characteristics (e.g., use of formative assessments, group-based activities) (Hew et al., 2021). In terms of subject discipline, meta-analyses mostly showed that the flipped classroom approach tends to be beneficial notwithstanding the discipline (e.g., Strelan et al., 2020, van Alten et al., 2019). Some meta-analyses (e.g., Bredow et al., 2021; Cheng et al., 2019; Låg & Sæle, 2019) documented slightly higher effect sizes for humanities than for STEM. Regarding implementation duration, some of the meta-analyses (e.g., Cheng et al., 2019; Wagner et al., 2021) found that flipped classroom studies with longer duration were associated with smaller effect sizes than studies of shorter duration, which might point towards a novelty effect (Clark, 1983). Concerning sample size, Låg and Sæle (2019) found that sample size had a significant impact on effect sizes, with smaller studies having larger effect sizes. Concerning publication characteristics, no significant differences were found in terms of publication type and year (Hew et al., 2021).

Main moderator findings for instructional design characteristics of flipped classrooms are presented in greater detail now because these can serve as implementation guidelines for flipped classrooms in the future.

Pre-class learning activities. Strelan et al. (2020) investigated in their meta-analysis the effects of different pre-class learning activities on student achievement in flipped classrooms and found the strongest effect for pre-class discussions ($g = 0.78$) and the weakest for reflections on pre-class material ($g = 0.35$). Besides, they reported a negligible difference between studies that used pre-class engagement exercises (e.g., quizzes) and studies that did not, concluding that pre-class testing is not a prerequisite for a successful implementation of the flipped classroom. Interestingly, in the meta-analysis by Bredow et al. (2021), effect sizes were indeed smaller when students had to complete pre-class assignments or quizzes than when they were not supposed to do so.

In-class learning activities. Most of the meta-analyses found no significant effect size differences between studies that implemented group-based activities and studies that did not (Låg & Sæle, 2019; van Alten et al., 2019). Strelan et al. (2020) also examined the effects of different in-class learning activities on student learning outcomes in flipped classrooms and found no remarkable differences between students engaged in group work (g = 0.46) and students working individually (g = 0.59). When working in groups, group size did not seem to be an important indicator. Teacher-centred approaches did not have a significant effect (g = 0.06); however, only four flipped classroom studies adopted such an approach. It is somewhat surprising that face-to-face cooperative learning did not have a positive effect on student learning outcomes, since previous meta-analyses (e.g., Kyndt et al., 2013) demonstrated its effectiveness. A possible explanation for this result might be that group-based learning activities were implemented in different ways and they might not always have satisfied Johnson and Johnson's (2009) cooperative learning criteria of positive interdependence and individual accountability. As noted by Erbil (2020), there is "no clear roadmap on how to incorporate cooperative learning methods in flipped classrooms" (p. 1) and further research is necessary in this regard.

Meta-analytic findings suggest no significant effect size differences between studies that implemented lecture activities during class and studies that did not (van Alten et al., 2019). It is still questionable whether lecture activities during class should be deployed in face-to-face lessons as these are already part of the out-of-class learning phase. If content from the instructional video is anyway repeated by the teacher, students might think that preparation for class is not necessary. As suggested by Lo and Hew (2017), a brief review and short lecture at the beginning of the lesson should be enough to stimulate students' memory and resolve any misunderstandings.

Use of formative assessments in general (out-of-class and in-class). Several meta-analyses have shown that effect sizes are significantly higher when formative assessments (e.g., quizzes) were implemented in flipped classrooms (Låg & Sæle, 2019; Lo et al., 2017; van Alten et al., 2019). This result can be explained by the so-called testing effect, which states that "tests enhance later retention more than additional study of the material, even when tests are given without feedback" (Roediger & Karpicke, 2006, p. 181). Bredow et al. (2021) found that using quizzes in class yielded even higher effect sizes than using quizzes before class. As mentioned before, students who had to complete pre-class assignments (e.g., worksheets or quizzes) actually achieved lower learning gains than students who did not have to complete such assignments. Bredow et al. (2021) suggested that such accountability measures might be less important in higher education settings because students possess higher self-regulation abilities.

Use of learning management systems (LMS). The use of learning management systems as a potential moderator was only investigated in the meta-analysis by Wagner et al. (2021). Findings suggest that the use of a LMS moderated the effect of flipped classrooms on student achievement. Effect sizes were higher in studies that did not employ LMS compared to studies that did use one. Wagner et al. (2021) provided an explanation for this unexpected finding by referring to the heterogeneous use of LMS in the different studies in terms of type, frequency of usage, and degree of interactivity. While some researchers integrated well-known LMS such as Moodle, which also enabled communication in the out-of-class learning phase, others only set up classroom websites on which learning resources were provided. However, findings have to be interpreted with caution since this meta-analytic finding relies only on a small number of primary studies. Future research is warranted regarding the effects of LMS on student achievement in flipped classrooms.

Explanations for the Low to Medium Effect Sizes in Previous Meta-Analyses

When looking at meta-analytic findings for the effectiveness of flipped classrooms, it seems that the potentials of this instructional approach were not fully exploited in the empirical studies. The aim of this subchapter is to provide reasonable explanations for the low to medium effect sizes that were found in previous meta-analyses.

First, flipped classroom research is characterised by a theory deficit. In 2015, Abeysekera and Dawson pointed out that "the flipped classroom approach is under-evaluated, under-theorised and under-researched in general" (p. 2). While many researchers responded to this plea by conducting empirical studies on the effectiveness of flipped classrooms, there still exists no universally agreed model or theory of the flipped classroom approach. Li et al. (in press) analysed 435 flipped classroom articles and found that approximately 65% of the articles made no connections to theory or a conceptual framework; rather, authors referred to a combination of pedagogical terms or approaches. In a similar manner, Wright and Park (2021) conducted a systematic review of flipped classroom studies in the field of K-16 science and maths education and found that of the 30 included studies, only 12 studies reported explicit or conceptual frameworks that guided the flipped classroom design. Lo (2018) tried to develop a theoretical framework for the flipped classroom approach by referring to Spector's (2016) model of six pillars of educational technology (i.e., communication, interaction, environment, culture, instruction, and learning). However, researchers still use different definitions of flipped classrooms, and consequently, flipped classroom implementations vary to a large extent. Different implementations, in turn, impede the evaluation of the effectiveness of flipped classrooms (DeLozier & Rhodes, 2017). Future research is encouraged to elaborate a robust theoretical framework of the flipped classroom approach, which elucidates the effects of flipped classrooms on student learning outcomes.

Second, flipped classroom research is characterised by an implementation deficit. Based on the empirical findings of prior studies, recommendations and guidelines for successful flipped classrooms have already been formulated (e.g., DeLozier & Rhodes, 2017; Lo & Hew, 2017; Lo, 2018). However, it seems that these guidelines are not carefully considered in implementing flipped classroom studies. The effectiveness of flipped classrooms, however, depends on how the flipped classroom approach and the different learning activities, for example, group-based learning activities, are realised. Careful attention should also be paid to sustaining instead of reducing face-to-face time in flipped classrooms (van Alten et al., 2019).

Third, a utilisation deficit might explain the low to medium effect sizes in previous meta-analyses. Researchers frequently mentioned that students' non-compliance to the intervention or their "instructional disobedience" (Elen, 2020), meaning that they do not study pre-class learning materials, is a serious problem in flipped classroom studies that diminishes treatment effects (e.g., He et al., 2016; van Alten et al., 2020a).

Fourth, aptitude-treatment-interaction (ATI) effects (Cronbach & Snow, 1977) might be another explanatory approach. Previous studies (e.g., Bhagat et al., 2016) have shown that high- and low-achieving students benefit to a different extent from the flipped classroom approach. The use of self-paced video learning particularly supports low-achieving students because they can watch the videos multiple times (Owston et al., 2011). However, they might rely on additional explanations and assistance from a teacher, which cannot as fully be provided in the out-of-class learning phase as in the in-class learning phase. High-achieving students have the advantage that they usually possess better self-regulatory learning (SRL) skills (Dent & Koenka, 2016), which appear to be an important requirement for flipped classroom instruction (Hewitt et al., 2014). It is assumed that low-achieving students do not automatically improve their SRL skills in flipped classrooms, but that they need SRL support (e.g., van Alten et al., 2020a; Wagner & Urhahne, 2021).

Fifth, a habituation effect, i.e., treatment losing its effect after some time, might explain the low to medium effect sizes. In some countries, e.g., the United States, students might already be used to this type of learning, and novelty effects that may enhance learning outcomes are therefore less likely. Meta-analytic findings (e.g., Wagner et al., 2021) pointed towards a novelty effect, which refers to the fact that learning gains decrease after some time as students get familiar with the medium and the instructional approach.

Bredow et al. (2021) showed in their meta-analysis that partially flipped courses (i.e., a combination of flipped and traditional lessons) lead to higher learning gains than fully flipped courses.

Higher learning gains at the beginning of a flipped classroom intervention may also be related to an experimenter effect, which refers to the fact that the experimenters' expectations influence students' learning outcomes. Experimenter effects are more likely in intervention studies with smaller sample sizes, which is a typical characteristic of flipped classroom studies. Educators' exaggerated beliefs in technology, for instance, that the use of digital media always leads to higher learning outcomes, might affect intervention results by becoming a self-fulfilling prophecy.

However, in 1994, Clark precisely pointed out that "media will never influence learning". Perhaps it is neither the medium (e.g., educational video) nor the instructional method (e.g., teacher-centred vs. student-centred) that influences students' learning outcomes (Wagner & Urhahne, 2021), but other desirable side effects of flipped classrooms. These include longer learning periods and time-on-task in the out-of-class learning phase, shorter instruction time in the in-class learning phase, and better fit to the prerequisites of the learners.

Implications for Educational Practice

Based on the theoretical and empirical research findings presented above, several instructional design guidelines for the successful implementation of flipped classrooms in different educational settings can be derived.

Pre-class learning activities. The design of multimedia learning materials used in the out-of-class learning phase of flipped classrooms (e.g., instructional videos) should be driven by our knowledge of human cognitive architecture. Based on Sweller's (2011) Cognitive Load Theory and Mayer's (2022) Cognitive Theory of Mutlimedia Learning and a large number of empirical findings, myriad principles for the design of multimedia learning environments have been established. These principles can help educational practitioners to develop their own effective multimedia learning materials or to analyse existing materials. It is not enough to provide learners with instructional materials, but materials need to be accompanied by meaningful learning activities. The ICAP-framework developed by Chi and Wylie (2014) distinguishes four different quality categories of learning activities and argues that if students are more engaged with the learning materials, from passive to active to constructive to interactive, their learning will improve. Meaningful pre-class learning activities include note-taking, online exercises (e.g., quizzes, ideally with computerised feedback), or online discussions (Lo & Hew, 2017; Lo, 2018; Strelan et al., 2020). To extend human interactions in the out-of-class learning phase, it is advised to implement an online communication platform or discussion forum for question-and-answer sessions (Lo & Hew, 2017; Lo, 2018). If instructional videos are utilised, a maximum duration of six minutes is recommended in the literature, while the pre-class activities should be finished within 20 minutes (Lo & Hew, 2017).

In-class learning activities. For the in-class learning phase, it is recommended for educational practitioners to not repeat too much of the content delivered in the out-of-class learning phase, but to start the lesson with a short review and question-and-answer session (Lo & Hew, 2017). Then, more time can be spent on active learning techniques such as responding to clicker questions (i.e., questions posted via audience response systems or so-called "clickers"), peer instruction, group-based learning, individual practices, cooperative learning activities ("think-pair-share"), student presentations, and discussions (DeLozier & Rhodes, 2017; Lo & Hew, 2017; Lo, 2018). If cooperative learning activities are implemented, Johnson and Johnson's (2009) cooperative learning criteria of positive interdependence and individual accountability need to be considered. Optimally challenging tasks are to be provided that are neither too easy nor too difficult (Lo, 2018). When completing the tasks, students should be supported by the teacher and their peers (Lo & Hew, 2017).

Use of formative assessments (out-of-class or in-class). Even though results concerning the use of formative assessments (either at home or in class) in flipped classrooms vary between different meta-analyses, it can be recommended to include formative assessment and regular feedback in flipped classrooms, since they support students' basic psychological needs for competence. In the out-of-class learning phase, students study on their own, and computer-generated feedback may help them realise whether they are on the right track (Lo, 2018).

Use of learning management systems (LMS). Although further research is needed with regard to the effects of LMS on student achievement in flipped classrooms, it can be argued that learning management systems (e.g., Moodle or Blackboard) are helpful because educational practitioners can monitor students' learning performance in the out-of-class learning phase and then tailor the in-class learning phase to the individual needs of the students (Lo, 2018). LMS thus help to combat the serious issue of students' non-compliance to the intervention, as instructors can check whether students studied pre-class learning materials. Besides, gamification elements such as points or badges may be incorporated into LMS to motivate student learning (Lo & Hew, 2017).

It remains to be hoped that the deficits in the theoretical foundation, implementation, and use that have been pointed out will lead to a well-founded revision of the promising flipped classroom approach. Those practices that have been shown to be particularly beneficial in the wide range of meta-analytic studies should be theoretically underpinned. Their application should be described in sufficient detail so that they can be easily implemented by teachers and effectively used by flipped classroom learners.

Evidence-Based Practice Recommendations:

- In the out-of-class learning phase, optimise the design of multimedia learning materials according to evidence-based design principles from multimedia research and complement them with active, constructive, and interactive learning activities.
- In the in-class learning phase, keep lecture time to a minimum so that more time can be spent on active learning techniques such as audience response ("clickers"), peer instruction, group-based learning, individual practices, cooperative learning activities ("think-pair-share"), student presentations, and discussions.
- Include formative assessments (e.g., quizzes) and regular feedback both in the in-class and out-of-class learning phases.
- Incorporate learning management systems (e.g., Moodle or Blackboard) to monitor students' learning performance and to tailor the in-class learning phase to the individual needs of the students.

Note

1 More detailed results are presented in the articles by Hew et al. (2021) and Kapur et al. (2022).

References

Abeysekera, L., & Dawson, P. (2015). Motivation and cognitive load in the flipped classroom: Definition, rationale and a call for research. *Higher Education Research & Development*, 34(1), 1–14. https://doi.org/10.1080/07294360.2014.934336

Akçayır, G., & Akçayır, M. (2018). The flipped classroom: A review of its advantages and challenges. *Computers & Education*, 126, 334–345. https://doi.org/10.1016/j.compedu.2018.07.021

Bernard, J. S. (2015). The flipped classroom: Fertile ground for nursing education research. *International Journal of Nursing Education Scholarship*, 12(1), 1–11. https://doi.org/10.1515/ijnes-2015-0005

Bhagat, K. K., Chang, C. N., & Chang, C. Y. (2016). The impact of the flipped classroom on mathematics concept learning in high school. *Educational Technology & Society*, 19(3), 134–142. https://www.jstor.org/stable/jeductechsoci.19.3.134

Biggs, J. (1996). Enhancing teaching through constructive alignment. *Higher Education*, 32(3), 347–364. https://doi.org/10.1007/BF00138871

Bishop, J. L., & Verleger, M. A. (2013). The flipped classroom: A survey of the research. In *120th ASEE national conference and exposition, Atlanta, GA (paper ID 6219)*. American Society for Engineering Education.

Bredow, C. A., Roehling, P. V., Knorp, A. J., & Sweet, A. M. (2021). To flip or not to flip? A meta-analysis of the efficacy of flipped learning in higher education. *Review of Educational Research*, *91*(6), 878–918. https://doi.org/10.3102/00346543211019122

Cheng, L., Ritzhaupt, A. D., & Antonenko, P. (2019). Effects of the flipped classroom instructional strategy on students' learning outcomes: A meta-analysis. *Educational Technology Research and Development*, *67*(3), 793–824. https://doi.org/10.1007/s11423-018-9633-7

Cheng, S.-C., Hwang, G.-J., & Lai, C.-L. (2020). Critical research advancements of flipped learning: A review of the top 100 highly cited papers. *Interactive Learning Environments*, *30*(9), 1–17. https://doi.org/10.1080/10494820.2020.1765395

Chi, M. T. H., & Wylie, R. (2014). The ICAP framework: Linking cognitive engagement to active learning outcomes. *Educational Psychologist*, *49*(4), 219–243. https://doi.org/10.1080/00461520.2014.965823

Clark, R. E. (1983). Reconsidering research on learning from media. *Review of Educational Research*, *53*(4), 445–459. https://doi.org/10.2307/1170217

Clark, R. E. (1994). Media will never influence learning. *Educational Technology Research & Development*, *42*(2), 21–29. https://doi.org/10.1007/BF02299088

Cronbach, L. J., & Snow, R. E. (1977). *Aptitudes and instructional methods: A handbook for research on interactions*. Irvington.

DeLozier, S., & Rhodes, M. (2017). Flipped classrooms: A review of key ideas and recommendations for practice. *Educational Psychology Review*, *29*(1), 141–151. https://doi.org/10.1007/s10648-015-9356-9

Dent, A. L., & Koenka, A. C. (2016). The relation between self-regulated learning and academic achievement across childhood and adolescence: A meta-analysis. *Educational Psychology Review*, *28*(3), 425–474. https://doi.org/10.1007/s10648-015-9320-8

Elen, J. (2020). "Instructional disobedience": A largely neglected phenomenon deserving more systematic research attention. *Educational Technology Research and Development*, *68*(5), 2021–2032. https://doi.org/10.1007/s11423-020-09776-3

Erbil, D. G. (2020). A review of flipped classroom and cooperative learning method within the context of Vygotsky theory. *Frontiers in Psychology*, *11*, 1157. https://doi.org/10.3389/fpsyg.2020.01157

Freeman, S., Eddy, S. L., McDonough, M., Smith, M. K., Okoroafor, N., Jordt, H., & Wenderoth, M. P. (2014). Active learning increases student performance in science, engineering, and mathematics. *Proceedings of the National Academy of Sciences of the United States of America*, *111*(23), 8410–8415. https://doi.org/10.1073/pnas.1319030111

Geiger, V., Deibl, I., & Zumbach, J. (2019). Flipped-Classroom: Ein pädagogisches Fehlkonzept? [Flipped-Classroom: A pedagogical misconception?] *Erziehung & Unterricht*, *1–2*, 169–179.

He, W., Holton, A., Farkas, G., & Warschauer, M. (2016). The effects of flipped instruction on out-of-class-study time, exam performance, and student perceptions. *Learning and Instruction*, *45*, 61–71. https://doi.org/10.1016/j.learninstruc.2016.07.001

Hew, K. F., Bai, S., Dawson, P., & Lo, C. K. (2021). Meta-analyses of flipped classroom studies: A review of methodology. *Educational Research Review*, *33*, 100393. https://doi.org/10.1016/j.edurev.2021.100393

Hewitt, K. K., Journell, W., & Zilonka, R. (2014). What the flip: Impact of flipped instruction on self-regulated learning. *International Journal of Social Media and Interactive Learning Environments*, 2(4), 303–325. https://doi.org/10.1504/IJSMILE.2014.067638

Johnson, D. W., & Johnson, R. T. (2009). An educational psychology success story: Socialinterdependence theory and cooperative learning. *Educational Researcher*, 38(5), 365–379. https://doi.org/10.3102/0013189X09339057

Johnson, L., Adams Becker, S., Estrada, V., & Freeman, A. (2015). *NMC Horizon Report: 2015*. Higher Education edn. The New Media Consortium.

Kapur, M., Hattie, J., Grossman, I., & Sinha, T. (2022). Fail, flip, fix, and feed - Rethinking flipped learning: A review of meta-analyses and a subsequent meta-analysis. *Frontiers in Education*, 7, 956416. https://doi.org/10.3389/feduc.2022.956416

Knogler, M., Hetmanek, A., & Seidel, T. (2022). Determining an evidence base for particular fields of educational practice: A systematic review of meta-analyses on effective mathematics and science teaching. *Frontiers in Psychology*, 13, 873995. https://doi.org/10.3389/fpsyg.2022.873995

Kyndt, E., Raes, E., Lismont, B., Timmers, F., Cascallar, E., & Dochy, F. (2013). A meta-analysis of the effects of face-to-face cooperative learning. Do recent studies falsify or verify earlier findings? *Educational Research Review*, 10, 133–149. https://doi.org/10.1016/j.edurev.2013.02.002

Låg, T., & Sæle, R. G. (2019). Does the flipped classroom improve student learning and satisfaction? A systematic review and meta-analysis. *AERA Open*, 5(3), 1–17. https://doi.org/10.1177/2332858419870489

Lage, M. J., Platt, G. J., & Treglia, M. (2000). Inverting the classroom: A gateway to creating an inclusive learning environment. *The Journal of Economic Education*, 31(1), 30–43. https://doi.org/10.1080/00220480009596759

Lee, E., & Hannafin, M. (2016). A design framework for enhancing engagement in student- centered learning: own it, learn it, and share it. *Educational Technology Research and Development*, 64(4), 707–734. https://doi.org/10.1007/s11423-015-9422-5

Li, R., Lund, A., & Nordsteien, A. (2023). The link between flipped and active learning: A scoping review. *Teaching in Higher Education*. https://doi.org/10.1080/13562517.2021.1943655

Lo, C. (2018). Grounding the flipped classroom approach in the foundations of educational technology. *Educational Technology Research and Development*, 66(3), 793–811. https://doi.org/10.1007/s11423-018-9578-x

Lo, C. K., & Hew, K. F. (2017). A critical review of flipped classroom challenges in K-12 education: Possible solutions and recommendations for future research. *Research and Practice in Technology Enhanced Learning*, 12(4), 1–22. https://doi.org/10.1186/s41039-016-0044-2

Lo, C. K., & Hew, K. F. (2022). Design principles for fully online flipped learning in health professions education: A systematic review of research during the COVID-19 pandemic. *BMC Medical Education*, 22(1), 720. https://doi.org/10.1186/s12909-022-03782-0

Lo, C. K., Hew, K. F., & Chen, G. (2017). Toward a set of design principles for mathematics flipped classrooms: A synthesis of research in mathematics education. *Educational Research Review*, 22, 50–73. https://doi.org/10.1016/j.edurev.2017.08.002

Mayer, R. E. (2022). Cognitive theory of multimedia learning. In R. E. Mayer & L. Fiorella (Eds.), *The Cambridge handbook of multimedia learning* (3rd ed., pp. 57–72). Cambridge University Press.

Owston, R., Lupshenyuk, D., & Wideman, H. (2011). Lecture capture in large undergraduate classes: Student perceptions and academic performance. *Internet and Higher Education*, 14(4), 262–268. https://doi.org/10.1016/j.iheduc.2011.05.006

Persky, A. M., & McLaughlin, J. E. (2017). The flipped classroom – from theory to practice in health professional education. *American Journal of Pharmaceutical Education*, 81(6), 1–11. https://doi.org/10.5688/ajpe816118

Roediger, H. L., & Karpicke, J. D. (2006). The power of testing memory: Basic research and implications for educational practice. *Perspectives on Psychological Science*, 1(3), 181–210. https://doi.org/10.1111/j.1745-6916.2006.00012.x

Ryan, R. M., & Deci, E. L. (2017). *Self-determination theory: Basic psychological needs in motivation, development, and wellness*. Guilford Press.

Schmidt, F. L. (2017). Statistical and measurement pitfalls in the use of meta-regression in meta-analysis. *Career Development International*, 22(5), 469–476. https://doi.org/10.1108/CDI-08-2017-0136

Sergis, S., Sampson, D. G., & Pelliccione, L. (2018). Investigating the impact of flipped classroom on students' learning experiences: A self-determination theory approach. *Computers in Human Behavior*, 78, 368–378. https://doi.org/10.1016/j.chb.2017.08.011

Spector, J. M. (2016). *Foundations of educational technology: Integrative approaches and interdisciplinary perspectives* (2nd ed.). Routledge.

Strelan, P., Osborn, A., & Palmer, E. (2020). The flipped classroom: A meta-analysis of effects on student performance across disciplines and education levels. *Educational Research Review*, 30, 100314. https://doi.org/10.1016/j.edurev.2020.100314

Sweller, J. (2011). Cognitive load theory. In J. Mestre & B. Ross (Eds.), *The psychology of learning and motivation: Cognition in Education* (Vol. 55, pp. 37–76). Academic Press.

The Flipped Learning Network (2014). The four pillars of F-L-I-P™. https://flippedlearning.org/wp-content/uploads/2016/07/FLIP_handout_FNL_Web.pdf

Turan, Z., & Goktas, Y. (2016). The flipped classroom: Instructional efficiency and impact of achievement and cognitive load levels. *Journal of e-Learning and Knowledge Society*, 12(4), 51–62. https://doi.org/10.20368/1971-8829/1122

van Alten, D. C. D., Phielix, C., Janssen, J., & Kester, L. (2019). Effects of flipping the classroom on learning outcomes and satisfaction: A meta-analysis. *Educational Research Review*, 28, 1–18. https://doi.org/10.1016/j.edurev.2019.05.003

van Alten, D. C. D., Phielix, C., Janssen, J., & Kester, L. (2020a). Effects of self-regulated learning prompts in a flipped history classroom. *Computers in Human Behavior*, 108, 1–13. https://doi.org/10.1016/j.chb.2020.106318

van Alten, D. C. D., Phielix, C., Janssen, J., & Kester, L. (2020b). Self-regulated learning support in flipped learning videos enhances learning outcomes. *Computers & Education*, 158, 104000. https://doi.org/10.1016/j.compedu.2020.104000

Wagner, M., Gegenfurtner, A., & Urhahne, D. (2021). Effectiveness of the flipped classroom on student achievement in secondary education: A meta-analysis. *Zeitschrift für Pädagogische Psychologie*, 35(1), 11–31. https://doi.org/10.1024/1010-0652/a000274

Wagner, M., & Urhahne, D. (2021). Disentangling the effects of flipped classroom instruction in EFL secondary education: When is it effective and for whom? *Learning and Instruction, 75,* 101490. https://doi.org/10.1016/j.learninstruc.2021.101490

Wright, G. W., & Park, S. (2021). The effects of flipped classrooms on K-16 students' science and math achievement: A systematic review. *Studies in Science Education, 58*(1), 95–136. https://doi.org/10.1080/03057267.2021.1933354

16

DESIGNING EFFECTIVE SYNCHRONOUS ONLINE LEARNING

Andreas Gegenfurtner, Svenja Bedenlier,
Christian Ebner, Özün Keskin and Marion Händel

Introduction

During the COVID-19 pandemic, educational institutions across the globe had to close, and regular lectures and seminars could no longer take place onsite. Additionally, students were forced to learn from home during so-called lockdowns. In contrast to distance education practiced before the COVID crisis, this new situation was subsumed under the term *emergency remote teaching* (Hodges et al., 2020). To switch from face-to-face to distance learning, teachers and educators adopted synchronous online learning as their new normal (Bond et al., 2021; Helm et al., 2021; Priatmoko et al., 2022), for example in K-12 education (Larson & Farnsworth, 2020), higher education (Gupta & Sengupta, 2021), and professional training (Gegenfurtner et al., 2020). Scholars have published numerous study reports and evaluations of synchronous online learning using webinars and video-conferencing platforms, for example in the fields of teacher education (Cronin, 2022), medical education (Toquero & Talidong, 2020), science education (Erickson & Wattiaux, 2021), and language learning (Kohnke & Moorhouse, 2022). Although the COVID-19 pandemic has boosted the design and implementation of synchronous online learning in many educational contexts, it has been widely practiced already before the pandemic (Gegenfurtner et al., 2018; Martin et al., 2017; Wang & Hsu, 2008), as learning and instruction afforded by videoconferencing scenarios have been around for about three decades, especially in the area of distance education (Bonk, 2020). Al-Samarraie (2019) and Correia et al. (2020), among others, describe different videoconferencing software systems available for teaching and learning purposes, including Zoom, Cisco WebEx, Microsoft Teams,

DOI: 10.4324/9781003386131-23

Google Meet, and Adobe Connect. Despite its frequent use, however, researchers and practitioners alike still discuss how to design effective synchronous online learning. This chapter reviews the findings of meta-analytic syntheses on synchronous online learning to offer some design recommendations for teachers and educators. First, we focus on the terminology used in research on synchronous online learning. Second, we synthesize the findings of meta-analyses that examined the effectiveness of synchronous online learning compared to synchronous face-to-face and asynchronous online learning. Third, we focus on instructional design elements that can moderate the effectiveness of synchronous online learning. Finally, we present a research agenda for future studies and offer evidence-based design recommendations for synchronous online learning environments. The chapter's guiding research question was: Which design characteristics influence the effectiveness of synchronous online learning?

Defining the term "synchronous online learning"

Synchronous online learning is an umbrella term that includes a number of different learning scenarios in which technology is used to bring teachers and learners from different locations together in real-time. As Martin et al. (2021, p. 206) put it, synchronous online learning "occurs when students and the instructor are together in 'real time' but not at the 'same place.'" Gegenfurtner and Ebner (2019) offer a glossary of terms associated with synchronous learning such as webinars and videoconferencing. The term "webinar" is often used synonymously with synchronous online learning. Webinars are defined as web-based seminars, in which students and teachers communicate live over the Internet across distant geographical locations. Shared virtual platforms with voice-over-IP technology and webcams are used to interact ubiquitously and synchronously in real time (Gegenfurtner & Ebner, 2019). The term "webinar" is a portmanteau combining the terms "web" and "seminar," indicating that student learning is situated in synchronous online learning environments, in contrast to (a) traditional seminars, in which student learning is situated in synchronous face-to-face learning environments at school or on campus, and in contrast to (b) asynchronous online learning environments, in which students and teachers interact online on learning management platforms, such as Moodle and wikis, but usually not synchronously at the same time but asynchronously at a time of their own choosing (Gegenfurtner & Ebner, 2019; Martin et al., 2021; Raes, 2022). Synchronous online learning is usually realized via videoconferencing sessions that display remote classrooms (Martin & Parker, 2014). Videoconferencing can be used for a variety of purposes, including non-educational team meetings or chats. We adopt Gegenfurtner and Ebner's (2019) definition of webinars as a special case of videoconferencing that serves an educational function.

		Modality	
		online	*offline*
Synchronicity	**synchronous**	webinars, virtual classrooms	face-to-face classrooms
	asynchronous	learning management platforms, videos	printed / mailed

FIGURE 16.1   Comparison of synchronicity and modality in learning environments with prototypical examples.

Source: adapted from Ebner & Gegenfurtner, 2019.

On a more general level, learning environments can be classified with regard to synchronicity and modality (Ebner & Gegenfurtner, 2019; Raes et al., 2020). *Synchronicity* refers to the "when" of interactions between students and their lecturers. Synchronous learning environments enable simultaneous and direct interactions, for example, during a Zoom webinar, while asynchronous learning environments afford temporally delayed and indirect interactions, for example on learning management platforms or when watching a video of a lecture on YouTube. *Modality* refers to the "how" of interactions: Online or offline. Online interactions are typically afforded by videoconferencing software using the Internet and computer devices, while face-to-face interactions occur onsite in lecture halls and seminar rooms in schools and campuses. Learning environments can be compared based on their levels of synchronicity and modality, as shown in Figure 16.1.

Meta-analyses of synchronous online learning

Several meta-analyses have addressed the effectiveness of synchronous online learning compared to asynchronous online learning and synchronous face-to-face learning. In this chapter, effectiveness is understood as a learning environment that leads to positive cognitive and affective outcomes. According to Phipps and Merisotis (1999) and Cunningham et al. (2021), effectiveness research typically includes measures of student learning outcomes (e.g., grades and test scores) and overall satisfaction. These two dimensions are also considered in the four meta-analyses on synchronous online learning presented in the following paragraphs.

Gegenfurtner and Ebner (2019) reported the outcomes of a meta-analysis of 15 randomized controlled trials that compared the effectiveness of synchronous online learning with synchronous face-to-face teaching and asynchronous online learning. Their meta-analysis suggested that learners in synchronous webinars had slightly higher post-test knowledge and higher knowledge gains than learners in asynchronous online (Cohen's $d = 0.04$) and face-to-face ($d = 0.16$) learning environments.

Ebner and Gegenfurtner (2019) meta-analyzed five randomized controlled trials that compared learning outcomes and learner satisfaction between learning environments. Their results indicated that learners showed higher learning outcomes (Hedges' $g = 0.06$) and higher satisfaction ($g = 0.12$) with webinars compared to asynchronous online learning environments. Across studies, learners also had higher learning outcomes ($g = 0.29$) and lower satisfaction ($g = -0.33$) in synchronous online learning compared to synchronous face-to-face instruction.

Martin et al. (2021) meta-analyzed 19 experimental and quasi-experimental studies that compared cognitive and affective educational outcomes between synchronous online learning and asynchronous online or face-to-face learning. Their findings suggested that cognitive outcomes in synchronous online learning were higher than those in asynchronous online learning ($g = 0.37$) but lower than those in synchronous face-to-face instruction ($g = -0.20$). Meanwhile, affective outcomes did not differ significantly between environments.

He et al. (2021) conducted a meta-analysis of seven randomized controlled trials in medical education that contrasted synchronous online and face-to-face learning using a subset of the studies included in Gegenfurtner and Ebner (2019). Their analyses suggested that knowledge outcomes ($g = 0.12$) and knowledge gains ($g = 0.15$) were higher in webinars than in face-to-face instruction. Contrary to Ebner and Gegenfurtner (2019), He et al. reported higher levels of learner satisfaction in synchronous online compared to synchronous face-to-face instruction ($d = 0.60$).

Overall, these meta-analyses suggest that synchronous online learning environments are effective in promoting student learning, particularly when the meta-analyses include well-controlled, randomized original research (Gegenfurtner & Ebner, 2019; He et al., 2021). We should also note that the effect sizes were small, indicating only slight advantages of synchronous online learning over asynchronous and face-to-face instruction. Moreover, the meta-analytic evidence on learner satisfaction is mixed, with higher satisfaction in synchronous online learning (He et al., 2021), higher satisfaction in synchronous face-to-face learning (Ebner & Gegenfurtner, 2019), and non-significant differences (Martin et al., 2021). Based on this available meta-analytic evidence, the next section elaborates on how different design features influence and moderate the effectiveness of synchronous online learning.

Influence of design features on webinar effectiveness

The meta-analyses reported in Section "Defining the term 'synchronous online learning'" of this chapter included a number of design features that can moderate how effectively learners develop knowledge and skills in synchronous online learning. These design features include the instructional format, knowledge type, webinar duration, webinar frequency, and access to archives, which we discuss in turn.

First, the instructional format has been shown to influence the effectiveness of synchronous online learning. We compare teacher-centered and student-centered formats. A teacher-centered format "'takes seriously the need to help students become knowledgeable" in ways that allow them to "develop an understanding of disciplines" (Bransford et al., 1999, p. 136). A prototypical example of a teacher-centered format in synchronous online learning is a teacher lecture in Zoom. In contrast, a student-centered format accounts for "the knowledge, skills, attitudes, and beliefs that learners bring to the educational setting" (Bransford et al., 1999, p. 133). Prototypical examples of a student-centered format in synchronous online learning are discussions and small-group activities in breakout rooms. The available meta-analytic evidence reported by Gegenfurtner and Ebner (2019) and Martin et al. (2021) suggests that students' learning outcomes are higher when the instructional format in synchronous online learning includes student-centered elements. Although there is a rich plethora of possibilities for designing student interactivity, the meta-analyses did not consider different kinds of these activities because of a low number of original research. Still, the cumulated effect sizes tend to suggest that students have higher cognitive outcomes when the synchronous online learning environment includes interactive instructional elements compared to purely lecture-based learning.

Second, knowledge type also influences the effectiveness of synchronous online learning. Based on Schraw's (2006) knowledge taxonomy, knowledge can be differentiated into declarative knowledge and procedural knowledge. Declarative knowledge includes knowledge about facts, episodes, schemata, and concepts, whereas procedural knowledge includes skills in the form of scripts, algorithms, and heuristics. He et al. (2021) reported higher effect sizes when synchronous online learning focused on procedural rather than declarative knowledge. Similarly, Gegenfurtner and Ebner (2019) reported higher levels of post-test knowledge when synchronous online learning was used to impart procedural performance rather than declarative knowledge. These findings tend to suggest that synchronous online learning, with its direct possibilities for synchronous communication and feedback, is particularly useful for gaining procedural knowledge.

Third, duration and learning time in synchronous online learning have been examined as a moderator of the effectiveness of synchronous online learning. Gegenfurtner and Ebner (2019) analyzed duration as a continuous variable and documented stronger increases in knowledge from the pre-test to the post-test in synchronous webinars with longer durations, $\beta = .997$. The duration was coded in minutes, reflecting the total length of a webinar meeting. Studies included in their meta-analysis examined synchronous online learning sessions ranging from half an hour to 25 hours ($M = 5.3$, $SD = 7.5$). Martin et al. (2021) analyzed duration as a categorical variable and compared total course durations that were shorter and longer than 15 weeks. They reported that synchronous online learning, compared to asynchronous online learning environments, was more effective in promoting cognitive outcomes only when the course duration was shorter than 15 weeks. A frequently asked question is how long a single session during synchronous online learning should be and if there is an ideal duration for a single online event. This question is hard to answer conclusively; it seems intuitive to assume that different course contents and course objectives require different amounts of learning time. Hence, a systematic meta-analytic comparison would ideally reflect and account for the scope and volume of courses compared. More research on duration and learning time in synchronous online learning is needed to provide evidence-based recommendations.

Fourth, and in addition to duration, the frequency with which synchronous online learning occurs has also been examined as moderators. Frequency in synchronous online learning is the number of events or meetings, ranging from a single session that is not followed-up to sessions that are repeated daily, weekly, monthly, etc. Research on frequency is still rare. Gegenfurtner and Ebner (2019) showed higher effects on knowledge outcomes and knowledge gains for repeated webinars than for single webinar events. Similarly, He et al. (2021) reported a higher effect size when synchronous online learning meetings were held more than once compared to single events. A possible reason for the positive effects of higher frequencies is the possibility of learners' repeated engagement with the course content.

Finally, access to archives seems to moderate the effectiveness of synchronous online learning. In their meta-analysis, He et al. (2021) found that learners who had access to additional information stored in archives benefited more from synchronous online learning than learners who had no access, potentially because access to archives "provides great opportunities for students to review lessons after class without time constraints" (p. 304). While He et al. did not define the term "archive," we speculate that it refers to learning management platforms in which learners have access to additional course materials, can read and download documents, and can re-watch video recordings of past sessions. Access to such materials seems to be beneficial for learners' knowledge acquisition.

In summary, these five design features are associated with the effectiveness of synchronous online learning. Based on consistent meta-analytic evidence, synchronous online learning environments tend to be more effective when they include student-centered interactive elements, when they are designed to teach procedural knowledge, when they are scheduled as repeated webinars in a series, and when learners get access to additional information stored in archives and learning management platforms.

Research agenda for future studies on synchronous online learning

Synchronous online learning has been used prior to the COVID-19 pandemic; however, because of lockdowns and homeschooling in K-12 education, higher education, and professional learning, the use of synchronous online learning environments has increased massively (Bond et al., 2021; Hacker et al., 2020; Helm et al., 2021; Priatmoko et al., 2022). Consequently, research on synchronous online learning has increased rapidly in the past two years. Four meta-analyses were summarized, all of which indicated that synchronous online learning is as effective as synchronous face-to-face instruction and more effective than asynchronous online learning in promoting student learning. In this section, we offer some evidence-based design recommendations—drawn from these rigorously performed meta-analyses—that teachers and instructional designers could follow when developing and conducting synchronous online learning environments.

Among these recommendations are (a) the inclusion of student-centered interactive elements rather than teacher-centered activities only, (b) focus on procedural rather than declarative knowledge, (c) repeated meetings instead of single events, and (d) access to additional resources on learning platforms. The available meta-analytic evidence concerning duration and learning time is mixed. These educational implications should not be followed blindly; instead, they need to be adapted and tailored to the specific affordances of course content and the learner population.

Reflecting on the meta-analytic evidence, it seems apparent that the number of available meta-analyses on synchronous online learning is still rather limited, as only four meta-analyses have been identified (Ebner & Gegenfurtner, 2019; Gegenfurtner & Ebner, 2019; He et al., 2021; Martin et al., 2021). We assume that more meta-analyses will be performed in the future because of the tremendous increase in original studies on synchronous online learning. While all primary studies included in the four meta-analyses were performed before emergency remote teaching, how the effectiveness of synchronous online learning might change during emergency remote teaching and afterward needs to be carefully considered. On the one hand, the COVID-19 pandemic might have been a booster for technology-enhanced education. On the other hand, synchronous online learning during emergency remote teaching might differ in quality because neither students nor educators had been prepared for this sudden, abrupt shift. Moreover, students' and educators' motivation to engage in synchronous online learning during emergency remote teaching, along with educators' technological pedagogical content knowledge (Koehler & Mishra, 2009), might have been lower than that during planned synchronous online learning courses.

What also seems apparent is the focus on learning outcomes in these meta-analyses. All meta-analyses were concerned with the effectiveness of synchronous online learning in promoting student learning and satisfaction compared to learning environments with different levels of synchronicity and modality. While such a focus is certainly interesting and useful, information on particular instructional design features tends to be underemphasized in meta-analytic syntheses. Consequently, in this section, we provide only a limited number of instructional design recommendations backed up by meta-analytic evidence. Again, we assume that more design recommendations will be identified in the coming years, as the number of meta-analyses will likely increase in the future. These recommendations and educational implications are needed to gain a more comprehensive understanding of particular instructional affordances that contribute to student learning, satisfaction, and motivation.

There are a number of instructional affordances that have already been addressed in single original studies, including the use of webcams, use of breakout rooms, integration of webinars into flipped classroom models, and use of webinars in hybrid teaching contexts (synchronous face-to-face and live-online teaching). First, the use of webcams seems significant for experiences of social presence, engagement, and learning (Bedenlier et al., 2021; Castelli & Sarvary, 2021; Händel et al., 2022; Raes, 2022). For example, in a study comprising 407 participants, Gerheş et al. (2021) reported that more than half of the learners were not willing to keep their webcams on during online classes. The reasons for turning off their webcams were the fear of being exposed, shyness, desire for privacy, and chances that other people might walk into the background. Similar reasons for students' nonuse of their webcams were evidenced in Bedenlier et al.'s (2021) study of 3,527 higher education students in Germany, in which they reported that female students were more likely to use webcams than male students. In addition, group size, level of formalization (lecture, breakout rooms, and self-organized learning groups), and webcam use by other stakeholders (lecturers and peers) seem to influence students' personal webcam use (Händel et al., 2022). Of course, for motivation, group awareness, and student-teacher interactions, a screen full of black tiles may be less satisfying than a screen full of smiling faces using webcams.

However, webcam use might not be beneficial per se. Studies on webcam fatigue indicate that videoconferencing can lead to exhaustion (Bailenson,

2021, Döring et al., 2022; Fauville et al., 2021). Hence, practitioners need to be aware that being visually present might be both beneficial and detrimental. A suitable compromise might be webcam use in highly interactive situations, such as in lively discussions (Jayasundara et al., 2022). Future meta-analytic studies can relate webcam use to synchronous online learning processes and outcomes to examine the extent to which learner visibility influences academic emotions, attention, group awareness, satisfaction, and knowledge gains.

A second candidate for future meta-analytic syntheses is the use of breakout rooms. Breakout rooms are spaces within webinar environments, such as Zoom, in which a small group of learners can interact separately from the whole group on the same or different tasks. Thus, they seem to afford possibilities for small-group interaction and learning. Li et al. (2021) and Ismailov and Laurier (2022) examined team-learning processes in breakout rooms. Although their descriptive analyses are highly informative, more rigorous and controlled studies are needed to examine the influence of synchronous online learning with breakout room sessions on cognitive and affective processes and outcomes relative to synchronous online learning without breakout room sessions. The use of webcams and breakout rooms can help facilitate social experiences during synchronous online learning, which seems associated with increased feelings of connectedness, increased positive affect, decreased feelings of loneliness, and decreased social threat (Kaveladze et al., 2022).

A third candidate to be further explored in the future is the integration of synchronous online learning into flipped classroom models. Traditionally, flipped classrooms are a combination of asynchronous online learning (typically with videos) for knowledge acquisition and interactive discussion and synchronous face-to-face learning in the classroom (Wagner et al., 2021). Because face-to-face classrooms were shut down during the pandemic, many educators used synchronous online environments for discussions with their learners in flipped classroom courses. However, it is still an empirical question to examine how effectively online learning can replace face-to-face classrooms as part of a flipped classroom approach.

Fourth, the use of synchronous webinars in the context of synchronous hybrid teaching might pose an interesting research object for future meta-analyses. In synchronous hybrid teaching settings, traditional face-to-face classes are also accessible via synchronous webinars, and students can decide how they want to participate. Hence, synchronous hybrid teaching might take "the best of both worlds" (Lindsay, 2004) and combine the advantages of synchronous online and face-to-face teaching. However, Raes et al. (2020) stated that most studies concerning this learning environment are still exploratory and lack quantitative foundations. Therefore, more research about student outcomes and pedagogical scenarios must be conducted before a meta-analysis is worthwhile.

Finally, in addition to the design characteristics discussed, research should also focus on the role of educators in synchronous online learning. Notably, Grammens et al. (2022) emphasized that synchronous online teaching requires specific competencies by teachers. In addition, according to the community of inquiry framework, teaching presence—comprising design, choice of content, and facilitation of a course through the educator—is ultimately aimed at fostering interrelated social and cognitive presences within the course (Garrison et al., 2010). The interrelationship between educator achievement goals and student evaluations of teaching quality during emergency remote teaching also illustrates the need for the consideration of student-teacher interactions. For example, professional teacher training with a focus on collaborative learning is related to higher student learning outcomes (Compen et al., 2021).

In summary, we offered evidence-based recommendations for the design of synchronous online learning in this section. Based on four meta-analyses, a number of design features were identified. However, we note that the available empirical evidence is still rather limited. As the COVID-19 pandemic has boosted the use and implementation of synchronous online learning at all levels of education, future research on the effectiveness of synchronous online learning tends to look bright and will rapidly increase in the years to come.

Evidence-based practice recommendations

- Across meta-analyses, synchronous online and offline seminars tend to produce comparable effect sizes for post-test knowledge when the design elements are identical.
- Synchronous online learning seems particularly effective for teaching procedural knowledge.
- Students tend to have higher cognitive outcomes when synchronous online learning includes interactive instructional elements compared to purely teacher-centered scenarios. These interactive elements can include videos, quizzes, audience response tools, breakout rooms, or group discussions.
- Evidence suggests that synchronous online learning is more effective when learners participate in multiple repeated meetings compared to single events and when learners have access to additional learning materials stored in online archives or platforms.
- Synchronous online learning can facilitate direct communication and experiences of social presence and is thus recommended in interactive sessions. In less interactive portions of synchronous online learning, it is acceptable not to use a webcam to minimize learners' videoconferencing fatigue.

References

Al-Samarraie, H. (2019). A scoping review of videoconferencing systems in higher education: Learning paradigms, opportunities, and challenges. *International Review of Research in Open and Distributed Learning*, 20(3). https://doi.org/10.19173/irrodl.v20i4.4037

Bailenson, J. N. (2021). Nonverbal overload: A theoretical argument for the causes of Zoom fatigue. *Technology, Mind, and Behavior*, 2(1). https://doi.org/10.1037/tmb0000030

Bedenlier, S., Wunder, I., Gläser-Zikuda, M., Kammerl, R., Kopp, B., Ziegler, A., & Händel, M. (2021). "Generation invisible?". Higher education students' (non)use of webcams in synchronous online learning. *International Journal of Educational Research Open*, 2, 100068. https://doi.org/10.1016/j.ijedro.2021.100068

Bond, M., Bedenlier, S., Marín, V. I., & Händel, M. (2021). Emergency remote teaching in higher education: Mapping the first global online semester. *International Journal of Educational Technology in Higher Education*, 18, 50. https://doi.org/10.1186/s41239-021-00282-x

Bonk, C. J. (2020). Pandemic ponderings, 30 years to today: Synchronous signals, saviors, or survivors? *Distance Education*, 41(4), 589–599. https://doi.org/10.1080/01587919.2020.1821610

Bransford, J., Brown, A. L., & Cocking, R. R. (1999). *How people learn: Brain, mind, experience, and school*. National Academy Press.

Castelli, F. R., & Sarvary, M. A. (2021). Why students do not turn their video cameras during online classes and an equitable and inclusive plan to encourage them to do so. *Ecology and Evolution*, 11(8), 3565–3576. https://doi.org/10.1002/ece3.7123

Compen, B., De Witte, K., & Schelfhout, W. (2021), The impact of teacher engagement in an interactive webinar series on the effectiveness of financial literacy education. *British Journal of Educational Technology*, 52(1), 411–425. https://doi.org/10.1111/bjet.13013

Correia, A.-P., Liu, C., & Xu, F. (2020). Evaluating videoconferencing systems for the quality of the educational experience. *Distance Education*, 41(4),1–24. https://doi.org/10.1080/01587919.2020.1821607

Cronin, S. (2022). Pandemic pedagogies, practices and future possibilities: Emerging professional adjustments to the working practices of university teacher educators. *Educational Review*, 74(3), 720–740. https://doi.org/10.1080/00131911.2021.1978397

Cunningham, M., Elmer, R., Rüegg, T., Kagelmann, C., Rickli, A., & Binhammer, P. (2021) Integrating webinars to enhance curriculum implementation: AMEE guide no. 136. *Medical Teacher*, 43(4), 372–379, https://doi.org/10.1080/0142159X.2020.1838462

Döring, N., Moor, K. D., Fiedler, M., Schoenenberg, K., & Raake, A. (2022). Videoconference fatigue: A conceptual analysis. *International Journal of Environmental Research and Public Health*, 19(4), 2061. https://doi.org/10.3390/ijerph19042061

Ebner, C., & Gegenfurtner, A. (2019). Learning and satisfaction in webinar, online, and face-to-face instruction: A meta-analysis. *Frontiers in Education*, 4, 92. https://doi.org/10.3389/feduc.2019.00092

Erickson, M., & Wattiaux, M. A. (2021). Practices and perceptions at the COVID-19 transition in undergraduate animal science courses. *Natural Sciences Education, 50*(1), e20039. https://doi.org/10.1002/nse2.20039

Fauville, G., Luo, M., Queiroz, A. C. M., Bailenson, J. N., & Hancock, J. (2021). Zoom exhaustion & fatigue scale. *Computers in Human Behavior Reports, 4,* 100119. https://doi.org/10.1016/j.chbr.2021.100119

Garrison, D. R., Cleveland-Innes, M., & Fung, T. S. (2010). Exploring causal relationships among teaching, cognitive and social presence: Student perceptions of the community of inquiry framework. *The Internet and Higher Education, 13*(1), 31–36. https://doi.org/10.1016/j.iheduc.2009.10.002

Gegenfurtner, A., & Ebner, C. (2019). Webinars in higher education and professional training: A meta-analysis and systematic review of randomized controlled trials. *Educational Research Review, 28,* 100293. https://doi.org/10.1016/j.edurev.2019.100293

Gegenfurtner, A., Schwab, N., & Ebner, C. (2018). "There's no need to drive from A to B": Exploring the lived experience of students and lecturers with digital learning in higher education. *Bavarian Journal of Applied Sciences, 4,* 310–322. https://doi.org/10.25929/bjas.v4i1.50

Gegenfurtner, A., Zitt, A., & Ebner, C. (2020). Evaluating webinar-based training: A mixed methods study on trainee reactions toward digital web conferencing. *International Journal of Training and Development, 24*(1), 5–21. https://doi.org/10.1111/ijtd.12167

Gerheş, V., Simon, S., & Para, I. (2021). Analysing students' reasons for keeping their webcams on or off during online classes. *Sustainability, 13,* 3203. https://doi.org/10.3390/su13063203

Grammens, M., Voet, M., Vanderlinde, R., Declercq, L., & De Wever, B. (2022). A systematic review of teacher roles and competences for teaching synchronously online through videoconferencing technology. *Educational Research Review,* 100461. https://doi.org/10.1016/j.edurev.2022.100461

Gupta, S. K., & Sengupta, N. (2021). Webinar as the future educational tool in higher education of India: A survey-based study. *Technology, Knowledge and Learning, 26*(4), 1111–1130. https://doi.org/10.1007/s10758-021-09493-7

Hacker, J., vom Brocke, J., Handali, J., Otto, M., & Schneider, J. (2020). Virtually in this together – How web-conferencing systems enabled a new virtual togetherness during the COVID-19 crisis. *European Journal of Information Systems, 29*(5), 563–584. https://doi.org/10.1080/0960085X.2020.1814680

Händel, M., Bedenlier, S., Kopp, B., Gläser-Zikuda, M., Kammerl, R., & Ziegler, A. (2022). The webcam and student engagement in synchronous online learning: visually or verbally? *Education and Information Technologies, 27*(7), 10405–10428. https://doi.org/10.1007/s10639-022-11050-3

He, L., Yang, N., Xu, L., Ping, F., Li, W., Sun, Q., Li, Y., Zhu, H., & Zhang, H. (2021). Synchronous distance education vs traditional education for health science students: A systematic review and meta-analysis. *Medical Education, 55*(3), 293–308. https://doi.org/10.1111/medu.14364

Helm, C., Huber, S., & Loisinger, T. (2021). What do we know about school-based teaching-learning processes in distance education during the Corona pandemic? – Evidence from Germany, Austria and Switzerland. *Zeitschrift für Erziehungswissenschaft, 24*(2), 237–311. https://doi.org/10.1007/s11618-021-01000-z

Hodges, C., Moore, S., Lockee, B., Trust, T., & Bond, A. (2020, March 27). The difference between emergency remote teaching and online learning. *EDUCAUSE review.* https://er.educause.edu/articles/2020/3/the-difference-between-emer.ency-remote-teaching-and-online-learning

Ismailov, M., & Laurier, J. (2022). We are in the "breakout room." Now what? An e-portfolio study of virtual team processes involving undergraduate online learners. *E-Learning and Digital Media, 19*(2), 120–143. https://doi.org/10.1177/20427530211039710

Jayasundara, J. M. P. V. K., Gilbert, T., Kersten, S., & Meng, L. (2022). How UK HE STEM students were motivated to switch their cameras on: A study of the development of compassionate communications in task-focused online group meetings. *Education Sciences, 12*(5), 317. https://doi.org/10.3390/educsci12050317

Kaveladze, B. T., Morris, R. R., Dimitrova-Gammeltoft, R. V., Goldenberg, A., Gross, J. J., Antin, J., Sandgren, J., & Thomas-Hunt, M. C. (2022). Social interactivity in live video experiences reduces loneliness. *Frontiers in Digital Health, 4,* 859849. https://doi.org/10.3389/fdgth.2022.859849

Koehler, M. J., & Mishra, P. (2009). What is technological pedagogical content knowledge? *Contemporary Issues in Technology and Teacher Education, 9*(1), 60–70.

Kohnke, L., & Moorhouse, B. L. (2022). Facilitating synchronous online language learning through Zoom. *RELC Journal, 53,* 296–301. https://doi.org/10.1177/0033688220937235

Larson, J. S., & Farnsworth, K. (2020). Crisis teaching online: Reaching K-12 students through remote engineering lab-based activities during the COVID-19 pandemic. *Advances in Engineering Education, 8*(4), 1–9.

Li, L., Xu, L., He, Y., He, W., Pribesh, S., Watson, S. M., & Major, D. A. (2021). Facilitating online learning via Zoom breakout room technology: A case of pair programming involving students with learning disabilities. *Communications of the Association for Information Systems, 48*(12), 88–100. https://doi.org/10.17705/1CAIS.04812

Lindsay, E. B. (2004). The best of both worlds: Teaching a hybrid course. *Academic Exchange Quarterly, 8*(4), 16–19.

Martin, F., Ahlgrim-Delzell, L., & Budhrani, K. (2017). Systematic review of two decades (1995 to 2014) of research on synchronous online learning. *American Journal of Distance Education, 31*(1), 3–19. https://doi.org/10.1080/08923647.2017.1264807

Martin, F., & Parker, M. (2014). Use of synchronous virtual classrooms: Why, who and how? *MERLOT Journal of Online Learning and Teaching, 10*(2), 192–210.

Martin, F., Sun, T., Turk, M., & Ritzhaupt, A. D. (2021). A meta-analysis on the effects of synchronous online learning on cognitive and affective educational outcomes. *International Review of Research in Open and Distributed Learning, 22*(3), 205–242. https://doi.org/10.19173/irrodl.v22i3.5263

Phipps, R., & Merisotis, J. (1999). *What's the difference? A review of contemporary research on the effectiveness of distance learning in higher education.* The Institute for Higher Education Policy.

Priatmoko, S., Hossain, B., Rahmawati, W., Winarno, S. B., & Dávid, L. D. (2022). Webinar among Indonesian academics during Covid-19, embracing the audiences. *PLoS One, 17*(3), e0265257. https://doi.org/10.1371/journal.pone.0265257

Raes, A. (2022). Exploring student and teacher experiences in hybrid learning environments: Does presence matter? *Postdigital Science and Education, 4*(1), 138–159. https://doi.org/10.1007/s42438-021-00274-0

Raes, A., Detienne, L., Windey, I., & Depaepe, F. (2020). A systematic literature review on synchronous hybrid learning: Gaps identified. *Learning Environments Research, 23*(3), 269–290. https://doi.org/10.1007/s10984-019-09303-z

Schraw, G. (2006). Knowledge: Structures and processes. In P. A. Alexander & P. H. Winne (Eds.), *Handbook of educational psychology* (2nd ed., pp. 245–264). Erlbaum.

Toquero, C. M., & Talidong, K. J. (2020). Webinar technology: Developing teacher training programs for emergency remote teaching amid COVID-19. *Interdisciplinary Journal of Virtual Learning in Medical Sciences, 11*(3), 200–203. https://doi.org/10.30476/ijvlms.2020.86889.1044

Wagner, M., Gegenfurtner, A., & Urhahne, D. (2021). Effectiveness of the flipped classroom on student achievement in K-12 education: A meta-analysis. *Zeitschrift für Pädagogische Psychologie, 35*(1), 11–31. https://doi.org/10.1024/1010-0652/a000274

Wang, S.-K., & Hsu, H.-Y. (2008). Use of the webinar tool (Elluminate) to support training: The effects of webinar-learning implementation from student-trainers' perspective. *Journal of Interactive Online Learning, 7*(3), 175–194.

17

IMPACTS OF WEB-BASED INQUIRY LEARNING ENVIRONMENTS ALIGNED WITH KNOWLEDGE INTEGRATION PEDAGOGY

Libby Gerard and Marcia C. Linn

Introduction: Authoring and Customizing Environments (ACEs)

Inquiry instruction designed using an Authoring and Customizing Environment (ACE) transforms classroom science learning by taking advantage of advances in learning science research and educational technologies (Linn et al., in press). To explore the impact of ACESs, this chapter synthesizes meta-analyses of inquiry instruction featuring ACEs and ACE features. ACEs empower partnerships among classroom teachers, discipline experts, software designers, and researchers to create and customize inquiry instruction to meet the needs of their community. ACEs make it possible to create inquiry activities by combining tested Open Educational Resources (OERs) and guidance aligned to a pedagogical framework. ACE designs incorporate features such as simulations, models, virtual labs, collaborative tools, extended reality, and videos. ACE designers take advantage of advances in Artificial Intelligence such as natural language processing to score students' written explanations and provide personalized guidance. ACEs also include the functions of a learning management system (LMS) to monitor student progress, record students' work, and allow for assigning guidance or grades. Designers combine OERs and guidance into inquiry units that members of the partnership can iteratively refine to meet the needs of students, teachers, or curriculum guidelines. We examine how research using ACEs is generating insights into the evolving interactions between interdisciplinary communities, the conceptualization of technology use in the classroom, and pedagogical frameworks (Pea & Linn, 2020).

DOI: 10.4324/9781003386131-24

ACEs Knowledge Integration (KI) Pedagogy

The Knowledge Integration (KI) pedagogy and other constructivist views have informed designs of ACEs (e.g. Linn & Eylon, 2011) including Concord Consortium (Pallant et al., 2020), Open SciEd (Edelson et al., 2021); Inq-IT (de Jong, 2019), nQuire-it (Aristeidou & Herodotou, 2020), and the Web-based Inquiry Science Environment (WISE: Linn & Eylon, 2011; Donnelly-Hermosillo et al., 2020). The KI pedagogy draws on four processes to promote integrated science understanding through ACE designs: (a) Eliciting current ideas and ways of thinking, including encouraging learners to generate the reasoning behind their ideas; (b) Discovering new ideas, for example, by engaging learners with scientific models or by interacting with peers; (c) Distinguishing among current ideas and new discoveries, for example, by seeking evidence from valid sources; and (d) Reflecting on the repertoire of ideas, for example, by encouraging learners to connect and sort ideas into a coherent view. To illustrate, Figure 17.1 shows how an ACE on Urban Heat Islands (UHI) engages students in the KI processes. At the same time, the authoring tools in the WISE ACE support teachers to monitor each student's progress and guide the class collectively toward integration of the target ideas.

ACE KI Assessments

To validly assess outcomes, KI assessments focus teacher and researcher attention on the links students are forming among target ideas. KI assessments differ from typical assessments because they reward students for using evidence to connect their ideas from everyday experience with ideas from instruction to form a response. For example, an assessment embedded in the UHI unit (see Figure 17.2) asks students to connect their ideas from experiences entering a car that has been parked in the sun, with their ideas from instruction about the greenhouse effect. The rubric assesses the degree to which students make links among ideas about solar energy transfer, energy transformation, and temperature. In addition to written explanation items, KI assessments include concept diagrams and opportunities to critique and revise fictional peer explanations (Liu et al., 2015). ACEs can use natural language processing to automatically score each student's written explanation according to a KI rubric. This makes the use of constructed response assessment items more feasible for teachers who need to grade 150+ students' explanations (Liu et al., 2016; Pallant et al., 2020).

Assessments are typically located at the start of an ACE unit to elicit students' ideas about the topic, at the end of the unit to gather students' connections among the ideas they have learned, and embedded within the unit to capture students' developing understanding. Further, automated scoring

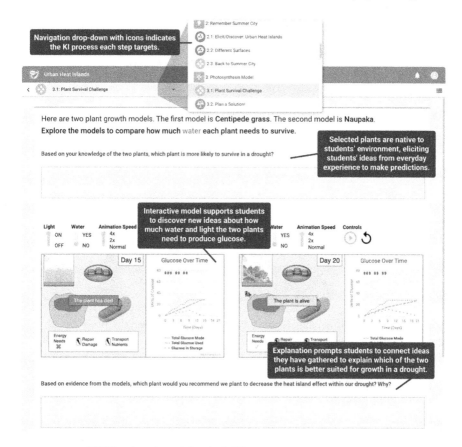

FIGURE 17.1 WISE urban heat islands ACE.

Source: Image from the Web-Based Inquiry Science Environment (WISE; https://wise.berkeley.edu)

within an ACE allows designers to create immediate student guidance, prompt students to revise their ideas, and evaluate the ability of the student to take advantage of the revision prompt (Gerard & Linn, 2022). Effective prompts enable students to rethink their reasoning, essentially capturing their Zone of Proximal Development (Vygotsky, 1978).

Student work is logged by the ACE and displayed for teachers in the ACE Teacher Tools. Teachers, examining logs of student progress, can evaluate how students respond to prompts and refine their explanations. Teachers can use the Teacher Tools to monitor student pacing, assess student reasoning, and assign guidance or grades. The teacher's use of the logged student-embedded assessment data within the ACE to give personalized guidance or inform the next day's lesson has shown to be instrumental in improving students' science learning outcomes (Gerard et al., 2011; Ibourk & Kendrick, 2021). Student work is also available to researchers in downloadable, de-identified log files.

On a cold winter day, Sam is walking to their car that is parked in the sun. Their car has not been driven for one week. How will the temperature inside the car feel?" Choose (a) Colder than the outside air, (b) Warmer than the outside air, or (c) Exactly the same as the outside air. Explain your choice	
KI Level	**Student Examples**
1	**Off-task** or **Irrelevant**	"I don't know"
2	**Vague or incomplete** ideas or links	"the air is warmer inside because it had no contact with cold air outside" "The car is hotter because it's been parked in the sun." *[accurate conclusion, no mechanism]*
3	**Partial link** Isolated normative idea OR Normative and non-normative ideas linked	"Since cars absorbed heat doesn't go anywhere, it warms up the car inside rather than the outside" *[heat is trapped inside of car]* "Energy from the sun warms up the car" *[explains energy source]*
4	**Full link** One complete and valid connection between 2 ideas	"the temperature will be hotter than the outside because the heat inside the car not escape and is trapped inside, the heat is added and added until is hotter than the outside" *[heat is trapped + reabsorbed]*
5	**Complex links** Two or more scientifically complete and valid connections	"Energy comes from the sun and is absorbed in the car to turn to heat. The heat is stuck in the car because the windows trap it making it hotter" *[energy from sun + solar radiation to heat + heat is trapped]*

FIGURE 17.2 Car on a cold day knowledge integration rubric.

Further, KI assessments have been extensively validated with middle school students. Results show that KI assessments fairly capture the progress of sub-groups including native and non-native English speakers (Boda et al., 2021; Liu et al., 2008).

Customizing ACEs Based on Evidence of Student Work

ACEs support partnerships of teachers and researchers to analyze student data, diagnose areas for customization, and improve the unit to better suit their students' needs. The pre-and post-assessments capture students' overall progress. The embedded assessments analyze the impact of specific activity designs. For example, partners have customized ACE units to increase/decrease scaffolding, strengthen opportunities for students' self-directed learning, or add investigations of science dilemmas located in the students' communities (Bichler et al., 2021; Gerard et al., 2022b; Matuk et al., 2015).

Customizing inquiry instruction in an ACE involves aligning the instruction to the needs of the students, while retaining the inquiry processes that ensure its success. The Curriculum Visualizer (Figure 17.3) supports the alignment of ACE customizations with the KI framework (Bradford et al., 2021). The Visualizer provides an interactive representation of how an ACE unit facilitates KI throughout inquiry. Each step in the unit is illustrated on a separate slide and color-coded for the KI process that the step targets, revealing the sequence and pedagogical intention of each step. Using the Visualizer, partners can easily add new activities from color-coded template slides, prompting them to consider the KI process engaged by the activity they intend to add. For example, (Figure 17.3) a 6th grade science teacher, a

FIGURE 17.3 Curriculum visualizer for urban heat islands.

Source: Google Slides is a trademark of Google LLC.

learning scientist, and a technology developer used the Visualizer to design modifications to the UHI unit (Bradford et al., 2022).

Impact of ACEs: Meta-Analyses and Cumulative Studies

To establish the value of ACEs, we report on relevant syntheses of studies featuring the impact of active learning, inquiry instruction, and technology-enhanced instruction on pre-college science learners. These syntheses either include ACEs or focus exclusively on ACEs. We also report on several studies that examine the cumulative benefits from sequences of ACE units.

These meta-analyses document the impact of ACEs on each student, including language learners. Reviews have explored comparison studies and longitudinal research. Cumulative impacts often highlight the value of technology, which reflects the role of the features of ACEs such as visualizations and collaborative environments. Further, researchers have studied the added advantage of online and teacher-personalized guidance during inquiry learning in the classroom.

Reviews of Inquiry Instruction that Include ACEs

Reviews and meta-analytic studies suggest that science instruction designed following inquiry pedagogy has promise (e.g. Alfieri et al., 2011; Freeman et al., 2014; Furtak et al., 2012; Lazonder and Harmsen, 2016; McElhaney et al., 2022; Minner et al., 2010). Alfieri et al. (2011) compared direct, inquiry, and guided inquiry instruction across 164 studies and found a negligible impact for science inquiry (d = .11), along with greater benefit for guided inquiry than for unguided inquiry. Freeman et al. (2014) analyzed 225 studies and found that active learning was substantially more effective than typical lectures (d = .50). Furtak et al. (2012) analyzed 37 studies of science instruction and found that inquiry was more effective than typical instruction (d = .50) and that among those studies, the teacher-guided inquiry was substantially more effective than unguided inquiry (d = .40). Lazonder and Harmsen (2016) analyzed 72 studies and found that guidance increased the impact of inquiry instruction (d = .50). McElhaney et al. (2022) concluded that guidance is needed for inquiry to succeed in science classrooms. Minner et al. (2010) analyzed 138 studies that included some form of inquiry and found that over half had a positive impact on conceptual understanding and only 2% had a negative effect. Taken together, these studies suggest that to realize the full benefit of inquiry instruction, some form of guidance is needed. These findings underscore the advantages of ACEs since they include tested features to help teachers guide inquiry as well as opportunities to design personalized guidance for each student.

Reviews and meta-analyses of promising technologies for inquiry instruction suggest the value of models, simulations, graphing technologies, collaborative tools, or personalized guidance (Bell, 2013; de Jong and Van Joolingen, 1998; Dillenbourg et al., 2009; Donnelly et al., 2014; Donnelly-Hermosillo et al., 2020; Gerard et al., 2015; Jeong et al., 2019; Lazonder & Harmsen, 2016; Matuk & Linn, 2018; Smetana & Bell, 2012). Each of these features has been supported in reviews and meta-analytic investigations. The impact of these features helps explain why inquiry learning is often found to be more effective than typical instruction.

Smetana and Bell (2012) found that 80% of studies (49 out of 61) showed an advantage for instruction featuring technology-enhanced simulations compared to typical instruction. They stressed that effective instruction included well-designed scaffolds for students, such as opportunities to reflect. Results of Smetana and Bell (2012) align with earlier meta-analyses showing that scientific visualizations impact science learning, especially when supported by teacher or technology scaffolds (de Jong and Van Joolingen, 1998).

Analyzing the impact of technology-enhanced graphing, Donnelly-Hermosillo et al. (2020) analyzed 42 studies involving over 7,000 students published over the past 30 years. They found that design studies refining guidance for graphing resulted in moderate improvement (d = .59) and that comparison studies comparing technology versus typical instruction also showed a moderate effect (d = .43).

Analyzing the impact of collaborative tools, several studies discuss benefits (Bell, 2013; Dillenbourg et al., 2009; Jeong et al., 2019; Matuk & Linn,

2018). Jeong et al. (2019) conducted a meta-analysis where they identified 316 outcomes from 143 studies published between 2005 and 2014. They reported an overall moderate effect for STEM collaboration tools (d = .51). In addition, they found that the effect was greatest for process outcomes, followed by knowledge and affective outcomes. Process outcomes included support for argumentation and turn-taking.

Meta-analyses show the advantage of typical versus technology-enhanced guidance. For example, Gerard et al. (2015) did a meta-analysis of 24 independent comparisons and found that automated adaptive guidance was significantly more effective than guidance provided in typical instruction, particularly for students with low prior knowledge (d = .34).

Combining the impacts of inquiry pedagogy and technologies featured in ACEs helps explain the uneven effects of studies of inquiry and studies of features of ACEs. The meta-analyses of inquiry pedagogy generally combine materials that use technology as well as those that do not. So some findings for inquiry are likely due to the value of simulations, graphing technologies, or automated guidance. Similarly, some studies of the impact of simulations, graphing, and guidance technologies likely reflect the value of inquiry pedagogy. Optimal instructional design benefits from a combination of features such as simulations as well as inquiry pedagogy. And, all the meta-analyses and reviews stress the importance of well-designed scaffolds and personalized guidance. ACEs offer designers support for implementing inquiry pedagogy such as Knowledge integration. ACEs also enable designers to combine inquiry technologies that enhance inquiry outcomes. And, ACEs support teachers to be effective guides by logging student work, displaying student progress, and synthesizing progress. In addition, ACEs support design partnerships to combine inquiry pedagogy and powerful technologies to scaffold learners.

Studies of Cumulative Learning from ACEs

One way to test the impact of ACEs is to analyze their cumulative impacts. Several studies have analyzed the cumulative benefits of studying ACE units over multiple years (Boda et al., 2021; Linn et al., 2006; Liu et al., 2015). In one study, Boda et al. (2021) studied the progress of 300 students using ACEs featuring graphing for multiple topics across three years of instruction, from sixth to eighth grade. Progress was measured using KI assessments administered in the Fall and Spring of each year. Overall, students who completed three years, scored at least one KI level higher at the end of the study, compared to their initial performance. For most students, this means they started with isolated ideas and gained the ability to make some connections between observations and evidence to support their explanations of scientific phenomena reflected in graphs from models or simulations. Students who benefited the most, started with KI scores between 1.5

and 2.5. These students started with either no ideas or only vague ideas. For these students, the curriculum led to KI scores that have at least partially correct normative scientific explanations. Gains were most pronounced in the first year. Student performance declined in the Fall of the second year. Gains in the second year were sustained in the third year, suggesting that two years of instruction were important for establishing robust understanding. Future studies explore the value of experiencing multiple ACEs featuring graphs.

Cumulative growth in Boda et al. (2021) was consistent across demographics, including gender and native English language status. There were negligible effect sizes for gender (d = .028) and native English language status (d = 0.131), consistent with earlier studies of KI instruction (Liu et al., 2015).

Exemplar: Urban Heat Islands ACE Unit

The WISE Urban Heat Islands (UHI) ACE, developed by a partnership among middle school science teachers, learning scientists, and technology developers, engages students in learning standards-aligned science concepts as they determine what causes a UHI, how the population density in cities contributes, and how urban designers can reduce the heat island effect (Bradford et al., 2022). People living in UHI experience higher summer temperatures than those living in suburban communities. Low-income communities and communities of color are most impacted by UHI, where they often experience severe heat-related illnesses.

The UHI ACE takes advantage of cutting-edge educational technologies to promote KI. We discuss how the unit leverages these technologies to implement each of the KI processes.

UHI: Eliciting Student Ideas

To implement the eliciting ideas process, the UHI unit asks students to predict the causes of an urban heat island, a personally relevant question for the audience (Gunstone & White, 1981). Students often predict that lack of shade, dark-colored buildings, concrete or asphalt surfaces, heavy traffic, or climate change generally cause UHIs. Each of these ideas can serve as a jumping-off point into the energy mechanisms underlying a UHI. Building on students' initial ideas entices them to explore the science topic. Yet, student ideas are often neglected in typical science instruction. Further, students need encouragement to share their ideas, especially if they fear that their ideas are incorrect or idiosyncratic or if they are unsure about which of the ideas they hold are relevant to the problem. Thus, effective instruction not only encourages students to express their ideas but also ensures that each student's idea is respected.

Adaptive Dialog

To elicit and respect student ideas, we tested an AI-based dialog, inspired by expert teacher guidance (Gerard et al., 2015; Ruiz-Primo and Furtak, 2007). Students selected an avatar from choices that reflected the racial and gender diversity of the class (Figure 17.4). The avatar started the conversation by asking a question that connected to student experience: "How does the temperature inside a car that has been parked in the snow on a sunny day feel?". Student responses often drew on their experiences, including, "the air is warmer inside the car because it had no contact with the cold air outside", or "the dark seats of the car make it hot". Using natural language processing (Riordan et al., 2020), the avatar detected the ideas in the student's response, acknowledged them, and continued the conversation by asking a question intended to elicit the reasoning underlying the students' responses. After two exchanges between the student and the avatar, the student was prompted to revise their initial explanation, informed by the new ideas they generated during the dialog.

Our results suggest that the dialog encouraged students to reflect on prior experiences, consider new variables, and incorporate additional science knowledge. In one study, 66 9th-grade students engaged in the Car on a Cold Day dialog at the start of the unit. They added 70 new ideas as they revised their explanations, and 79% of these new ideas connected to normative science concepts (Gerard et al., 2022a). These results confirm that students start with multiple ideas about the topic. They also demonstrate how an AI dialog

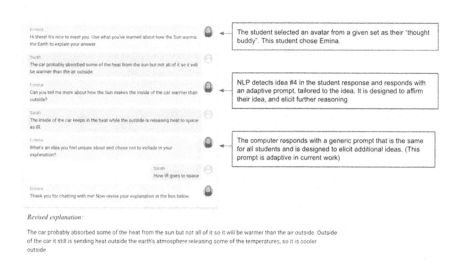

FIGURE 17.4   Adaptive dialog in the urban heat island unit.

Source: Image from the Web-Based Inquiry Science Environment (WISE; https://wise.berkeley.edu)

can support students to elaborate their predictions based on the rich reper-toire of ideas they hold from prior experience.

UHI: Discovering Evidence

To engage students in discovering evidence for their prediction, the UHI ACE enables students to use computational thinking to design a Snap! Model of the situation. Snap! is an open-source block-based programming language that can be embedded within an ACE (Goldenberg et al., 2020). Modeling activities allow students to see "under the hood" of a model. For example, students can test their prediction that the color of the city buildings contributes to the heat island effect.

Designing a Model with Snap!

Using a block-based programming language like Snap! students can mod-ify model rules to test their predictions, run the model, and see the output of their rules in a graph or dynamic visualization. Modifying and refining the model's rules based on the output can strengthen student under-standing of the scientific mechanisms governing the color of the buildings (Figure 17.5).

The UHI unit features three progressively more difficult programming challenges that support students to explore the heat island phenomenon and generate a solution for a fictitious neighborhood (see Figure 17.4). In a Snap! programming challenge, students can test the impact of adding reflective roofing to buildings. Students set the value for a Reflective Roof variable by selecting and dragging existing blocks into gaps in the pre-built program.

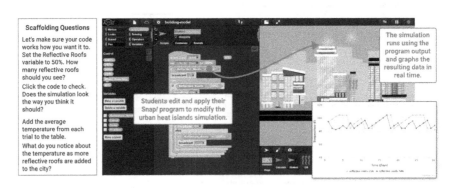

FIGURE 17.5   Snap! activity that asks students to test the impact of reflective roofs on the temperature for a city section.

Source: Image from WISE featuring Snap!

The model visualizes the student the code in the animations and graphs, to support reflection and iterative refinement of their program. In this lesson, students gained confidence and knowledge of programming while also strengthening science understanding (Bradford et al., 2022).

UHI: Distinguishing Among Ideas

To support students to distinguish among the results from using the computational model, the UHI ACE includes two activities. First, students collaborate to compare the results from their modeling activities. They compile their results from the model exploration in a composite graph or table. Then, using an Idea Basket, students contribute ideas to a class discussion and seek consensus. Second, to distinguish among their ideas about how models work, students engage in a rule-sorting activity (Wiese & Linn, 2021).

Rule Sorting

Rule sorting helps students distinguish between what the computational model does and the underlying science. The rule sorting item proposes potential rules the model might follow. Some rules align with the science in the model (e.g. *if heat energy is created the temperature increases*); others are contradicted by the model (*if solar radiation hits grass, it always turns into heat energy*) or are imprecise (e.g. *if the variable Grass Coverage is set to 75%, make more grass*). The item then asks students to indicate which rules they think the model is following (see Figure 17.6). By distinguishing among the rules that govern the model, rules that depict the science underlying the model, and rules that may be intuitive but not helpful, students clarify and extend their understanding of the role of models in scientific advancement. This activity strengthens the students' ability to engage in computational thinking.

UHI: Reflecting on Ideas to Form Connections

The process of reflection provides an opportunity to form connections among the ideas that emerge in the unit and build a coherent view. In UHI, the unit guides students to connect the ideas they have gathered about city surface features such as grass, reflective roofs, or asphalt, with ideas about solar radiation absorption, reflection, transformation, and temperature. To support students in making these links, students use a Data Synthesizer to integrate the results of their investigation and write explanations supported by personalized guidance to communicate their conclusions.

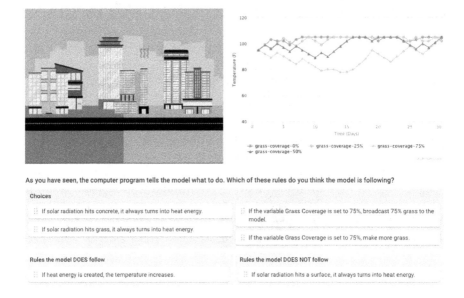

As you have seen, the computer program tells the model what to do. Which of these rules do you think the model is following?

Choices

⠿ If solar radiation hits concrete, it always turns into heat energy.	⠿ If the variable Grass Coverage is set to 75%, broadcast 75% grass to the model.
⠿ If solar radiation hits grass, it always turns into heat energy.	⠿ If the variable Grass Coverage is set to 75%, make more grass.

Rules the model DOES follow

⠿ If heat energy is created, the temperature increases.

Rules the model DOES NOT follow

⠿ If solar radiation hits a surface, it always turns into heat energy.

FIGURE 17.6 Rule selection item in urban heat islands unit.

Source: Image from the Web-Based Inquiry Science Environment (WISE; https://wise.berkeley.edu)

Data Synthesizer

In a culminating activity, UHI features a diagramming tool and Data Synthesizer. The activity prompts students to design a city grid to reduce the temperature in "Summer City", keeping in mind what they learned from Summer City residents (e.g. one likes roads so she can quickly drive to work; another wants more grass to play soccer), and what they have discovered about the relationship between each surface type and temperature change from programming the model. Once students have created their grid, they input their values for each block of city surface into the Data Synthesizer (see Figure 17.7). The graph displays the city temperature for their grid, in comparison to the initial layout in Summer City. The student is prompted to explain how much cooler Summer City would be if they followed the student's plan and why. This activity encourages students to connect the science ideas they have learned about radiation and reflection/absorption to generate a solution for a heat island.

Personalized Guidance and Explanation Revision

Finally, students are supported to form connections among their ideas by writing KI explanations and refining them in response to automated, adaptive guidance. Students respond to an explanation prompt at the beginning

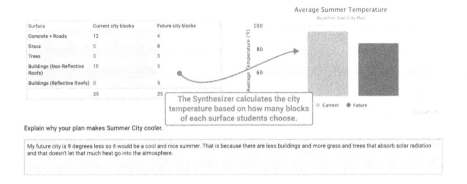

Average Summer Temperature
Based on Your City Plan

Surface	Current city blocks	Future city blocks
Concrete + Roads	12	4
Grass	0	8
Trees	3	3
Buildings (Non-Reflective Roofs)	10	5
Buildings (Reflective Roofs)	0	5
	25	25

The Synthesizer calculates the city temperature based on how many blocks of each surface students choose.

Explain why your plan makes Summer City cooler.

My future city is 9 degrees less so it would be a cool and nice summer. That is because there are less buildings and more grass and trees that absorb solar radiation and that doesn't let that much heat go into the atmosphere.

FIGURE 17.7   Data synthesizer.

Source: Image from the Web-Based Inquiry Science Environment (WISE; https://wise.berkeley.edu)

and end of the unit that asks them about how human activities are contributing to rising temperatures. Students write their explanations and submit them. Their explanation is automatically scored using craterML natural language processing, based on the 5-point KI rubric. Guidance is assigned based on the score level to help the student move one level up in the rubric. The guidance calls for a mechanism to explain an observation common at that score level. For example, a typical level 3 response on the KI rubric is one that expresses the isolated idea that "CO2 makes the air warmer". The adaptive guidance prompts the student to revisit a relevant model of global climate, "to find out how carbon dioxide in the atmosphere affects the global temperature" KI guidance has shown to be more effective than specific guidance to build coherent understanding (Vitale et al., 2016).

UHI Exemplar: Summary

As seen in the example of UHI, new ACE features to support each of the KI processes are rapidly emerging due to convergence of advances in AI, OER, and learning sciences research. Teachers can use an ACE to teach standards-aligned science concepts such as energy transfer and transformation in the exploration of pressing societal dilemmas such as climate change and urban heat islands. Features such as adaptive dialogs, block-based programming, and personalized guidance for data-based explanations are areas of active research in science education. Research partnerships of science teachers, learning scientists, environmental scientists, and software designers ensure that new ACE features are a result of synthesizing expertise in pedagogy, science, and technology. Partners use the Curriculum Visualizer to customize the unit for the needs of their classroom.

Impact of ACE Features on Student Inquiry

The UHI case illustrates how cutting-edge ACE features, when combined using KI pedagogy, support teachers to help students build integrated understanding during inquiry. These features and others have been refined in comparison studies over the past decade to improve the alignment with pedagogy. WISE in particular has been iteratively refined by a partnership for over 25 years to take advantage of technology advances for supporting teachers to guide students in KI (Linn et al., 2003; Linn et al., in press). Each feature has been refined based on multiple classroom comparison trials, in which students are randomly assigned to one of two conditions using the ACE branching functionality (see Figure 17.8). The partnership uses the study outcomes to strengthen the feature and unit overall.

This chapter illustrates classroom studies of ACE features in the WISE environment that were conducted in the last ten years and published in peer-reviewed journals. Each study produced empirical evidence for the link between a feature, KI pedagogy, and student learning outcomes. It is the combination of such tested features within an ACE unit that makes inquiry instruction effective.

Design of Features for Eliciting

ACEs leverage technology to elicit each student's ideas about the target topic (Figure 17.8). Students can test these ideas, refine them, or strengthen them as they discover new ideas and distinguish among their growing repertoire of ideas. In one study, randomly assigned student pairs (N = 78) used the WISE Thermodynamics ACE for either: student choice of their investigation pathway from a set of options or random assignment to one of the investigation pathways (Chen et al., 2020). Choice students more often used the virtual model in the pathway to test their predictions than pairs who were assigned to a pathway. Further, Choice students also ran more informative experiments to test their predictions. In short, when students express their initial ideas, they have the chance to evaluate which of their ideas are more promising than others. If students fail to express an idea during instruction, they may retain it and return to it after the science lesson is over rather than testing and refining it (diSessa, 2006; Linn et al., 2006).

Design of Features for Discovering

Interactive models have been well documented as an effective ACE feature for fostering student science learning (de Jong and Van Joolingen, 1998; Linn et al., 2003). Visualizations illustrate ideas that are too small (molecular level)

ACE feature	Feature Design	Comparison Study	Findings
Eliciting Ideas			
Virtual Model to Predict Engineering Design Features	A virtual model elicits student ideas for how they will design a physical solar oven.	Students engaged in either planning or reflecting by using a virtual model of a solar oven before building the physical solar oven or after, respectively.	Students in the planning condition used the model in an exploratory manner, while students in the reflecting condition used the model to confirm the results of their physical solar ovens. Using the model during the planning phase helped students to better integrate their ideas about energy (McBride et al., 2016).
Student Choice of Investigation Pathway	Authors use branching to enable students to select different pathways in the same unit	In a Thermodynamics unit, students either choose to investigate how to keep a hot drink hot, or how to keep a cold drink cold, based on their interest - or were assigned to a pathway.	Students who were able to choose their investigation focus demonstrated a higher rate of following through and carrying out the experimental tests that they planned compared to the no-choice students (King Chen et al., 2019).
Discovering Ideas			
Automated Guidance	AI algorithms are used to instantaneously diagnose student written explanations in the unit, and assign guidance tailored to the student response.	Designed two forms of guidance to support students learning of climate change. *Specific:* guidance communicated ideas that were missing or inaccurate in student responses. *Knowledge integration:* guidance provided hints to motivate learners to analyze features of their response and seek more information.	While *specific* guidance typically produced larger accuracy gains on responses within the curriculum unit, *knowledge integration* guidance produced durable understanding measured by a novel essay at posttest (Vitale, McBride & Linn, 2016).
Scaffolds for learning with Dynamic Visualizations	Students are prompted to write explanations that call for them to gather evidence from a dynamic visualization	When students interacted with a dynamic visualization of energy transformation in Photosynthesis, typical guidance provided text explanations while inquiry-oriented guidance asked students to generate their own explanations about three key energy transformation concepts.	Both reading and generating explanations helped students interpret the visualization, but generating explanations was more beneficial. Students who generated explanations were better able to extract salient information and distinguish among multiple ideas (Ryoo & Linn, 2013).
Dynamic versus Static visualizations (See Figure ACE)	Dynamic visualizations of energy and matter transformations	Students experienced either dynamic or static visualizations embedded when learning in the Photosynthesis unit. The viz's were equivalent except for being static/dynamic.	English Learners and Non-English Learners in the dynamic condition engaged in more talk turns to interpret photosynthesis and considered more ideas when forming explanations of photosynthesis (Ryoo & Bedell, 2017).
Distinguishing ideas			
Idea Manager for Peer Collaboration	Students write ideas; tag and sort them along various attributes; and exchange them with classmates. At culminating points students graphically organize their ideas to prepare explanations.	In a Mitosis unit, students were prompted to select one of their ideas to add to the Public Idea Basket, and then to select a peer's idea to compare their idea to. Students were prompted to compare to either a peer's idea that was similar to theirs, or different from their own.	Students who selected a peer's idea that was different from their own, rather than similar, made significantly greater improvement when revising their explanations (Matuk & Linn, 2018).
Rule Sorting (See Figure Rule Selection)	Computer models operationalize real-world behaviors of variables through programmed instructions. Rule items propose potential model rules and ask students which ones the model is following.	In an Assessment, students explored three computer models and responded to both Rule Sorting tasks and typical science questions.	Compared to the "typical" questions about the science content alone, rule sorting items elicited deeper science thinking, with 2–10 times more responses including reasoning about scientific mechanisms (Weise & Linn, 2020).
Interactive Graphs	Graph is linked to a simulation depicting the relationship between mass, volume, and density. Students use the graph to select test cases.	In a Density unit 8th-grade students were assigned to *Analyze*: Students plot a given set of data points to help clarify the relationship between mass, volume, and buoyancy, and then interact with a simulation to improve their plotting accuracy. Or - *Generate*: Students choose their own data points, and then interact with a simulation to test and revise their choices.	*Analyze* students were more likely to construct accurate graphs but *Generate* students were more likely to develop a coherent understanding of density and buoyancy. *Generate* students considered the mass-volume ratio by intentionally testing points and identifying patterns whereas *analyze* students displayed less deliberate exploration of the graph (Vitale, Applebaum & Linn, 2019).
Connecting ideas			
Annotator + Adaptive Guidance	Revising explanations is a typical way that scientists distinguish among ideas. Students often find it difficult to revise. The Annotator helps them figure out how to link new ideas with their existing ideas by critiquing a fictional peer's explanation using pre-authored labels.	In a unit on Photosynthesis, and a unit on Plate Tectonics, students received computer-based guidance on their explanations mid-way through the unit. Half of the students received the Annotator plus one round of adaptive guidance and the other half received two rounds of adaptive guidance.	Students using the Annotator who initially displayed unintegrated ideas were more likely to make integrated revisions to their explanations, than students receiving automated, adaptive guidance. These students also made greater knowledge integration revisions on the posttest one week later (Gerard & Linn, 2022).
Concept Diagram	Students are given a set of icons and types of links. They select which icons to use, and which link to use to illustrate the scientific relationships in a system.	In a unit on evolution, high school student dyads in one condition compared their concept maps against an expert map while dyads in the other condition conducted a peer-review	Both groups improved their maps significantly; they used different criteria in critique. Students in expert-map condition focused on concept-focused criteria like concept classification while students in the peer-review condition used more link-focused criteria like link labels and missing connections (Schwendimann & Linn, 2016).

FIGURE 17.8   ACE feature refinement for engaging students in KI processes.

or too slow (climate change, evolution, plate tectonics) to observe directly. Visualizations allow for slowing down to observe variable interactions that you cannot see physically (solar ovens design choices). As shown in Figure 17.8, studies demonstrate how dynamic visualizations stimulate verbal sense-making, among native and non-native English speakers (Ryoo & Bedell, 2017). Students benefit from guidance to help them discern evidence from the model. For example, when students write explanations based on interactions with a model, they benefit more than when they observe the model and read an explanation. Similarly, when they write explanations and receive hints to improve the explanation, they benefit more than when they receive corrective feedback (Vitale et al., 2016).

Design of Features for Distinguishing

Tools that help students to compare ideas promote distinguishing. This might involve comparing the explanatory power of the ideas in your repertoire by making each idea visible in a graph (Vitale et al., 2019), comparing the rules that govern a dynamic scientific model (Wiese and Linn, 2021) or comparing your explanation to a peer's (Matuk and Linn, 2018). The WISE Idea Manager for instance guides students to contribute an evidence-based idea that they want to share with the class to the public Idea Basket (Figure 17.8). Then, they are prompted to select a classmates' idea from the Basket and compare them. Matuk and Linn (2018) compared prompting students to select a peer's idea from the public Idea Basket that was different from their own idea, versus prompting students to select a peer's idea that was similar to their own. Students who were prompted to diversify their ideas showed significantly greater pre- to post-test gains. Comparing different ideas encouraged students to distinguish the evidence supporting each idea to understand why they differed.

Design of Features for Connecting

ACEs support students to make connections by writing explanations or creating concept diagrams that link evidence to a local science dilemma, and revising their explanation or diagram using AI-fueled guidance. Studies also demonstrate the value of an Annotator where students critique a peer's explanation before refining the connections among their own ideas (Figure 17.8). When the peer's explanation surfaces key science ideas the teacher wants the students to consider as they revise their own explanations, students benefit (Schwendimann & Linn, 2016). The Annotator is an ACE feature that guides this process (Gerard & Linn, 2022) and improves students' ability to use guidance to revise, a practice integral to science learning.

Evidence-Based Practice Recommendations

1. Align the design and assessments for an ACE unit using a research-based pedagogical framework such as KI. (Minner et al., 2010).
2. Create partnerships with science teachers, education researchers, and software designers to design inquiry curricula using an ACE and to customize the instruction using evidence from their classroom implementations (e.g. Gerard et al., 2015).
3. Combine tested ACE features including interactive graphs, dynamic visualizations, collaboration tools, opportunities to construct explanations, and automated, adaptive guidance to implement the pedagogical framework for each ACE inquiry unit. (Donnelly-Hermosillo et al., 2020).
4. Design a sequence of ACE inquiry units to reinforce KI across grade levels and achieve robust understanding (Liu, 2015).

Discussion and Next Steps

ACEs connect powerful educational technologies with current research on science education pedagogy such as KI. Meta-analyses of the impact of inquiry environments that include ACEs (e.g. Donnelly-Hermosillo et al., 2020; Gerard et al., 2015; Lazonder & Harmsen, 2016; Minner et al., 2010) and reviews of inquiry instruction (Furtak et al. 2012; Krajcik and Mun, 2014) document the value of inquiry instruction in science. Further, alignment of inquiry instruction and assessment using learning science pedagogy ensures that the impacts are validly measured (Linn & Eylon, 2011).

Meta-analyses and reviews illuminate the impact of specific ACE features as well as combinations of these features in inquiry instruction. Features include interactive graphs, dynamic visualizations, collaboration tools, opportunities to construct explanations, and automated guidance. ACEs capture student work using embedded assessments, empowering research partnerships to customize the features based on empirical results from design and comparison studies conducted in multiple science classrooms. These customizations both strengthen students' science learning and offer future designers powerful examples of effective customizations. The studies of ACE features underscore the advantages of ACEs that incorporate adaptive guidance, including automated guidance based on AI tools such as natural language processing or machine learning.

ACE features are developed, tested, and refined in partnership with science teachers. Using the Curriculum Visualizer partners, customize and test inquiry features to better connect the ACE features, such as personalized guidance, to students' lives and concerns, while leveraging KI pedagogy. Examples of successful customizations inspire new users of units such as UHI to identify refinements that meet the needs of their students.

The studies of cumulative learning discussed in this chapter demonstrate the benefits of teaching ACE inquiry units across grade levels (e.g. Liu et al., 2015). When students encounter a series of ACE units following a coherent pedagogy, they have the opportunity to connect ideas across topic areas. They also become proficient in interpreting data representations such as graphs as they encounter them in multiple contexts. Further, students develop methods for interrogating models and simulations and refine them in new contexts. As students learn science using ACEs, they also hone their collaboration skills, learning to take advantage of the insights of their peers. When teachers use a series of ACE units, they too gain proficiency in inquiry teaching, using logged student data, and planning customizations. More studies of cumulative impacts of ACEs are needed to clarify the mechanisms governing student lifelong learning.

ACEs are emerging as a valuable contributor to effective science instruction. ACEs support research partnerships to efficiently design new ACE units, use customization tools to adapt existing ACEs for new topics and contexts, and continuously refine their practice. Many groups are designing OERs that authors can incorporate into ACEs. Researchers are continuously adding investigations of the impact of inquiry instruction that help distinguish between the overall value of inquiry and the contributions of inquiry technologies. Extensions and syntheses of this ongoing work are needed to strengthen the field.

References

Alfieri, L., Brooks, P. J., Aldrich, N. J., & Tenenbaum, H. R. (2011). Does discovery-based instruction enhance learning? *Journal of Educational Psychology, 103*(1), 1–18. https://doi.org/10.1037/A0021017

Aristeidou, M., & Herodotou, C. (2020). Online citizen science: A systematic review of effects on learning and scientific literacy. *Citizen Science: Theory and Practice, 5*(1).

Bell, P. (2013). Promoting students' argument construction and collaborative debate in the science classroom. In *Internet environments for science education* (pp. 143–172). Routledge.

Bichler, S., Gerard, L., Bradford, A., & Linn, M. C. (2021). Designing a remote professional development course to support teacher customization in science. *Computers in Human Behavior, 123.* https://doi.org/10.1016/j.chb.2021.106814

Boda, P. A., Bathia, S., & Linn, M. C. (2021). Longitudinal impact of interactive science activities: Developing, implementing, and validating a graphing integration inventory. *Journal of Research in Science Teaching, 58*(2), 225–248. https://doi.org/10.1002/tea.21653

Bradford, A., Bichler, S., & Linn, M. C. (2021). Designing a workshop to support teacher customization of curricula. In E. de Vries, J. Ahn, & Y. Hod (Eds.), *Proceedings of the 15th International Conference of the Learning Sciences – ICLS 2021* (pp. 100–115). International Society of the Learning Sciences.

Bradford, A., Gerard, L., Lim-Breitbart, J., Miller, J., & Linn, M. C. (2022). Computational thinking in middle school science. In C. Chinn, E. Tan, C. Chan, & Y. Kali (Eds.), *Proceedings of the 16th International Conference of the Learning Sciences – ICLS 2022* (pp. 839–846). International Society of the Learning Sciences.

Chen, J. K., Bradford, A., & Linn, M. (2020). Examining the impact of student choice in online science investigations. In Gresalfi, M. and Horn, I. S. (Eds.), *The Interdisciplinarity of the Learning Sciences, 14th International Conference of the Learning Sciences (ICLS) 2020*, Volume 3 (pp. 1705–1708). International Society of the Learning Sciences.

de Jong, T. (2019). Moving towards engaged learning in STEM domains; there is no simple answer, but clearly a road ahead. *Journal of Computer Assisted Learning*, 35(2), 153–167.

de Jong, T., & Van Joolingen, W. R. (1998). Scientific discovery learning with computer simulations of conceptual domains. *Review of Educational Research*, 68(2), 179–201.

Dillenbourg, P., Järvelä, S., & Fischer, F. (2009). The evolution of research on computer-supported collaborative learning. In *Technology-enhanced learning* (pp. 3–19). Springer.

Donnelly, D. F., Linn, M. C., & Ludvigsen, S. (2014). Impacts and characteristics of computer-based science inquiry learning environments for precollege students. *Review of Educational Research*, 84(4).

Donnelly-Hermosillo, D. F., Gerard, L. F., & Linn, M. C. (2020). Impact of graph technologies in K-12 science and mathematics education. *Computers & Education*, 146, 103748.

Edelson, D., Reiser, B., et al (2021) Developing research-based instructional materials to support large-scale transformation of science teaching and learning: The approach of the OpenSciEd middle school program. *Journal of Science Teacher Education*, 32(7), 780–804. https://doi.org/10.1080/1046560X.2021.1877457

Freeman, S., Eddy, S. L., McDonough, M., Smith, M. K., Okoroafor, N., Jordt, H., & Wenderoth, M. P. (2014). Active learning increases student performance in science, engineering, and mathematics. *Proceedings of the National Academy of Sciences*, 111(23), 8410–8415. https://doi.org/10.1073/pnas.1319030111

Furtak, E. M., Seidel, T., Iverson, H., & Briggs, D. C. (2012). Experimental and quasi-experimental studies of inquiry-based science teaching: A meta-analysis. *Review of Educational Research*, 82(3), 300–329. https://doi.org/10.3102/0034654312457206

Gerard, L., Bichler, S., Bradford, A., & Linn, M. C., Steimel, K., & Riordan, B. (2022a). Designing an adaptive dialogue for promoting science understanding. In Oshima J. Mochizuki, & Y. Hayashi (Eds.), *Proceedings of the 2nd Annual Meeting of the International Society of the Learning Sciences (ISLS)*. ISLS.

Gerard, L., Bradford, A., & Linn, M. C. (2022b). Supporting teachers to customize curriculum for self-directed learning. *Journal of Science Education & Technology*.

Gerard, L. & Linn, M. C., (2022). Computer-based guidance to support students' revision of their science explanations. *Computers & Education*, 176

Gerard, L., Matuk, C., McElhaney, K., & Linn, M. C. (2015). Automated, adaptive guidance for K-12 education. *Educational Research Review*, 15, 41–58.

Gerard, L. F., Varma, K., Corliss, S. C., & Linn, M. C. (2011). A review of the literature on professional development in technology-enhanced inquiry science. *Review of Educational Research*, *81*(3), 408–448.

Goldenberg, D., Mark, J., Harvey, B., Cuoco, A., & Fries, M. (2020) Design Principles behind beauty and joy of computing. *Paper presented at the Curriculum Initiatives Meeting at SIGCSE.*

Gunstone, R. F., & White, R. T. (1981). Understanding of gravity. *Science Education*, *65*(3), 291–299.

Ibourk, A., & Kendrick, M. (2021) Elementary students' explanation of variation of traits and teacher's feedback using an online embedded assessment tool. *International Journal of Science Education*, *43*(8), 1173–1192.

Jeong, H., Hmelo-Silver, C. E., & Jo, K. (2019). Ten years of computer-supported collaborative learning: A meta-analysis of CSCL in STEM education during 2005–2014. *Educational Research Review*, *28.*

Krajcik, J. S., & Mun, K. (2014). Promises and challenges of using learning technologies to promote student learning of science. In N. G. Lederman & S. K. Abell (Eds.), *The handbook of research on science education* (pp. 337–360). Routledge.

Lazonder, A. W., & Harmsen, R. (2016). Meta-analysis of inquiry-based learning: Effects of guidance. *Review of Educational Research*, *86*(3), 681–718.

Linn, M. C., Clark, D., & Slotta, J. D. (2003). WISE design for knowledge integration. *Science Education*, *87*, 517–538.

Linn, M. C., Donnelly-Hermosillo, D. & Gerard, L. (in press). Synergies between learning technologies and learning sciences: Promoting equitable secondary science education. *Handbook of research on science education volume III*. Routledge Press.

Linn, M. C., & Eylon, B.-S. (2011). *Science learning and instruction: Taking advantage of technology to promote knowledge integration*. Routledge.

Linn, M. C., Lee, H.-S., Tinker, R., Husic, F., & Chiu, J. L. (2006). Teaching and assessing knowledge integration in science. *Science*, *313*, 1049.

Liu, O. L., Lee, H.-S., Hofstetter, C., & Linn, M. C. (2008). Assessing knowledge integration in science: Construct, measures, and evidence. *Educational Assessment*, *13*(1), 33–55

Liu, O. L., Rios, J. A., Heilman, M., Gerard, L., & Linn, M. C. (2016). Validation of automated scoring of science assessments. *Journal of Research in Science Teaching*, *53*(2), 215–233.

Liu, O. L., Ryoo, K., Linn, M. C., Sato, E., & Svihla, V. (2015). Measuring knowledge integration learning of energy topics: A two-year longitudinal study. *International Journal of Science Education*, *37*(7), 1044–1066.

Matuk, C. F., & Linn, M. C. (2018) Why and how do middle school students exchange ideas during science inquiry? *International Journal of Computer-Supported Collaborative Learning*, *13*, 263–299.

Matuk, C. F., Linn, M. C., & Eylon, B. S. (2015). Technology to support teachers using evidence from student work to customize technology-enhanced inquiry units. *Instructional Science*, *43*, 229–257.

McElhaney, K. W., Mills, K., Kamdar, D., Baker, A., & Roschelle, J. (2022, August). A summary and synthesis of initial OpenSciEd research: Draft version [White paper]. Digital Promise. Retrieved from: https://digitalpromise.org/wp-content/uploads/2022/08/OpenSciEd-Research-Agenda-Synthesis-Aug_2022.pdf

Minner, D. D., Levy, A. J., & Century, J. (2010). Inquiry-based science instruction - what is it and does it matter? Results from a research synthesis years 1984 to 2002. *Journal of Research in Science Teaching, 47*(4), 474–496.

Pallant, A., Lord, T., Pryputniewicz, S., & McDonald, S., (2020). Models for developing explanations of earth's dynamic plate system. *Science Scope, 45*(4).

Pea, R. & Linn, M. C. (2020).Personal perspectives on the emergence of the learning sciences: 1970s–2005. *Frontiers in Education, 5*.

Riordan, B., Cahill, A., Chen, J. K., Wiley, K., Bradford, A., Gerard, L., & Linn, M. C. (2020). Identifying NGSS-aligned ideas in student science explanations. *Paper presented at the Thirty-Fourth AAAI Conference on Artificial Intelligence*, New York, NY.

Ruiz-Primo, M. A., & Furtak, E. M. (2007) Exploring teachers' informal formative assessment practices and students' understanding in the context of scientific inquiry. *Journal of Research in Science Teaching, 44*(1), 57–84.

Ryoo, K. and Bedell, K. (2017), The effects of visualizations on linguistically diverse students' understanding of energy and matter in life science. *Journal of Research in Science Teaching, 54*, 1274–1301.

Schwendimann, B. A., & Linn, M. C. (2016), Comparing two forms of concept map critique activities to facilitate knowledge integration processes in evolution education. *Journal of Research in Science Teaching, 53*, 70–94.

Smetana, L. K., & Bell, R. L. (2012). Computer simulations to support science instruction and learning: A critical review of the literature. *International Journal of Science Education, 34*(9), 1337–1370.

Vitale, J., Applebaum, L., & Linn, M. C. (2019). Coordinating between graphs and science concepts: Density and buoyancy. *Cognition and Instruction, 37*(1), 38–72.

Vitale, J. M., McBride, E., & Linn, M. C. (2016). Distinguishing complex ideas about climate change: Knowledge integration vs specific guidance. *International Journal of Science Education, 38*(9), 1548–1569.

Vygotsky, L. S. (1978). *Mind in society: The development of higher psychological processes*. Harvard University Press.

Wiese, E. S., & Linn, M. C. (2021). "It must include rules": Middle school students' computational thinking with computer models in science. *ACM Transactions on Computer-Human Interaction*.

PART VIII

Discussion

18

INCREASING THE EFFECTIVENESS OF DIGITAL LEARNING

Richard E. Mayer

Introduction

How can we optimize student learning in digital learning environments such as multimedia lessons, instructional videos, video demonstrations, digital text, learning with pedagogical agents, and learning in immersive virtual reality? This is the focus of the chapters in Parts II, III, and IV. These chapters provide useful research-based reviews of how to design technology-supported learning environments grounded in research-based theories of learning in digital environments. The chapters are written by leading researchers in the field. In addition, the chapters suggest that design principles can be moderated by boundary conditions such as the prior knowledge of the learner or the content of the learning material. This work shows the progress that is being made in accumulating evidence-based and theory-grounded principles of instructional design for digital environments (Mayer, 2021; Mayer & Fiorella, 2022a).

Table 18.1 summarizes five types of digital learning environments that are examined in these sections: multimedia lessons, which include words and graphics; instructional video, such as a video of an instructor explaining a series of slides; video demonstrations, such as a video in which an instructor writes out the step-by-step solution to a math problem on the board as she explains each step; digital text, which involves printed words on a computer screen; pedagogical agents, who are onscreen characters designed to aid learning; and immersive virtual reality, in which the learner puts on a head-mounted display and is transported to a computer-generated three-dimensional world to learn new academic material.

DOI: 10.4324/9781003386131-26

TABLE 18.1 Examples of Digital Learning Environments

Name	Description	Chapters
Multimedia lessons	Lesson involving words and graphics	2, 3, 4, 5, 6, 7, 8, 9, 10
Instructional video	Lesson involving video of instructor delivering a lecture	6, 7, 9
Video demonstration	Lesson involving video in which a model shows how to perform a task	8, 9
Digital text	Lesson including onscreen printed text	3
Pedagogical agents	Lesson showing an onscreen character intended to foster learning	9
Immersive virtual reality	Lesson in which learner wears a head-mounted display, creating an artificial three-dimensional environment	10

Table 18.2 summarizes 11 evidence principles of instructional design for digital learning environments that are examined in these sections. I briefly summarize these principles in the subsequent sections of this chapter.

Signaling Principle

The signaling principle is that people learn better from a digital lesson when the core material is highlighted (Mayer, 2021; van Gog, 2022). For example, suppose you are viewing a video demonstration of how to perform a new task, including a concurrent spoken explanation. Learners might be overwhelmed by the lesson and not know where to look. When the instructor mentions a new term, the learner might not know which part of the video corresponds to it. This situation can create *extraneous processing* (i.e., cognitive processing that does not support the instructional goal), in which the learner wastes precious cognitive resources on scanning around the screen in search of where to look.

How can we help guide the learner's visual attention? One approach, described in Chapter 8 by van Gog et al., is to implement eye movement modeling examples (EMMEs) in which a series of dots or circles is superimposed on the video image to indicate where the model is looking in sync with the explanation (EMME; van Gog, 2022). EMMEs are intended to guide the learner's visual attention, and therefore can be considered a form of *visual signaling*, i.e., cues that are added to a digital lesson that highlight where to look on the screen. In Chapter 8, van Gog et al. also suggest that EMMEs can help learners improve their perceptual or cognitive strategies for how to allocate their visual attention in subsequent digital lessons.

TABLE 18.2 Evidence-Based Design Principles for Digital Learning Environments

Principle	Description	Chapters
Signaling	Add cues that highlight the core material	2, 3, 6, 7, 8, 9
Segmenting	Break a continuous lesson into meaningful parts	2, 3, 6, 7
Embodiment	Incorporate human features in graphics and pedagogical agents	3, 6, 7, 9
Embodiment	Show video demonstrations from first-person perspective	7
Embodiment	Display positive human emotion in speech and gesture	9
Coherence	Eliminate unneeded words and graphical elements	2, 3, 7
Contiguity	Place corresponding words and graphics near each other on the screen or in time	2, 3, 10
Redundancy	Eliminate captions that duplicate speech except for learning in a second language	2, 3, 7
Generative activity	Includes interactive activities such as glossaries, questions, and prompts to summarize	3, 7, 10
Modality	Explain graphics with spoken words rather than printed words	2, 3
Animation	Present appropriate graphics as animation rather than static graphics	2, 3
Personalization	Use conversational or polite wording	3, 9
Digital reading	Present printed text with adequate luminosity and without scrolling	3

In Chapter 2, Schuler et al. summarize several meta-analyses showing that signaling produces small-to-medium effect sizes on learning outcomes (e.g., Alpizar et al., 2020, reported $d = 0.38$ based on 44 effect sizes; Richter et al., 2016, reported $r = 0.17$ based on 45 effect sizes; and Schneider et al., 2018 reported $g = 0.53$ based on 145 effect sizes), where visual signaling included devices such as arrows, circles, pointing, spotlights, color, and verbal signaling included boldface font and headings. Concerning boundary conditions, there is some evidence that signaling works best for students with low prior knowledge.

In Chapter 6, Merkt and Huff show that dynamic lessons such as videos need dynamic signals such as spotlights, colors, or flashing that are synchronized to the terms mentioned in the spoken explanation. Similarly, in Chapter 7, Hoogerheide and Sepp suggest using cues to direct the learner's attention during instructional videos, such as having the instructor gaze or gesture toward the relevant part of the graphic as she mentions it. Furthermore, in Chapter 9, Beege et al. provide evidence that pedagogical agents are effective when they point to specific diagram components rather than when they display more general gestures.

Overall, there is consensus among the authors that signaling can be an effective design element in digital lessons. This includes both visual signaling such as pointing, circling, or adding arrows and verbal signaling such as special fonts and headings.

Segmenting Principle

The segmenting principle is that people learn better when a digital lesson is presented as learner-paced segments rather than as a continuous presentation (Mayer, 2021; Mayer & Fiorella, 2022b). For example, suppose a student is viewing an hour-long instructional video from an introductory college course showing a college instructor standing next to a series of slides as she lectures. The video contains a lot of new information, so after several minutes the student feels overwhelmed and starts to miss important points and gives up on trying to make sense of the material.

What can be done to help relieve the learner from cognitive overload? One approach suggested by several chapter authors is to break a digital lesson into smaller segments, in which the lesson pauses, and the learner can control when to go on to the next part. For example, Merkt and Huff, in Chapter 6, and Schuler et al. in Chapter 2, summarize a meta-analysis by Rey et al. (2019) showing that segmenting is an effective design feature for digital lessons with an effect size $d = 0.36$ based on 56 comparisons, including when the breaks are determined by the system or by the learner. Chapter 6 also summarizes a study by Merkt et al. (2022) reporting that learners paused video lessons at meaningful structural breakpoints or when they were having difficulty. Similarly, in Chapter 7, Hoogerheide and Sepp suggest implementing segmenting, especially when instructional videos are long and complex, although they note it is not yet clear how long the breaks should be and whether they should be determined by the instructor or the student. In Chapter 3, Salmeron et al. show how segmenting can be extended to lessons consisting of multimedia digital texts.

Overall, there is agreement among the authors for the segmenting principle. Further work is needed to determine the proper length of a segment, whether learner-selected segments are as effective as system-selected segments, and whether adding generative activities during the pauses can further aid learning.

Embodiment Principle

When an instructor delivers a lecture, the learner may be affected not only by the content of the lesson but also by the way the instructor presents the material. Several chapters provide evidence for the embodiment principle, which holds that people learn better when the instructor exhibits human-like gestures, eye-gaze, and facial expressions (Chapters 3, 6, 7, 9; Fiorella, 2022; Mayer, 2021). The embodiment principle can be extended to include adding human-like features to elements in graphics, as suggested in Chapter 3; having onscreen instructors display positive emotion, as suggested in Chapter 9; and showing video demonstrations from a first-person perspective rather than a third-person perspective (Chapter 7). For example, in Chapter 9, Beege et al. summarize meta-analyses showing that onscreen pedagogical agents are more effective when they display positive emotion through gesture and voice and when they display human-like gestures.

Coherence Principle

You might be tempted to try to make a digital lesson more interesting by adding features such as interesting stories or cute photos to go along with it. The advice of several chapter authors is to adhere to the coherence principle: Don't include unneeded words or graphical elements (Chapters 2, 3, 7; Fiorella & Mayer, 2022a; Mayer, 2021). For example, in Chapter 7, part of Hoogerheide and Sepp's very first tip for effective instructional design is to "avoid seductive details"—which are interesting but irrelevant text or images. Although they are intended to make a lesson more interesting, seductive details have been shown to have a negative effect on learning outcomes. In Chapter 2, Schuler et al. provide evidence for seven multimedia design principles, including the coherence principle. They point to eye-tracking evidence that seductive details draw attention away from the essential material in a multimedia lesson (Alemdag & Cagiltay, 2018). In Chapter 3, Salmeron et al. show that students have more difficulty reading from onscreen text and graphics than from print media and suggest that adherence to multimedia design principles such as the coherence principle are particularly important in digital reading venues.

Contiguity Principle

In a video lesson, an instructor speaks as she explains the current slide, or the narrator describes a graphic as it is presented. In these cases, the spoken words and corresponding words and graphics are presented at the same time, which can be called temporal contiguity (Fiorella & Mayer, 2022a; Mayer, 2021). In Chapter 10, Petersen and Makransky advocate adhering to the temporal contiguity principle when designing learning experiences in immersive virtual reality. In Chapter 2, Schuler et al. summarize a meta-analysis by Ginns (2006) in which temporal contiguity resulted in a large effect size of $d = 0.78$.

Another form of continuity is spatial contiguity, which involves placing printed words next to the part of a graphic they refer to (Fiorella & Mayer,

2022a; Mayer, 2021). In Chapter 2, Schuler et al. summarize a meta-analysis by Ginns (2006) reporting an effect size of $d = 0.72$ and a meta-analysis by Schroeder and Cenkci (2018) reporting an effect size of $g = 0.63$ favoring the spatial contiguity principle. In Chapter 3, Salmeron et al. also call for implementing both temporal contiguity and spatial contiguity in designing digital lessons.

Redundancy Principle

Consider an instructional video or narrated animation in which the instructor lectures as corresponding graphics are presented, in line with the contiguity principle that was just described. You might be tempted to add onscreen captions that repeat what the instructor is saying, but doing so would violate the redundancy principle, which cautions against adding redundant material to a lesson (Kalyuga & Sweller, 2022; Mayer, 2021). For example, in Chapter 7, Hoogerheide and Sepp note that adding redundant information that is related to the instruction goal can hinder learning, such as when a printed caption simply repeats what the instructor is saying or an illustration is added that simply represents an object already described in the text. In Chapter 2, Schuler et al. summarize meta-analyses by Adesope and Nesbit (2012) and Mayer and Fiorella (2014) that report adding captions is not helpful when the lesson consists of spoken text and graphics. In Chapter 3, Salmeron et al. point out that an important boundary condition is that adding captions can be helpful when learning in a second language.

Generative Activity Principle

Sitting at a computer and watching an instructional video, a narrated animation, or a series of multimedia slides can seem like a passive learning experience. What can we do to make digital learning more engaging? One approach is to insert generative learning activities, i.e., behaviors that the learner engages in during learning that are intended to improve learning, such as generating a summary or answering a practice question (Fiorella & Mayer, 2015, 2022b). For example, in Chapter 3, Salmeron et al. call for adding interactive features to digital texts such as hyperlinks, digital glossaries, inserted questions, annotation tools for note-taking, and hotspots that can produce sounds or graphics when tapped, in line with meta-analyses by Furenes et al. (2021) and Clinton-Lisell (2021). A boundary condition is that too much interactivity can lead to distraction and a feeling of being lost in the lesson, so students may need guidance. When designing instructional videos, Hoogerheide and Seep (in Chapter 7) suggest incorporating generative learning activities such as summarizing, explaining, answering practice questions, or even asking learners to make their own instructional videos. When designing learning in immersive virtual reality, Petersen and Makransky (in Chapter 10) also recommend incorporating generative learning activities, which are intended to help keep learners focused on the core content of the lesson. In short, several authors provide evidence-based support for the generative learning principle, which calls for asking learners to engage in appropriate generative learning activities during learning.

Modality Principle

Should the words in a digital lesson be printed on the screen or spoken by an instructor? Several chapter authors present evidence for the modality principle, which holds that the words in a multimedia presentation should be spoken rather than printed (Chapters 2 and 3; Castro-Alonso & Sweller, 2022; Mayer, 2021). The theoretical rationale is that when the screen contains both graphics and printed text, the learner experiences split attention, in which the learner cannot be looking at the words if they are looking at the graphics and vice versa. For example, in Chapter 2, Schuler et al. describe meta-analyses by Ginns (2005), Mayer and Fiorella (2022b), and Reinwein (2012) supporting the modality principle. Some important boundary conditions include that the modality principle applies most strongly when the material is complex and fast-paced, when the text is short and contains familiar words, and when learners lack extensive prior knowledge.

Animation Principle

Suppose you want to show a procedure, process, or chain of events. Would it be better to present them as a series of static illustrations or as an animation? According to the animation principle, proposed by several chapter authors (Chapters 2 and 3), it is best to use animation to depict change over time (Lowe et al., 2022). For example, in Chapter 2, Schuler et al. summarize several meta-analyses that yielded small effect sizes favoring animation over static pictures (Berney and Bétrancourt, 2016; Höffler and Leutner, 2007; Ploetzner et al., 2020). Importantly, Schuler et al. note that animations work best for specific situations showing a change over time that is relevant to the instructional goal, especially when the change cannot be easily portrayed in a static picture. Animations should be used sparingly for a specific purpose and can benefit from incorporating other principles such as signaling and segmenting.

Personalization Principle

Digital learning has the potential to be a lonely and alienating experience. What can we do to make the learner feel that the instructor cares about them and is working with them, so the learner works harder to make sense of the material? One simple approach, advocated by several chapter authors (Chapters 3 and 9) is for the instructor to use wording that is conversational and polite, which Mayer (2021) has called the personalization principle. For example, in Chapter 9, Beege et al. note that pedagogical agents have been shown to be more effective when they use conversational language rather than formal language or polite wording rather than direct wording. Personalization can serve as a social cue that helps the learner feel a better social connection with the instructor (Mayer, 2021), but it works best when it is used sparingly.

Digital Reading Principle

Finally, in Chapter 3, Salmeron et al., provide evidence-based suggestions for how to present digital text: Use adequate luminosity and avoid the need for scrolling.

Conclusion

Overall, the chapters in these sections provide a wealth of evidence-based recommendations for how to maximize the instructional effectiveness of digital lessons. I congratulate the authors on providing an up-to-date and comprehensive review of what we know about how to design computer-based learning experiences ranging from instructional video to learning with pedagogical agents to learning in immersive virtual reality. These chapters not only show the current state of the field, but also help form the basis for future advances in the field. These can include determining the boundary conditions for design principles, clarifying the underlying theories, and devising better measures of learning processes and learning outcomes.

Acknowledgment

Preparation of this chapter was supported by Grant N000142112047 from the Office of Naval Research and Grant 2201020 from the National Science Foundation.

References

Adesope, O. O., & Nesbit, J. C. (2012). Verbal redundancy in multimedia learning environments: A meta-analysis. *Journal of Educational Psychology, 104*(1), 250–263. https://doi.org/10.1037/a0026147

Alemdag, E., & Cagiltay, K. (2018). A systematic review of eye tracking research on multimedia learning. *Computers & Education, 125,* 413–428. https://doi.org/10.1016/j.compedu.2018.06.023

Alpizar, D., Adesope, O. O., & Wong, R. M. (2020). A meta-analysis of signaling principle in multimedia learning environments. *Educational Technology Research and Development, 68*(5), 2095–2119. https://doi.org/10.1007/s11423-020-09748-7

Berney, S., & Bétrancourt, M. (2016). Does animation enhance learning? A meta-analysis. *Computers & Education, 101,* 150–167. https://doi.org/10.1016/j.compedu.2016.06.005

Castro-Alonso, J. C., & Sweller, J. (2022). The modality principle in multimedia learning. In R. E. Mayer & L. Fiorella (Eds.), *The Cambridge handbook of multimedia learning* (3rd ed., pp. 261–267). Cambridge University Press. https://doi.org/10.1017/9781108894333

Clinton-Lisell, V. (2021). Stop multitasking and just read: Meta-analyses of multitasking's effects on reading performance and reading time. *Journal of Research in Reading, 44*(4), 787–816. https://doi.org/10.1111/1467-9817.12372

Fiorella, L. (2022). The embodiment principle in multimedia learn. In Richard E. Mayer & L. Fiorella (Eds.), *The Cambridge handbook of multimedia learning* (3rd ed., pp. 286–295). Cambridge University Press. https://doi.org/10.1017/9781108894333

Fiorella, L., & Mayer, R. E. (2015). *Learning as a generative activity.* Cambridge University Press. https://doi.org/10.1017/CBO9781107707085

Fiorella, L., & Mayer, R. E. (2022a). Principles for reducing extraneous processing in multimedia learning: Coherence, signaling redundancy, spatial contiguity, and temporal contiguity principles. In R. E. Mayer & L. Fiorella (Eds.), *The Cambridge handbook of multimedia learning* (3rd ed., pp. 185–198). Cambridge University Press. https://doi.org/10.1017/9781108894333

Fiorella, L., & Mayer, R. E. (2022b). The generative activity principle in multimedia learning. In R. E. Mayer & L. Fiorella (Eds.), *The Cambridge handbook of multimedia learning* (3rd ed., pp. 339–350). Cambridge University Press. https://doi.org/10.1017/9781108894333

Furenes, M. I., Kucirkova, N., & Bus, A. G. (2021). A comparison of children's reading on paper versus screen: A meta-analysis. *Review of Educational Research, 91*(4), 483–517. https://doi.org/10.3102/0034654321998074

Ginns, P. (2005). Meta-analysis of the modality effect. *Learning and Instruction, 15*(4), 313–331. https://doi.org/10.1016/j.learninstruc.2005.07.001

Ginns, P. (2006). Integrating information: A meta-analysis of the spatial contiguity and temporal contiguity effects. *Learning and Instruction, 16*(6), 511–525. https://doi.org/10.1016/j.learninstruc.2006.10.001

Höffler, T. N., & Leutner, D. (2007). Instructional animation versus static pictures: A meta-analysis. *Learning and Instruction, 17*(6), 722–738. https://doi.org/10.1016/j.learninstruc.2007.09.013

Kalyuga, S., & Sweller, J. (2022). The reducny principle in multimedia learning. In R. E. Mayer & L. Fiorella (Eds.), *The Cambridge handbook of multimedia learning* (3rd ed., pp. 212–220). Cambridge University Press. https://doi.org/10.1017/9781108894333

Lowe, R. K., Schnotz, W., & Boucheix, J.-M. (2022). The animation composition principle in multimedia learning. In R. E. Mayer & L. Fiorella (Eds.), *The Cambridge handbook of multimedia learning* (3rd ed., pp. 313–323). Cambridge University Press. https://doi.org/10.1017/9781108894333

Mayer, R. E. (2021). *Multimedia learning* (3rd ed). Cambridge University Press. https://doi.org/10.1017/9781316941355

Mayer, R. E., & Fiorella, L. (2014). Principles for reducing extraneous processing in multimedia learning: Coherence, signaling, redundancy, spatial contiguity, and temporal contiguity principles. In R. E. Mayer (Ed.), *The Cambridge handbook of multimedia learning* (2nd ed., pp. 279–315). Cambridge University Press. https://doi.org/10.1017/9781108894333

Mayer, R. E., & Fiorella, L. (Eds.). (2022a). *The Cambridge handbook of multimedia learning* (3rd ed). Cambridge University Press. https://doi.org/10.1017/9781108894333

Mayer, R. E., & Fiorella, L. (2022b). Principles for managing essential processing in multimedia learning: Segmenting, pre-training, and modality principles. In R. E. Mayer & L. Fiorella (Eds.), *The Cambridge handbook of multimedia learning* (3rd ed., pp. 243–260). Cambridge University Press. https://doi.org/10.1017/9781108894333

Merkt, M., Hoppe, A., Bruns, G., Ewerth, R., & Huff, M. (2022). Pushing the button: Why do learners pause online videos? *Computers & Education, 176*, 104355. https://doi.org/10.1016/j.compedu.2021.104355

Ploetzner, R., Berney, S., & Bétrancourt, M. (2020). A review of learning demands in instructional animations: The educational effectiveness of animations unfolds if the features of change need to be learned. *Journal of Computer Assisted Learning, 36*(6), 838–860. https://publons.com/publon/10.1111/jcal.12476

Reinwein, J. (2012). Does the modality effect exist? and if so, which modality effect? *Journal of Psycholinguistic Research, 41*(1), 1–32. https://publons.com/publon/10.1111/jcal.12476

Rey, G. D., Beege, M., Nebel, S., Wirzberger, M., Schmitt, T. H., & Schneider, S. (2019). A meta-analysis of the segmenting effect. *Educational Psychology Review, 31*, 389–419. https://doi.org/10.1007/s10648-018-9456-4

Richter, J., Scheiter, K., & Eitel, A. (2016). Signaling text-picture relations in multimedia learning: A comprehensive meta-analysis. *Educational Research Review, 17*, 19–36. https://doi.org/10.1016/j.edurev.2015.12.003

Schneider, S., Beege, M., Nebel, S., & Rey, G. D. (2018). A meta-analysis of how signaling affects learning with media. *Educational Research Review, 23*, 1–24. https://doi.org/10.1016/j.learninstruc.2018.06.006

Schroeder, N. L., & Cenkci, A. T. (2018). Spatial contiguity and spatial split-attention effects in multimedia learning environments: A meta-analysis. *Educational Psychology Review, 30*(3), 679–701. https://doi.org/10.1007/s10648-018-9435-9

Van Gog, T. (2022). The signaling (or cueing) principle in multimedia learning. In R. E. Mayer & L. Fiorella (Eds.), *The Cambridge handbook of multimedia learning* (3rd ed, pp. 221–230). Cambridge University Press. https://doi.org/10.1017/9781108894333

19

DESIGN OF DIGITAL LEARNING ENVIRONMENTS

Balancing theoretical, methodological, empirical, and technological approaches

Raija Hämäläinen

Parts V–VII of the book attempt to facilitate a better understanding of how to design digital learning for different needs by distinctively balancing the learning use of technology for research at the interfaces of theoretical, methodological, empirical, and technological approaches. On the one hand, this reflects the nature of research in the area, but on the other hand, achieving a more in-depth overall picture requires that the reader have previous knowledge in the area. The concerns of the chapters in these sections include overviews (Gerard & Linn; van den Beemt) and reviews utilising the results of meta-analyses (Schlag et al.; Kollar et al.; Wagner et al.; Gegenfurtner et al.; Havard et al.; and Hunsu et al.). As described by the authors, the goals, methods, and origins of the presented technologies vary. This is understandable, as the contexts and the forms of learning and interaction activity also vary greatly. This complexity is increased by the fact that digital learning environments can be used to support other forms of teaching, such as classroom teaching, and teaching can be mainly or entirely based on digital technologies. Conceptually, digital learning environments are multidimensional, depending on the perspective from which the research area is approached.

It is well-known that, at their best, digital learning environments have clearly been found to add value to learning by, for example, supporting the acquisition of basic spelling and reading skills (Lyytinen et al., 2021); activating multiple skills among science learners, such as measuring, controlling variables, and formulating hypotheses (Ben Ouahi et al., 2021); achieving higher cognitive gains (Lamb et al., 2018); rehearsing dangerous or expensive learning situations (Myers et al., 2018); and illustrating hard-to-understand topics (Mikeska et al., 2021). However, numerous studies have reported challenges in individual or collaborative learning in

DOI: 10.4324/9781003386131-27

digital learning environments (García-Morales et al., 2021; Zabolotna et al., in press). Thus, despite the long history of research in digital learning, the crucial question is still how to design an effective digital learning environment. Sections V–VII seek answers to this topical question.

Most of the technologies and devices presented in the book were originally developed for uses other than education, namely, for entertainment, professional, and manufacturing endeavours, which has lowered their prices. This, in turn, has led learning researchers to think about how to take advantage of new technologies when designing digital learning environments to support learning, such as through games (Schlag et al.), using sensors and wearables (Havard), audience response systems or clickers (Hunsu et al.), social media (van den Beemt), and webinars and videoconferencing (Gegenfurtner et al.).

Three contributions approach the design of digital learning environments from a more theoretical approach: the pieces by Kollar and colleagues on computer-supported collaborative learning (CSCL), by Wagner and colleagues on flipped classrooms, and by Gerard and Linn on web-based inquiry learning environments using knowledge integration pedagogy for science, technology, engineering, the arts, and mathematics (STEAM) subjects from a theory-based premise. The articles by Kollar et al. and Wagner et al. represent the research branch of digital learning environments that have a theoretical grounding (regarding CSCL and flipped classrooms, respectively). Both works draw comparisons—between learning that takes place in digital environments and that without technology or between forms of digital learning implemented in two different ways. Gerard and Linn's article summarises the evidence on the impact of digital inquiry environments and recommends future steps. In the next section, I begin my commentary on two articles that contribute to gamification and sensor-based learning in the context of digital environments. Then, I reflect on digital learning in a social context via the articles in Part VI. Finally, I discuss two articles that introduce approaches to designing and evaluating digital classrooms in Part VII.

Part V focuses on game-based and sensor-based learning in digital environments. First, the article by Schlag and colleagues called "Effectiveness of gamification in education" illustrates and discusses the use of gamification and its potential in education. This work builds on decades of research in game-based learning. Thus, it is already well-known that, at its best, gamification is an effective way to foster cognitive, affective/motivational, and behavioural learning outcomes (see e.g., De Freitas, 2018; Lämsä et al., 2018). The article begins with brief introductions to game elements. Next, they theorise gamification, introduce empirical research, and provide recommendations on how to use game elements to foster psychological needs for autonomy, competence, and social relatedness. Finally, moderating variables are discussed in relation to the effects of gamification on learning outcomes, as are some limitations of the game-based learning approach. There is a need for further empirical studies on how to advance gamification with learning research and vice versa, for example, how to take advantage of multimodalities in serious game design.

Second, Havard's article on sensors and wearables provides an overview of possible enhancements to learning and human performance through instructional and non-instructional interventions. The argument is that these devices change the nature and dynamics of how individuals acquire, store, and retrieve information, virtually eliminating the disconnect between humans and computers. A key aspect is that wearables include a variety of body-borne sensory, communication, and computational components that may be worn under, over, or within clothing. The definition of "wearables" is blurred; technologies are developing rapidly, and it can be challenging to define when a technology is wearable. For example, headset wearables for VR were not included in this study. However, Havard does include a discussion of several other technologies (e.g., smartwatches, wristbands, smart jewellery, eyewear, headsets, and e-textiles) and illustrates how they may influence learning and performance through their support of a variety of learners, learning strategies, and learning environments. Sensors and wearables are used in diverse contexts (e.g., military, healthcare, business, and industry), but in terms of empirical results, the article illuminates that we should consider this an emerging, rather than an established, research area. Furthermore, previous studies have highlighted that while these technologies impart advantages, new ethical challenges and dilemmas need to be considered in the design of digital learning environments when sensors and wearables are applied (Goodyear, 2017).

Part VI focuses on digital learning in social contexts. The article by Kollar and colleagues aims to give an overview of meta-analytic evidence of the effects of CSCL on learning. The title of the article, "Computer-supported collaborative learning," implies its limits: the review stems from an apparently narrow perspective of CSCL research; that is, it focuses on a specific line of quantitative, (quasi-)experimental research. Critically examined, the title is misleading, as it neglects the diversity at the fertile intersection of CSCL and analytical approaches (see e.g., Arvaja & Hämäläinen, 2021; Baker et al., 2021). As a result, a reader unfamiliar with the subject may get a very narrow picture of CSCL research. Despite this limitation, the article provides solid empirical evidence for principles underlying the effective design of CSCL. Furthermore, the authors claim that adding computer support to collaborative learning indeed boosts the effectiveness of that learning. One of the most interesting findings of this study is that when certain tools are combined in a CSCL setting, the positive effect can disappear. Kollar et al. indicate that the effectiveness of CSCL seems to be associated with a broad range of variables, such as learners' educational levels and intervention duration. This reflects the crucial and evolving question of CSCL: "Why does CSCL seem to work in some situations and fail in others?" Currently, various physiological measures are being applied in CSCL research to understand learning and interaction processes more deeply (Malmberg et al., 2019). This study by Kollar et al. indicates that further analysis across the different CSCL contexts is needed to increase our knowledge of how various learning processes can successfully be triggered when designing CSCL. Furthermore, so far, hardly anything has been known about the development of CSCL across time. Therefore, in addition to meta-analysis, long-term empirical follow-up studies of CSCL are essential for the future design of effective digital learning environments.

Social media has changed the culture of schools in an unprecedented way. Before social media, students were physically present in classrooms, and the social environment consisted of the students in the class and the adults working there (typically the teacher). Nowadays, in addition to the physical classroom, students may be part of some other social community, via social media, during class. Therefore, classroom activities may be influenced in real-time by external contacts—friends, parents, or, in the worst case, bullies. As stated by Van den Beemt, social media continues to play a key role in education and educational research, and the article tackles the advantages and disadvantages of this phenomenon. It is crucial to remember that social media were never developed for education, and this proves a challenge for effective inclusion in learning and teaching. At the same time, because students are actively using social media, teachers and educational institutions are forced to develop practices to deal with the accompanying downsides (e.g., disturbance, distraction, and teachers' lack of familiarity with rapidly evolving forms of social media environments). Thus, Van den Beemt claims that teachers are in need of professional development regarding the use of social media. This is in line with previous notions regarding teachers' ICT competencies, which encompass a set of ICT-related skills, knowledge, and attitudes that seem to vary greatly between teachers (Hämäläinen et al., 2021). As a response to this challenge, there is an indication from van den Beemt that teachers are looking for ways to incorporate social media into their teaching. Furthermore, evidence of positive results from social media use regarding engagement and motivation seems to be convincing. However, empirical results on how social media affects learning are yet to come, and it is currently unknown whether social media contributes positively or negatively to overall learning results.

In the article, "Clickers for effective learning and instruction: An examination of the effects of audience response systems in the classroom," Nathaniel Hunsu, Isaac D. Dunmoye, and Taiwo R. Feyijimi examine how clickers are used in various contexts to facilitate participation and interaction. Their contribution is an excellent addition, not only to the literature on Audience Response System (ARS) systems (also called clickers) but also to broader digital learning environment research. In general, there is an ongoing reform towards more inquiry-based teaching approaches in digital environments. Therefore, within the design and implementation of digital learning environments, the essential question is how to activate learners and orchestrate them in real-time (see Roschelle et al., 2013). Sawyer (2004) has highlighted that teaching is a creative activity that includes improvisation related to the collaborative and emergent nature of effective classroom practice. Furthermore, Lehesvuori et al. (2018) have argued that in learner-centred teaching approaches, student contributions should be explicitly taken into account as part of classroom interactions. In modern educational practices, technologies can be applied to the creative orchestration of classroom activities, taking into account learners' contributions, and activating learners. The advantage of clickers is that they enable teachers to apply real-time student participation in the classroom via laptops, tablet computers, and smartphones. Too often, research into digital learning environments degenerates into a debate about the appropriateness of a single approach. It is more important to understand when, how, and why, for example, ARS systems should be used. Hunsu and colleagues offer interesting and reflective perspectives on the effectiveness of clickers within existing theoretical and empirical literature. Furthermore, they offer theory-based considerations for the implementation of effective clicker-based instruction.

The final part of the book consists of three articles and focuses on designing digital classrooms. The flipped classroom approach to implementing digital learning is increasingly being discussed, investigated, and implemented in almost all possible disciplines and educational institutions around the world. As a result of this explosive popularity, a considerable number of review articles have already been published on the topic (see e.g., Hendrik & Hamzah, 2021; Hew et al., 2021; Wright & Park, 2022). The article by Marlene Wagner, Andreas Gegenfurtner, and Detlef Urhahne contributes to this ongoing discussion by providing an overview of meta-analytic evidence for the effectiveness of flipped classrooms. In the flipped classroom context, they focus on instructional design characteristics, which have an impact on effectiveness. Generally, the flipped classroom approach seems to be effective in many disciplines. Several design characteristics, such as pre-class activities, in-class learning activities, the use of formative assessments, and learning management systems, are briefly introduced as potential starting points when designing flipped learning. Finally, the article gives guidelines for the successful implementation of flipped classrooms in various educational settings. While increasingly popular, failed experiments have also increased. At the moment, it is not clear how many of the failed flipped learning experiments have actually been published. A major pedagogical problem in authentic settings is that schools are flooded with new pedagogical methods and learning content. Thus, in addition to investigations regarding the effectiveness of flipped classrooms, it would be important to seek how to understand and support teachers' professional agency amid educational changes (see Vähäsantanen, 2015).

The paper by Andreas Gegenfurtner, Svenja Bedenlier, Christian Ebner, Özün Keskin, and Marion Händel focuses on the design of effective synchronous online learning. The authors argue that they provide an overview of recent reviews and meta-analyses on the effectiveness of webinars compared to asynchronous digital and synchronous face-to-face environments. They define effectiveness as a learning environment that leads to positive affective or cognitive outcomes. The authors conclude that webinar-based learning environments seem to be effective for promoting learning. At the same time, it is well-known in the literature that productive synchronous or asynchronous online learning does not happen automatically. As a response to this need, Gegenfurtner and colleagues have developed design principles to guide teachers, trainers, and educators in designing effective webinar-based learning environments. First, synchronous online learning should be designed to impart procedural knowledge. Second, the impact can be increased via interactive instructional elements (e.g., videos, breakout rooms). Third, multiple repeated webinars seem to be more influential than single webinar events. Fourth, they recommend allowing learners to have access to additional learning materials. Finally, this type of learning should facilitate direct communication via, for example, webcams. According to Gegenfurtner and colleagues, digital learning environments can be differentiated and analysed based on their synchronicity and modality levels. In digital learning environment research, different methods contribute to our understanding of synchronicity and modality. In particular, the research trend in synchronicity (the timing of interactions between students and their lecturers) is a timely investigation. Currently, various methods are being developed to understand how these individual- and group-level processes evolve. In the design of digital learning environments, it is increasingly important to reveal not only the timing of these interactions but also how learners resonate with various digital learning environments in their talk, body movement, facial expressions, and physiology.

As stated above, most of the technologies that come into classrooms are not primarily developed for the needs of learning and teaching, but teaching practices need to adapt to the technological development of society and strive to utilise the available technologies as optimally and flexibly as possible. This leaves much responsibility for quality to the teachers' disciplined improvisation, and teachers are in need of evidence-based support for their teaching practices and professional learning (see Eteläpelto et al., 2014; Hämäläinen & Vähäsantanen, 2011). The last article of the book, "Impacts of Web-based Inquiry Learning Environments Aligned with Knowledge Integration Pedagogy" by Gerard and Linn, offers an example of systematic research-based knowledge for designing and implementing digital learning. Their approach provides further evidence for the positive impact of inquiry instruction in science learning, which is well documented. However, despite decades of research on designing and developing science education, too many students are still falling behind in their mathematics and science learning. Thus, novel approaches based on the integration of learning theories, multimodalities of the data, and the current advantages offered by technological development are needed to provide teachers and schools with the necessary knowledge and tools to implement effective inquiry pedagogy in science learning. The authors illustrate that novel Authoring and Customizing Environment (ACE) features to support knowledge integration can be designed via the integration of AI, open education resources, and learning sciences research. What is particular to their approach is over twenty-five years of systematic research into methods that support teachers in guiding students in knowledge integration. At their best, the advantages of ACEs that incorporate adaptive and automated guidance seem to hold the potential to contribute to large-scale educational change.

In my opinion, the research-based design of digital classrooms is particularly important; with the technologicalization of society, it is reasonable to ask whether non-digital classrooms even exist anymore. Indeed, the infiltration of various technological devices and software into learning and teaching practices is forcing teachers to design digital classrooms in their everyday work. However, recent analyses of large-scale assessment data, such as the Programme for the International Assessment of Adult Competencies (PIAAC), the Teaching and Learning International Survey (TALIS), and the International Computer and Information Literacy Study (ICILS), show that teachers' skills have simply not kept up with the needs of a digitalising society (De Wever et al., 2021; Fagerlund et al., 2022; Hämäläinen et al., 2021, 2019). For example, according to the ICILS 2018 (Fraillon et al., 2019), less than half of teachers actually use information and communications technology (ICT) in their teaching on a daily basis (see also De Wever et al., 2021). The central approach to addressing these challenges is to increase teachers' research-based knowledge, especially on the design of digital classrooms.

Today's teaching and learning attempt to optimise the changes brought about by digitalisation in society. Despite this, in authentic settings, discussions about the effectiveness of digital learning environments easily drift into arguments about whether learning environments are "good or bad for learning." Although in certain learning situations, the advantages of digital environments are recognised, critiques assert that effective digital learning environments are yet to be developed (e.g., Lavidas et al., 2022; Olofsson et al., 2021). The articles in Parts V–VII strike a balance among the different extremes of hype, potential, and limitation in regard to the effectiveness of the design of digital learning environments. At the same time, they present state-of-the-art evidence on the effects of designing digital learning environments. These articles enable a better understanding of this contemporary topic, and several future research lines are presented. Interestingly, the issue of whether digital environments are harmful or beneficial seems to depend on many contextual features, and when analysing learning and interaction in digital settings, in addition to learning outcomes, the contextual perspective needs to be considered.

References

Arvaja, M., & Hämäläinen, R. (2021). Dialogicality in making sense of online collaborative interaction: A conceptual perspective. *The Internet and Higher Education*, *48*, 100771. https://doi.org/10.1016/j.iheduc.2020.100771

Baker, M. J., Schwarz, B. B., & Ludvigsen, S. R. (2021). Educational dialogues and computer supported collaborative learning: Critical analysis and research perspectives. *International Journal of Computer-Supported Collaborative Learning*, *16*(4), 583–604. https://doi.org/10.1007/s11412-021-09359-1

Ben Ouahi, M., Ait Hou, M., Bliya, A., Hassouni, T., Ibrahmi, A., & Mehdi, E. (2021). The effect of using computer simulation on students' performance in teaching and learning physics: Are there any gender and area gaps? *Education Research International*, *2021*. https://doi.org/10.1155/2021/6646017

De Freitas, S. (2018). Are games effective learning tools? A review of educational games. *Journal of Educational Technology & Society*, *21*(2), 74–84. http://www.jstor.org/stable/26388380

De Wever, B., Hämäläinen, R., Nissinen, K., Mannonen, J., & Van Nieuwenhove, L. (2021). Teachers' problem-solving skills in technology-rich environments: A call for workplace learning and opportunities to develop professionally. *Studies in Continuing Education*, 1–27. https://doi.org/10.1080/0158037X.2021.2003769

Eteläpelto, A., Vähäsantanen, K., Hökkä, P., & Paloniemi, S. (2014). Identity and agency in professional learning. In S. Billet, C. Harteis and H. Gruber (Eds.), *International handbook of research in professional and practice-based learning* (pp. 645–672). Springer. https://doi.org/10.1007/978-94-017-8902-8_24

Fagerlund, J., Leino, K., Kiuru, N., & Niilo-Rämä, M. (2022). Finnish teachers' and students' programming motivation and their role in teaching and learning computational thinking. In *Frontiers in education* (Vol. 7). Frontiers Media SA. https://doi.org/10.3389/feduc.2022.948783

Fraillon, J., Ainley, J., Schulz, W., Friedman, T., & Duckworth, D. (Eds.). (2019). *Preparing for life in a digital world: IEA International Computer and Information Literacy Study 2018 international report*. International Association for the Evaluation of Educational Achievement. https://doi.org/10.1007/978-3-030-38781-5

García-Morales, V. J., Garrido-Moreno, A., & Martín-Rojas, R. (2021). The transformation of higher education after the COVID disruption: Emerging challenges in an online learning scenario. *Frontiers in Psychology*, *12*, 616059. https://doi.org/10.3389/fpsyg.2021.616059

Goodyear, V. A. (2017). Social media, apps and wearable technologies: Navigating ethical dilemmas and procedures. *Qualitative Research in Sport, Exercise and Health*, *9*(3), 285–302. https://doi.org/10.1080/2159676X.2017.1303790

Hämäläinen, R., De Wever, B., Nissinen, K., & Cincinnato, S. (2019). What makes the difference–PIAAC as a resource for understanding the problem-solving skills of Europe's higher-education adults. *Computers & Education, 129,* 27–36.

Hämäläinen, R., Nissinen, K., Mannonen, J., Lämsä, J., Leino, K., & Taajamo, M. (2021). Understanding teaching professionals' digital competence: What do PIAAC and TALIS reveal about technology-related skills, attitudes, and knowledge? *Computers in Human Behavior, 117,* 106672. https://doi.org/10.1016/j.chb.2020.106672

Hämäläinen, R., & Vähäsantanen, K. (2011). Theoretical and pedagogical perspectives on orchestrating creativity and collaborative learning. *Educational Research Review, 6*(3), 169–184. https://doi.org/10.1016/j.edurev.2011.08.001

Hendrik, H., & Hamzah, A. (2021). Flipped classroom in programming course: A systematic literature review. *International Journal of Emerging Technologies in Learning (iJET), 16*(2), 220–236. https://doi.org/10.3991/ijet.v16i02.15229

Hew, K. F., Bai, S., Dawson, P., & Lo, C. K. (2021). Meta-analyses of flipped classroom studies: A review of methodology. *Educational Research Review, 33,* 100393. https://doi.org/10.1016/j.edurev.2021.100393

Lamb, R. L., Annetta, L., Firestone, J., & Etopio, E. (2018). A meta-analysis with examination of moderators of student cognition, affect, and learning outcomes while using serious educational games, serious games, and simulations. *Computers in Human Behavior, 80,* 158–167. https://doi.org/10.1016/j.chb.2017.10.040

Lämsä, J., Hämäläinen, R., Aro, M., Koskimaa, R., & Äyrämö, S. M. (2018). Games for enhancing basic reading and maths skills: A systematic review of educational game design in supporting learning by people with learning disabilities. *British Journal of Educational Technology, 49*(4), 596–607. https://doi.org/10.1111/bjet.12639

Lavidas, K., Apostolou, Z., & Papadakis, S. (2022). Challenges and opportunities of mathematics in digital times: Preschool teachers' views. *Education Sciences, 12*(7), 459. https://doi.org/10.3390/educsci12070459

Lehesvuori, S., Ramnarain, U., & Viiri, J. (2018). Challenging transmission modes of teaching in science classrooms: Enhancing learner-centredness through dialogicity. *Research in Science Education, 48*(5), 1049–1069. https://doi.org/10.1007/s11165-016-9598-7

Lyytinen, H., Semrud-Clikeman, M., Li, H., Pugh, K., & Richardson, U. (2021). Supporting acquisition of spelling skills in different orthographies using an empirically validated digital learning environment. *Frontiers in Psychology, 12,* 566220. https://doi.org/10.3389/fpsyg.2021.566220

Malmberg, J., Haataja, E., Seppänen, T., & Järvelä, S. (2019). Are we together or not? The temporal interplay of monitoring, physiological arousal and physiological synchrony during a collaborative exam. *International Journal of Computer-Supported Collaborative Learning, 14*(4), 467–490. https://doi.org/10.1007/s11412-019-09311-4

Mikeska, J., Howell, H., Dieker, L., & Hynes, M. (2021). Understanding the role of simulations in K–12 mathematics and science teacher education: Outcomes from a teacher education simulation conference. *Contemporary Issues in Technology and Teacher Education, 21*(3), 781–812. https://citejournal.org/volume-21/issue-3-21/general/understanding-the-role-of-simulations-in-k-12-mathematics-and-science-teacher-education-outcomes-from-a-teacher-education-simulation-conference/

Myers, P. L., Starr, A. W., & Mullins, K. (2018). Flight simulator fidelity, training transfer, and the role of instructors in optimizing learning. *International Journal of Aviation, Aeronautics, and Aerospace, 5*(1), 6. https://doi.org/10.15394/ijaaa. 2018.1203

Olofsson, A. D., Lindberg, J. O., Young Pedersen, A., Arstorp, A. T., Dalsgaard, C., Einum, E., ... Willermark, S. (2021). Digital competence across boundaries— Beyond a common Nordic model of the digitalisation of K-12 schools? *Education Inquiry, 12*(4), 317–328. https://doi.org/10.1080/20004508.2021.1976454

Roschelle, J., Dimitriadis, Y., & Hoppe, U. (2013). Classroom orchestration: Synthesis. *Computers & Education, 69*, 523–526. https://doi.org/10.1016/j. compedu.2013.04.010

Sawyer, R. K. (2004). Creative teaching: Collaborative discussion as disciplined improvisation. *Educational Researcher, 33*(2), 12–20. https://doi.org/10.3102/001 3189X033002012

Vähäsantanen, K. (2015). Professional agency in the stream of change: Understanding educational change and teachers' professional identities. *Teaching and Teacher Education, 47*, 1–12. https://doi.org/10.1016/j.tate.2014.11.006

Wright, G. W., & Park, S. (2022). The effects of flipped classrooms on K–16 students' science and math achievement: A systematic review. *Studies in Science Education, 58*(1), 95–136. https://doi.org/10.1080/03057267.2021.1933354

Zabolotna, K., Malmberg, J., & Järvenoja, H. (in press). Examining the interplay of knowledge construction and group-level regulation in a computer-supported collaborative learning physics task. *Computers in Human Behavior, 138*, 107494. https://doi.org/10.1016/j.chb.2022.107494

INDEX

Pages in **bold** refer to tables.

For Product Safety Concerns and Information please contact our EU
representative GPSR@taylorandfrancis.com
Taylor & Francis Verlag GmbH, Kaufingerstraße 24, 80331 München, Germany

www.ingramcontent.com/pod-product-compliance
Lightning Source LLC
Chambersburg PA
CBHW070933050326
40689CB00014B/3189